FAMILY LIFE IN

17TH- AND 18TH-CENTURY AMERICA

FAMILY LIFE IN
17TH- AND
18TH-CENTURY
AMERICA

JAMES M. VOLO AND
DOROTHY DENNEEN VOLO

Family Life through History

GREENWOOD PRESS
Westport, Connecticut • London

Library of Congress Cataloging-in-Publication Data

Volo, James M., 1947–
  Family life in 17th- and 18th-century America / James M. Volo and Dorothy Denneen Volo.
      p. cm. — (Family life through history, ISSN 1558–6286)
  Includes bibliographical references and index.
  ISBN 0–313–33199–5 (alk. paper)
  1. Family—United States—History—17th century. 2. Family—United States—History—18th century. 3. North America—History—Colonial period, ca. 1600–1775. I. Title: Family life in seventeenth- and eighteenth-century America. II. Volo, Dorothy Denneen, 1949– III. Title. IV. Series.
HQ535.V65 2006
306.850973′09032—dc22   2005026302

British Library Cataloguing in Publication Data is available.

Library of Congress Catalog Card Number: 2005026302
ISBN: 0–313–33199–5
ISSN: 1558–6286

First published in 2006

Greenwood Press, 88 Post Road West, Westport, CT 06881
An imprint of Greenwood Publishing Group, Inc.
www.greenwood.com

Printed in the United States of America

The paper used in this book complies with the Permanent Paper Standard issued by the National Information Standards Organization (Z39.48–1984).

10 9 8 7 6 5 4 3 2 1

CONTENTS

INTRODUCTION

THE FUNCTIONS OF THE FAMILY

The knowledge gained by the experiences of childhood, the formal training required to earn a living, the formation of adult values, and the rearing of a new generation were all intimate functions of the family during the colonial period. The family was the mechanism by which children passed to successful adulthood, acquiring the skills, the values, and the philosophies of their forebears, their community, their church, and their nation. The family also served to transmit cultural ideals, societal standards, and historical awareness to children, and family structure and order helped to mitigate the sometimes wild fluctuations in the political and economic life of communities surviving on the fringe of civilization in an organized and distinctive way. The functions of the colonial family can be separated into four general themes: religious, economic, educational, and supportive. The relative importance of each theme varied as the colonial period progressed, but all four functions continued to characterize the overall purposes of the family throughout the period.

For children in particular, family religious instruction remained uniquely important because they received religious enlightenment at home at an earlier age and in a more appropriate manner than any formal religious training institution could have effectively done given the sparse population density and remote nature of colonial settlement. Moreover, many early immigrants to America were highly sectarian in their beliefs, and their doctrines generally rejected formalized ceremonies and traditional

The colonial family was a network of parents, grandparents, aunts, uncles, and siblings that formed a supporting structure for society.

religious organizations. As a method of religious instruction and a means of religious support, the family supplied an ethical atmosphere based on the particular tenets of its religious sect that helped to maintain core beliefs. In this regard religious sects tended to be more narrowly focused on discrete principles and their effect on the individual than did organized churches, which were more directly concerned with social programs for all their members. Sectarian groups were often self-led or formed around a particularly charismatic leader, whereas churches generally had a trained authoritarian ministry and a long-standing dogmatic tradition. In this regard the colonial family, being organized within highly sectarian communities, enabled the practice of worship outside the formal settings of a church organization, and it reinforced for both children and adults the doctrines and principles of a generally more narrow set of strongly held truths than those propagated by formal churches. Nonetheless, many colonial sects eventually evolved into remarkably well-organized and authoritarian churches of their own with sophisticated and discrete sets of doctrines.

The primary economic function of the family was to provide the daily necessities of life to every person. Family members were fed, clothed, and sheltered in a manner commensurate with the social and economic status of their household. For colonials experiencing subsistence living, meeting this function required the cooperation of the entire family. For the families of tradesmen, laborers, or craftspersons residing in a more urban setting, the colonial economy was filled with uncertain trends and political obstacles to success. In all but the most affluent families, children were considered economic assets and an essential part of the work force. By custom, the labor of children belonged to their father until set free at the age of majority Adult children, brothers, sisters, and grandparents living in the household were also expected to contribute . "At harvest time, extra help was required, and the presence of family members provided a cooperative force which was needed to harvest the wheat and corn, butcher the hogs, or perhaps build a barn. Although this activity was primarily economic, the social contract during these times was part of the sustenance which bound and maintained the families."[1]

The educational function of the family was one by which parents (and grandparents) transferred their values and skills to the next generation. All facets of family life, not just formal training, were involved in this process. The overheard conversations of the adults, the way they lived, the way they dealt with others in the community, and the way they carried out their own daily duties were of particular importance for instructing children. It was often essential to the well-being of the family, possibly even its survival, that children performed any task correctly and with dispatch.

Formal education, as in a school, was viewed in many different ways in the colonial period. New England Puritans and frontier Scotch-Irish seemed most positively impressed by schools, but southern aristocrats and sectarian Quakers and Pietists often distrusted institutionalized instruction. This dichotomy created a regional pattern of educational development that ranged from home schooling to university education.

Finally, the family provided emotional, social, and financial support as well as physical protection to each member of the household and to the wider community of relatives. In the colonial period the role of each individual was somewhat better defined than at present, but the consequences of faulty parenting or other flaws in family relationships were not so well understood as they are today. Ideally the father headed the household with stern guidance and loving care; and the mother provided comfort in good times and sympathy and understanding in the face of difficulty. The presence of children provided emotional support for parents and guaranteed caring aid in their old age. The extended family also provided support. Uncles, aunts, and cousins often lived nearby and were available for daily counsel, economic assistance, and active defense in times of trouble. Local militias were often composed almost entirely of relatives. These several functions of the family, which will be further discussed in detail, allowed each family member to adapt to the outside world and overcome the peculiar challenges of life in the colonial period.[2]

The colonies that made up British North America were initially established over a long period of one hundred and twenty-five years from Jamestown, Virginia in 1607 to the colony of Georgia in 1732. The development of the thirteen mainland colonies did not happen in a vacuum. In the 17th century England saw substantial immigration not only to the Atlantic seaboard of North America, but also to Bermuda, Barbados, Jamaica, and the Leeward Islands of St. Kitts, Nevis, Antigua, and Montserrat. More than 100,000 persons moved to the Caribbean alone, and another 100,000 immigrated to the "English" plantations in Ireland. Records suggest that no fewer than 250, 000 persons left Britain between 1607 and 1660, and it is possible that as many more emigrated by the end of the 17th century.[3]

The earliest English colonists at Jamestown in 1607 called their New World home Virginia in honor of Elizabeth Tudor, the never-married Virgin Queen who had ruled from 1558 to 1603, but they carefully named their first settlement in the New World after the reigning Stuart monarch, James I. Seventeenth-century Royalists called the southernmost colonies of the 17th century the Carolinas in honor of James's brother and successor, Charles I. The Catholics may have called their colony Maryland after the biblical mother of Christ, but the actual Mary in question remains a matter of historical debate. Parts of New Netherlands were renamed New York and New Jersey after members of the Royal family when the English took the colonies from the Dutch in the 1660s; and Pennsylvania and Delaware were named for their respective founders, Sir William Penn and Lord De la Warr. Georgia, founded in 1732, was dedicated to the reigning British monarch, George II. Only one group refused to name its new home in North America for a person. The Pilgrims, who began to arrive in 1620, referred to their rocky settlements on the northeast Atlantic coast simply as New England.

The circumstance of having separate names for different portions of the British colonies, unlike the French who called their entire colony New France, well mirrored the character of British colonial settlement in North America. The colonial structure of British North America was almost as confused as the many names that described it. Some colonies were virtually self-governing while others were ruled by governors appointed by the Crown. Still others were managed under the jurisdiction of proprietors or trustees. For example, Virginia in 1624, had its governance transferred from the board of directors of a limited stock company to a royal governor appointed by the Crown. No two colonies were governed in exactly the same manner, and it should be remembered that no two were settled by a single distinct and homogeneous population of immigrants. Even Puritan New England had its dissenters, nonconformists, and outright rebels.

Unlike the French and Spanish colonies in the New World, which were generally ruled from abroad as extensions of a comprehensive empire, most of the British colonies were virtually independent political entities in their formative years. Indeed the governance of each British colony was not only unique; it was viewed with a certain independence and reliance on self-determination. The glorious Revolution of 1688 seems to have been a watershed event in this regard. When James II became King of England, he attempted to cancel many of the royal charters under which the colonies had been formed. He succeeded in combing the entire Atlantic coast from Maine to Delaware into the Dominion of New England and placing them under the authority of a single royal governor, Sir Edmund Andros. William III, who succeeded the deposed James II, reissued many of the original charters in a modified form. Nonetheless, under William's modified plan Massachusetts was partitioned, and both it and the new colony of New Hampshire formed from within its boundaries became royal colonies. Oddly, Massachusetts kept control of Maine even though it was thereafter physically separated from it. Meanwhile Rhode Island retained its right to elect its own government, and Connecticut retained its original charter by refusing to yield it up and hiding it in the hollow of an oak tree.[4] With the stroke of a pen, King William not only dismembered the Dominion of New England, but he also eliminated many of the legal precedents that were based on Roman and Biblical law and set up the courts and government of the realm based on English common law. Laws and proceedings that had been common practice throughout the empire were suddenly no longer recognized, and not until 1726 was the mass of legal confusion that ensued corrected.

The royal colonies of New York and New Jersey were particularly unfortunate in their court-appointed governors, many of whom proved to be arrogant, dishonest, or incompetent. The proprietary colonies of Pennsylvania and Maryland were somewhat more fortunate in their governance. Pennsylvania was briefly converted into a royal colony, but the proprietorship of the Penn family was reinstated by the beginning of the 18th century. Maryland underwent a political and military upheaval in 1688 because its founder, George Calvert, the First Lord Baltimore, had been a Catholic. It was thought that the Catholics in Maryland might support the deposed king, James II, who was friendly to Papists, instead of the stalwartly Protestant William III. It is not surprising therefore, that William appointed a Protestant royal governor in response to a petition by the colony's Protestant settlers.

Of the approximately 200,000 people who crossed the Atlantic to settle in British North America in the 17th century, sixty percent (120,000) went either to Virginia or Maryland. The peak period of this immigration was during the three decades after 1630. The two southern colonies originally known as the Carolinas began as a single entity, but by 1710 a separate royal governor was appointed to each. This date marks the separation of

North and South Carolina. The tract of land that became Georgia in 1732 was given to a set of eight trustees under a limited charter, but at its expiration the governance of the colony reverted to the Crown.

Delaware remains an enigma in the colonial period, and it is almost certain that Lord De la Warr never saw the colony named for him. Delaware was originally founded by the Swedes. It was captured by the Dutch and then seized by the English. Delaware was claimed by both Maryland and Pennsylvania in the early colonial period and was considered part of the latter throughout most of the 18th century. It did not gain recognition as an independent colony until the eve of the American Revolution. Similarly, Maine was considered part of Massachusetts and Vermont part of New York until after the War of Independence.

Confined to the margins of the Atlantic coast by the claims of Catholic France and Spain, the overwhelmingly Protestant Anglo-American colonies faced the persistent hostility of their neighbors—rooted in the deep and genuine religious and political antagonisms formed during the Protestant Reformation of the 16th and 17th centuries. These hostilities dominated much of the thinking and politics of many generations of Anglo-Americans. Early colonists attempted to transplant the emotionalism of the religious and theological controversies raised by the Protestant Reformation in Europe to the colonies in America. The Catholic kingdoms of Europe, which had little success in stopping the Protestant movement that swept their domains in the 16th century, refused to allow heretics to contaminate their holdings in the New World. Protestants felt a similar antipathy toward Catholics of all nationalities, distrusting them and believing that they represented the Antichrist. This belief, strongest during the 17th century, colored the functioning of colonial governments as well as the social, economic, and cultural order everywhere in Anglo-America.

Colonial society was based on an acute awareness of class. Gradations in the social order were openly recognized and accepted by persons of all ranks. Even in the colonial wilderness, the gentleman was accorded his deference and respect, and custom assigned the middle and lower classes to their established places on the rungs of the societal ladder. Nonetheless, transition from one class to another in British North America was not infrequent and may have been accomplished with greater ease than anywhere in Europe. Yet even with the presence of social mobility distinctions between ethnic and economic groups remained clearly defined.

A physician noted in 1744 that "vulgar behavior ... always proceeded from ... narrow notions, ignorance of the world, and low extraction, which is indeed the case with most of our aggrandized upstarts in these infant countries of America who never had an opportunity to see, or if they had, the capacity to observe the different ranks of men of polite nations or to know what it is that really constitutes that difference of degrees." Nonetheless, the physician noted a declining subordination of "inferiors to superiors" outside his home colony of Maryland. "I find they are not quite so scrupulous about bestowing titles [in New England] as in Maryland." Unknown even to himself, the good doctor was witnessing and recording the beginnings of a great revolution—the breakdown of a class structure that had held sway over people's lives since Medieval times and a growing unity among the people of a more common sort.[5]

This book focuses on family life in the mainland colonies in the 17th and 18th centuries. Particularly, the interaction of parents and children, the methods of parenting, and the molding of young lives have been analyzed. A comparative study of all the disparate family groups that came to America in the colonial period with regard to these principles would be most interesting, but with the exception of the New England Puritans there are few solidly researched accounts of family life and childrearing in early America.[6]

Yet, good historical research should raise questions even if they cannot immediately be answered. It is by this means that meaningful contributions to understanding are made. This book uses the record established in diaries and journals, personal letters, church documents, and published material contemporary with the colonial period. Through the investigation of these sources and through reference to previous studies in American social history, many valuable insights have been gained and a number of areas for further study have been identified.

NOTES

1. Alvin E. Conner, *Sectarian Childrearing: The Dunkers, 1708–1900* (Gettysburg, PA: Brethren Heritage Press, 2000), 119.

2. For a more detailed analysis of family functions, see ibid., 111–40.

3. Surviving records have proved too fragmentary to permit precise estimates. Moreover, many persons may have moved two or even three times.

4. The act of hiding the charter made no practical difference in terms of its legitimacy, but Connecticut tradition makes much of it, nonetheless.

5. Carl Bridenbaugh, ed., *Gentleman's Progress: The Itinerarium of Dr. Alexander Hamilton, 1744* (Chapel Hill: University of North Carolina Press, 1948), xxiv.

6. Conner, 2.

Part I
The Role of Family

1
Folkways

Whoever wishes to go to the New World
Should be sure to take a sack of money
And also a strong stomach
So he can withstand the demands of the ship.
                                        —An immigrant to Pennsylvania, 1751[1]

WAVES OF MIGRATION

Recent demographic research reveals that immigration to the New World from Europe was not a random flood of unrelated and diverse people, but a sequential movement of several distinct groups, each with its own unique cultural characteristics. Even though the ethnic composition of the United States has changed since colonial times, and fewer than twenty percent of those now living in America can trace their ancestors to the 17th or 18th centuries, the cultural, social, and religious characteristics of these first immigrants have persisted into our own time and remain powerful influences in politics, society, culture, education, and lifestyle.

Social historian David Hackett Fischer has identified more than a dozen qualitative features of colonial family life and culture that he calls "folkways." Not to be confused with the anecdotes, beliefs, stories, superstitions, and sayings of ancient or primitive peoples more properly categorized as "folklore," folkways are recognizable patterns in speech, family structure, marriage, child rearing, social order, and religion characteristic of advanced societies. Fischer deals only with the folkways of the four groups of immigrants to North America with British roots and ignores to a great extent the early non-English speaking settlers of the middle Atlantic colonies of New York, New Jersey, and the interior sections of Pennsylvania. Nonetheless, his signal work is essential reading for those doing research in the arenas of cultural and social history during the American colonial period. Moreover, while not all of the folkways Fischer identifies seem eligible for inclusion in a study focused on family life, once the concept of *persistent distinctive customs* has been established, it is very difficult to avoid its application in that context.[2]

Of all the European nations that came to the New World, the Spanish, the French, and the English had the greatest effect on its culture. While all three nations tried to maintain a hegemony among the sugar islands of the Caribbean, Spain, which discovered America in 1492 and later absorbed the New World possessions of Portugal, focused its interests primarily in South America, Central America, Mexico, and the great Southwest of the present-day United States. The French generally directed their colonial aspirations toward Canada, the Great Lakes Region, and the lands drained by the Mississippi River. They would gladly have driven the Anglo-American colonials into the sea had they been capable of doing so, but seven decades of woodlands warfare failed to dislodge the stubborn British. Nonetheless, the Anglo-American colonies were restricted by political circumstances and geography to a thin strip of seemingly insignificant colonies on the Atlantic coast of North America. These colonies were largely dysfunctional as discrete political, military, and economic entities, and they were greatly overshadowed in their importance to the British trading empire by the handful of wealth-producing sugar islands in the Caribbean.

The interactions of the three great nations of Europe during the next 300 years in North America were complex in nature and far reaching in their effect. As an example, a small woodland skirmish between a score of French and British irregulars in western Pennsylvania in 1754 touched off a world-wide conflict known as the Seven Years' War, which spread quickly to India and the Far East, and ultimately involved most of the major kingdoms of Europe. The intervening political, economic, social, and religious issues during this period were intricate and numerous, and they serve the academic community as a basis for historical research, hypothesis, and theory. Nonetheless, it can be said of this period with simplicity and with some accuracy that the Spanish discovered America and plundered it of its wealth; the French cherished it and were largely absorbed by it; and the English coveted it, made a large part of it their own, and then lost most of it to their own offspring.

Seven major groups migrated to British North America in the 17th and 18th centuries: four distinct waves of Britons (the English and Scotch-Irish identified by Fischer), the Dutch, the Germans, and the Africans. Other immigrants included small groups—mostly workmen and artisans—of Swedish, French, Swiss, Italian, Portuguese, and Spanish extraction, but these groups had little lasting influence on the culture of Anglo-America due either to their small numbers or their absorption into another culture. All brought to the colonies that they founded, developed, and defended the basis for many regional variations in government, business, culture, society, and family life. This helped to create an expansive pluralism in America that remained one of the most important cultural characteristics affecting the history of the United States.[3]

At least four great waves of English-speaking colonists migrated to North America between 1620 and 1775. Each of these came willingly and had its own religious affiliations, speech patterns, social ranking, and family structure. While the four waves of English language speakers shared, with few exceptions, an adherence to the Protestant faith and a respect for the precedents of English law, they spoke different dialects, built their houses differently, held diverse views on business and farming, and had different conceptions of public order, power, freedom, and family obligations. These discrete peoples settled in New England, in a wide region of the tidewater region of the greater Chesapeake Bay known collectively as Virginia, in the lower Delaware River Valley, and in the backcountry of Georgia and the Carolinas.[4]

Overlapping this influx of English-speaking immigrants was a stream of people from the lowlands and the central heart of continental Europe who entered North American principally through the Hudson River Valley and New York Bay. The Calvinist Dutch and their religious brethren, the Flemish Walloons and French Huguenots, had a significant influence on the culture of English North America in this region, and many 19th-century authors, principally Washington Irving, incorporated colonial Dutch customs into the folklore of New York. The greatest concentrations of Dutch colonials were initially to be found in the settlement of New Amsterdam on the island of Manhattan and along the Hudson River to the head of navigation near Albany at Fort Orange. From these mid-17th century outposts, the Dutch penetrated the frontier of central New York, expanding their influence along existing Indian trails, rivers, and tributaries.

The Dutch were joined in the 18th century by a flood of German-speaking peoples known as the Palatines, who established scattered settlements on the New York frontier in the early 1700s. Before the American Revolution, a massive influx of German speakers entered the continent through Philadelphia and New Jersey. Misnamed the "Pennsylvania Dutch," these Germans ultimately formed isolated communities of Lutherans, Moravians, Anabaptists, Mennonites, and other Pietist religious sects mainly in Pennsylvania, New Jersey, and New York. Their descendants retained their language, traditions, and culture for many generations although none had a living memory of the Old World.

Finally, a separate group of immigrants—of African descent—was brought unwillingly to American shores as slaves. The early history of race-based slavery in North America is poorly documented and inconclusive, yet it seems certain that none of the founders of the first English colonies anticipated a dependence on slave labor. Rather, they thought to rely on their own labor, the labor of hired servants, or on the system of white indentured labor common in their homeland. While the first black Africans brought to the English colonies in Virginia were formerly thought to have been exclusively slaves, recent research suggests that many of them were indentured servants or even free craftsmen many generations removed from the soil of Africa.[5] In 1625, there were about 460 white indentured servants in Virginia and as few as 22 blacks, some of whom may have been slaves.

Black slaves from Africa had been used as agricultural workers since the 16th century by the Portuguese on their plantations in the Azores. In large measure, race-based black slavery was cemented in the British colonies by its introduction in 1627 to Barbados, where commercial sugar production was first undertaken by the English. While Englishmen had come ashore on Bermuda as early as 1583 and had touched on St. Lucia and Grenada in 1605 and 1609, respectively, no major English colony had been established in the West Indies before 1623, when a large settlement was made on St. Kitts (St. Christopher). However, Barbados had a better harbor and a more strategically important position among the islands of the Caribbean. During the final quarter of the 17th century, there were more settlers, both black and white, on the small sugar island of Barbados than in all the mainland English colonies.

A very large number of black slaves, possibly 80 percent of the population, were among the first settlers of Barbados. Moreover, the proportion of blacks to whites increased as poorer whites were forced off the best sugar-producing lands by the bigger and richer planters who could afford more slaves. By the 1690s, white immigration to the island had all but ceased. According to a report written to the Board of Trade, "[White] people no longer come to Barbados, many having departed to Carolina, Jamaica, and the Leeward Islands in hope of settling the land that they cannot obtain there [in Barbados]."[6]

Estimates of the number of Africans forcibly removed from their homelands and brought to the colonies over the two centuries from the founding of the first English colonies to the American Revolution vary so widely that "it is a telling demonstration of the communications gap" between historical researchers and the writers of textbooks.[7] Both the lowest and highest estimates were calculated in the decades before the American Civil War by partisan authors involved in the anti-slavery crisis. These estimates, ranging from a questionable low of 2 million to a implausible high of 40 million, have been made more problematic by a lack of accurate knowledge concerning the proportion of black slaves

Plantation slaves like these worked in large gangs assigned to particular tasks. They were often managed in the fields by other blacks who served as "drivers."

born in America as compared with those born in Africa and imprecise estimates of the proportion of imported Africans brought to British North America rather than to the West Indies or other parts of the Americas before the Revolution. Moreover, many slaves entering Virginia and the Carolinas may have been counted twice as they were re-exported by ship from one colony to another as part of the intercolonial trade in human beings. Although this might amount to a "negligible error" if the level of this traffic was small, the error from this source alone could be far more substantial if the size of the inter-colonial slave trade was also more extensive than formerly thought.[8] Estimates based on unanswered questions like these may have caused some of the "chronic exaggeration of the [slave] trade still found in the historical literature."[9]

Curiously, few 19th- and 20th-century texts have gone beyond the repetition of what has been described as "guesswork." Little further work has been done to increase the potential knowledge of the extent of slavery, and "nothing at all" has been added, apparently, to "the actual knowledge represented in the textbooks and general works" on the subject. Notwithstanding an academic interest in accurately estimating the number of Africans brought to Anglo-America, the importation of a single enslaved person should be viewed with dismay and revulsion. A reasonable estimate of the number of African slaves brought to the North American mainland during the colonial period, based on the most recent historical research, hovers around 400 thousand.[10] There is no need to inflate this estimate to condemn the practice of slavery.

Regardless of their number, the distinction among blacks who were African-born or American-born, freemen, indentured servants, or slaves quickly blurred in the colonies.[11] By the beginning of the 18th century, the tragedy of race-based slavery in perpetuity had been firmly established in Anglo-America. Not only were the slaves sentenced to a lifetime of servitude, their offspring were also carried into bondage upon their birth. There was no precedent in English law for such an inherited status up to that time, but the vile practice of breeding new generations of slaves from the old was carried out nonetheless under the guise of following Roman and Biblical precedents.[12]

As late as the 1760s, the British were justifying race-based slavery in the islands and in the southern mainland colonies with arguments similar to this one written by a magistrate on the Board of Trade: "Rice, indigo, naval stores, and lately hemp ... cannot be raised and extended but by the labour of slaves supplied by the African Trade." A colonial observer from South Carolina noted, "During the summer months the climate is so sultry, the air so poisoned by marshy swamps, that no European without hazard can endure the fatigues of labouring in the air." This tenet of the pro-slavery rationale, which remained a standard weapon in the arsenal of arguments used by southern apologists for generations, led to the dubious conclusion that blacks were racially suited to their servile status and therefore predestined to serve as laborers.[13]

AGE DISTRIBUTION

It has been estimated that the ages of the immigrants to the English colonies were fairly random in their distribution. Records from the late colonial period, after the French and Indian Wars, indicate that only the elderly, those over sixty (less than 1%), seem to have been under represented. Of the remaining ninety-nine percent, the largest group (39%) was composed of those between 25 and 59 and the smallest (25%) by children under 14. The remaining group (35%) was remarkable in that it was composed of older teenagers and young adults between 15 and 24. "[A]mong those ... still young and healthy enough to endure a long sea voyage, the tales they heard of freedom and opportunity in the New World and of the crying need for cheap labor made their hearts leap with that stranger joy of hope."[14]

In sharp contrast to the near-absence of female immigrants to New France and New Spain, women and girls made up approximately half of the early English colonists.. Although most Puritans came to New England in family groups and single men dominated those that came to Virginia, by the middle of the colonial period the male-female ratio was more equal in the southern colonies than in New England. In the later colonial period, male immigrants outnumbered females by a ratio of 3 to 2.[15]

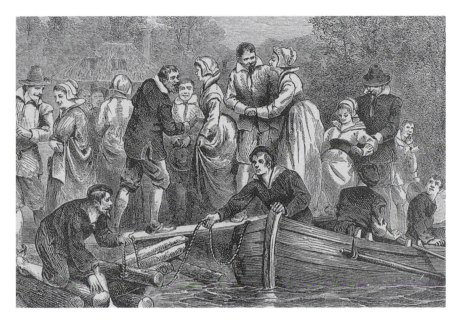

Women of good reputation had no trouble finding husbands in the colonies. Colonial men favored young women of childbearing years who had "healthy" figures and obedient dispositions.

LITERACY

It is generally accepted that the Puritans of New England and the Quakers of the middle colonies could read as the periodic reading of Holy Scripture was a cornerstone of their religious belief. It is also generally assumed that the elite among the Royalists that came to the Chesapeake colonies were as well educated as their counterparts in Britain. Although their spelling and grammar leave much to be desired by late-Victorian standards, the many surviving diaries, journals, and letters written by the officers and common soldiers of the provincial armies show that these men were literate by 18th-century standards. Many German and Dutch immigrants may also have been literate in their native language.

Numerous anecdotes and misconceptions about the level of illiteracy among frontier settlers have survived, however. Some of these have been kept alive by well-meaning, but otherwise misguided, docents and local antiquarians right up to the present time. Some unwary historians have been led to believe that the literacy of the frontiersmen was uniformly low, and that their speech patterns and written vocabulary were of inferior quality. Careful research suggests that this was not the case. In the 17th century, men on the frontier seem to have had a literacy rate of approximately 50 percent. This figure improved to 65 percent by the early 18th century possibly because the Scotch-Irish who flooded the frontier during this period strongly supported formal education for their children.[16]

The standard used for defining literacy in these cases was "the ability to sign one's name, a skill that runs parallel [to] though slightly below reading proficiency and likewise runs parallel [to] though slightly above the ability to write." As would be expected, literacy varied greatly with wealth and social class, but it also varied from one ethnic group to another. Based on the examination of wills, deeds, and other public documents German Protestants and French Huguenots may have been 90 percent literate. Precise estimates for the Scotch-Irish are not available, but surviving documents from the mid-18th century show that fewer than 30 percent of lowland Scots used a "mark" rather than a signature, suggesting that as many as 70 percent could write. Literacy rates in the coastal settlements seem to have been higher in the early colonial period than they were later and, less surprisingly, higher among the gentry and craftsmen than among the growing number of laborers. These patterns in America mirror similar findings for Britain at the same time.[17]

The availability of books and other reading materials can sometimes be used as a good indicator of literacy. In the colonial period, a few exceptional families owned large collections of books (forty or fifty volumes was considered a vast library even in the late 18th century), but a lack of books in colonial communities not does not necessarily indicate widespread illiteracy. Rather, it reflects the poor availability of books in general and the priority given to transporting tools, provisions, livestock, and firearms rather than books to a colonial wilderness. Nonetheless, most estates that reached probate included at least a few books in their inventories, generally primers, prayer books, practical handbooks on farming, and treatises on medicine. An unusual number of books on mathematics and surveying can be found, denoting not only literacy but numeracy and even mathematical acumen. The most common book to be found in British North America was the Bible.

Levels of literacy were also closely associated with gender. Males may have been twice as likely as females to be literate among southern and middle Atlantic settlers. In New England the difference, while marked, was not so pronounced. This evidence needs to be viewed with great care, however. Women were often taught to read so that they could read the Bible for themselves and to their children. Sometimes female children were promised reading lessons during their tenure as indentured servants. Apparently, however, many women who could read were not taught to write because society saw no need for them to do so. With no legal standing in court, women rarely had the opportunity to sign the types of documents that might survive the ravages of time. In contrast to the 19th century, when women were prolific writers of personal accounts, few colonial women left diaries or journals. The use of written evidence as the only indicator of literacy may have resulted

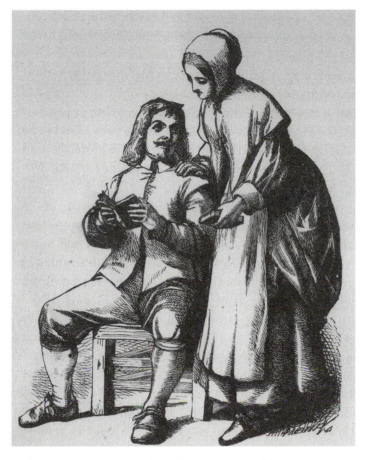

Both men and women read. In the colonies the ability to read may
have been higher than in Europe.

in a serious underestimation of the number of female readers during
this period.[18]

REGIONAL CHARACTER

Although the ethnic composition of modern America has changed dra-
matically since colonial times, many distinctive folkways have persisted
into the 21st century in regions settled by the seven major groups in the
17th and 18th centuries. This was no mere accident of geography. The part
played in the development of British North America by factors such as the
place of origin of the immigrant population cannot be overstated. Equally
important, if not more so, was the religious affiliation of the immigrants,
which was often tied to their place of origin. Questions surrounding

religion and the establishment of state-sponsored churches loomed especially large in the colonial period as legitimate causes for social strife, the confiscation of property, imprisonment, rebellion, and even execution. No fewer than seven of the colonies founded by the English in the 17th century were established specifically for religious motives. Five of these colonies were established by English Puritans in New England: Plymouth (1620), Massachusetts Bay (1630), New Haven (1638), Connecticut (1639), and Rhode Island (1644). The other two were the Catholic colony of Maryland (1633) and the Quaker colony of Pennsylvania (1682).

Rather than founding a sanctuary of religious toleration, the Puritans of New England drove from their midst all those who did not believe in their form of theocracy. Moderates like Roger Williams, Anne Hutchinson, and their followers removed themselves from the Plymouth colony to form their own settlements rather than accept the strict orthodoxy of the Puritan elite. Nonetheless, the societies formed in the Massachusetts Bay colony, New Haven, Rhode Island, and Connecticut were cut essentially from the same cultural cloth. For several decades there was an amazing cooperation between church and government leaders throughout New England, yet with time the influence of the ministers and religious zealots diminished or was undermined by internal tensions, environment, and a reassertion of the traditions of English self-government and self-determination.[19]

The Anglican aristocrats of the Chesapeake Bay area, with the force of an established religion behind them, were no more tolerant than their New England neighbors, disenfranchising all dissenters including Calvinists, Presbyterians, Quakers, and Catholics (even in Catholic-founded Maryland). Notwithstanding their position as members of the established church, Anglicans, and especially their clergy, retained an unsavory reputation among the followers of other Christian sects in the colonies for being indolent, high-living, and scandalous persons.[20]

This lack of religious toleration was not reserved for the colonials of the 17th century. The Scotch-Irish Presbyterians populating the backcountry frontiers of the Carolinas, Virginia, and Pennsylvania in the mid-eighteenth century were not so well organized in their intolerance, but their individual disdain for those outside their kindred groups drove most Calvinists, Pietists, and Quakers north to the friendlier borderlands of Pennsylvania and New York before the Revolution. There is also ample evidence from late in the colonial period of the intolerance—a general repugnance, agitation, and anxiety toward Anglicans and Congregationalists—preached by the English evangelist George Whitefield. Having toured Philadelphia and other cities in 1739, Whitefield set off the Great Awakening, the first "great and spontaneous" religious movement among the American people. The reaction of "Old Light" Christians to those following the "New Light" of the Great Awakening can be summed up by the negative observations of Dr. Alexander Hamilton, a member of the established church, "The spirit of enthusiasm has lately possessed the [New Light] inhabitants of the forests [and] it has been a common practice for companies of 20 or 30 of these hair brained [*sic*] fanatics to ride thro' the woods singing psalms."[21]

In sharp contrast to their mainstream counterparts, the elite among the English and Welsh of William Penn's Quaker colony actively sought out a diversity of European Protestant Pietists, including groups of related peoples from Central Europe loosely known as Germans. Thereby the Quakers hoped to expand the boundaries of their own sect by exhibiting tolerance and open-mindedness toward others. In this hope they were largely frustrated. The German speakers tended to form their own isolated communities, both in Pennsylvania and in central New York, rather than be assimilated into English Quakerism. By their self-imposed isolation, the Germans achieved a far greater social solidarity than many other groups in the colonies. A decade after the American Revolution, many communities founded by German-speaking immigrants in New York, New Jersey, and Pennsylvania "still spoke German, married other Germans, went to German churches, and lived near or next to German neighbors."[22]

The Dutch colonials had roots among the most cosmopolitan people in Europe. The Netherlands, the country of origin of those we commonly call Dutch, is almost invariably identified with the seventeen discrete lowland provinces of northeastern Europe. Yet only the seven northernmost of these provinces surrounding the watershed of the River Maas, the delta of the River Schnede, and the Zuider Zee, were politically united. The southern provinces were known during the colonial period as the Spanish Netherlands or Flanders (present-day Belgium). Formal treaties from as early as 1579 (Peace of Utrecht) referred to the seventeen provinces collectively as "the Lands of the United Netherlands," yet maps from the colonial period labeled the country as "The United Provinces" or "Dutch Republic," and the entire region was commonly referred to as Holland because of that state's prominence among the northern provinces. The individual provinces were deliberately protective about their territorial boundaries. Nonetheless, during their wars of religion with Catholic Spain, and later with Catholic France, the people of the area assembled a collective self-portrait and some sort of patriotic self-consciousness that made them Dutch.[23]

The religious wars of the Protestant Reformation and the Catholic Counter-Reformation, generally encompassing the Thirty Years' Wars (1618–1648), displaced many people from their homes, and the Dutch Republic became an asylum for anti-Catholic religious dissenters from throughout Europe. In a land surrounded by the sea and filled with a diversity of refugees from all over Europe, many of the Dutch turned to overseas trade to make a living. Soon endless trains of river barges and a forest of masts could be seen lining the quays of all the port cities of the Dutch Republic. The republic's principal city, Amsterdam, was a port of great antiquity. In the seventeenth century it was the largest port in the world and one of the most cosmopolitan cities in Europe. Other Dutch ports such as Texel, The Hague, and Antwerp also became great centers of trade.[24]

The colonial town of New Amsterdam grew slowly, but it was destined to reflect much of the character of its namesake. In 1609, one year after Henry Hudson discovered the river that bears his name, a Dutch trading vessel entered Lower New York Bay. The vessel had come to barter beads, knives, hatchets, and cloth for furs with the Raritan nation, a Native American tribe that inhabited the western shore across from the large hilly island occupied by their neighbors, the Manhattans. By 1640, a fort (called Fort William for William of Orange) had been built, and blockhouses for the garrison were erected at the tip of Manhattan Island. A ten-foot wall separated these buildings from the hinterland (Wall Street), and several churches and windmills were built within its precincts. A fine house was built for the colonial governor, and a gallows was erected at the water's edge as a warning to potential criminals or malcontents. The Dutch militia drilled on the common, and several cannon were placed in a well located battery to defend the anchorage. Outlying settlements such as Flushing, Bergen, Bushwick, Haarlem, Ostend, Utrecht, Nassau, and Staten Island were named after places in the old Netherlands, and retained their significance even after a squadron of five English warships entered the harbor at New Amsterdam and took possession of the town from the Dutch colonials in 1664. The residents of the region surrounding Manhattan Island, and later those at the outpost at Fort Orange (Albany) accepted the change in governance with little difficulty mainly because the English brought the promise of a considerable increase in trade. The most significant change for most Dutch colonials was the renaming of the port city and the colony for the English Duke of York (later King James II).

In nine of the colonies established by the English, including the city of New York, Anglicanism was the official religion. In much of the former Dutch colony and in the Dutch holdings along the Hudson and in the Mohawk Valley, however, the residents were left free to follow whatever religions they chose and to continue their reliance on the relationship between tenant and Dutch patroon (large landowner). In the Hudson Valley, besides the Dutch, there were French, Walloons, Palatines, and English. On the island of Manhattan the Dutch were numerically the greatest portion of the 5000 residents, but politically, socially, and economically they quickly lost power to the English speaking population. In 1700 Dutch burghers in New York made up two-thirds of the population in Duchess and Ulster counties, three-quarters in Orange County, five-sixths in Kings County, and nine-tenths of all those living near Albany. In New Jersey they comprised more than three-quarters of all residents in Bergen and Somerset counties.[25]

Many Dutch colonials practiced race-based slavery and were comfortable with its continuance even after their governance had passed to the English. Dutch farmers commonly owned slaves in two's and three's rather than in the large numbers characteristic of Southern colonial plantations. The status of black slaves on Dutch farms was little different from that of white indentured servants and contract laborers. The entire business operation of some Dutch concerns in New York was left to the personal initiative of the slaves who worked there without the intercession of any white other than a hired overseer.

The slaves who were first brought to the Americas came from cultures and religious backgrounds as diverse as their many dialects. Upon arrival in the colonies, they found themselves intermingled with other Africans who held a wide range of beliefs and practiced a multiplicity of rites. The desire to hold true to ancestral customs was a strong one and some slaves would periodically steal away to neighboring farms to join with others from the same ethnic group. Lacking an understanding of African cultures and having no desire to cultivate one, many slaveholders did their best to prevent these liaisons and to strip the slaves of their native culture. Effectively, however, much of African culture was merely driven underground, to be practiced in secret and transformed by exposure to other African customs and to European language and culture. This ongoing and complex process spanned generations and created, especially in the South, a whole new set of African-American folkways.

Historians investigating the survival of African cultural features among New World blacks agree that in Latin America and the islands of the West Indies "survivals from African religion [and culture] are not only to be encountered everywhere, but such carry-overs are so distinct that they may be identified with particular tribal groups." Conversely, the same authorities "have been put to great effort to prove that in North American black society any African cultural vestiges have survived at all."[26] This dichotomy suggests that there is a need to examine more closely the different slave systems of the Western Hemisphere, including the need to know much more about the impact on slavery of different social systems under the Spanish, Portuguese, French, English, and British colonials.

THE ENGLISH PURITANS: NEW ENGLAND

The earliest English immigrants—Jamestown settlers in Virginia (1607) and the Pilgrims of Plymouth, Massachusetts (1620)—shared many characteristics with the immigrants that followed them, but they were too few to warrant inclusion as discrete migrant waves. Nonetheless, the first mass migration into the English colonies was made by Puritans very much like the Pilgrims of the 1620s. The Plymouth plantation had grown slowly at first, with a few score new arrivals each year, but a great flood of Puritan migration began in 1630 when 700 English colonists arrived in a single season. By 1640, more than 21,000 people had come to the shores of New England. "The [Puritans] came to America not only because they were unable to realize their religious aspirations in old England. They were also driven by a profound disquiet over the state of contemporary English society." The Puritan movement was religiously and socially conservative, and it valued strict social order and community control in order to "conform as closely as possible to traditional English conceptions of the ideal, well-ordered commonwealth." By 1660 the New England colonies had twice the population of those in the Chesapeake Bay although the latter colonies were a generation older.[27]

Surrounded by available and generally vacant land,[28] many Puritans quickly moved away from the centers of authority, spreading out their settlements along the Massachusetts coast or forming new colonies along the rivers of Connecticut. Although seemingly scattered in an overwhelming wilderness, each independent settlement featured certain common characteristics such as a tightly constructed form of government, a formally covenanted social structure, and a dominant voice among its religious leaders. Puritans counseled Christian obedience, but their doctrines unfortunately left the policing of the boundaries between righteousness and sinfulness to the judgment of the secular authorities. This judgment generally reflected the interests and beliefs of those persons attracted to the Puritan sect in Britain. Among yeoman farmers and artisans, who together constituted a super majority of the population, were an extraordinary number of persons familiar with law and government and also deeply involved with the practice of religion. The social and cultural structure of the region remained dominated by this minority of magistrates and ministers for many decades. This perception may be skewed somewhat by the tendency of lawyers, government officials, and preachers to leave more copious written records than craftsmen or agricultural workers.[29]

No other part of British North America could claim such a high proportion of university graduates as New England. Additionally, government documents, court proceedings, sermons, godly treatises, diaries, and correspondence authored by the social elite may have been better preserved in antiquity and more extensively used than other sources by well-meaning but generally provincial 19th-century historians. The genesis of this historical bias has been attributed to the work of New England historian George Bancroft, who immediately after the American Civil War proposed that the roots of the political and cultural development of the United States ran not back to the history of early Virginia, but back to the history of Plymouth and the New England colonies. According to Bancroft and the generation of Ivy League historians that followed his lead, Southern history before the Civil War could serve only as "a negative example of what America had to overcome before it could finally realize its true self."[30]

A later generation of 19th-century historians uncovered additional records from dissenting churches; land, probate, and tax records from towns and villages; colonial census records (taken before the official U.S. Census was established); and other demographic data to expand their view of society to include the contributions of a wider segment of the colonial population in the development of American fundamentals. Ironically, this "new" view more closely parallels that of the writings of the colonials themselves.[31]

THE ENGLISH ROYALISTS: CHESAPEAKE

The second wave of English immigrants—very much like the Jamestown settlers of 1607—was composed of a small Royalist elite and a larger number of indentured servants and laborers from the south of England. They flowed sporadically into Virginia riding the changing tides of civil strife in England from approximately 1642 to 1725. Those best described as the gentry or the aristocracy arrived in America in the greatest numbers during the English Civil Wars (1642–1649) and during the Puritan controlled Republican Period (1649–1658). By coming to America these royalists avoided both the trauma of a war-torn nation and the injustices heaped upon those who continued to support the Crown by the Lord Protector, Oliver Cromwell, and his Puritan supporters.

The flow and counterflow of Royalists and Puritans across the Atlantic is a significant characteristic of Anglo-American immigration in the 17th century. Elizabethan England (1558–1603) had been generally tolerant of the Puritans, viewing them as a nuisance rather than a threat. During the reign of James I (1603–1625), they were persecuted and the number of immigrants increased slightly, but the great Puritan migrations to New England took place during the truly repressive reign of Charles I (1625–1649). The years of the English Civil War actually saw a reverse flow of immigrants as one-third of young Puritan males returned to England to fight in the Parliamentary armies. During the Republican period, with both the monarchy and the House of Lords abolished, many Royalists and some Catholics (Papists) migrated to Virginia and Maryland to avoid Puritan repression—a trend that was reversed with the Restoration of the monarchy in 1660.

Nonetheless, during this period of internecine strife many royalist families found a good life, abundant land, and a satisfactory income in the North American wilderness. The wealth to be realized from growing tobacco in the Chesapeake was second only to that available from growing sugar in the West Indies. Yet there was no vacant land in the islands while there were thousands of fertile acres available in Virginia and the Carolinas. The total number of persons migrating to this region during this period was perhaps 45,000. The surviving population in 1660 was reduced to half this number by disease, starvation, and Indian attacks.

Between 1661 and 1665, the Carolinas were opened to occupation by the younger sons of the Royalist aristocracy, who were more interested in making money from trade and farming than finding religious toleration or supporting Royalist causes.

THE ENGLISH QUAKERS: PENNSYLVANIA

The third wave of English immigrants was composed of persons from Wales and the northern midlands of England who came to the Delaware Valley between 1675 and 1715. Because of the fine climate, the abundant game and vegetation, and the good relations fostered by the Penn family with the local Indian tribes, most of the early settlers survived. Of the approximately 23,000 immigrants in this group, most were Quaker tradesmen, artisans, and farmers, who formed a more egalitarian social order than that of New England or tidewater Virginia.

The persecution of Quakers in Britain under the Test Act of 1673 had led William Penn to devise his plan for a Quaker colony in the New World, and the rigid enforcement of the act over the next decades increased Quaker migration to America. These immigrants made extraordinary efforts to develop the Delaware River Valley and southeastern Pennsylvania, and they strongly influenced the unique character of the colonial frontiersman and settler. Penn personally directed the development of the land he had been granted. By the beginning of the 18th century, Penn's own efforts and those of his heirs, who took an active role in organizing the province, had created the most successful of the English colonies as measured by contemporary standards.

Penn recruited his Quaker population disproportionately from among the Cheshire and Welsh farmsteads of England. For generations these farmers had successfully carved a living in a difficult environment, and they combined their religion and their agricultural experience into a spiritual framework that well served the economically challenging conditions of a new land. This led to Pennsylvania's unchallenged economic dominance in the colonial period.

THE SCOTCH-IRISH: THE FRONTIER

The fourth wave of English-speaking immigrants were composed mostly of persons of Scotch-Irish descent from the borderlands of Britain and Ireland. They settled in the Appalachian backcountry of the southern colonies from 1718 to 1775. The widely used term *Scotch-Irish* is actually a misnomer. Scots from Ireland might be more precise. This group shared a common language and history with the other Anglo-cultural groups in much the same way that any subject people might be influenced by the culture of its conquerors. Under the encouragement of James I, many Scots, perhaps 50,000, had immigrated to Ulster in Ireland. They were a hardy and clannish people who regarded the native Irish as "semi-savages, uncivilized, and unfriendly." There was practically no intermarriage between the Presbyterian Scots and the Roman Catholic Irish. The Scotch in Ireland had been tenants and cottagers under the rule of English land-lords, and under the brief reign of the pro-Catholic James II they were "openly persecuted, their industries dissolved, their holdings seized, [and] their lives and livelihood in constant danger."[32] Not even the accession in 1688 of William of Orange, a Protestant, could stem the tide of persecution as absentee English landlords turned the Scots off their land. Under these conditions emigration to America became a promising enterprise.[33]

The attitudes of the Scotch-Irish in America reflected a long and tumultuous history. The accession of the royal Scottish house of Stuart on the death of Elizabeth I had combined the ancient Welsh, English, and Scottish thrones into a single British monarchy for the first time in 1603. James Stuart was simultaneously King James I of England and King James VI of Scotland. The general attitude of peaceful religious coexis-tence exhibited by James, a Scotch Presbyterian with Catholic sympathies, led to an immediate decline in the influence of Puritans in govern-ment. More overt Catholic predilections by James's successor, Charles I, provided a religious impetus to the English Civil Wars and fueled a rampant religious intolerance during the period of the Republic and the Restoration of the Stuart line. The Glorious Revolution of 1688 replaced James II with his own daughter Mary and her Dutch husband, William of Orange. William, a protestant, had been the focus of anti-Catholic and pro-Calvinist intrigue since boyhood, and he found little support among the largely Presbyterian Stuart loyalists especially after Mary's death early in his reign.

The death in 1715 of Mary's sister Anne, the last Stuart monarch of Great Britain, caused the Scots to lose the final shreds of their political influence. The accession of George I of the German House of Hanover alienated many Scots from the British Crown. A number of Jacobean plots and insurrections followed as the Scots tried and failed to regain the British throne for one of the legitimate descendants of James II then living in Europe. Five decades of rebellion, persecution, and repression followed, particularly in 1715, 1719, and 1745. The violent repression of the Scottish highlanders by the Hanoverian kings, particularly after the decisive battle of Culloden in 1746, ended any practical hope of renewing the Stuart Dynasty.

Thereafter, the power of the clans was gone forever, as was the old cattle economy of the highland chiefs that had dominated Scottish culture and family life. A growing number of English landlords introduced sheep to the Scottish and Irish hill country, clearing entire counties of tenant farm-ers to make way for their vast woolly herds and driving many Scots from Britain during the next decade.[34] Scottish families immigrating to America tended to draw their kinfolk to follow even from as far away as Ireland.

"Within a generation or two, by a gentle and ironic twist of history, the Scots of Scotland and the Scots of Ireland became in the public mind one folk known only, then and now, as Scotch-Irish."[35]

It is not difficult to understate the hatred that formed between the Scottish Presbyterians and the English Anglicans during this period. Having chaffed under the yoke of Hanoverian rule in Scotland, and under mean-spirited absentee English landlords in northern Ireland, the Scotch and Scotch-Irish Presbyterians formed a great hatred for the institutions of English government. This was especially true when London attempted to force Anglicanism upon them. Many Scots who settled in North America were found either to be actively anti-English or at least unwilling to coop-erate with English colonial authorities. Ardently Presbyterian, the Scots were hostile to both Congregationalists and Anglicans. At the same time that they scorned the religiously tolerant but dissident Quakers because of their self-proclaimed pacifism, they reluctantly endured the Catholics because of French support for the Stuart pretender to the throne. Even their Presbyterian contemporaries in Britain criticized the Scotch-Irish in America, claiming that their attitudes were "productive of confusion" and that they advocated "the most wicked and destructive of doctrines and practices."[36]

The first Scotch-Irish settlement in America was established in 1632 along the eastern shore of Maryland, but the migration began in earnest around 1719 after a series of bad harvests in Ulster and a failed Jacobean revolt in Scotland. The Scotch-Irish who began to arrive in America in 1728 turned largely toward the Maryland, Virginia, and Carolina fron-tiers, but the Susquehanna River served as a psychological barrier to further migration for a number of years. A smaller number of Scotch-Irish families arriving in Philadelphia turned into northern New Jersey. The peak years of Scotch-Irish emigration thereafter were 1741, 1755, and 1767, but members of this group continued to trickle onto the frontiers in lesser numbers by passing through the older settlements to live on the edge of civilization until the outbreak of the American Revolution.[37]

More than 90 percent of the backcountry settlers had Scottish roots, with the remainder being composed almost entirely of German-speaking immi-grants.[38] The total number of persons of Scottish ancestry migrating to these regions during these periods may have been in excess of 250,000. However, tracing the movements of these Scotch-Irish immigrants has proved dif-ficult for historians and genealogists because a large number of British colonists to New England or Virginia were also Presbyterians with Scottish or Irish surnames but were not part of this distinct migrant group.[39]

THE DUTCH: NEW YORK

Some of the earliest explorations of the northeastern Atlantic seacoast were conducted under Dutch patronage. Henry Hudson, Adrien van

Block, and Giovanni da Verrezano all represented Dutch commercial interests in the days before Britain had developed its trading empire. Given
an early start in the exploration and settlement of the New Netherlands
colony in the 17th century, the directors of the Dutch West India Company
in Holland nonetheless had great difficulty in finding settlers of an
appropriate type from among the natives of the United Provinces. The
Dutch had no reason to leave their homeland for the New World. Life in
Holland was easy, rich, and peaceful. Their cities were cosmopolitan, their
entertainments sophisticated, and their politics uncluttered by dynas-
tic squabbling. Religious toleration was practiced throughout all seven
Dutch provinces, but cultural diversity was not their forte. Refugees and
dissenters were welcome, but they were expected to live their lives as the
Dutch did—a national characteristic that was unacceptable to the early
English Puritans who tried to live there.[40]

The directors of the Dutch West India Company therefore enlisted a
number of foreign religious refugees among their settlers to America. The
company's orders required all settlers to be at least nominal members
of the Dutch Reformed Church (a Calvinist faith), which may account
for the large proportion of Walloons and Huguenots that answered the
call. Walloons were French-speaking Calvinists from the southernmost
provinces of the Spanish Netherlands (Flanders). The Huguenots were
Protestant refugees from within France. Both the Walloons and Huguenots
were targets of the relentless persecution of the Catholic regimes of Spain
and France, respectively. Although Walloon immigration to America was
never significant, a great wave of Huguenot emigration began in 1685
when the Edict of Nantes was revoked and French Protestants were once
again made subject to open religious persecution.

The early activities of the Dutch West India Company in America are
not clear in the historical record mainly because its business records were
systematically destroyed in the 19th century before interested historians
could amass a significant body of research from them. Yet, surviving letters and other miscellaneous documents reveal much of the early history
of the Dutch colony of New Netherlands. For example, when the Dutch
Reformed minister Jonas Michaelius arrived in New Amsterdam in 1628
to oversee the organization of the Dutch Reformed religion in the colony,
he was shocked to find a substantial number of Spaniards, Portuguese,
and Italians—all nominally members of some protestant sect—living in
the colony. Many of these persons were less than wholehearted devotees
of sectarian Dutch Calvinism.[41] Michaelius and his successors moved to
enforce a strict adherence to the Calvinist faith, but in 1653 the directors
of the Company in Holland, valuing profit over orthodoxy, ordered the
toleration of variations in worship as long as they were held in diplomatic
privacy. Direct persecution of Catholics was halted, and a small conclave
of Sephardic Jews, those whose ancestry lay in the Iberian Peninsula, was
tolerated by the colonial Dutch government.[42]

By the time of the American Revolution there were seventeen houses of worship in the city of New York representing fourteen different religions or sects. The Anglicans were the largest group in the city, but the Presbyterians outnumbered them in the rest of the colony. There were three Anglican churches, three Dutch churches (each belonging to a different sect), and two Presbyterian meeting houses. There was one house of worship for each of the following: Judaic, Lutheran, New Light Lutheran, Calvinist, Moravian, Anabaptist, Huguenot, and New Light Scottish. There was no Catholic Church as such, but a priest, originally from Maryland, had openly instituted a weekly Sunday Mass and had ministered to the small Catholic population for several years by rotating his base of operations through several private homes.[43]

Dutch immigration to New Netherlands in the 1640s survived the change to English governance under the managers appointed by the Duke of York in 1664, and it was bolstered by accession to the English throne of William of Orange in 1688. As hereditary ruler of Holland, William was the virtual ruler of the United Provinces. His acceptance of the English throne created an alliance of Dutch and English interests against the Catholic Bourbon kingdoms of France and Spain that helped to reawaken and reinforce anti-Catholic sentiment in the English colonies. William and Mary had driven James II from the English throne, and continued animosity between those loyal to James and those supporting William helped to fuel a violent upheaval in New York known as Leisler's Rebellion. Sparked in part by questions of royal authority, a Dutch rebel named Jacob Leisler raised a group of his countrymen, seized Fort William in lower Manhattan, and attempted to gain control of the colony in 1691. Forces loyal to James under another Dutchman, Peter Schuyler held Albany. Ironically, the unrest continued until agents of William and Mary jailed Leisler two years later for treason even though he was ostensibly acting in their behalf.[44]

A decade of war with France following James's deposition created an alliance of Dutch and English interests in Europe that helped to reinforce Anglo-Dutch cooperation in the colonies. Dutch emigration to America remained significant until about 1735. Hundreds of families came by boat to the present site of New Brunswick, New Jersey to ascend the rivers that emptied into New York Harbor, and advanced north and west into New Jersey and Pennsylvania. They also established Dutch settlements on the upper Hudson River with names like Poughkeepsie, Kinderhook, and Watervliet. A number of Dutch settlements scattered along the route known as the Old Mine Road (U.S. Route 209) from Ulster County, New York, south into the Delaware Water Gap of Pennsylvania and beyond quickly dominated the region. In 1737, no fewer than four Dutch Reformed churches served both sides of the Delaware River from present-day Port Jervis, New York, to the Water Gap—a distance of only forty miles. The influence of the Dutch was so strong that several families with

Leisler's Rebellion was a symptom of the confusion caused in the colonies by political upheavals many thousands of miles away. While Leisler was initially supported by the Crown, he was ultimately hanged for overstepping his authority.

English roots were attending Dutch churches and speaking the Dutch language as their own within two decades of their arrival.[45]

THE GERMANS: PENNSYLVANIA

The earliest German-speaking immigrants to America in the 17th century have been described as "poor and alienated, and, to some extent, suffer[ing] from the religious persecution of that era." Many represented the dominant culture of the Rhineland in central Europe. A few were formally educated, most were capable farmers and husbandmen, and many were skilled tradesmen who needed only economic opportunity and political stability to be self-sufficient. Although these characteristics did not cause them to stand out among other immigrant groups, they did form a subculture of German-speaking peoples, founded in commonly held religious principles derived from the Protestant Reformation. "These religious principles were applied to their daily lives, further shaping the form of the subculture and dictating the values by which these hardy people lived." This influence of religion on daily life was particularly true among adherents of the Anabaptist and German Pietist movements.[46]

Much like their English-speaking counterparts, Germans immigrated to America in waves. The first movement, which began around 1683, though not numerous, consisted of well-organized radical Pietist groups that moved to Pennsylvania to find religious toleration. William Penn's agents traveled through southwestern Germany and Switzerland, converting some residents to Quakerism and interesting others in removing to Pennsylvania. The British government also circulated pamphlets and other propaganda encouraging German immigration to Anglo-America throughout the loosely knit principalities of central Europe.

The first major success in finding willing German immigrants came in 1710 after one of the most disastrous agricultural seasons in recent European history. More than 2,000 Palatine Germans traveling in ten ships contracted to serve as tenants and laborers for Robert Livingston, who had founded plantations on the Hudson River in New York with a view to establishing the commercial production of naval stores such as masts, pitch, and hemp for the British Royal Navy. The Palatines became disgruntled when the project lost the support of the government, and many ultimately removed to the Delaware River Valley and Berks County in Pennsylvania, where their cultural legacy can still be observed. A smaller group of Palatines traveled up the Hudson River to settle in the Mohawk Valley or on the Schoharie land grant in central New York.

From 1717 through the next half century, a different type of immigrant arrived from Germany, seeking an independent life based on the availability of inexpensive land and an unfettered opportunity to improve themselves economically. In one year, almost 12,000 German-speaking immigrants arrived in Pennsylvania, and the Quaker-controlled government became uneasy lest the province become a minor German "state within a state." However, subsequent declines in the absolute number of new immigrants allayed these fears somewhat.[47]

Around 1740, a new flood of Germans began to enter the colonies, and the pace of this immigration did not falter until the advent of the American Revolution. The large majority of these immigrants settled in parts of southeastern Pennsylvania, but many others moved into the backcountry of Maryland and Virginia or joined their comrades in central New York. Several shiploads of immigrants landed in Halifax, Nova Scotia, around 1750, and others landed in Massachusetts and Maine. A group of Palatines whose ship was blown off course for New York landed instead in Philadelphia. Striking overland for New York City on the Old York Road, many of them became enamored of the region through which they were passing and chose to settle in Pennsylvania and New Jersey. These Pennsylvania Germans (incorrectly called Pennsylvania Dutch) maintained close relations among themselves well beyond the revolutionary period.[48]

During this long period of immigration almost 85,000 Germans were recruited by land speculators or by those hoping to realize a profit from transporting them to their destinations. Many of these immigrants had been adversely affected by the adoption of new farming methods in the Rhine Valley that supplanted the older common field system with a more intensive, capitalistic form of cultivation. European landowners increasingly enclosed common fields for their own private use; raised the fees charged to tenants for grazing livestock on common lands; and banned meetings of the village assembly of tenants and agricultural workers. While small subsistence farming still existed, a growing population pressure caused the extant common fields to quickly disappear as the peasants divided their lands into smaller and smaller parts to provide fields for their children. To stem this tide of land partition some governments in the Rhineland outlawed marriage for persons under twenty-five and attempted to interfere with the traditional inheritance customs of the villagers.[49]

The residents of these Rhineland villages, however, were not powerless rural peasants unfamiliar with politics. They often took a direct role in dealing with offensive local aristocrats by appealing to higher authorities when they perceived a threat to their interests. Many of those who chose to come to North America had been "inhabitants of strong, tightly knit nuclear villages [that] had struggled with the local nobles, who were trying to increase their presence, status, and wealth in society." These clashes with the European nobility did not cause the villagers to immigrate to America, but they did help to establish a pattern of political awareness that would resurface among those who came to the colonies. The best interests of their local community usually shaped their collective political will, and in Pennsylvania or New York they would resolve their conflicts with the agents of the British Crown by appealing to their colonial legislatures and governors.[50]

Letters from friends and relations already in America served as an added impetus to continued immigration, and Germans generally left Europe in small groups composed of other members of their village or town. Although peasants were supposed to pay a fee and receive permission to emigrate from the landowner to whom they owed allegiance, most left without paying and without permission. A single peasant from the village of Hoffenheim immigrated to Pennsylvania in 1720 in response to new pressures placed upon the village by the local ruler. During the next three years almost three dozen of his fellow villagers followed him to America.

The prospect of free or very cheap land caused many Germans to abandon a livelihood scratching in the worn-out garden patches of Europe for the promise of a better life in America where "plantations" of three hundred and four hundred acres were promised. Early immigrants to British North America reported that "there was so much land and freedom from encumbrances on its use that one might never again face poverty." There was land enough to provide for extensive agriculture by first-generation immigrants with plenty left over for all their children when they came of age.[51]

The promise of religious freedom or toleration, often stressed by historians as an incentive for immigration, has perhaps been overemphasized as one of the causes of German migration to Anglo-America. The British colonial governments generally enforced the legal standing of the established church through a universal system of tithes. Yet the population was generally free to practice and support the religion of their choice as long as they still paid for the maintenance of the Anglican Church and the livelihood of its ministers. This system of religious tithes was much the same as that used throughout Germany. Nonetheless, most Germans ultimately settled in regions where there was little enforcement of an allegiance to the established church beyond the collection of money. Whether this was due to the indifference of the King's officials, the influence of their own large numbers or other unidentified factors defies resolution. More important to them than religious toleration, German immigrants found that in America they were free from having their sons drafted into the man-power starved armies of minor 18th century nobles. They were also freed from having their property confiscated by the undisciplined, plague-carrying foragers that had ravaged central Europe during decades of religious and political warfare.[52]

By 1750, immigrants from Wurttemberg, Baden-Durlach, Breisgau, Speyer, Lower Neckar, and the City of Ulm had joined those from the Palatine Electorate, settling the far northwestern portion of New Jersey and penetrating westward into the region surrounding Reading and Harrisburg, Pennsylvania. These Germans separated themselves from the English in southeastern Pennsylvania, a process aided by their own lack of the English language. Traveling through this region in 1775, Joshua Gilpin noted, "I never knew before the total want of a language for in this respect we might as well have been in the middle of Germany." The German settlers were joined during the American Revolution by thousands of deserters from the Hessian regiments fighting for the British Crown, who simply blended into the background of German settlements.[53]

Not all German settlers separated themselves from the English in this way. Some played an important role in the colonial politics of Pennsylvania. Many German men swore allegiance to the British Crown in the early part of the 18th century and became naturalized citizens with the right to vote in colonial elections. Although most refused to seek or to hold office because of their religious scruples, they used their numbers and their ethnic solidarity to help sway the Quaker-controlled colonial legislature. In 1755, after General Edward Braddock's defeat at the hands of the French and Indians in western Pennsylvania, a mob of Germans carried the mutilated corpses of frontier settlers into Philadelphia to dramatize to the pacifist Quaker assembly that self-defense had become a matter of life and death. Although many German Pietists also believed in pacifism, they immediately pressured the Quakers in the legislature to provide a string of frontier forts for their defense. In 1765 immediately after suffering the depredations of Pontiac's Rebellion, 2,700 Germans became naturalized—easily ten times the usual number for an entire year. Germans—pacifists and nonpacifists alike—understood that an uncontrolled Indian presence on the borders of the colony might roll back the frontier and make land in the heartland of Pennsylvania not only untenable but also unaffordable.

THE AFRICANS

Almost all the Africans who came to America were brought in as slaves and their descendants remained in bondage for generations. Africans were the most numerous Old World immigrants to North America before the middle of the 18th century.[54] Ethnologists have determined that the lineage of most African Americans can be traced to only a few dozen tribes that inhabited the western part of the African continent. These tribal societies were largely agricultural. In contrast to white Europeans, who had no practical knowledge of its cultivation, west African blacks were thoroughly familiar with the basic food crop of the 17th-century colonies: rice. "It is important to consider the fact that literally hundreds of black immigrants were more familiar with the planting, hoeing, processing, and cooking of rice than were the European settlers that purchased them."[55] While not all were experts in rice farming, most black slaves who came to America were already experts in other farming methodologies and animal husbandry. The patterns and rhythms of the agricultural cycle were not imposed on these people by European owners but retained from their West African forebears. Although the trans-Atlantic African slave trade was outlawed by mutual agreement between Britain and the United States in 1808, race-based slavery was continued by fostering a "natural increase" among those held in bondage.

In British North America, the ideal of a master-slave relationship steeped in Christianity fed the myth of the benevolent planter-patriarch who oversaw the simple, helpless, and heathen Africans. With time, however, it was not unusual for slaves to outnumber whites not only on the plantations but also in racially mixed Christian churches. This manifestation of the plantation missionaries' success was misleading, however, because it represented only one component of a slave's religious experience. In the secrecy of their cabins and amid "brush" or "hush arbors," slaves met free from the owner's gaze to practice a religion that addressed issues other than a slave's subservience to his master. The struggle for freedom and deliverance was often the subject of Judeo-Christian prayer, and these themes attributed to the persecuted Israelites of the Old Testament resonated well with black worshipers. Through prayer, song, and "feeling the spirit," slaves gained renewed strength through hope. Their informal

prayer meetings were filled with spirituals, which perpetuated a continuity with African music and performance. Outlawed by slave owners,
the drums that had once been a vital part of their spiritual expression
were replaced by rhythmic hand-clapping and foot-stomping known as
"shouting." Rather than truly adopting white Christian principles, the
slaves had simply adapted the Christian religion to themselves.[56]

Slave children did not belong to their parents but were generally considered the property of the mother's master. The father and the father's
master, should he be a different person than the mother's owner, were
denied any standing in regard to the offspring of slave unions. The offspring of a free man and a slave woman was, thereby, a slave; yet the
offspring of a slave and a free woman was considered to be freeborn even
if the woman was black. Even the children of a white master by a slave
mother were born slaves under British colonial law. In the case of a dispute in this regard, with very few exceptions, whenever a slave's human
rights came into conflict with a master's property rights, the courts invariably decided in favor of the master.

Some blacks of African heritage came to America as freemen, wage
earners, sailors, artisans, and craftspersons. Many of these moved out
onto the frontiers to escape white prejudice in the coastal communities.
Nonetheless, some historians question whether common notions characteristic of American racial prejudice preceded slavery or whether they
developed largely after blacks came to be viewed as plantation laborers.[57]
While this view was particularly common in the southern colonies, race-
based slavery was not isolated in the south. It was a legally recognized
institution throughout the British colonies, and many New England communities counted large numbers of black slaves among their populations
as late as the 1840s.[58]

A number of features distinguished slave labor in the northern colonies from that in the South. In the North, slaves were set to the same
tasks that white laborers were accustomed to perform, and they worked
as individuals or in small groups as did whites. Many were household
servants, dock workers and sailors, or artisans and crafts persons. In the
South, almost all blacks served as field hands, toiling to produce food,
livestock, or staple crops for export. Gang labor was common on large
Southern plantations. Those having fifty or more slaves generally divided
their workers into two gangs. The most able-bodied men, and sometimes
women, were known as plow-hands. Less capable workers were designated as hoe-hands. On some plantations, trash-gangs were assigned
to such light work as weeding and yard cleanup. This last group often
included children, elderly persons, or others having limiting physical
factors. The gang was generally headed by a slave driver, usually chosen
from among the male slaves of the gang.

The work experience and acclimatization to the colonial environment
of free blacks and black indentured servants differed little from that of

whites immigrants in similar circumstances. Native Americans on the frontiers were no more tolerant of blacks invading their lands than they were of whites. Black families were just as likely to be attacked and slain on the frontier as were white families, and blacks were given no special consideration when it came to adoption or torture. A significant exception was the Florida wilderness where Indians and escaped black slaves seem to have formed an alliance to resist both the Spanish and the English that lasted well into the 19th century. Free black craftsmen and servants seem to have preferred to live in an urban setting and were twice as likely to live in cities as slaves, who were primarily agricultural workers. In cosmopolitan areas, blacks found opportunities for employment, exposure to black culture and religious communities, and the company of other freemen and artisans. However, the majority of free blacks lived on the margins of poverty and were subject to detention and questioning by the authorities without cause. Moreover, they were continually encouraged to enter into indenture agreements or to sell themselves into slavery.

The systematic physical abuse of black freemen was generally limited to the rural areas of the South, but all blacks were exposed to some form of racial prejudice by the vast majority of whites throughout British North America.[59] Free blacks lived hard lives, yet many displayed fortitude, courage, and a sense of dignity throughout. Nonetheless, a minority of free blacks condoned slavery, used slave labor in their businesses, and even owned slaves. Black tradesmen and artisans, in particular, owned many of their fellow black workers, an arrangement often entered into in lieu of an apprenticeship agreement. Incredibly, many of these black slaves were family members and close relatives, who received the protection of the law in many colonies because of their status as slaves.[60]

NOTES

1. Quoted in Aaron Spencer Fogleman, *Hopeful Journeys: German Immigration, Settlement, and Political Culture in Colonial America, 1717–1775* (Philadelphia: University of Pennsylvania Press, 1996), 72.

2. David Hackett Fischer, *Albion's Seed: Four British Folkways in America* (New York: Oxford University Press, 1989), 8–9.

3. Ibid., 6–11. The authors are thankful to Fischer for his use of the term *folkways* to describe these characteristic categories.

4. Ibid., 6.

5. David Brion Davis, *Slavery in the Colonial Chesapeake* (Williamsburg: Colonial Williamsburg Foundation, 1994), 5.

6. Quoted in Peter H. Wood, *Black Majority: Negroes in Colonial South Carolina from 1670 through the Stono Rebellion* (New York: W.W. Norton, 1996), 7–8.

7. Philip D. Curtin, *The Atlantic Slave Trade: A Census* (Madison: University of Wisconsin Press, 1975), 13.

8. Ibid., 145.

9. Ibid., 235.

10. Ibid., 268.

11. Philip A. Bruce, *Economic History of Virginia in the Seventeenth Century: An Inquiry into the Material Condition of the People, Based on Original and Contemporaneous Records* (New York: MacMillan, 1896), 573.

12. J. P. Mayer, ed., *Journey to America, by Alexis de Tocqueville* (1832; reprint, New Haven: Yale University Press, 1960), 61.

13. Both quotations from Wood, *Black Majority*, 85.

14. Robert Leckie, *A Few Acres of Snow: The Saga of the French and Indian Wars* (New York: John Wiley and Sons, 1999), 259.

15. Fischer, *Albion's Seed*, 610, 610n.

16. Ibid., 716.

17. Selma R. Williams, *Demeter's Daughters: The Women Who Founded America 1587–1789* (New York: Atheneum, 1976), 109.

18. See Dorothy Denneen Volo and James M. Volo, *Daily Life in Civil War America* (Westport: Greenwood Press, 1998); and James M. Volo and Dorothy Denneen Volo, *Encyclopedia of the Antebellum South* (Westport: Greenwood Press, 2000).

19. Gerald N. Grob and Robert N. Beck, eds., *American Ideas, Source Readings in the Intellectual History of the United States: Foundations, 1629–1865* (New York: Free Press, 1963), 4.

20. Carl Bridenbaugh, ed., *Gentleman's Progress: The Intinerarium of Dr. Alexander Hamilton, 1744* (Chapel Hill: University of North Carolina Press, 1948), 206.

21. Ibid., 10.

22. Fogleman, *Hopeful Journeys*, 12.

23. Simon Schama, *The Embarrassment of Riches: An Interpretation of Dutch Culture in the Golden Age* (New York: Vintage Books, 1997), 54.

24. G. J. Marcus, *The Formative Centuries: A Naval History of England* (Boston: Little, Brown, 1961), 197.

25. North Callahan, *Royal Raiders: The Tories of the American Revolution* (New York: Bobbs-Merrill, 1963), 126.

26. Stanley M. Elkins, *Slavery: A Problem in American Institutional and Intellectual Life* (New York: Grosset and Dunlap, 1963), 102–3.

27. Jack P. Greene, *Pursuits of Happiness: The Social Development of Early Modern British Colonies and the Formation of American Culture* (Chapel Hill: University of North Carolina Press, 1988), 21–22.

28. Much of the native population of coastal New England had succumbed to a series of epidemic diseases brought from Europe by fishermen and coastal traders, leaving cleared fields and untended orchards for the English to occupy.

29. Louis B. Wright, *The Cultural Life of the American Colonies* (Mineola, NY: Dover Publications, 2002), 101.

30. Quoted in Jack P. Greene, *Pursuits of Happiness*, 3.

31. Foremost in the field of precise historical scholarship in the nineteenth century were Jared Sparks, Peter Force, and Francis Parkman. They exerted an influence out of proportion to their number largely because they occupied the halls of academia, particularly at Harvard University where each had attended. With the exception of their coverage of tidewater Virginia, each had his own set of prejudices that tended to maximize the contributions of New England and minimize those of southern and backcountry society. See Daniel Blake Smith, "The Study of the Family in Early America: Trends, Problems, and Prospects," *William and Mary Quarterly* 3rd series, 39 (1982), 4.

32. Paul Swain Havens, *Chambersburg: Frontier Town, 1730–1794* (Chambersburg, PA: Craft Press, 1975), 16–17.

33. Ibid., 18.

34. Bryan Perrett, *The Real Hornblower: The Life and Times of Admiral Sir James Gordon, GCB* (Annapolis: Naval Institute Press, 1997), 130.

35. Havens, *Chambersburg*, 19–20.

36. Quoted in Parke Rouse Jr., *The Great Wagon Road from Philadelphia to the South* (New York: McGraw-Hill, 1973), 59.

37. Havens, *Chambersburg*, 21.

38. Fischer, *Albion's Seed*, 606.

39. See the chart in Fischer, 804.

40. For addition information see Schama, *Embarrassment of Riches*.

41. Louis B. Wright, *The Atlantic Frontier: Colonial American Civilization, 1607–1763* (New York: Alfred A. Knopf, 1951), 164–68.

42. Ibid., 10.

43. See Bruce Bliven Jr., *Under the Guns: New York, 1775–1776* (New York: Harper and Row, 1972), 18

44. Leisler served as interim governor but was later hanged for plotting treason.

45. Peter O. Wacker, *The Musconetcong Valley of New Jersey: A Historical Geography* (New Brunswick, NJ: Rutgers University Press, 1968), 42; and George W. Cummins, *History of Warren County* (New York: Lewis Historical Publishing, 1922), 73.

46. Alvin E. Conner, *Sectarian Childrearing: The Dunkers, 1708–1900* (Gettysburg: Brethren Heritage, 2000) 1.

47. Havens, *Chambersburg*, 26.

48. Wacker, *The Musconetcong Valley of New Jersey*, 35–36.

49. Fogleman, *Hopeful Journeys*, 25.

50. Ibid., 48.

51. Quoted in Ibid., 33.

52. Ibid., 35.

53. Wacker, *The Musconetcong Valley of New Jersey*, 50–51; and Joshua Gilpin, "Journey to Bethlehem," *Pennsylvania Magazine of History and Biography*, XLVI (1922), 25.

54. Curtin, *Atlantic Slave Trade*, 3.

55. Wood, *Black Majority*, 59–60.

56. See Volo and Volo, *Encyclopedia of the Antebellum South*, 214.

57. Kenneth Morgan, *Slavery and Servitude in Colonial North America* (New York: New York University Press, 2000), 4.

58. Connecticut, for example, had 3,000 slaves among its population as late as 1848.

59. Ervin L. Jordan Jr., *Black Confederates and Afro-Yankees in Civil War Virginia* (Charlottesville, VA: University Press of Virginia, 1995), 9, 22.

60. John W. Blassingame, *Black New Orleans* (Chicago: Chicago University Press, 1973), 33.

2
Family Structure

In every Anglo-American culture, the nuclear family was the normal unit of residence, and the extended family was the conventional unit of thought.
                                            —David Hackett Fischer, Historian

Almost every rural household possesses a loom and a swarm of children, who are set to work as soon as they are able to spin and card.
                                            —Governor Henry Moore to the Board of Trade

A WORLD OF SURVIVORS

Most immigrants to British North America came in family groups. As noted in the previous chapter, the ages of these immigrants appear to be randomly distributed. However, the quality of the documentary evidence for these estimates is inconsistent. Records from the late colonial period, after the French and Indian Wars, indicate that only the elderly, those over sixty (less than 1%), seem to have been underrepresented among immigrants. Of the remainder the largest group (39%) was composed of those between age 25 and 59; the smaller (25%) by children under 14. The remaining 35 percent was remarkable in that it was composed of older teens and young adults between 15 and 24—those young enough and perhaps healthy enough to endure a long sea voyage.[1]

Women and girls made up approximate half of the earliest immigrants to the New England colonies because they came as part of a family group. This was in sharp contrast to the almost total lack of female representation in the Chesapeake colonies. In the later colonial period, male migration overall seems to have dominated that of females by an average ratio of 3 to 2. Rather than this reflecting fewer women immigrants, it seems to have resulted from many more young men coming to look for work in America. The need for wage laborers seems to have shifted the gender statistics somewhat even in New England. "[T]he tales they heard of freedom and opportunity in the New World and of the crying need for cheap labor made their hearts leap with that stranger joy of hope."[2] In the same period, the mix of genders became more equal in the southern colonies where the increased demand for labor was being supplied by male slaves.[3]

An outstanding feature of the colonial period was the expansion of the entire population both numerically and spatially. However, such a result was far from preordained. The earliest immigrants to Jamestown and Plymouth suffered extraordinary rates of mortality in the first years of their settlement, and they were largely isolated in their initial coastal settlements by a reliance on supply vessels from England. In Plymouth, the crude death rate from all causes approached 50 percent in the first year, and in Jamestown it reached an astounding 70 percent due largely to disease and starvation. Yet, the death rate in Europe was no less grim. The mid-17th century decades were the only ones since the time of the

The earliest immigrants to New England were families. Fathers, mothers, aunts, uncles, and children—whole households—moved to the New World. Only the elderly were underrepresented.

Black Death in the 13th century in which the population of the western world actually declined.[4]

As the immigrants to Virginia and New England gained a better knowledge of their environment, established more dependable connections with the Old World, and began trading with their colonial neighbors, the extremely high death rates went down. Although more than 20,000 immigrants sailed to Massachusetts between 1630 and 1640, the flow thereafter "stopped and ran in reverse, as many Massachusetts Puritans sailed home to serve in the [English] Civil War." Those who remained "became the breeding stock for America's Yankee population." Nonetheless, the persistent early mortality among many colonials, especially among young parents, had a profound impact on the structure of colonial family life.[5]

The mortality rate was high almost everywhere in the Western world in the 17th and 18th centuries, but the open spaces and clean waters of North America were thought to provide a more healthful climate. Nonetheless, throughout British North America the absolute death rate was always higher near swampy areas or wetlands that supported mosquito-borne diseases like malaria and yellow fever; where there was no potable water save that in streams and rivers; or where contagious diseases, such as smallpox and measles, were introduced from Europe. Measles, considered a childhood nuisance today, was a serious and often fatal illness even among adult populations in colonial times. According to contemporary journals and diaries the colonial population was bombarded with an annual series of health challenges. In the Spring people of all ages were subject to pleuresies, inflamatory fevers, distempers, and colds. Summer was the season of epidemics of cholera, dysentery, typhoid, assorted fevers, and both bloody and black fluxes, and winter brought rheumatic pains, consumption, and lung disease. At any time of the year, an accidental wound or ulcer could harbor a fatal infection. Autumn seems to have been the healthiest season of the year with its moderate temperatures and abundance of newly harvested food.

The need to preserve foodstuffs through the winter caused much of the food eaten by colonials to be dried or heavily salted. The resulting undifferentiated diet of preserved meats and dried vegetables ultimately led to serious physical difficulties, including outbreaks of scurvy. This disease—common among seamen, but equally devastating to landsmen—was thought to originate from the highly salted provisions and bad water commonly found on sea voyages. In fact, the main cause of scurvy was a deficiency of Vitamin C, which could be made up by adding fresh vegetables and fruits to the diet. These were generally unavailable to colonists until late spring, but early-sprouting wild scallions and cabbages or teas made from spruce buds could serve as a remedy. Native Americans had suggested the latter remedy early in the 17th century. Anglo-colonials soon learned to store potatoes, yams, turnips and other root vegetables capable of retaining their vitamin C content through the winter months.

Citrus fruits were unavailable in the mainland colonies, but an alternative prophylactic against scurvy was thought to be the use of vinegar or rum in small daily doses of about half a pint.

Scurvy was a terribly debilitating affliction. If unremediated it could, and did, cause death, especially among children and the aged. William Hutchinson experienced the ravages of the disease in 1739 and lived to write about it in great detail only because he was given fresh provisions in time to save him from death. Hutchinson's description of the symptoms of scurvy is one of the most graphic recorded in the 18th century.

[A]fter eating a hearty breakfast of salt beef, I found myself taken with a pain under my left breast, where I had formerly received a dangerous blow. From this time the … scurvy increased upon me, as it had done upon many others, a good while before me; and I observed that they … became black in their armpits and hams, their limbs being stiff and swelled, with red specks, and [they] soon died… . I thus struggled with the disease 'till it increased so that my armpits and hams grew black but did not swell, and I pined away to a weak, helpless condition, with my teeth all loose, and my upper and lower gums swelled and clotted together like a jelly, and they bled to that degree, that I was obliged to lie with my mouth hanging over the side of my [bed], to let the blood run out, and to keep it from clotting so as to chock me … . [W]ith fresh provisions and fomentations of herbs I got well in … eighteen days.[6]

Massachusetts, more fortunate than Virginia, was blessed with a cooler climate that proved healthier for immigrants than the warm tidal flats of the Chesapeake. In fact, water temperatures off the New England coast were cooler by several degrees (Fahrenheit) in the 17th century than they are now. Biting cold may have frozen over salt marshes and increased the incidence of frostbitten fingers and toes, but deadly insect- and water-borne illnesses were diminished by the colder climate. Though high by modern standards, the mortality rate in Plymouth, where drinking water came from a nearby spring, may have been lower than in England during the same period. Moreover, many early Chesapeake Bay settlements, situated on low-lying tidal estuaries with military defense in mind, were badly located in terms of health. The periodic invasion of salt water and sediment made the river water brackish and unfit for human consumption, and the waste products of human habitation, including fecal matter floated back and forth on the daily tides, bringing typhoid and dysentery. Mortality in the tidewater may have been twice that of both New England and Europe in the same period, with roughly two-thirds of Virginia settlers succumbing to disease while the colony was under the direction of the Virginia Company. After 1624, a redistribution of settlers to higher ground, with access to fresh-water springs and free flowing creeks, cut the annual mortality rate in half.[7]

In Virginia, white aristocrats, indentured servants, and African slaves all died in appalling numbers that were roughly equal to their proportions in the population. This fact belies the idea that Africans were better suited than whites for work in the hot, humid conditions of the South. Yet, this absurd theory was not put to rest until the 19th century when John Quincy Adams noted that white Europeans cultivated the land in Greece and in Italy, whose climates were hotter than those of Virginia or the Carolinas. Ironically, while white and black immigrants from Africa died at about equal rates in the southern colonies, those blacks brought to Massachusetts in the early colonial period were twice as likely to die as whites from pulmonary infections contracted during the cold New England winters.[8]

As noted earlier, parental death among the colonials had a number of unforeseen consequences. In some parts of Maryland, the death of one marriage partner could be expected within seven years of the marriage ceremony. In other parts of the Chesapeake, 25 percent of children could expect to lose at least one parent by age 5, 50 percent by age 13, and 70 percent by age 21. "Parental death was such an integral part of the fabric of life that it was the norm for most children."[9] Because only one child in four could expect the support and counsel of both parents into their adult years, most sons and daughters were required to learn at an early age to deal responsibly with the common burdens of family life. Many children had to form new relationships with stepparents, step-siblings, and half-brothers or half-sisters.

Oddly, even though men were thought to die at an earlier age than women, there were many single-parent male households in the Chesapeake colonies of the 17th century. Many colonial communities suffered a shortage of mature women and a surfeit of motherless children. Not only did male immigrants exceed females by as much as three to one, but pregnancy and the rigors of childbirth resulted in a high premature death rate among young women. The need to find care for young orphans from among their kin created a powerful cohesive force not only among relatives, but in the wider unrelated community as well. The rearing of orphaned children was a common experience for most families in the early colonial period. The quasi-kinship ties formed among families and their unrelated foster children helped to provide for community cohesion and a network of social interconnections in later years.

Many women, initially devastated by the loss of a husband, found that their status as a widow gave them a newfound freedom. As long as they maintained their bereaved status and refused a new marriage, most women for the first time in their lives had the ability to make their own decisions without being overruled by a father or husband. Widows had more influence in managing the family wealth, business, or estate than might otherwise be the case. The widows of artisans or of tavern- and shopkeepers often continued the businesses long after their husband's death, and a remarkable number of licensed establishments in the colonies seemingly had no male proprietor that anyone could remember. The

Both older and younger women were among the
early settlers to New England because the Puritans came as family groups.

wives of these men had also been their business partners helping to run
the establishment, providing food and clean clothing for the workmen or
boarders, and sometimes maintaining the accounts.

Many dangers faced colonial children before they reached maturity.
A modern social scientist has noted:

Country children did not die from disease in such numbers as city children, where
crowding, open sewers, and general filth fostered the spread of germs, but rural
children were exposed to other hazards. They drowned in rivers, lakes, ponds,
and wells; fell to their deaths from trees and haylofts; succumbed to snakebite,
bee stings, and tetanus; were trampled by runaway horses; and perished by fire
and the fast-spreading rabies of mad dogs and woodland animals. In addition, of

course, respiratory infections, ruptured appendixes, and other common medical emergencies claimed their toll in city and country alike.

Overall child mortality in the colonial period varied between 20 and 30 percent, a far cry from the 1 percent rate of present-day North America.[10] Nonetheless, those who survived into their twenties had a reasonable expectation of living to the age of 70 years promised in the Bible (Psalms 90:10): "The days of our years are three score years and ten; and if by reason of strength they be fourscore years, yet is their strength labour and sorrow; for it is soon cut off, and we fly away." While the *average* life span of colonials may have been in the 40-to-50-year range, this statistic was largely due to the inclusion of a great number of infant and early childhood deaths, which dragged the average life expectancy down. Most of those that survived the ravages of disease and childhood accidents proved to be healthy, strong, and agile adults. There was a positive correlation between the stage of life and the expectant term of future survival. A man of 21 might expect to live until 69; one reaching 50 might live expect to live until 74; and one surviving until 70 could expect an additional decade of life. This improvement was probably due in part to a reduced likelihood of death by accident as older men avoided more physically demanding and dangerous activities in the pursuit of their livelihoods. Similar life expectancies held true for women, with the exception of those between 20 and 40 years, whose life expectancy was 5 years less than their male counterparts largely due to the dangers inherent in childbearing. Once out of their childbearing years, women could expect to live as long as comparably aged men. Colonial-era cemeteries are peppered with the graves of infants, but they also contain many grave markers for elderly persons who lived for 70 or even 80 years.[11]

POPULATION GROWTH

Unlike the early immigrants to Virginia, who were generally single men, early New Englanders generally came to America in family groups, or at least as married couples. The steady increase in colonial population in New England during the last half of the 17th century was fueled by fertility rates that seemingly tested the biological maximum for women having a normal span of childbearing years. It was not uncommon to have families with twelve or fourteen children of whom 70 or 80 percent survived to adulthood. Even with the likelihood of early death during pregnancy adversely affecting the life expectancy of young women, the population of New England increased from 20,000 to 100,000 by the end of the 17th century. Almost all of these were descended from the survivors of those immigrants who had sailed from England in the 1630s.

From 1700 to 1750, the population of New England increased to 400,000—virtually doubling during each of the previous twenty-five-year periods and creating tremendous pressure for the expansion of settle-ments as parents found that they could no longer partition their land among their children into practical units for farming. It should be noted that in a population growing as rapidly as this "more than half of the people alive in the colonies [in 1750] were necessarily under the age of sixteen." Almost all of this phenomenal growth resulted from a natural population increase through legitimate births among the small nucleus of families that had survived the privations and dangers of the previous century.[12]

In colonial times a man's right to have sexual relations with his wife was absolute, and few wives would have been supported by the wider community of matrons in demanding that their husbands desist from such activity or employ contraceptives. So strong was the approval given to parenthood, indeed, that bachelors and spinsters were objects of scorn, and childless couples were viewed as disfavored by God. Contraceptive devices, both practical and conjectural, were available, but they were nei-ther openly advertised nor commonly used. Some of the crude mechanical contraceptives were effective, but many concoctions employed by women to prevent conception were ineffective or even dangerous. Furthermore, husbands had little or no interest in limiting the size of their brood. In a society so dependent on labor, children old enough to work had an important economic value that could not be dismissed simply due to the inconvenience of pregnancy and childbirth.[13]

Consequently, colonial women were exposed to the rigors of almost continuous pregnancy, interrupted only by a painful and dangerous labor and by months of nursing. So frequent were these bouts with nature that many women, conceiving again before fully recovering from a previous pregnancy, gave birth to underweight or feeble infants that were prime candidates for an early death. "Even in a society where large families were the norm and were valued, wanted, and needed for practical reasons, at least some women must have dreaded the cyclical round of conception, pregnancy, labor, parturition, nursing, and again conception."[14]

White women emigrating from Europe generally nursed for two years, creating a natural contraceptive effect during that period, but pregnancy intervals of twelve or fifteen months were commonly recorded in family Bibles, journals, diaries, and other documents. However, such short terms between pregnancies were almost always associated with the miscarriage or early death of an earlier child, whose period of breast-feeding would be short or nonexistent. In such cases, the contraceptive benefits of lactation were removed. African women brought to America as slaves preferred to breast-feed for three years, thereby somewhat extending the time between births. Their choice may have been a cultural one as many reindustrialize peoples erected a ban against sexual relations between husband and wife while the woman was nursing as was certainly the case among Native American peoples.[15]

Prevailing positive attitudes towards large families allowed a widower to quickly remarry a younger woman after the death of a first wife—who had borne him several children and had likely succumbed in childbirth—only to produce a whole new brood of offspring. Many of these marriages were of the "May-December" variety, and the young wife was often little older than the eldest children from a previous marriage. Moreover, the proud sire was often an aging grandparent by the time his third or even fourth wife presented him with his last child.

TYPES OF HOUSEHOLDS

Families can take many functional and acceptable forms, and a variety of household structures could be found in colonial America. While each individual family is unique, families in general can be categorized according to a handful of archetypes. Colonial families generally fall into one of four categories identified by social historians: nuclear families, extended families, stem-nuclear families, and clan-like families. Each of these familial structures has its own peculiar characteristics.

The true *nuclear family* was composed of a married couple living with their children under the same roof and apart from all other relatives. A *stem-nuclear family* occurred when a son married, moved with his bride (or vice versa) into their parents' home, and raised the next generation there creating a three generation homestead. Stem-nuclear families were almost completely absent from the initial generation of settlers due to high death rates and low population density, but in some regions, where the availability of arable land was low, they ran to the third, fourth, or even fifth generation. An *extended family* structure, much like the nuclear one for individual parents and minor children, was less a matter of living arrangement than a kinship network among blood relatives living within the same community but in separate households. Only in old age were parents likely to move in to live with a married child. A widowed mother or sister might live next door to a married child or sibling, functioning in a separate household of their own while being bathed in the reflected protection of close and loving relations. In the *clan-like family* structure, the basic unit of habitation was clearly nuclear, but the members of each clan claimed a common ancestry, usually carried a common name, and, most importantly, recognized a common identity beyond the bounds of the nuclear family that was largely unaffected by any daily living arrangement. Although it was rarely the case in British North America, clan-like families might just as easily live in different colonies as live in different houses in the same village. It was the acknowledged continuity and maintenance of ancestry that defined the clan.

Studies of southerners in the antebellum period of the 19th century noted a strong sense of obligation among blood relatives commonly known among social historians as kinship ties.[16] A number of other words and expressions have come down to us expressing this same obligation: *kinfolk, blood kin, blood ties,* and *kissing cousins* are among a few. The kinship network has been noted as one of the most conservative and inviolable of Southern institutions, but the kinship connections that gave structure to all types of families and groups of immigrants were equally important elsewhere especially in the early colonial period. They were "a source for support, cooperation, loyalty, and sharing in times of need and joy." In every type of family structure common to the colonial period never-married adults, orphans, the disabled, widowed, or otherwise helpless or needy could usually find some type of accommodation under the kinship umbrella where they might live in relative security.[17]

THE NEW ENGLAND FAMILY

Almost all of the Puritans who came to New England arrived in family groups that had been established for many decades in Britain. The family structure among these immigrants was clearly nuclear in that the core of the family almost always consisted of a single married couple and their children, but it was nonetheless remarkably different from that of almost all of the other immigrant groups because of the external influences brought to bear on the family by the agencies of church and theocratic government. The term *covenanted nuclear family* is often used with respect to these Puritan families of the 17th century in order to emphasize this characteristic difference.

The people of the Massachusetts Bay Colony were part of a Pietist religious movement generally rooted in Calvinism, and they thought of themselves as God's chosen people sent into the wilderness much like their Biblical forbearers. The covenant made between God and Abraham, which extended to all nations through his "seed" (as recorded in Genesis 22:18), was thought to be binding upon the Puritan family as well, passing from the Almighty through the head of household, to the children, and even to the household servants, slaves, and apprentices. So central was the idea of the family covenant in the Puritan theocracy that it was extended to the wider community and its civil government as well.

The leading families of colonial New England did not spring from the soil of America. They came from the wealthier classes of British society, and they were already adept at exercising their will on the lower classes. Good order was expected of all families and family members, and it was often enforced by outside agents, who acted with the dual authority of church and state. Strict conformity to community edicts regarding social behavior, moral codes, and religious doctrines was fervently demanded and harshly enforced. Parents and heads of households were bound to those biblical principles that the theocracy sought to engender with the force of law, and all those under their roof—their wives, children, kindred, wards, servants, and acquaintances—were expected to follow the moral and social precepts found in the Scriptures and submit to the lawful will of the householder or suffer enforcement by the wider community.

While male heads of household were most common, female householders were not unusual, and they could also evince formidable authority within the covenanted family unit. Apprentices were expected to be subservient to both their masters and mistresses, and younger children to both their parents, all their elder siblings, and any adult relatives. Even adult children who had formed their own households were required to obey their parents, and those who refused might be placed under the jurisdiction and subjugation of the government. "An obedient son followed the trade of his father, a good girl gave up her virginity only to her husband and a commoner knew his place and respected his betters." Unfortunately, a civil discipline based on doctrinal precepts rather than individual rights, if left unfettered, sometimes turned to subjugation, with colonial magistrates promulgating and enforcing laws based on privately held religious scruples or personal interpretations of Scripture. Situations like these caused no end of trouble among disputing social and religious factions in many early settlements.[18]

The extended family structure often included grandparents, married children, and, of course, grandchildren. The head of the household was always given the seat of honor at the head of the table, often the only chair in the room with armrests and decorations.

Because of the emphasis on the solidarity of the covenanted family unit, single living by any individual was unacceptable to the larger community. Those attempting to lead a solitary life were often forced to reside within a family group for the moral good of the community—even if they were otherwise unrelated by blood to the other members of the household. An elderly widowed grandmother was expected to reside in the household of her adult children; unmarried daughters lived with their parents or within the household of a brother or married sister; and orphans were placed with respected families in the community even if unrelated to them.

Family order in the Puritan home was based primarily on age. Blood relationship, rank, and gender were less important to the household

Adult children rarely shared a roof with their elderly parents. Each young man set out to find a wife and form his own household. Nonetheless, a widowed parent could usually find refuge with an adult child if the need arose.

hierarchy than among other immigrant groups. Inheritance practices, which usually reserved the estate of the parents for the eldest son, caused the Puritan family to develop much like those of the traditional English feudal aristocracy. On his death the head of the household invariably left his house to one of his sons, but rarely to more than one. A single household with many children might contain an adult son about to marry, a male child not yet in his teens, and a number of other sons in between. Many wills reveal a pattern by which older men regularly conferred a "portion" on their youngest sons in the form of a partition of land or a sum of money with which to build homes, start businesses of their own, or fund their educations some years in the future.

Unforeseen financial burdens and single parenthood brought on by the early death of a spouse were reasons for "sending out" supernumerary children from the household. This custom was particularly popular among Puritans, who sent their prepubescent children to other respectable homes to learn a skill or to apprentice them to a trade. Samuel Sewall sent out his three daughters—Hannah to learn housewifery, Elizabeth to learn needlework, and Mary to learn to read and write. His son, Samuel, was bound as an apprentice as would be expected in a region where almost half the households were headed by artisans or craftsmen. While the parents intentions may have been in their child's best interests, the separation necessitated by common apprenticeship practices was sometimes a painful personal experience. Sewall made the following entry on Hannah's departure: "[M]uch ado to pacify my dear daughter, she weeping and pleading to go [home] with me."[19]

Maintenance of the family wealth and its equitable distribution among the children was of utmost concern to New England Puritans, especially in the second and third generations after initial settlement. Parents were legally obligated to provide their "always obedient and respectful" children with a portion of the family property or with training in some lawful calling or employment. Parents who neglected this responsibility were subject to fines, sanctions, or other penalties placed on their estates. Numerous deeds of gifts and inheritances show men detaching adjoining parts of the main farmstead into parcels of several "score acres" capable of providing a "comfortable living" for their male children when they married. Daughters were more often endowed with money, linens, or furniture. Nonetheless, marriage contracts between the families of a prospective bride and groom regularly provided for the building or purchase of a separate home for the new couple at the expense of both. Some men gained the assistance of the courts in arranging for the parceling of portions or guaranteeing money for the training of any young children borne to them in their old age, but such matters were usually managed on a private basis.[20]

The Puritan family featured a large number of children and few, if any, servants. Between the founding of the Plymouth colony in 1620 and the

The early death of a parent, especially that of a male head of household, had a profound effect on the surviving members of the family beyond the normal sadness and mourning one would expect. Educations might be forfeit; the family's social status might be put in jeopardy; and a wife was suddenly thrust into the unfriendly world of widowhood.

outbreak of the Revolutionary War in 1775, the average number of children born to families in New England rarely fell below 7 and often reached 9 or 10. The New England family was generally insular—respectful of aunts, uncles, nephews, nieces, and other blood relatives (especially if they were older), but most strongly devoted to the two generations (parents and children) forming the nuclear household. In this respect, it was child-centered and much like the modern American family.[21]

New England women generally married in their early twenties (22 to 23), and there was a low incidence of recorded prenuptial pregnancy. The courtship of a prospective married couple was developed under the watchful eye of their parents and adult relations, and any sustained period of privacy was almost impossible. Nonetheless, many engaged couples managed to find a

Young couples sometimes sought the advice of friends and relatives, who acted as intermediaries during courtship.

few private moments that produced inconvenient pregnancies. These are evidenced in the historic record as a large number of eight- and nine-month births immediately after marriage. Ironically, the number of seven-month births—almost certainly a signal of prenuptial sexual activity—was much lower in the 18th century than in the 17th century despite the common view that the earlier century was more repressive of sexual misconduct. As long as the offending couple married quickly, these lapses in judgment seem to have been treated differently from the cases of "fornication" that pepper the Puritan court records.

The punishment of fornication, usually discovered through the pregnancy of the woman, included fines and physical chastisement for both parties if they were known. The authorities wished to discover the identity of the father not only to punish him, but also to make him financially responsible for his offspring. Otherwise, it was thought that the responsibility might devolve onto the community. A paternity case from 1686 placed four men under suspicion of being the father of a single child. Could the mother have been so promiscuous in a sexually restrained community that she could not identify the father? Under these circumstances "it becomes difficult to sustain the traditional picture of seventeenth-century New England as being extremely strait-laced and repressive in anything pertaining to sex."[22]

The structure and ordering of the covenanted family functioned well enough for several generations of Puritans in America, but as the 17th century closed, the division and subdivision of property among children and grandchildren increased. This "parceling" and "splintering" of holdings in New England, with its generally rocky and unforgiving soils, was accompanied with an inevitable breakdown in the concept of the covenanted family structure. Faced with the prospect of making a living from a parcel of land a small fraction of the size farmed by their grandparents, succeeding generations were forced to move away from the original settlements. While land was still abundant in America, it was not always freely available. Native Americans controlled most of the region in the 17th century, and proprietary rights and grants made to joint stock companies made access to new land problematic and costly. Moreover, the process by which wilderness tracts were transformed into productive acres was physically demanding and time consuming.

Moreover, the change in New England from an undifferentiated covenanted family structure rooted in Puritanism to a more diverse and secular form tended to follow the parallel drift of the overall transformation of colonial religious thought throughout the 17th and 18th centuries. The old Puritanism, characterized by rigid religious intolerance and formal family structure, drifted slowly toward a more liberal toleration of most mainstream Protestant religions and the less-structured family orders that were characteristic of the enlightened 18th century. Beginning in the 1660s, the old Puritan culture became less dominant as diverse religious and secular expressions found root in the expanding New England colonies. This was particularly true of the Anglican (Episcopal) religion, which, aided by its designation as the established church, made inroads into the bastions of the old Puritan Calvinism.

Yet the true Puritanism of the covenant—the original Religion of Grace or Holy Experiment that had taken root in Plymouth in the 1620s—persisted and was never completely lost. Embraced by many of the pillars of the community during the 18th century, it came again into full flower among a significant minority of the New England population during the American Victorian period.[23] This New England conservatism has been characterized as "a hypocritical morality, a new-rich respectability, a sentimentality pretending to religion, and an enameled cruelty." Yet after 1700, it was "always" comprised of a small but "solid lump" of persons resistant to both religious and secular liberalism.[24] Jonathan Edwards, the implacable enemy of such religious hypocrisy, noted in the 1740s, "It is not unusual ... for persons, at the same time they come into church and pretend to own [to] the covenant, freely to declare to their neighbors, that they have no imagination that they have any true faith in Christ or love for him."[25]

THE PLANTATION ARISTOCRACY

The colonies surrounding the Chesapeake were populated largely by those persons faithful both to the Anglican Church and to the royal prerogatives espoused by the monarchs of the 16th and 17th century. In the early colonial period, no more uncompromising enemy of the New England Puritans could be found in British North America than these royalist adherents to the Church of England.

Among the southerners of Virginia, the Carolinas, Maryland, and, later, Georgia, the sense of a wider extended family and the value of family connections were more prevalent than among the introspective and self-reliant Puritans of New England. "Family" tended to be a more comprehensive term in the South that included, besides parents and their immediate offspring, a wide variety of blood relations including aunts, uncles, brothers, sisters, and cousins. To maintain the integrity of the family structure, the female relatives would gather to trace the family tree from long before the rise of the Stuart kings. Intermarriage between second and third cousins was promoted to strengthen the connections within the extended family. Nowhere else in colonial American was the status of an extended family of cousins more closely followed or revered.

Although half the white population of the tidewater had come to the colonies as indentured servants, generations of close and sometimes carefully planned intermarriage spread the 17th-century royalist blood so thin that by the middle of the 18th century, almost all the influential families in the South could claim some form of aristocratic right to position and power. Kinship-neighborhoods, sometimes encompassing whole counties, developed during the late 17th and early 18th centuries as estates were divided and subdivided among children and then recombined by the intermarriage of second and third cousins. Cousin marriages were almost unheard of in Puritan New England, but in the tidewater colonies before the American Revolution, there were only a few thousand independent freeholding families from which to choose a spouse and even fewer that could be considered aristocratic plantation owners.

Nonetheless, outside marriage into an influential family with aristocratic roots had distinct advantages for small southern landowners, with the whole family gaining status from a single marital union. Whether through birth, marriage, or myth, support of the southern gentry was indispensable for the man or family that hoped to rise in society, politics, or business. Yet few southerners succeeded in attaining a social level much above the station of their birth, and it was not unusual to separate the social order even among property owners into *common folk* and *gentle folk.* Those marrying up in the social order were often viewed with equal portions of envy by their peers and contempt by their betters.

Family was the most conservative and inviolable of southern institutions. It went without saying that southern gentlemen came from good stock. The parentage and pedigree of the majority of plantation owners were considered aristocratic, at least, and those with questionable family connections were viewed with suspicion and subject to gossip and ridicule. To maintain their high social position and authority, it was important for Southerners to have a strong sense of obligation to their blood relatives. A number of words and expressions have come down to us expressing this obligation, but the term *kinship* probably serves best to describe this strong sense of a wider family among southerners.

With kinship came advantage and obligation within the family order. Older kin were a source of advice and counsel, as well as property, loans, and other forms of financial aid. Moreover, in a time when there were few or no formal schools, educating the next generation was often undertaken by family members thereby ensuring "the smooth and efficient transmission of both practical knowledge and shared values."[26] In this regard, the male head of the family was often considered a patriarch, a term used by many contemporaries to describe them. He welded wide powers in terms of choosing proper marriage partners or disposing of family property. Viewing himself in these terms, William Byrd of Virginia noted, "Like one of the Patriarchs I have my flocks and my herds, my bond-men and bond-women, and every sort of trade amongst my own servants, so that I live in a kind of independence of everyone but Providence. However this sort of life is attended without expense, yet it is attended with a great deal of trouble. I must take care to keep all my people to their duty, to see all the springs in motion and make everyone draw his equal share to carry the machine forward."[27]

Birth into one of the leading families of the South brought prominence and the presumption of ability—whether it was present or not. Southerners believed that character was inherited just as surely from one's father or grandfather as land, money, and slaves were inherited. So pervasive was this assumption that kinsmen were given positions as sheriffs, justices of the peace, militia captains, or county lieutenants by influential relatives without the slightest charge of favoritism by anyone within the system.[28]

Fathers were protective of their daughters, providing their sons-in-law with influence, if not money. Unmarried daughters were often given the position of companion to their fathers or other elder male relative. Granddaughters were treated in much the same way by their grandfathers or great uncles, especially in the absence of their father. Men were similarly solicitous of their nieces, daughters-in-law, and all their children. Siblings were treated in a hierarchical manner with all the male offspring being given a superior position over their sisters.

The inferior position of female siblings implied an obligation that was placed upon brothers to defend their honor. A brother could intervene in the affairs of his sisters and their circle of friends with or without their permission. At times these brothers could take on a very combative stance when dealing with a sister's reputation. Female cousins came under the same type of protection. As women were not permitted to correspond with men who were not relatives, many young women had no knowledge of men who were not their blood kin until after their marriage. Even then their social relationships with males were limited to the friends and acquaintances of their husbands. Southern men also felt obliged to counsel, support, and defend, not only their own families, but all females and minor children placed under their protection.

A more sizeable portion of the southern population was considered to be part of the social and ruling elite when compared with similar persons in other regions of the colonies. Whereas ministers and magistrates ruled New England society, wealthy southern planters saw themselves and their class as the natural leaders of their communities, whose wants were rightly supplied by the labor of the rest of society. As many as 10 percent

It would be an error to believe that fathers were not intimately concerned for the education and welfare of their daughters. Young women were taught to manage a household of their own. They were also expected to be able to read the bible and provide a basic education to their own young children.

of southern white adult males belonged to this group. Slaves and servants supplied their labor just as serfs had supported the feudal aristocracy of Europe. Yet few in the southern master's social class actually had aristocratic roots, and for some of the gentry, the need to maintain a large body of servants was greatly intensified by the lack of blood ties to some genuine form of royalty. Planters with an English heritage might claim their descent from the Cavaliers of the English Civil Wars of the 1640s. No mere followers of the Stuart kings, their planter ancestry might be derived from dukes, earls, knights, and loyal squires who had ridden at Nasby. This claim helped the planters to define themselves in historically acceptable terms. There were enough southern families with legitimate family trees of this sort—the Lees, the Fairfaxes, and the Randolphs, for instance—to maintain the "truth" of the wider fiction.

Southern families were usually composed of two parents and five or six legitimate children, but the child mortality rate in the South was considerably higher than elsewhere. Almost half the children born to households in the Chesapeake never reached adolescence. This caused family size to be appreciably lower in the South than in New England. Many marriages ended at an early age when one of the partners died of disease or in childbirth. The average age at marriage for women was only 18, four to five years younger than in other regions. Early marriage may have extended a robust woman's childbearing years somewhat. Moreover, the rate of prenuptial pregnancy was quite high, approaching 40 percent in some areas, and the fathering of children out of wedlock was also quite high, with almost 12 percent of children being born on the wrong side of the blanket. While southern men seem to have been given a pass in this regard, southern women faced severe social penalties for sexual activity outside of marriage that could extend to virtual social ostracism, personal disgrace, and disavowal by their families.

Nowhere was the overwhelmingly rural nature of Southern society more deeply obvious than in the tidewater. In the social hierarchy, just below the plantation aristocracy was a large group of small farmers who exhibited many of the social characteristics of the "yeomanry" of England. More than 60 percent of the southern male population "owned no land at all, and very little property of any other sort." The landless majority was almost evenly split between free tenant farmers and those in servitude (either as indentures or slaves). The planter aristocracy generally responded to the deference of the white underclasses and to the submission of their black slaves with benevolence and chivalric obligation. The Southern elite voluntarily assumed the role of benefactor and knight errant to all other levels of their society. This obligation was extended to poor relations, visitors, tutors, clerks, servants, and anyone who came into their sphere of influence in an ambiguous, but serious, way. Many planters were genuinely concerned for the physical and moral welfare of their slaves but only in terms of continued racial separation and subjugation. Although their numbers were quite small, the planter aristocracy successfully dominated southern society for almost two centuries by applying their wealth and political influence to the wheels of government and society.[29]

THE MIDDLE COLONIES

The Society of Friends, or Quakerism, was begun in 17th-century England by George Fox and Margaret Fell. The first adherents to the new sect—many of whom were of Welsh ancestry—were drawn largely from farmers who lived on the fringe of the cultural, economic, and social mainstream. Quakerism was a radical religion that attracted these generally independent people by preaching the virtues of the family as the basic disciplining and spiritualizing authority in society as opposed to that of magistrates and church prelates. Thanks in part to their devotion to the decentralization of authority, many Quakers were more comfortable in the vast spaces of the American forests than were the New Englanders, who had come from more densely populated villages in the southeast of England.[30]

Quakers and other minor religious sects were initially prosecuted under the laws of many colonies in British North America. Only in Pennsylvania were they allowed full suffrage and participation in the colony's governance. In the 1660s, under the pressure of a royal order by Charles II, many colonies stopped openly persecuting Quakers and allowed them to hold meetings. Official intolerance endured in many forms in places like Massachusetts and Connecticut into the 18th century. Yet the Quakers had an effective advocate at the Court of St. James in the person of William Penn a favorite of Queen Anne (1701–1714) who achieved the repudiation of laws against Quakers in Connecticut, Massachusetts, and Rhode Island. By 1706, Quakers had become the first officially tolerated heretics in the colonies.[31] Official toleration was in the main a political and involuntary expedient adopted in response to the developing rise of reason and humanism known as the Enlightenment. Nonetheless, by the 1730s Quakers were generally tolerated everywhere and in some places were considered "almost respectable."[32] On this widening stage of religious toleration, the Quakers were able to transform the Pennsylvania wilderness into one of the most successful colonies in British North America.

Quakers devoted themselves to their religious duties by creating a family structure of nearly autonomous moral households. These were almost always nuclear in nature. Everything in the Quaker household— wives, children, and business—was subjected to a familial order based in a strict personal morality. The burden of producing, sustaining, and incorporating morality, and civic and economic virtues, into the household was taken on by the entire family and supported by the community. Outside

A family was fortunate if four of its children reached their teen years
like this group of upper class siblings.

authorities such as an intolerant established priesthood, an authoritarian
upper class, or even a pedantic university system were considered "not
only unnecessary but even pernicious."[33]

The Quaker family was very similar to the modern American family
with its child-centered outlook. The family unit was moderately nuclear
with an average of five children and only one or two servants or farm
workers. Rarely did Quaker families have more than seven children. The
average age of women at marriage was 24, and prenuptial pregnancies
were so low that they were considered uncommon.

The level of parental authority was based on the willfulness and personality of the individual, and Quaker parents repudiated the use of fear
and physical punishment as the principle means of disciplining their

children. Grandparents were respected, but they were not venerated as were those in New England. Mature children left the strict authority of their parents upon their marriage and the establishment of a separate household. Both of these requirement were necessary for adult men to leave the home of their father. Aunts, uncles, nieces, and nephews were considered extended family members, but cousins took on an added importance somewhere between the eminence placed on them in the South and the general neglect they experienced in New England. The importance of these wider kinship relationships may have resulted from the Quaker penchant for staying apart from all but their relatives and members of their faith.

The Quaker community gave unprecedented moral authority within the household and within the congregation to the women of their sect. Quakers thereby radically changed the traditional structure of the English household, especially in the areas of authority over child-rearing, court-ship, and marriage. Women were encouraged to discuss and legislate on "women's matters" in specially designed women's meetings set up for the primary purpose of controlling courtship and marriage within the community. No fewer than twelve female "ministers" have been identi-fied as being active between 1690 and 1765 in the region of initial Quaker settlement.[34]

Quaker fathers devoted a great deal of their energy to the accumula-tion of land, which would be devolved onto their sons, or would other-wise benefit their daughters in marriage. The availability of large tracts of undeveloped land in southeastern Pennsylvania was one factor that caused the overwhelming majority of Quaker children in America to marry other Quakers locally and stay within the Quaker meeting dis-cipline. Consequently, the Quakers quickly found themselves related to one another not only by religion but also by a web of shared genet-ics. This kinship was partly responsible for the strong community ties exhibited by a community of people who were otherwise defiantly anti-institutional.[35]

The first town named by Penn was Chester, founded in 1682 and situated on the Delaware River. Here the land claim boundaries of Pennsylvania, Delaware, and New Jersey almost came together. The basic unit of Quaker settlement was the family farm of about 250 to 300 acres—an initial size to which much was added with time. The holdings were widely dispersed, and Quaker farmers were accustomed to moving about on horseback over a mildly undulating or flat countryside. By 1720, every township in Penn's original grant to the Quakers had a meeting house. Pennsylvania roads, unlike those in other sections of the colonial countryside, tended to form as the spokes of a wheel, with the meeting house at the hub. Remnants of this characteristic road pattern can be observed even today in this region of the state. Gettysburg, Pennsylvania (noted for the American Civil War battle fought there in 1863) exhibits this pattern of development.

THE SCOTCH-IRISH

The exact characteristics of family structure in the backcountry are difficult to pin down because those living in the American borderland left fewer written records than those of other immigrant groups. This is not to say that they were significantly less literate, but rather that the harsh conditions of life and survival on the frontier left little time for reflective journalizing or thoughtful authorship. Nonetheless, the Scotch-Irish are known to have retained many of the folkways that they practiced on the borderlands of Northern Britain and Ireland. These they seem to have adapted to the American environment with little change. Post Civil War studies conducted in the 19th and 20th centuries affirm that the fundamental social structure and family orders common to Britain and Ireland were transplanted to America almost intact.

The basic unit of the family was clearly nuclear, but each household was surrounded by an extended circle of social contacts that was stronger and more influential than those found among other English-speaking groups in America. For centuries in Europe, the Scotch and Irish peoples had based their social structure on the clan—not precisely the tartan plaid Highland clans identified by well-meaning but slightly delusional Victorian sociologists, but clans composed of related families who lived near and supported each other when danger threatened.

Concurrent with the great Puritan migration to America that began in 1630 was an influx of Scottish families to Ireland. In one two-year period in the 1630s, at least 10,000 Scots transplanted themselves to Irish soil, and the total migration to Ireland may have exceeded 50,000 persons. The subsequent migration of these Scotch-Irish to America began as a trickle half a century (and two generations) later and became a flood in the first half of the 18th century. No random movement of families, the movement of the Scotch-Irish was a classic example of a serial migration in which one family in the clan leads the way to be followed by a steady stream of kinfolk who settle in the same general region of the country.

As an example, after the death of his first wife in 1743, Benjamin Chambers returned to Ulster in Ireland to encourage the friends and neighbors he had left behind to emigrate to Pennsylvania and to bring his three sisters back with him to America in the expectation that they would help him to raise his motherless children. Once again, after he had remarried in 1753, Chambers traveled to England to speak before Parliament as an agent for the proprietors and to find additional Scotch-Irish families to serve as settlers. Chambers proved an effective proponent of emigration, and he was granted a tract of land, now called Chambersburg, by Thomas Penn, one of the three proprietors of Pennsylvania.[36]

This type of serial migration produced populations in the backcountry uniquely related to one another. The word *family* in this regard "meant not merely a nuclear or extended family but an entire clan." Moreover, the clan system was uniquely suited to a people carving out homes from among lands that for thousands of years were the unquestioned domains of sometimes primitive and hostile native peoples. It spread rapidly throughout the southern backcountry and provided a power base for the removal from their ancestral lands of several formidable tribes of native Americans including the Shawnee, Creek, Choctaw, Chickasaw, Catawba, Cherokee, and other tribes of the southeast woodland.

DUTCH HOUSEHOLDS

The Dutch tended to settle on large grants of lands called patents, which were given to wealthy men (patroons) willing to bring in settlers as rent-paying tenants or subdivide the land. Here, they carved out individual farmsteads of manageable size while leaving the unimproved acreage as a common holding to be distributed at a later date among the patentees or their children, or to be sold to outsiders. Although surrounded by English-speaking neighbors from the beginning of the 18th century, the Dutch generally retained most of their distinctive ways by forming small enclaves of homes and farmsteads around a central Dutch Reformed Church. Consequently, Dutch culture did not generally spread far beyond the boundaries of their 17th-century settlements.

The early Dutch formed two-parent nuclear families with many more children than their corresponding generation in the United Provinces. While many couples they had more children than the average colonial household in other regions, not all Dutch parents did so. Infant mortality was high—especially among those in rural areas—but not extremely so, and the number of single heads of households (widows and widowers) was much smaller than previously thought. A Dutch couple could expect to experience the early death of at least one child, but most of their children would survive into old age.

In the 1680s, William Penn described Dutch families living along the Delaware River as having "fine children, and almost every house full; rare to find one of them without three or four boys, and as many girls; some six, seven, or eight sons." Seven related Dutch families of the same generation living in Tappan, New York, between 1688 and 1734 had a total of 65 children—an average of about 9 live births per family. Almost a third of these died in the first year of life or in "youth." The large number of children in Dutch families would rank high among the average family sizes found in New England, however, the Puritans of Massachusetts may have been more likely to leave illegitimate births unrecorded. Dutch attitudes toward premarital and extramarital sexual relationships "are not easy to discover, but a general absence of comment and the perhaps purposeful failure to record a marriage or birth date" may reflect a tactful effort to obscure an embarrassing fact of Dutch colonial life.[37]

The Dutch family structure was different from that of the English in that the household contained more slaves. In the 1740s many more Dutch families than English ones were slave owners. This may have reflected the significant role played by the Dutch in the 17th-century slave trade. These slaves, rarely numbering more than a half dozen, often occupied the same structure as the family, working alongside the family members and sleeping in the garrets or kitchen spaces. Notwithstanding the presence of forced labor, the Dutch were noted as being hardy, frugal, industrious, pious, brave, hospitable to a fault, and addicted to cleanliness.[38]

Dutch family order was much more hierarchical in areas influenced by the culture of New England than those in the Hudson Valley or on the Albany frontier, and it retained much of its 17th-century European flavor in Manhattan, Staten Island, and parts of New Jersey. Dutch colonial men generally married between the ages of 23 and 25, depending on whether they lived in a city or a small settlement. Male residents of New Amsterdam or Albany (Fort Orange) tended to marry at a later age, possibly because they were attempting to establish themselves in trade or were waiting to come into an inheritance. Farmers living in the hinterland married younger because land was abundant, and it was to their advantage to build a house, find a wife to serve as a helpmate, and begin their family. Women throughout the colony married at an average age of just over 22 years, almost exactly the same age as the young women of Massachusetts Bay Colony. Dutch women were "renowned for their premarital chastity." Any Dutch girl or woman whose reputation was questionable was absolutely prohibited from marriage. Wives retained possession of their marriage portions after the nuptials, and if widowed had control of their own money and any inheritance.[39]

THE GERMAN VILLAGE

German Pietists and English Quakers populated the heart of the colonies in the region surrounding Philadelphia. The German family was more hierarchical and patriarchal than that of their English Quaker neighbors, but in other respects it was very similar. This similarity was largely due to the fact that both groups followed the same essential religious compass. The German immigrants, on the whole, were sober and collected, and their pietist religions valued simplicity, justice, and mercy. They tried to revive plainness of dress and manner in their everyday lives. They exhibited many of the aspects of their Old World European peasant culture and village-based political systems. Nonetheless, there was a great diversity among them as they generally came from separate political entities rather than a single national state. A good number of Palatine Germans settled in the Mohawk Valley of central New York near the settlements of German Flats and Palatine. Others settled in west central Pennsylvania and Maryland. Studies of German family names suggest that they made up a small but significant segment of the population in North Carolina, Tennessee, and Kentucky.

Many persons identified as German were actually from Switzerland, Alsace, Westphalia, Silesia, Saxony, or other Teutonic regions of Europe. Research in this regard suggests that the first sizable German migration to British North America (about 1710) was composed of people from many diverse communities. Most German immigrants were from the lower Rhineland. Approximately 42 percent came from the Palatine Electorate west of the Rhine, yet many others came from as far north as the fringes of the Baltic Sea near Denmark or from Czech border towns like Dresden. Statistical conclusions regarding place of origin may be imperfect because the residents of the villages, cities, and minor geopolitical entities characteristic of central Europe had been for many decades in a high state of mobility. There was a constant back-and-forth flow of agricultural workers and their families seeking seasonal employment or permanent homes. This movement was exacerbated by recurrent famines and pestilence, and decades of religious and political persecution especially during the Thirty Years' Wars (1618–1648).

Almost all the German immigrants to British North America identified themselves by their religious affiliation. "[Religious] sects in central Europe, stimulated in their mobility by the political and religious fragmentation of the German-speaking world, drew aside in self-protection just as the Pilgrims and Puritans had done."[40] Germantown, located north of Philadelphia, boasted a great mixture of dialects and religions considered German. Along a two-mile stretch of the main highway passing though the town were churches built by Lutherans, Mennonites, Anabaptists, Moravians, Baptists, Amish, and Calvinists. The Lutheran and Calvinist Germans were largely from within the same theological compass as most mainstream English Protestants, but the others pietist sects were generally viewed as radicals more closely associated with the English Quaker movement. The peculiar ways of these radical pietists, with their group migrations and close knit settlements, made them highly visible to contemporaries and also to later historians.[41]

The German Baptist Brethren, in particular, attempted to reinstitute many early Christian customs, such as the washing of feet and complete immersion for baptism, from which practice they became known as "Dunkers." The Dunkers, known in England as the Church of the Brethren, eschewed religious bickering and denominational controversies as unchristian. They preferred within their religious congregations soft-spoken, contemplative, and reaffirming sermons as compared to those fire and brimstone bouts with oratory characteristic of New England churches. Puritan ministers often espoused dogmatic confrontation and a brutal adherence to orthodoxy, while among the German Brethren it was thought that there should be no force in religion. "Individuals should be guided by their conscience, not by secular or ecclesiastic fiat."[42] The

Brethren movement started in Schwarzenau and spread up and down the middle Rhine Valley. Ninety percent of the approximately 300 original Dunker immigrants came from Schwarzenau, Krefeld, or Friesland.[43]

The total number of German-speaking Pietist immigrants to Anglo-America may have reached 6,000 in colonial times. The largest single entity, between 2,000 and 4,000, was composed of Mennonites, who concentrated their settlements in Pennsylvania in central Lancaster County, in the upper portions of Chester, Philadelphia, and Bucks counties, and in southern Northhampton County. They were among the first sects to seek a democratic religious way of life. The Amish, with whom the Mennonites are often confused, were an offshoot of the Church of the Swiss Brethren from Switzerland, Alsace, and the Palatinate. They settled largely in Lancaster County were their culture is still plainly visible. The initial number of Amish immigrants was less than 300, but they appear to have supported a very high fertility rate. The total of Schwenkfelders and Waldensians was no more than 300 persons making them the smallest of the German immigrant pietist sects in British North America.[44]

The Moravians (Fratres Unitas) were among the least fanatical of the pietist sects that came to America, but they were among the best-financed immigrants to British North America. They must also have been a healthy and hardy lot since only one of the 830 Moravian immigrants to America is known to have died on the passage from Europe, a death rate thirty-eight (38) times smaller than that for all German immigrants during the period. This amazing accomplishment may also have been due to the fact that the Moravians provided their own ships from Europe and overland transportation to the American settlements, thereby avoiding many of the exploitive and deceitful practices of outside agents.[45]

The Moravians had become one of the most important Protestants groups in central Europe at the beginning of the seventeenth century. Nonetheless, they suffered decades of persecution in the Thirty Years' War (1618–1648) being hounded from their homes until only a few faithful aristocratic families were left in the sect by the end of the century. In 1722, almost the entire surviving Moravian congregation could be found on the estate of their protector, Count Nikolaus von Zinzerdorf of Saxony. From there they began to spread their faith to the West Indies, Africa, Asia, and North and South America. From their London center they influenced John Wesley, a leader in the evangelical movement in the Anglican Church and the founder of Methodism.

By 1735, many Moravians had turned their efforts to the New World. Their beliefs were loosely related to those of the Lutheran faith with connections to the teachings of John Huss and John Wycliffe. Although they professed a common unity among all Christians, this goal proved too high minded for most Moravians who were dedicated to a narrower field of church dogma. About 20 percent of all Moravian immigrants spoke some English, which helped them in their apostolic efforts in British America.

However, Moravians, like the Quakers, refused to take an oath or to bear arms in times of war. Consequently, they were viewed with a good deal of suspicion by the majority of other settlers on the American frontier.[46]

Beginning in 1735, the first Moravians entered North America through Philadelphia. Seventeen of the original immigrant families had aristocratic origins, and 20 percent of all Moravian males have been identified as clergy. The headquarters of the Moravian mission in America was located for a long time in the town of Bethlehem on the banks of the Lehigh River in Pennsylvania. From here they established additional settlements, particularly at Nazareth, to which they built a substantial wagon road. The Moravians conscientiously paid the Indians for the land that they settled. In fact by 1755, they had paid for it several times distributing funds to various groups of Indians over the years as new claims were made against them. In 1775, they completed an enormous stone structure for Count Zinzerhoff that may well have been the largest residence built for a single person in British North America up to that time. Zinzendorf never occupied it.[47]

Using the Moravian community as a springboard, Zinzerhoff attempted to establish himself as the head of the German Lutheran Church in Philadelphia, but the resistance of other Protestant groups to this idea caused a great deal of friction within the wider German community. Anti-Moravian sentiment was so strong outside southeastern Pennsylvania that the sect was virtually prevented from making settlements elsewhere. Nonetheless, during 1743, two Moravian preachers, Leonhard Schnell, a German, and Robert Hussey, an English convert from Anglicanism, traveled south through Maryland and the Shenandoah River Valley, making converts as far south as the Carolinas and Georgia. Soon their missionary work bore fruit as other Moravians began settlements at Bethabara, Bethania, and Salem in North Carolina. From Salem, the Moravian preachers set out to preach on the frontier, "miraculously [preserving] some of the Christian virtues of medieval monasticism: altruism, self-denial, meditation, industry, frugality, and selfless submission to discipline." However, these communities proved to be the only meaningful successes recorded by the movement outside Pennsylvania.[48]

Moravian family life was formed around the structure of a missionary community, and many of its private family qualities are somewhat obscured by the overcoat of their communal religious practices. "For them the religious community, not the home village, was the focal point of their collective strategy, and for some Moravians the process of migration itself played a special role in building their ideal communities."[49] Moravians divided their communities into "living groups" separated by gender, age, and martial status. It was not enough to have a community composed of clergy, artisans, craftsmen, tradesmen, farmers, housewives, and children. While such a structure shattered the basic concept of a nuclear family, it is not completely clear to what extent traditional parent-child relationships were effected. It is certain that the religious leaders of the community believed that the living groups needed to be properly compartmentalized for Moravian social order to be deemed correct. However, the extent to which these living groups interacted is unclear. A Moravian minister detailed the composition of the living groups of a community of 130 persons at Bethabara, North Carolina, in the following list:

18 Married couples	36
Widowers	3
Widows	4
Single Sisters [adult women]	3
Older Girls	12
Younger Girls	5
Single Brethren [adult men]	36
Older Boys	20
Younger Boys	11
Total	130[50]

It is clear that there were far more males (88) in the community than females (42), and fewer married persons (36) than those adults who were single or who had lost a partner (46). The number of older and younger children may represent the generally high birth rate among all colonials in this period especially if some of the unmarried adults were also products of the married or once-married household families.

The Moravian discipline initially promised to be much like that which they had experienced in Europe. In this regard most German family units could be identified as living in an extended family format within a social order similar to the village of their origin. Notwithstanding temporary emergencies, however, large numbers of relatives rarely lived under the same roof. One of the characteristics of this lifestyle was the *strassendorf,* or single street village. This pattern of settlement was one of strips of land running back from a long center street somewhat like ribs from the spine of a fish. The houses stood apart from one another along this center causeway with access to fresh water usually at the rear of the properties. Immediately behind each house, the villagers usually kept an orchard or garden patch, while further away they tilled their fields for profit, grazed their animals, and cut their firewood and lumber. Different villagers might own other properties scattered about the region, but *strassendorf* villages found among the first generation of settlers rarely contained more than ten or twelve homes. Moreover, partition of properties among half a dozen adult children left a crazy-quilt of land ownership in the second and third generations as parents tried to "portion" each child. This factor

and the general availability of land elsewhere forced succeeding generations to abandon the *strassendorf* structure as landless offspring moved
onto the frontier. Thereafter, German communities tended to take on a
structure similar to that of the English Quaker villages.

Germans rarely married anyone outside their own nationality, which in
a small community quickly built up an understructure of acknowledged
kinship. As the population increased, stress was placed on the cohesive-
ness of the German community. This effected the sectarian communities
most because they hoped "to maintain the purity of their religion through
its expression in their daily lives."[51]

German families were large. On the whole they were larger than
those of the Quakers averaging about 9 pregnancies per married couple.
Approximately 75 percent of the children survived into adulthood.
Documentation from late in the period involving 30 families from southeastern Pennsylvania shows an average of 7 children per family, but
family size in this sample ranged from 3 to 23 persons. German widowers seemingly remarried quickly after the death of a wife. Some men had
as many as five wives in sequence and may have had children by each
one. "This mixing of generations posed problems: the third or fourth wife
could be the same age as the oldest child by the first wife." Widows had
few legal powers with regard to the family land in Pennsylvania, but the
laws of other colonies, especially Virginia, gave them some legal standing
in the courts in this regard.[52]

Prenuptial sexual activity was neither more nor less prevalent among
German settlers than it was elsewhere. However, children who deviated
from the community's norms were generally considered to bring shame
upon the family, particularly the father, who often viewed such transgres-
sions as a personal failure in parenting. Alexander Mack Jr., writing to the
Elder of his congregation in 1776, noted the failure of his daughter and
her fiancé in this regard with sympathy.

I can therefore not very well avoid telling you a bit about the present situation....
It is true, my Hannah had thought at first that her sin was not so great because
they had been engaged never to leave each other, and both she and her husband
[they married after the pregnancy was discovered] indeed intend to prove this.
However, she realizes her error and recognized her misdeed. She wants me to ask
you especially for your forgiveness as she has always held a special love for you,
because she believed that you feared the Lord. She would be especially grateful
if you prayed to the Lord for her that he might have mercy on her condition and
request, for she does not want to remain behind completely.[53]

Detected fornication was punishable in this sect by avoidance (sometimes called shunning). Hannah was placed on full avoidance under the
discipline of the church. She was refused communion and had her membership among the Brethren withdrawn. Even her own family was not

permitted to eat with her. Ironically, Mack's other daughter Sarah was also placed under the discipline of the congregation, but in not so complete a manner. Sarah's offense was that she married outside the religious community; had sought out a marriage license from the local magistrate (a great sin among the sectarian German Brethren); and had formed a union with a man who had not yet completed his apprenticeship (probably a violation of his indenture). Mach noted with regard to the failures of his children, "Before God I cannot declare myself entirely blameless even though I did certainly think I had used great diligence and sent many sighs [prayers] to the Eternal Love for these two poor children."[54]

AFRICAN FAMILIES

The demographic condition of families of African descent in British North America is difficult to ascertain because the overwhelming majority were slaves who left no personal accounts of their lives until the middle of the 19th century.[55] The actual place of origin of African slaves is somewhat obscured by the common practice of using of the point of sale on the coast of Africa as a point of origin in the colonial records. Seven coastal regions have been identified as the origins of Africans brought to the Americas as slaves. These are Senegambia, Sierra Leone, the Windward Coast, the Gold Coast, the Blight of Benin, the Blight of Biafra, and the central southeast African coast. Records kept in this manner tend to conceal a much richer and more diverse cultural background, encompassing possibly dozens of ethnic groups and regional tribes. Some of these ethnic groups were identified in the 19th century, and they include the Wolof, Malinke, Temne, Fulbe, Susu, Mende, Koso, Sherbro, Basa, Akan, Kromantees, Fon, Gun, Popos, Yoruba, Nupe, Benin, Ibo, Efik, Ibibo, Calabahs, Bantu, and Hausa groups, and several regional groups from the Congo or Mozambique.[56] More recent research suggests that the greatest number of Africans brought to Virginia and the Carolinas were drawn from among the Bantu-speaking people of the Niger Delta and the Gold Coast.[57]

Until very late in the 18th century "virtually no white men had ever seen anything of the African interior," and contemporary European statements as to the conditions prevalent there were almost completely conjectural. Certainly there was a widespread and highly successful determination on the part of the coastal slave-trading tribes to keep out white slavers. Except at the coastal stations, the trade in slaves was controlled entirely by blacks, many of whom were Muslim slave raiders from the interior. In the Niger Delta, the trade was organized by the Oracle, a judicial-religious body that condemned hundreds of persons to be enslaved and acted as an intermediary agency between the coastal tribes and those in the interior. Likewise, the Ashanti, a tribal group located in the heart of the slave raiding country, became as powerful as some feudal European states. They developed tradition-based legal institutions, a tax and revenue system,

White slave traders rarely ventured out of sight of their ships, purchasing slaves on the coast, where the likelihood of contracting tropical diseases was lower than in the interior. African families were often ripped apart at the outset.

and a military organization that could field tens of thousands of warriors for extended campaigns. Groups like the Oracle and the Ashanti helped to structure operative agreements, "effective over hundreds of square miles," that made it possible to exclude Europeans from a vigorous slave trade economy.[58]

Slavery had existed in Africa for centuries (as of this writing, it still exists in Sudan and other countries), but there was a sharp difference between the domestic tribal slavery of the village and the deplorable state into which deported captives were delivered by Europeans. Throughout West Africa, the authority of the elders was unquestioned, yet in a wide variety of political and semipolitical settings, the rule of law was followed over any absolute dictatorship. "African political institutions, moreover, were developed in sufficient complexity that they were able to provide stable governments for groups as large as two hundred thousand, some of them lasting for centuries." Under Ashanti law, a slave could marry, own property, swear an oath, serve as a witness in legal cases, and own a slave himself. All of these competencies were denied to slaves in British North America.[59]

It would be premature to generalize about the impact the slave trade had on Africa. The negative consequences seem too obvious to state.

The position that slavery was due solely to European demand, as some antislavery partisans argued, is simply false. Yet the demographic consequences of physically removing any large number of people from a society "can have meaning only in relation to the size of the society, the time period concerned, the age and sex composition of the emigrants and the society from which they depart." The social and political implications of removing between ten and twenty million people from African society may not correspond directly to the number that were exported. One imponderable consequence is the effect of European contact on the native people of Africa. It is well known, for instance, that Old World diseases virtually wiped out many of the American Indian populations of the New World, but very little is known of the epidemiological history of East Africa. It is therefore impossible to gauge at present the effect of any European or American diseases introduced to the African continent. Conversely, at least two American food crops—manioc and maize—were successfully adapted to widespread use in Africa, helping to organize an agricultural economy that could support a heavily concentrated population in a relatively limited area. Yet, the overall social and political effects of the slave trade on Africa remain unknown. Slave raiding, slave catching, and the entire slave economy that surrounded exportation may have transformed a previously peaceful agricultural society into a highly militarized one, or it may have reflected a society already prone to solve its disputes through military means, producing prisoners of war who, if not killed or exchanged, might be enslaved and sold. "The African adaptation to the demand for slaves might be to change military tactics and strategy to maximize the number of prisoners, without actually increasing the incidence or destructiveness of warfare." Without further research in this area, the answers are simply not known.[60]

Most of the people brought as slaves to British North America came from cultures based on farming and herding rather than on hunting and warfare, and they were, therefore, well versed in common agricultural tasks and animal husbandry. Nineteenth-century thought considered persons from agricultural cultures to be tractable and unlikely to revolt and therefore to be prime candidates for enslavement. Yet the economies of West Africa were characterized by a high degree of specialization and division of labor. Ironworkers, weavers, carpenters, carvers, and basket makers were "all clearly defined occupational groups, and their clothing, tools, and other products were made not simply for their own use but also for sale."[61] The work expected of slave and the tasks to which they were put varied with time and the economic condition of the region into which they were brought, but the vast majority of these tasks involved farming.

The proportion of African-born to American-born blacks influenced family formation, marriage age, the relative family size, reproduction rates, and culture especially in the deep South where dependence on African-born slaves continued into the 1760s. Moreover, gender ratios, age structure, and distribution of relatives among the various plantations were generally under the control of the slave owners and were therefore neither random nor uniform. Generally, there was a gender imbalance in the slave trade with males, especially young males, outnumbering females. This was partly because women were more highly valued as agricultural workers in Africa than men, who filled the roles of hunter and defender in many tribes. Conversely, adult men were more highly valued in America because they could contribute the strength of muscle needed to clear land, build canals to drain swamps, and break the virgin soil. In the American South slaves worked at tasks like these during almost all the daylight hours for at least six days a week.

In the 17th century, there was little attempt to breed slaves domestically because slaves who died or were worn out with hard work could be more easily and quickly replaced by those imported from Africa than by those raised from childhood in America. Moreover, adult female Africans were often well advanced into their childbearing years, the younger women having a greater value in Africa than at the trading stations. African born women invariably nursed their babies for up to three years, and the lactation had a natural contraceptive consequence. With fertility low, mortality high, and an imbalanced gender ratio, family formation among black slaves in America was negatively impacted.

Although the black population of the colonies was heavily dependent on a continued influx of Africans from 1690 through 1740, the natural increase in American-born blacks ultimately became significant as American-born black women reached their childbearing years. In 1700, many black slaves were brought directly from Africa, but by 1775 only 20 percent were African-born. With births of male and female infants running about equal, the gender ratio quickly closed. Young men and women, freed of the need to adapt to a new environment, began to create a natural and rapid increase in their numbers. Black American-born women began having children at a younger age than their African-born mothers and grandmothers. They generally bore six children in their lifetimes on average while African-born women bore only three. As their fertility increased the mortality rate among American-born adults also seems to have waned. Only in the Deep South did mortality continue to outstrip the natural increase in births. As plantations in the Chesapeake increased in number and size, the opportunities for blacks to marry and have children increased also. Every time a black slave gave birth, the slave owner acquired a new slave. In the decade before the Revolution, 56 percent of slaves in the Carolinas had been born in America, while in Virginia and Maryland, this proportion rose to 90 percent. A contemporary plantation mistress noted, "[Slave] women are generally shown some indulgence for three or four weeks previous to childbirth … [and] they are generally allowed four weeks after the birth of a child, before they are compelled to go into the field. They then take the child with them."[62]

A closely knit family structure stood at the base of all the political, economic, and legal institutions in Africa, but the slave family in America was an intrinsically unstable institution. No colony recognized marriage between slaves. Marriage for the white population was considered a legal medium by which property was handed down to legitimate heirs. Since slaves could have no property, the law saw no reason to recognize the union of slaves as binding. The slaves seem to have coveted marriages blessed by clergy, however. Some morally scrupulous planters encouraged marriage ceremonies in opposition to the immorality of open promiscuity, and they found that such a policy decreased the incidence of runaways and discouraged fighting among the slave population. A tradition of "jumping the broom" is thought to have been developed by those slaves denied a formal wedding ceremony as a physical manifestation and finalization of their union. Female slaves did not take the name of their husbands but generally retained the family name of the slave owner.

Slave courtship and marriage "abroad," as that between persons on different plantations was called, was generally discouraged because it allowed slaves to travel beyond the owner's holdings. Small holdings and a dearth of available partners, however, made the practice more common. Husbands were generally issued weekend passes permitting them to leave after a half day of work on Saturday and to return Monday morning after visiting their wives and children abroad. Many planters went to considerable lengths to avoid breaking up families because of the great unrest it caused. Unfortunately, however, mortgage foreclosures, loan repayments, and inheritances brought many slaves to the auction block with no concern for the family unit. Executors of estates often divided slaves into lots of equivalent value for distribution to heirs. Additionally, planters often made gifts of slaves to their children, especially as wedding presents.

NOTES

1. Robert Leckie, *A Few Acres of Snow: The Saga of the French and Indian Wars* (New York: John Wiley and Sons, 1999), 259.

2. Ibid., 259.

3. David Hackett Fischer, *Albion's Seed: Four British Folkways in America* (New York: Oxford University Press, 1989), 610, 610n.

4. Ibid., 111–12.

5. Ibid., 16–17.

6. William Hutchinson, *A Treatise on Naval Architecture* (Liverpool: T. Billinge, 1794), 286–89.

7. Jack P. Greene, *Pursuits of Happiness: The Social Development of Early Modern British Colonies and the Formation of American Culture* (Chapel Hill: University of North Carolina Press, 1988), 14.

8. Fischer, *Albion's Seed*, 52.

9. Greene, *Pursuits of Happiness*, 15.

10. Firth Haring Fabend, *A Dutch Family in the Middle Colonies, 1660–1800* (New Brunswick, NJ: Rutgers University Press, 1991), 43.

11. John Demos, *A Little Commonwealth: Family Life in Plymouth Colony* (New York: Oxford University Press, 2000), 192.

12. T. H. Breen, *The Marketplace of Revolution: How Consumer Politics Shaped American Independence* (New York: Oxford University Press, 2004), 63.

13. William Peirce Randel, *The American Revolution: Mirror of a People* (Maplewood, NJ: Hammond, 1973), 87.

14. Fabend, *A Dutch Family in the Middle Colonies*, 45.

15. Demos, *A Little Commonwealth*, 133n.

16. See James M. Volo and Dorothy Denneen Volo, *Encyclopedia of the Antebellum South* (Westport, CT: Greenwood Press, 2000).

17. Fabend, *A Dutch Family in the Middle Colonies*, 38.

18. William S. Sachs and Ari Hoogenboom, *The Enterprising Colonials: Society on the Eve of the Revolution* (Chicago: Argonaut, 1965), 11.

19. M. Halsey Thomas, ed., *The Diary of Samuel Sewall, 1674–1729*, vol. 2 (New York: Farrar, Straus and Giroux, 1973), 314.

20. Quoted in Demos, *A Little Commonwealth*, 63.

21. Ibid., 27.

22. Ibid., 153.

23. Chard Powers Smith, *Yankees and God* (New York: Hermitage House, 1954), 184.

24. Ibid., 228.

25. Quoted in ibid., 240.

26. Fabend, *A Dutch Family in the Middle Colonies*, 38.

27. Quoted in Kenneth Morgan, *Slavery and Servitude in Colonial North America* (New York: New York University Press, 2000), 78.

28. Fabend, *A Dutch Family in the Middle Colonies*, 38.

29. Fischer, *Albion's Seed*, 374–75.

30. Ralph Bennett, ed., *Settlements in the Americas: Cross-Cultural Perspectives,* (Newark, DE: University of Delaware Press, 1993), 146.

31. Smith, *Yankees and God*, 232.

32. Ibid., 230–31.

33. Bennett, *Settlements in the Americas*, 149.

34. Ibid., 169.

35. Ibid., 152–53.

36. Paul Swain Havens, *Chambersburg: Frontier Town, 1730–1794* (Chambersburg, PA: Craft Press, 1975), 41.

37. Fabend, *A Dutch Family in the Middle Colonies*, 40–41.

38. Simon Schama, *The Embarrassment of Riches: An Interpretation of Dutch Culture in the Golden Age* (New York: Vintage, 1997), 78.

39. Ibid., 79.

40. Bernard Bailyn, *The Peopling of British North America: An Introduction,* (New York: Alfred A. Knopf, 1986), 33.

41. Aaron Spencer Fogleman, *Hopeful Journeys: German Immigration, Settlement, and Political Culture in Colonial America, 1717–1775* (Philadelphia: University of Pennsylvania Press, 1996) 102.

42. Alvin E. Conner, *Sectarian Childrearing: The Dunkers, 1708–1900* (Gettysburg, PA: Brethren Press, 2000), 11.

43. Fogleman, *Hopeful Journeys,* 54.

44. Ibid., 103.

45. Ibid., 126.

46. Ibid., 56.

47. Ibid., 72.

48. Parke Rouse Jr., *The Great Wagon Road from Philadelphia to the South* (New York: McGraw-Hill, 1973), 78.

49. Fogleman, *Hopeful Journeys*, 101.

50. Ibid., 124.

51. Conner, *Sectarian Childrearing,* 1.

52. Ibid., 113.

53. Quoted in ibid., 117.

54. Quoted in ibid., 118.

55. Even among records left after the colonial period, there are questions of authenticity, perspective, and propaganda.

56. Philip D. Curtin, *The Atlantic Slave Trade: A Census* (Madison: University of Wisconsin Press, 1975) 245.

57. Stanley M. Elkins, *Slavery: A Problem in American Institutional and Intellectual Life* (New York: Grosset and Dunlap, 1963), 93.

58. Ibid., 95–96.

59. Ibid., 97.

60. Curtin, *The Atlantic Slave Trade*, 271–72.

61. Elkins, *Slavery*, 95.

62. Horatio T. Strother, *The Underground Railroad in Connecticut* (Middletown: Wesleyan University Press, 1962), 195.

Part II
The Role of Father

3

Patriarch

Such a father could curse God and brave hell itself to insure his child's recovery.[1]

—Lisa Wilson, historian

To maintain the order of his household and his own authority, a man was required to assert a bold personality, to maintain a consistent outward character, and sometimes to take forceful measures to insure the uninterrupted functioning of his home. Consequently, colonial fathers of the 17th and 18th centuries are often pictured as harsh, cold, and controlling men imbued with zealous religious fervor and a scrupulous fixation on the rigorous upbringing of their children in terms of their bodies, their minds, and their souls. Of prime importance in the upbringing of children was that they be God-fearing, knowledgeable in the doctrines of their religion, and shielded from the deadly sins of overindulgence, permissiveness, and indolence during their formative years.

Colonial fathers considered themselves to be reincarnations of the imposing biblical patriarchs of old. This picture of colonial fatherhood is often portrayed as a misguided system of male-dominated instruction and government, which would not be replaced by a more affectionate and openly loving form of parenting until the Victorian Era. This bias is perhaps engendered by the righteous tenor found in much of colonial writing. Further investigation, however, reveals a different picture of fathers in the colonial period that is not so far removed from those of the 19th or even the 20th centuries.

Certainly the letters of colonial fathers to their children often lack the romantic language, enlightened sentiment, and tender endearments of later centuries. However, this apparent poverty of language should not automatically be interpreted as evidence of a want of affection toward the members of their families. Few loving fathers today put such sentiments on paper. While colonial men were quick to take up the pen and record their thoughts on doctrinal and technical subjects, the same men were seemingly reticent about recording their personal emotions. They sometimes recorded nothing that could be considered warm and loving with respect to their offspring anywhere except in their last will and testament. Nevertheless, in their children's infancy, many colonial men sought out detailed information concerning their health, growth, and well-being. They likewise recorded the small achievements of their toddlers, the mastery of their adolescents, and the accomplishments of their adult offspring. Moreover, with a degree of parental pride consistent with biblical humility, they boasted of these occurrences in their diaries and reported them to their friends and relations in letters and conversations. Moreover, as their children passed through adulthood, fathers remained solicitous of their well-being and were quick to counsel them as to the future course of their lives.

Colonial fathers derived their authority from four sources. The Scriptures gave them wide authority as the head of their family. Their church order, especially in communities founded by religious sects, required that they properly organize their households or face the scrutiny of the elders or the magistrates. Their employment—be it farm, craft, or trade—imposed on them a practical necessity to manage their businesses and often required the cooperation of family members, including wives and children, as integral parts of the work force. Finally, the custom of the day required that children submit absolutely to paternal authority until they reached their majority and that women submit to the will of their husbands. Fathers thought this authority to be their natural God-given right. They did not hesitate to use it, nor did they apologize for its use.[2]

In most colonial families, the Scriptural image of God as the father of all humanity seems to have served as a divine example for the male parent, and the Bible itself served most men as a template for dealing with specific problems concerning childrearing. Scriptural references were constantly used to prop up paternal authority by emphasizing its God-givenness. Yet there were two differing themes in the Bible from which the character of paternal authority might be extracted. Punitive actions with regard to fatherly authority were more strongly expressed in the Old Testament, while the theme of a loving and caring authority, lacking the punitive aspects, predominated in the New Testament. The responsibility of the father, according to colonial consensus, was to rear his children and order his household in a caring and nurturing manner as suggested by the New Testament, while withholding the coercion and use of force openly sanctioned in the Old. Any father who behaved too harshly toward his family was subject to the disapproval of his neighbors. "Ye fathers," warned the Bible (Ephesians 6:4), "provoke not your children to wrath but bring them up in the nurture and admonition of the Lord."[3]

Depending largely on the force of their own personalities, colonial fathers usually laid down the law and then enforced it compassionately because of their affection for their wives and children. In times of trouble, fathers instructed their children in the power of hopeful prayer and used biblical references to help make sense of difficult or frustrating situations. A man was charged with the stewardship of his children's bodies and souls no less than he was of any other valuable property. Men guided their children, even in adulthood, with a loving but firm hand.

The correction of wayward children and their submission to paternal authority were equally compelling characteristics of colonial parenting. A child's duty to obey was unequivocal. Philip Fithian wrote to his father in 1769, "The duty of a child to a parent is obedience, love, and all kinds of regard."[4] The instruments of paternal power used to discipline children ranged from verbal chastisement to corporal punishment, which sometimes bordered on physical abuse by modern standards. Nonetheless, the young were allowed their age-typical misadventures with little or no punishment. The withholding of allowances, the threat of delayed inheritance, or other financial penalties were reserved for older children, teenagers, and young adults. Fathers also resorted to manipulative methods that played on the conscience of the child and associated disobedience or misbehavior with guilt. This method was particularly effective when accompanied by biblical allegories or religious injunctions. In no case were children to be treated as anything but children, in contrast to the present day when childrearing has become intertwined with individual rights and juvenile prerogatives. Colonial fathers were always certain to vigorously assert their parental authority—especially in their written admonitions to older children, but actual physical corrections or counseling sessions were usually carried out in an atmosphere of mutual obligation, contemplative restraint, and loving discipline.

Although colonial fathers were urged to maintain a generational distance from their children, they were constantly looking for everyday opportunities for pious instruction on a personal level. They were alert to those evils that might endanger the spiritual salvation of their children's souls. In good times, they taught their children to recognize the nature of God's blessings and to credit Him with bestowing on them those talents and strengths of character that might allow them to succeed. Children were warned to never be so blatantly prideful as to proclaim themselves "self-made" men or women. When the mercy or intervention of God was seemingly withheld, fathers emphasized resignation to the will of the Creator and a patient, if not cheerful, submission to the Divine plan. Even the untimely death of a sibling or other relative could be used to teach

surviving children about the fragility of life, the inevitability of death, and
the imminent benefits of true godliness.

The distress engendered by the illness or death of a child could often
wrest a torrent of tender and affectionate admissions from even the most
stern and reserved father. On the death of his oldest son in 1679, Wait
Winthrop wrote, "I lost my hope, and the greatest part of my comfort."
Samuel Bradstreet wrote of a son lost in 1678, "He was a lovely child
exceeding forward, every way desirable, most dearly beloved by me in this
life and as much lamented since his death." Samuel Sewall, a prodigious
diarist, was fated to lose eight of his fourteen children before they reached
their adult years. Such repeated losses would sorely test any man's faith,
yet he seemingly resigned himself to God's will: "The Lord help[ed] me
thankfully and fruitfully to enjoy them [while they lived]." Other men
reasoned and bargained with God for the health of their living offspring
or for the salvation of the souls of those that were taken from them. They
"took out their religious arsenals to counter assaults on their families.
They even risked their souls to save their child[ren]." Some men blamed
their own weakness of character, lapses of good judgment, or transgres-
sions of the moral code for the suffering of their offspring. Others scolded
God for his lack of mercy or threatened him with the denial of their love if
their petitions went unanswered. In a period when men believed fiercely
in God's involvement in their day-to-day lives, and when they counted
on his benevolence and good will to insure the ultimate fate of their own
souls, assertions of this nature were not to be taken lightly.[5]

It seems reasonable that individual fathers combined many levels of
authority and stern intimidation, depending on their own personalities.
The colonial realms of social, political, and economic power were ruled by
men, and men were always considered the heads of their households. By
authority of the Scriptures, men were subservient to God and wives were
subservient to their husbands. Yet husbands commonly wrote of their
wives as companions or helpmeets. In the home, parental authority was
usually shared between husband and wife to a far greater degree than
some observers might have acknowledged. The level of maternal authority during the colonial period is difficult to judge mainly because women
produced many fewer written documents than their husbands and were
reticent about criticizing them even in writing. Most men almost certainly
upheld and supported the authority of their wives. "It [is] difficult to
believe that [wives] were not equal partners, in substance if not in role, in
most issues that faced the family."[6]

During the colonial period, both parents were urged through sermons
from the pulpit and through learned treatises on childrearing to agree as
to the course of governance for their children, and both mother and father
were expected to contribute to their proper upbringing. Samuel Chandler,
writing from his dormitory at Harvard of himself and his brothers and
sisters, noted that, from his infancy, both his parents "clothed us, gave

Men were expected to take part in the governance of the wider community. This informal role as community leader was often accomplished through talk and discussion with neighbors.

us food for the nourishing of our bodies, protected us from evils, and instructed us in every branch of learning [of] which they themselves were capable, [and] spared no cost for our education nor thought any pains too great to be taken that [were] for our advantage."[7]

Cotton Mather in *A Family Well-Ordered* (1699) and Benjamin Wadsworth in *The Well-Ordered Family* (1712) outlined parental responsibilities for both fathers and mothers based on an overall firmness of conviction heavily tempered by love. Verbal and physical corrections, leavened with tenderness rather than fear, were to be used to instill reverence for parental authority. "Let not your authority be strained with such harshness, and fierceness, as may discourage your children," wrote Mather. "[Y]our authority should be tempered with kindness, and meekness, and loving tenderness, that your children may fear you with delight and see that you love them, with as much delight."[8] Colonial fathers provided extremely strong guidance and control by present-day standards, leaving the mother as the intercessor, who blunted the impact of the sometimes overly dogmatic stances of her husband as mothers have done for many ages.[9]

One book that circulated widely in America between the turn of the 17th and 18th centuries was Francis Osborn's *Advice to a Son* (1656). Osborn's work was somewhat more formal than the parenting instructions that could be gleaned from sermons or biblical passages. It dealt with education, the improvement of assets, love and marriage, travel, government, and religion. The emphasis throughout was rooted in a tough-minded pragmatism. For instance, he advised that "an over passionate prosecution of learning" might draw a man away from "an honest improvement in his estate." He also suggested that a son should "marry well for a great estate is the surest palliative for the inconveniences [expenses] of wedlock: submit quietly to whatever power sits in the saddle of sovereignty; in matters of religion, undiscovered hypocrisy is less dangerous than open profaneness; conscience must be kept tender, but not so raw as to occasion imprudence." Although Osborn's book was fully compatible with colonial attitudes toward worldly success, some of his contemporaries, especially devout Pietists, considered his advice to be conceited and irreligious.[10]

Once their children were beyond infancy, fathers began to parent in a manner different from that of mothers. While both took responsibility for the physical welfare of their children, the father concentrated on the children's spiritual health by instructing them in the tenets and doctrines of the family religion. He usually led the family in daily prayer and continued to instill those religious practices attendant to a life rooted in scriptural imperatives. It was usually the father who counseled his children to turn to the Bible and to supplicant prayer in times of distress, to protect their souls from imminent evil, and to glorify God at all opportunities. "Accept of my love and don't forsake a father's advice, who, above all things, desires that your soul may be saved in the day of the Lord," wrote John Williams to his son in 1706. "God knows that the catechism in which I instructed you is according to the word of God and so will be found in the Day of Judgment."[11]

Fathers also instructed their children in the proper rules of both private and public secular behavior. For fathers without access to schools or without tutors practiced in etiquette who might instill civility in their children there was no alternative than to carry on this training in a family setting. This was the case for most colonial families. To some extent the content of this training was the same for both boys and girls—the avoidance of awkward behaviors such as staring, fumbling, or stammering, or unseemly behaviors such as speaking out of turn, failing to acknowledge the primacy of their elders (or their social betters), or otherwise deporting themselves in an inappropriate manner. Childish chatter was considered particularly inappropriate. Josiah Cotton admonished his children "not to speak when others are speaking, not to talk too much or all at once, nor to speak before they think." Proper manners for children included a whole protocol of behaviors based on social position and respect for one's elders. Silence was golden, and the general chaos of childlike play was to be avoided when adults were about. Children were warned "not to contend or fight with each other" as part of their amusement. They should not seat themselves first at table nor stand between others and the warmth of the fire, nor address their elders without the use of proper titles or familial terms such as father, mother, grandfather, or aunt.[12]

A major test of children's behavior was the deportment that they exhibited at dinner. "In some families children stood behind their parents and other grown persons, and the food was handed back to them—so we are told. This seems closely akin to throwing food to an animal, and must have been [common] among people of very low station and social manners. In other houses they stood at a side table; and trencher in hand, ran [moved] over to the great table to be helped to more food." Generally,

Children were to be seen and not heard. They were not permitted to frolic on the floor or fight during meals. This man has obviously lost control of his household and is taking out his frustrations on the servant girl. Note the look of discomfort on the face of his wife seated at the table.

when children were seated at the table with the family, they were to eat in silence, finish as quickly as possible, and leave as soon as they were given permission. "They were ordered never to seat themselves at the table until the blessing had been asked and their parents told them to be seated. They were never to ask for anything on the table; never to speak unless spoken to; always to break bread, not to bite into a whole slice; never to take salt except with a clean knife; not to throw bones under the table; [nor] look ... earnestly at any other person that was eating."[13]

There were, of course, a whole series of semiprivate and public occasions that marked the comings and goings of the family and the wider community. These were usually characterized by the consumption of large amounts of food and beverage. It was important that children be seen to behave properly and politely in this context. Family feasts of this sort often celebrated the life cycle of the family. There were lying-in feasts, birthing feasts, baptismal feasts, churching feasts, feasts when children were swaddled, feasts on the beginning of school or an apprenticeship, betrothal feasts, wedding and anniversary feasts, feasts for setting up house, feasts to celebrate recovery from an illness, and feasts that followed the setting of a gravestone. Neighborhood feasts, set for a particular time span and with a more formal protocol, proclaimed the order and safety of the community and affirmed the life cycle of the collective society. There were many occasions for such gatherings: the completion of a church project, such as the installation of a new window, an organ, or choir loft; the launching of a new vessel or the return of one thought lost at sea; the news of a military victory or the conclusion of a triumphal peace; and the birth of a royal child or grandchild. Although many Protestant sects, including Calvinists and Quakers, were "especially hostile to seasonal or annual feasting," the celebration of saint's days and holy days based on the traditional Christian calendar could not be suppressed by the ministers with their sermons vilifying Roman popery.[14]

Colonial families, like families in all times and places, sometimes had to deal with the phenomenon of the absentee father. Conditions at the time required men to be away from home for long periods. Just going to town for weekly or monthly supplies took an entire day—perhaps overnight; trips to market with produce or livestock often took a week; and spying out or improving new land on the frontiers might require a man to be absent from his home for many months. For instance, under the laws of some colonies, he might be required to occupy a land claim for a certain number of days per year to maintain the title to it. In the case of families pursuing a subsistence living on the frontier, the father might have to go to town for several weeks to earn money to purchase manufactured items, seed, livestock, or tools. Surveyors, fur traders, missionaries, sailors, fishermen, and whalers were often away from their families for many months or even years, and the early death of some fathers from natural causes or work-related injuries was inevitable. The death of a father had a profound effect on their sense of security. The absence of a father, whether temporary or permanent, put a heavy burden on the wife if there were no adult sons to fill the void. In addition to her own work, she had to assume all the responsibilities of the total household and the farm or business if there was one.

Colonial fathers were the patriarchs of their households, but most were also loving counselors, good providers, and dedicated protectors—not only of their families' physical well-being but also of their souls. True authority in a colonial patriarch derived not simply from a man's undisputed legal power over his wife, children, servants, or slaves, but also from his ability to subdue within himself those flaws of character that he normally attributed to lesser men: unbridled passion, unrestrained anger, ungodliness, idleness, and economic dependence.[15]

NOTES

1. Lisa Wilson, *Ye Heart of a Man, The Domestic Life of Men in Colonial New England* (New Haven: Yale University Press, 1999), 133.

2. Alvin E. Conner, *Sectarian Childrearing: The Dunkers, 1708–1900* (Gettysburg, PA: Brethren Heritage, 2000), 88.

3. Ibid., 88.

4. Philip Fithian to his father, Joseph, 28 September 1769, http://www/indiana.edu/~jah/teaching/2003_09/sources/ex2_father.shtml (acessed March 2005).

5. Quoted in Wilson, *Ye Heart of a Man*, 133.

6. Conner, *Sectarian Childrearing*, 102.

7. Wilson, *Ye Heart of a Man*, 116–17.

8. Ibid., 119.

9. Conner, *Sectarian Childrearing*, 105.

10. Lawrence A. Cremin, *American Education: The Colonial Experience, 1607–1783* (New York: Harper and Row, 1970), 75–76.

11. Quoted in Wilson, *Ye Heart of a Man*, 132.

12. Josiah Cotton (1723), quoted in Wilson, 127.

13. Alice Morse Earle, *Home Life in Colonial Days* (New York: Macmillan, 1993), 102–3.

14. Simon Schama, *The Embarrassment of Riches: An Interpretation of Dutch Culture in the Golden Age* (New York: Vintage, 1997), 185.

15. Kathleen M. Brown, *Good Wives, Nasty Wenches, and Anxious Patriarchs: Gender, Race, and Power in Colonial Virginia* (Chapel Hill: University of North Carolina Press, 1996), 321–22.

4

Wise and Seasonable Counsels

Accept of my love and don't forsake a father's advice, who, above all things, desires that your soul may be saved in the day of the Lord.
—John Williams, 1706

Colonial fathers were quick to take corrective steps when they observed those flaws developing in their own children that their society attributed to persons of lesser character. They took seriously their role as counselor and advisor to their children, grandchildren, and other relatives. Some men also took on the role of leader in their church, their community, their protective forces, or their colonial government. They sometimes served as military commanders, delegates to the colonial legislature, or advisors to the governor. Late in the 18th century, some of these same men advised their fellow citizens to undertake commercial boycotts, separation from Britain, and even armed rebellion. A few of them became leaders of a new nation.

Like fathers today, colonial fathers were deeply concerned for their children's future. Daughters were expected to learn proper housekeeping and fine needlework and to find husbands to care for them. Fathers hoped that their girls would find honest and well-to-do husbands, and they often devolved money and land on them to sweeten their eligibility. Sons needed to settle into permanent, honest, and reliable careers. Colonial father loved their daughters and their sons equally well, but they expended a great deal more effort in guiding their sons to choose an appropriate education and career. At the same time, fathers were acutely aware that their sons' career decisions had to be framed within the larger context of what might prove most beneficial for the future of the entire family. With family size often approaching a dozen children at times, individual career choices were limited by the parents' ability to provide a suitable living for all their offspring. Most fathers felt that the greatest need was to educate their eldest sons well, and find them careers that would generate the largest possible income so that the sons could help their brothers and sisters who followed after them. Blatant nepotism especially with regard to the advancement of nephews seems to have been an accepted fact of colonial life. A less common means of improving the family fortune was to marry off a daughter or a niece into a wealthy or influential family, which might aid its in-laws at some future time. Such cross family connection were very important.

Ezekiel Williams, for instance, hoped that after his eldest son was established in his career, he might "be enabled to do justice to my other children." Although the desires of the eldest son were given great attention the counsels of a father were likely to channel the boy into certain occupations that produced revenue or generated influence. Younger sons were often left at liberty to follow their own "learned and virtuous" inclinations with respect to employment or career. Joseph Green, the father of fourteen children, ten of them boys, found that he could afford a college education for only two—one sent to the ministry and the other set to scholarship. The remaining boys were apprenticed as tailors, blacksmiths, and carpenters, or found places aboard ships as sailors—considered at the time one of the least desirable career choices by most parents. The younger of the two college-bound sons, John, then at Harvard, recalled that immediately after his father's death—a particularly trying time for the family finances—there was talk among his uncles of removing him from school and "putting" him to some other less costly career.[1]

Sons expected and seriously considered the counsel of their fathers, and some valued it highly. Isaac Sherman wrote that he understood "the incumbent duty of a young man to consult and advise with those who are acquainted with the various maneuvers of mankind; especially with a kind indulgent parent, who always [counsels] the good of his children."[2] Benjamin Trumbull wrote obligingly to his father, "I have always enjoyed your wise and seasonable counsels.... [Y]ou have withholden nothing in your power to bestow that which might serve for my advantage." Thomas Williams, on the other hand, complained bitterly about his father's advice in a letter to his elder brother Eliphalet, a minister, "Father has a mind I should keep school." Thomas considered the life of a school master difficult and poorly paid work. "Is it reasonable to trudge and sweat a whole day at ABC's for 18 or 20 pence when a farmer won't at the scythe [earn] under half a Crown at least!"[3]

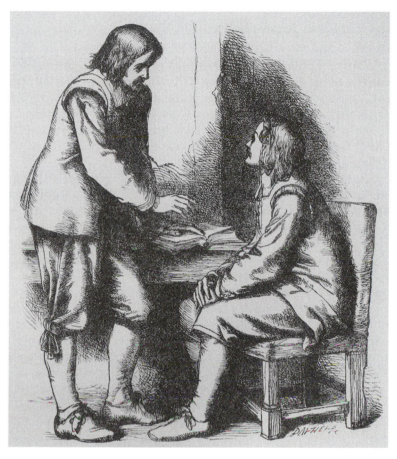

While fathers were considered the absolute authority in their homes, most dealt with their children in a dispassionate and controlled manner that emphasized good counsel rather than iron will.

Colonial fathers felt some obligation to devote the life of at least one son to God's ministry, but they understood that such a career required a formal college education and provided few financial rewards. Ministers were thought to work for loftier rewards than money, including influence in the community and respectable social status. Nathan Miles, a Congregational minister, wanted his son, Elisha, to follow him into the pulpit, but Elisha went off to be a soldier, his mind according to his father, having been "more and more weaned from heavenly entertainments."[4]

Few fathers wrote scornfully of their sons entering a trade, "for trade was the means by which men attained ... leadership and prestige."[5] The surest road to prosperity and prestige in British North America was through the merchant's counting house, and although the planter aristocracy of the South attained social significance and contributed greatly to the intellectual leadership of the colonies, Southerners also respected trade as a means to turn a penny.[6] The prestige attained by countless craftsmen, tradesmen, shipmasters, and merchants served as examples for all ranks of the colonial population. A favorite tract of the colonial merchant class, *A Cloud of Faithful Witnesses Leading to the Heavenly Kingdom* by William Perkins, demonstrated through scriptural references how God led the faithful to worldly success. Another work suggested as reading material by many fathers to their sons was Cotton Mather's *Magnalia Christi Americana,* which was filled with "glorious examples of how God would crown heroic virtue with [financial] success."[7]

Of course, many sons chose to ignore the advice of their fathers. Josiah Cotton, for example, was quite disturbed by his son's choice of a career as a ship's officer. His concern was based on fear for his son's physical well-being and a concern for his spiritual salvation. He wrote to his son, Theophilas, "Sailors, one would think, should be the best of men, they're being, as we say, but a step between them and death; and yet experience shows that they are commonly the worst."[8] William Livingston, governor of New Jersey, wrote to his son John on his becoming a ship's officer, "When you are obliged to associate with the common mariners, I would have you act towards them with becoming familiarity and freedom, without assuming any airs of superiority on account of your connections, but I would by no means have you enter into their vulgarisms and low-lived practices, for which they themselves will rather despise you; and above all, that you must carefully avoid contracting that abominable custom, so common among seamen, of profaning the name of God by oaths and imprecations." In giving his blessing to his son before his voyage, Livingston noted, "Let me entreat you not to forget your Creator in the days of your youth, to remember your duty to the great God, who alone can prosper you in this life and make you happy in that which is to come."[9]

Ezekiel Williams, preferring a career for his son, John, as a clerk, initially counseled him to avoid the study of law: "[I] am very willing you should study law or any other studies that may be useful to you in life … but as I suppose you do not mean to practice law for a livelihood … you should learn to write well … [as I] might be able to get a berth for you for awhile as a clerk." Some time later, John made clear to his father the finality of his decision to become a lawyer. The elder Williams finally acquiesced, "If you choose to practice law I shall not hinder you as I believe it not a dishonest calling, and as there are many worthy men in that profession, tho' I should not have wished that for you, if your genius and inclination had led you otherwise."[10]

Many fathers expressed a wish that their children "be more concerned for work, than for wages."[11] A popular book, *A Treatise of the Vocations* (1603), also written by William Perkins, circulated widely in the colonies. Perkins expounded an elaborate doctrine connecting heavenly salvation to diligent labor at some honest trade or vocation. Protestants, particularly those with a Puritan or Quaker background, strongly countenanced Perkins' gospel of work. Today the gospel of work is often referred to as the "Protestant Work Ethic." Thomas Bacon, who would found a charity school for poor children of both genders, noted the necessity to instruct children "in the Knowledge and Fear of God, and inure [them] to useful Labour ... before being put out as apprentices." He also wrote, "Ignorance and indolence among the lower class of people in these colonies are no less prejudicial to the common interest, or dangerous to the constitution, than popery and idleness."[12]

Colonial fathers insisted on their children receiving a good education because they feared "that ignorance would beget idleness, and idleness, which was a waste of God's precious time ... [and was] one of the worst sins."[13] Thomas Shepard, writing to his son at Harvard in 1672, warned, "Abhor therefore one hour of idleness as you would be ashamed of one hour of drunkenness."[14] Cotton Mather wrote and spoke against idleness on numerous occasions. "Idleness, alas! Idleness ... of which there never came any goodness! Idleness, which is the reproach of any people." Mather believed that idleness, and particularly the refusal to work, was a sin against God himself.[15]

Fathers hoped that their children would follow in their footsteps. This naval officer appears to have little to fear concerning his son's choice of a career.

Colonial fathers also wrote extensively to their children emphasizing good judgment, prudence, and modesty and inveighing against waste, extravagance, and ostentatious vanities such as opulent clothing, lavish wigs, and the use of makeup—all of which characterized an Italianate style fashionable among young English dandies known as Macaronis. They glorified those virtues that led men to apply themselves to their earthly callings with cheerful diligence. They valued a calm demeanor, prudence, frugality, industry, and chastity in their daughters. They enjoined their children to be sober and thrifty and to carefully manage their time and their assets. God would reward industry, thrift, and pious diligence with prosperity, prominence, and influence. In fact, success in business and society was considered by most colonists to be an outward sign of inner godliness. Thus the industrious and pious person, whether man or woman, farmer, craftsman, professional, or housewife could expect to prosper with the help of the Almighty.[16] Nonetheless, some children were "naturally of [a] very mischievous disposition; at times highly passionate; and prone to evil." As they "grew older and became less in the presence of [their] parents, [they] often set at naught all their counsel to walk in the counsel of the ungodly."[17]

William Livingston warned his 18-year-old son against the dangers of profligacy:

I must press upon you to be saving of your money, and not to spend it unnecessarily. If you do not observe this direction, you will find by woeful experience that you have rejected the most salutary advice.... [But] I do not intend that you should ever appear mean ... nor grudge little expense upon proper occasions, when you must either part with your money or appear contemptible; as when you are necessarily engaged in company, and they go rather farther in the expenses of the club than you could wish; in such case and in others that will occur, one must sometimes conform against his inclinations, to save his character, and afterwards make it up by retrenching some other expenses and a greater economy.[18]

Colonial men also served as counselors to relatives outside their immediate households, giving advice about a wide range of topics. In New England, this role rarely extended beyond the circle of siblings, but in the southern colonies, men saw themselves as the natural leaders of their extended families and the larger plantation community. They sometimes behaved in a haughty and condescending manner reminiscent of the old nobility of Europe, marrying off their daughters as if sealing treaties between feudal estates and demanding positions of authority in local organizations. This voluntary assumption of the roles of counselor, benefactor, and knight errant to all other levels of their society was no mere attempt at social bravado. Men among the southern elite felt obliged to counsel and defend, not only the members of their own families, but all females and minor children placed under their protection.

Newcomers to America often relied on relatives or close friends who had proceeded them to provide information about how to prepare for life in the colonies. A letter from Robert Parke, an Irish Quaker in Delaware County, Pennsylvania, to a relative who was planning to come to the colonies with her own family in 1725 reveals much about their relationship and about colonial America.

This goes with a salutation of Love to thee ... hoping it may find you all in good health, as I with all our family in general are in at this present writing and have been since our arrival, for we have not had a day's sickness in the family since we came to [this] country, blessed be God for it. My father in particular has not had his health better in these ten years ... his ancient age considered....

Thee writes in thy letter that there was talk went back to Ireland that we were not satisfied in coming here, which was utterly false.... There is not one in the family but likes the country well and would if we were in Ireland again come here directly, it being the best country for working folk and tradesmen of any in the world.... As to what thee [wrote] about the Governor's opening letters it is utterly false and nothing but a lye; and anyone except bound servants may go out of the country when they will and servants when they serve their time may come away if they please, but it is rare any are such fools to leave the country except men's business requires it.

Land is of all prices even from ten pounds, to one hundred pounds a hundred [acres and] grows dearer every year by reason of vast quantities of people that come here yearly from several parts of the world, therefore thee and thy family, or any that I wish well, I would desire to make what speed you can to come here the sooner the better. [Father] bought a tract of land consisting of five hundred acres for which he gave 350 pounds. It is excellent good land but none cleared except about 20 acres, with a small log house and orchard planted. [W]e are going to clear some of it directly for our next Summer's fallow. We might have bought land much cheaper but not so much to our satisfaction.

Sister I desire thee may tell my old friend Samuel Thronton that he could ... not do better than to come here.... The best way for him to do is to pay what money he can conveniently spare at that side and engage himself to pay the rest at this side and when he comes here if he can get no friend to lay down the money for him, when it comes to the worst, he may hire out 2 or 3 children, and I would have him cloath his family as well as his small ability will allow.... If I had not respect for him and his family I should not have writ[ten] so much for his encouragement.

[F]ind no iffs [sic] nor ands in my letter ...Dear Sister I would not have thee doubt the truth of what I write, for I know it to be true tho' I have not been long here. I would have you cloath yourselves well with woolen and linen, shoes and stockings and hats for such are dear here and yet a man will sooner earn a suit of cloathes here than in Ireland, by reason workman's labour is so dear.[19]

As the colonial period waned, the influence of religion and of religious thought also waned, to be replaced in many cases by a mixture of pious superstition and enlightened rationalism. The movement from rigid theological thought to a more flexible secular thought that paralleled these developments percolated through the American upper classes throughout the 18th century as the influence of the ministers and the old religions declined, to be replaced by the thinking of politicians and the rise of mercantilist economics. Colonial men were quick to add the knowledge of politics and business to their interests. In some cases, these interests became preoccupations overshadowing, but never eliminating, the primacy of religious values.

Rather than aspiring to the ministry, men now strove to expand their business enterprises or to gain prominence in the colonial legislature. This new thinking was often reflected in the tone with which fathers counseled their children. Once steeped in biblical allusions, divine mandates, and an absolute morality, by the eve of the Revolution good counsel had taken on a more secular form that emphasized economic success and recognized the natural rights of man, majority rule, and an early form of moral relativism.

A trend in the late colonial period toward the development of advanced political concepts brought with it greater personal freedom and religious toleration. Among the philosophies that highlighted the colonial period were those of John Locke and Jeremy Bentham. Although both men were English and had never visited the colonies, their works had far-reaching consequences in British North America. Separated by almost a century, both nonetheless emphasized the importance of reason over tradition and custom, and both were champions of religious toleration, political rights, and the human condition.

Locke's work, especially that on human understanding, had considerable influence on Bentham. However, Locke argued his case logically and supported it by citing biblical references and historical precedents whereas Bentham combined an empirical approach and deductive scientific argument to account for the principles underlying his theories. For Locke, morality came from God through the dictums of the Old Testament, and political governance came from the will of the people through the social contract: "Thus every man, by consenting with others to make one body politic under one government, puts himself under an obligation to everyone of that society to submit to the determination of the majority." For Bentham, on the other hand, both morals and political governance could be ascribed to psychological hedonism—a utilitarian view that attributed most human actions to either the pursuit of pleasure or the avoidance of pain.[20]

In 1689, Locke returned to England from a self-imposed exile in the Netherlands, where he had gone to escape the arbitrary reign of James II. In the same year, he wrote two treatises on government to vindicate William III (William of Orange) and the English Whigs for their part in deposing James during England's Glorious Revolution of 1688. Locke's *Second Treatise on Civil Government* accomplished much more than this temporary and limited objective, providing the theoretical foundation for the American Revolution, modern constitutionalism, and representative democracy. Although he made considerable use of the concept of natural reason, Locke was careful to credit "those grants God made of this world to Adam, and to Noah and his sons ... [having] given the earth to the children of men." No part of Locke's argument is rooted in any premise that does not start with the deity: "The rules that they [men] make for other men's actions must ... be conformable to the law of Nature—i.e., to the will of God."[21] Locke's rationale was particularly attractive to Anglo-American Deists, such as Benjamin Franklin, Thomas Jefferson, and Thomas Paine.

Bentham, in contrast, sought no divine authority for his theories. In *Introduction to the Principles of Morals and Legislation*, he writes, "Nature has placed mankind under the governance of two sovereign masters, pleasure and pain. It is for them to point out what we ought to do, as well as to determine what we shall do." Personal inclination, or *utility*, not only served as an explanation for human actions, it also defined good and evil. Bentham, who called his theory utilitarianism, wrote, "If he [a man] is inclined to think that his own approbation or disapprobation ... is a sufficient foundation for him to judge and act upon, let him ask himself whether his sentiment is to be the standard of right and wrong, with respect to every other man, or whether every other man's sentiment has the privilege of being a standard to itself." Bentham assumed that the utility principle, rather than Locke's deity, was the foundation of all morality and law. Utility, rather than God, "approves or disapproves of every action whatsoever according to the tendency it appears to have to augment or diminish happiness."[22] Although Bentham's theories were extreme for his day, surprisingly similar concepts were echoed by many moderate men throughout 18th-century Anglo-America.[23]

As the apparent philosophical conflict between the divine right of kings and human rights became more extreme, it increasingly spilled over into the public arenas of politics, government, and economy. By the 1760s, with the threat of the French in Canada virtually eliminated, much of the philosophical neutral ground had disappeared, making it impossible for most colonials to hold any but the most extreme positions on the topic. Nonetheless, a number of mediators tried to ameliorate the coming crisis or at least to tone-down the rhetoric. These men took on the role of counselor, not only to their own families, but to the entire community.

John Witherspoon, for example, presented a series of lectures on moral philosophy at Princeton in 1768 that centered on the union of Enlightenment thinking and biblical revelation with respect to tolerance, patriotism, and natural rights:

When we are speaking of kind affections, it will not be improper to observe that some unbelievers have objected against the gospel, that it does not recommend private friendship and the love of our country. But if fairly considered, as the Scripture, both by example and precept, recommends all particular affections ... insisting on the forgiveness of injuries and the love of enemies.... The love of country to be sure, is a noble and enlarged affection, and those who have sacrificed their private ease and family relations to it, have become illustrious, yet the love of mankind is still greatly superior.... The great law of love to others, I shall only say further that it ought to have for its object their greatest and best interest, and therefore implies wishing and doing them good in soul and body.... Our duty to others, therefore, may be all comprehended in these two particulars, justice and mercy.[24]

Benjamin Franklin, a true symbol of the Enlightenment, was the first American colonist to be world renowned. Best known as a scientist, inventor, and wit, Franklin served, nonetheless, as a political and moral counselor to the colonial population during much of the mid-18th century. In his autobiography, he wrote, "I think it principally owing that I had early so much weight with my fellow-citizens ... and so much influence in public councils." Sadly, Franklin failed his own son, William, in the role of parental counselor. William Franklin was the royal governor of New Jersey before and during the War of Independence, and the rebel father and loyalist son became bitterly opposed during the crisis and never fully reconciled their differences.[25]

In honor of the thirteen united colonies, the elder Franklin "enumerated" an equal number of moral virtues and proffered them for the consideration of his fellow citizens, carefully crafting his appeal to include both secular and religious overtones. Some of his virtues may be familiar to modern readers:

The names of these virtues, with their precepts, were: (1)Temperance. Eat not to dullness: drink not to elevation. (2) Silence. Speak not but what may benefit others and yourself: avoid trifling conversations. (3) Order. Let all your things have their place: let each part of your business have its time. (4) Resolution. Resolve to perform what you ought: perform without fail what you resolve. (5) Frugality. Make no expense but to do good to others or yourself: i.e., waste nothing. (6) Industry. Lose no time; be always employed in something useful: cut off all unnecessary actions. (7) Sincerity. Use no hurtful deceit; think innocently and justly, and, if you speak, speak accordingly. (8) Justice. Wrong none by doing injuries, or omitting the benefits that are your duty. (9) Moderation. Avoid extremes: forbear resenting injuries as much as you think they deserve. (10) Cleanliness. Tolerate no uncleanliness in body, cloaths, or habitation. (11) Tranquility. Be not disturbed at trifles, or at accidents common and unavoidable. (12) Chastity. Rarely use venery but for health or offspring, never to dullness, weakness, or the injury of your own or another's peace or reputation. (13) Humility. Imitate Jesus and Socrates.[26]

In these precepts, Franklin expounded a secular humanism that reflected not only his own enlightened philosophy but also a long tradition of English and American moral thought. Almost all of them could be found in the writings of fathers to their children. As counselor to the nation,

Franklin sought to retain the chief virtues cherished by 17th-century Puritans but to drop the theological sanctions and biblical rhetoric that went with them. Although a self-proclaimed Deist, Franklin, more than any other man of his day, tried to formulate an ethical position that would be true to the spirit of both enlightened secularism and the Judeo-Christian religion.

Colonial men communicated to their children, their relations, and their neighbors a system of ethics, morality, and society that was simultaneously in keeping with the religious toleration and God-centered political theories proclaimed by John Locke in the 17th century, the almost atheistic utilitarianism espoused by Jeremy Bentham in the 18th century, and the moral precepts of traditional Protestantism. Combining reason and a secular conscience, they successfully blended the ideals of courage, duty, and liberty with the theological concepts of love, obligation, and godliness.

NOTES

1. Quoted in Lisa Wilson, *Ye Heart of a Man, The Domestic Life of Men in Colonial New England* (New Haven: Yale University Press, 1999), 27.

2. Louis B. Wright, *The Cultural Life of the American Colonies* (Mineola, NY: Dover Publications, 2002), 44.

3. Quoted in Wilson, *Ye Heart of a Man*, 31–32.

4. Quoted in ibid., 34.

5. Wright, *The Cultural Life of the American Colonies*, 34.

6. Ibid., 44

7. Ibid., 38.

8. Quoted in Wilson, *Ye Heart of a Man*, 33.

9. William Livingston to John Livingston (1780), quoted in William Bell Clark, *The First Saratoga, Being the Saga of John Young and His Sloop-of-War* (Baton Rouge: Louisiana University Press, 1953), 41.

10. Quoted in Wilson, *Ye Heart of a Man*, 33.

11. Samuel Seawell (1720), quoted in Wilson, *Ye Heart of a Man*, 25.

12. Quoted in Carl Bridenbaugh, ed., *Gentleman's Progress: The Itinerarium of Dr. Alexander Hamilton, 1744* (Chapel Hill: University of North Carolina Press, 1948), xix.

13. Wright, *The Cultural Life of the American Colonies*, 25.

14. Quoted in ibid., 25.

15. Quoted in ibid., 25.

16. Ibid., 28–29.

17. Quoted in Alvin E. Connor, *Sectarian Childrearing: The Dunkers, 1708–1900* (Gettysburg, PA: Brethren Heritage, 2000), 185.

18. Clark, *The First Saratoga*, 42.

19. Quoted in Alden T. Vaughn, (ed.), *America before the Revolution, 1725–1775* (Englewood Cliffs, NJ: Prentice-Hall, 1967), 26–27.

20. Richard N. Current and John A. Garraty, (eds.), *Words That Made American History: Colonial Times to the 1870s* (Boston: Little, Brown, 1965), 73.

21. John Locke, quoted in ibid., 74–75.

22. Jeremy Bentham, Chapter 1, *Introduction to the Principles of Morals and Legislation* (Oxford: n.p., 1823), http://www.utm.edu/research/iep/b/bentham.htm (accessed March 2005); and http://www.la.utexas.edu/research/poltheory/bentham/ipml/ipml.c01.html (accessed March 2005).

23. Having graduated from Oxford in 1764, Bentham spent the rest of his life writing, but he made little effort to publish what he wrote until the last decade of the 18th century. See Bentham, http://www.la.utexas.edu/research/poltheory/bentham/ipml/ipml.c01.html.

24. Quoted in Gerald N. Grob and Robert N. Beck (eds)., *American Ideas: Source Readings in the Intellectual History of the United States: Foundations, 1629–1865* (New York: Free Press, 1963), 130–31.

25. Ibid., 128.

26. Ibid., 125.

5

Educator

Schools of learning are approved and appointed by God, and of great
importance for the benefit of God's People ... [being] one way of raising
up Prophets.... [T]here is much more need of schools now, when those
extraordinary Prophets are wanting.

—Charles Chauncy, 1671[1]

The continued existence of discrete societal groups such as Puritans,
Quakers, or Moravians depended in large part on their ability to transfer their value systems with its attendant traditions and mores to their
children. While these values can be conserved, they rarely do so without
evolving somewhat over the span of almost two centuries. The cause of
these changes is often rooted in economic or political realities outside the
control of individual parents. The rate of change, however, is often dependent upon the methods that parents choose to use in transferring values
from one generation to the next. Many facets of family life were involved
in this process. Among these were the examples set by parents as they
lived and carried out their own daily duties, and the expectations—
academic, social, or religious—that they communicated to their children.
Also important was the influence of close relatives, particularly grandparents, who passed on to the new generation the culture of former times
thereby moderating somewhat the cultural innovations made by younger
less experienced parents.[2]

In colonial times as today, the two most important periods during the
rearing of children were the first five years and the teenage years. During

the child's early years, the authority of the parent was established and a system of internal controls was inculcated in the child. The most highly prized of these controls in the colonial period was obedience. It was the one thing that most parents insisted upon, yet even good parents could be inconsistent in exercising their authority within the family. "Since there was no institutional protocol to follow [as there would have been in a school], the discipline of children varied with the rank of birth, just as it does in the present time. The older child has a father who is younger, more immature, more ambitious, and usually in poorer economic circumstances. Therefore, this child is controlled, worked more, and expectations of him are greater. The father of the younger child has matured, mellowed, and is in better economic circumstances, so this child is given more advantages and is subject to fewer controls."[3]

Even under the best of circumstances the teen years were often marked by confrontation, a daily contest of wills easily recognized by any parent who had gone through it with a previous child. Constancy and predictability by the parent usually blunted these inevitable clashes between generations. The importance of grandparents as mitigating agents under these circumstances is obvious. They had passed through the process and could help to relieve unnecessary confrontations and distress. Ironically, as family size grew the intensity of a strict discipline with its punitive overtones seems to have diminished giving way to an expected conformity of behavior among all ages, the youngest taking their lead from their older sisters and brothers.

Once good behavior was established, a father turned to the more practical matter of educating his children to be diligent and self-supporting adults. Of course, men tended to focus on the educations of their sons, preparing them for careers in politics, a trade, a profession, or other aspect of the world of work. Mothers took a more active part in teaching their daughters a woman's role in the household. As concerned as colonial fathers were about vocational training, they did not simply substitute manual skills for an academic education. As one historian has pointed out, "It remained for the twentieth century to achieve that confusion."[4]

Religion was the foundation of all colonial education. Beginning with the imperative found in Psalms 1:7, "The Lord is the beginning of Knowledge," fathers emphasized that truly godly men "[made] religion their business, their choice, their delight, at all times."[5] While Puritans emphasized that human beings were born in a state of sin, they also recognized that they were rational and intelligent beings capable of improvement. "Without instruction and refinement," wrote Phillip Fithian, "men are advanced but a little above their fellow creatures the brutes; they are ignorant of themselves and of the wonderful works of Providence."[6] A comprehensive education might not make people less sinful, but it could help them come to a better understanding of God's works and purposes. As written in

Deuteronomy 6:5–7: "Thou shalt teach them diligently unto thy children, and shalt talk of them when thou sittest in thine house, and when thou walkest by the way, and when thou liest down, and when thou risest up."[7] Even families of minimal means required their minor children to learn to "read the Bible and write a legible hand" by the time they reached adolescence. Reading and writing not only reinforced the child's religious life, but they suggested a mastery of the fundamental skills needed to pursue further self-directed study. Nonetheless, many children, especially those in the most rural areas of the colonies, failed to meet these minimum expectations never going "beyond the ability to spell out their catechism and to scrawl their names."[8]

The emphasis placed on reading in an era when books were expensive, few in number, and difficult to acquire reflects to some degree a characteristic tenet of colonial Protestantism, which relied on the personal interpretation of the Scriptures and the obligation to consult pious books and treatises as guidepost to salvation. Fathers constantly worried lest their children, while engaged in secular pursuits, might forget their basic religious learnings or "grow up barbarous in the wilderness."[9] Fithian noted, "It is then no wonder if the vicious tempers of some men, always prone to mischief, debauch the best principles of education.... Men of letters have it in their power to refine and often reform mankind, to correct their principles, and check their vices.... [T]hey can better form their own path ... [and] their sentiments and precepts."[10]

From the very beginning, there was a popular sentiment among New Englanders in favor of the establishment of community schools on a variety of levels. Connecticut required every town of 80 families to support an elementary school, and those with 500 families to establish the equivalent of a high school. Massachusetts did likewise, requiring every town of 50 families to appoint a schoolmaster. The citizens of the Bay Colony also established the first college in British North America at Boston (Harvard) to insure a continuous crop of ministers. Enterprises like these were also based in biblical teaching, "The things that thou hast heard of me [Jesus] before many witnesses, the same commit to faithful men, who shall be able to teach others also."[11] *New England's First Fruits*, written in 1643 (probably by Henry Dunster) and published in London some years later, described Harvard College: "The Edifice is very fair and comely within and without, having in it a spacious Hall where they meet at common lectures and exercises, and a library with some books to it, the gift of our diverse friends.... [B]y the side of the College [is] a fair Grammar School, for the training up of young scholars, and fitting them for Academical Learning."[12]

Much of New England, therefore, had a generally widespread and comprehensive system of community schools by the beginning of the 18th century. New York, under Dutch rule, saw little in the way of public

With higher education being rare and expensive, a young man had to dedicate himself to independent study.

education (a single school in 1633), yet under English rule the Dutch were motivated to establish additional schools of their own, perhaps as an attempt to maintain their own culture in the face of an influx of English residents. On the whole, the members of the Dutch Reformed Church showed more interest in education than their Anglican neighbors. They established public schools for girls and boys in New Amsterdam, Brooklyn, Flatbush, Bushwyck, Wiltwyck, and Harlem in New York, and one in Bergen in New Jersey. The Dutch maintained their interest in education right up to the beginning of the revolution. By comparison, in 1741 New York City had only six English schools, and two decades later, at the end of the French and Indian Wars, it had only ten.

The greatest number of schools established during the colonial period appeared in cities like New York, where a growing population and increasing affluence made such endeavors practical. Philadelphia, with its diverse population of Quakers, Germans, and Scotch-Irish, established some of the best schools and most comprehensive curricula in British North America before the American Revolution. All public schools established in the colonies shared certain characteristics: They all emphasized religious matters, taught the Lord's Prayer and the Ten Commandments, and used the Bible as a major source of instructional material. Beyond this, reading, writing, sums, and manners seem to have dominated the curricula. Declamation and rhetorical skills thought to be the stuff of early education, in fact, did not come into the course of study until late in the period when they came to largely characterize 19th century educational practice.[13]

Planters and merchants in Virginia, Maryland, and the Carolinas generally sent their children to private schools or provided tutors in their homes. Hundreds of advertisements for tutors appeared in the southern press in the colonial period. These tutors were uniformly male and generally impoverished, but filled with "erudition and experience." They took their students through a wide range of studies, and some parents preferred their tutorials to semesters in private schools, colleges, or even universities.[14]

In the colonial South, wealthy parents sent their children to private schools in England to an extent undreamed of by their New England counterparts. The following advertisement appeared in the *Virginia Gazette* for November 1769: "At the Academy in Leeds, which is presently situated in the county of York, England, young gentlemen are genteelly boarded and diligently instructed in English, the classics, modern languages, penmanship, arithmetic, merchant accounts, mathematics, modern geography, experimental philosophy, and astronomy for twenty guineas per annum if under twelve years of age, by Mr. Aaron Grimshaw an able master. Drawing, music and dancing are extra charges."[15]

With many Southern parents sending their children to England for an education, less pressure was brought to bear on the local community to foster public education. One of the first private schools in the colonial South was established in Maryland by the Jesuit order, but with the ascendancy of the established Anglican Church in the colony in the middle of the 17th century, the Catholics found it hard to maintain anything other than a rudimentary grammar school system. Nonetheless, after his visit to America in the early 19th century, Alexis de Tocqueville reported that the Catholics had created an extensive system of institutions of higher learning in Maryland. Ironically, he also reported that these colleges were "full of Protestants."[16] The backcountry of the Carolinas had few schools, but ministers, missionaries, and itinerant schoolteachers traveled there. The Society for the Propagation of the Gospel in Foreign Parts, an Anglican agency, actively sent forth its missionaries to the frontiers during the 18th century to battle dissenters, papists, and the unorthodox. The Scotch-Irish brought with them a high respect for education, but they relied almost solely on their learned and widely traveled Presbyterian ministers to spread a classical form of academic education throughout the frontier communities.

Quaker families, suspicious of any government-run agency, generally eschewed public schooling, but they did manage to teach their children to read, write, and calculate in some manner. Although they were more interested in teaching their children practical skills, adult Quakers were generally well educated, and they personally gave their children the fundamentals of academic learning. The German immigrants, with the notable exception of the Moravians, were largely of peasant stock, however, and they showed only a passing interest in classical or academic pursuits, preferring only to train their children in what they considered practical and utilitarian.[17] Dunker children were reared within a system of closely held and purposeful dictates based on the Bible and the demands of rural life that rejected public education as infecting the community with secular influences. The elders among the semiliterate German Brethren were so skeptical of formal schooling that even Sunday schools were prohibited until the 19th century. Nonetheless, both the Quaker and German orders were by their nature and dedication to the precept of individuality quite flexible allowing members to accommodate their educational practices to their personal religious beliefs.[18]

If they could afford to do so, fathers took great pains to expand their children's experiences of the world beyond the boundaries of formal education so that they might "grow in grace and knowledge" and not seem provincial as adults. In his diary of 1723, Josiah Cotton expressed the hope that "my sons (provided they are not educated at the college) may, when they are about fourteen or sixteen years old, spend about a twelve month at Boston to study mathematics and anything that might be useful: and my daughters also spend some time there, not to render them prouder, but to better their behavior, and by going to school to acquaint themselves with such knowledge, as there are not advantages for in the country." For their daughters, fathers often sought "religious virtue and industry" rather than experience and polish, while for their sons they strove to provide instruction leading to "some lawful profession," "an industry blessed by God," or at least a "decent support in life."[19]

While an adequate fundamental education could be provided by tutors, ministers, or the parents themselves, providing a higher (college) education remained a problem. Colleges and universities have long been viewed as repositories of knowledge in America, established to train the best minds to deal with advanced philosophical concepts, if not with technical and professional training. The historical record is replete with calls to establish institutions of higher learning in the colonies. While some parents were so eager to provide a comprehensive formal education for their children that they sent them "almost as infants" to England for a decade or more to be better educated, for most parents this problem was best solved by community action rather than by long separation from their loved ones.[20]

Consequently, eleven major colleges were established in America during the colonial period, chiefly through the efforts of private parties or sectarian religious groups. Among those in the northern and middle colonies were Harvard (1636), Yale (1701), Princeton (the College of New Jersey, 1746), the University of Pennsylvania (1751), Columbia (King's College, 1754), Brown (1764), Rutgers (1766), and Dartmouth (1770). In the southern colonies, there were William and Mary (1693), Hampton-Sydney College (1776), and Transylvania College (1780).

One of the Puritan founders of Harvard College noted in 1643, "After God had carried us safe to New England ... one of the next things we longed for and looked after was to advance learning and perpetuate it to posterity." The immediate goal of the founders of Harvard was to produce a new generation of preachers, "dreading to leave an illiterate ministry to the churches when our present ministers shall lie in the dust." However, it was largely through the collective action of the laymen of the community rather than of its men of the cloth that a college was established to make learning—religious, classical, and traditional—more accessible.[21] Yale in Connecticut was a haven for those Congregationalists who were less dogmatic than their Puritan brethren in Massachusetts. Princeton was founded by Presbyterians and Columbia by the Dutch Reformed Church. Notwithstanding these sectarian origins, the curriculum at most early colleges generally followed the pattern first established at Harvard.[22]

Zeal for an educated ministry prompted the founding of many other colleges. Francis Nicholson, governor of Maryland, emphasized the relationship between learning and the maintenance of a cadre of ministers for the established Anglican Church. "[I]nstructing our youth in the orthodox religion, preserving them from the infection of [heretical] tenets and fitting them for the service of church and state in this uncultivated part of the world are our cheerful end and aim."[23] Largely through Nicholson's efforts, the College of William and Mary was established in Williamsburg in 1693 to advance learning, promote piety, and provide for "an able and successive ministry" in both Maryland and Virginia. Even though the two schools were founded a half century apart, the organization and curricula of William and Mary were initially very similar to those of Harvard except for the sectarian differences between Puritan and Anglican theology. Nonetheless "for a decade after its founding [William and Mary] remained little more than a grammar school" while Harvard flourished as a beacon of academia. Not until the 18th century did the teachers at the Virginia college begin to make independent educational breakthroughs.[24]

Once begun, however, the academic innovations instituted at William and Mary were extraordinary. It was the first school to cultivate an intelligent and meaningful study of American history as opposed to a solitary focus on English tradition. It also took the lead in engendering the study of natural science and the practice of law. A remarkable feature of William and Mary was the introduction of an elective system that allowed a choice of studies among those taught by a faculty newly organized into departments by content. Moreover, in 1760 the faculty at William and Mary was the first to introduce the modern lecture system, a major departure from the practice of hearing lessons recited by individual students from memory. By 1779, the school had abolished its grammar school and its department of divinity studies and established in their stead departments of modern languages and constitutional and court law and a school of medicine. Thomas Jefferson wrote, "William and Mary, in Williamsburg, since the remodeling of its plan, is the place where are collected together all the young men of Virginia under preparation for public life.... It is true that the habit of speaking the modern languages cannot be so well acquired in America; but every other article can be acquired at William and Mary as at any place in Europe."[25]

Ironically, many of the faculty at William and Mary in the latter part of the 18th century were themselves graduates of Princeton, then known as the College of New Jersey, a popular destination for many children of southern planters. Princeton's influence was not really felt until 1745, after which it was enormous. Under the leadership of Samuel Davies, later president of the school, a great number of the graduate alumni began to frequent the communities along the colonial frontiers, propagating the Presbyterian faith and providing academic instruction. In the half-settled border regions, they established some very good private schools and served as tutors to the children of the largely Scotch-Irish population. This spread of Scotch-Presbyterian sentiment helped to create a strong support for the American Revolution among the backwoodsmen of Virginia and the Carolinas.[26]

Graduates of the College of Philadelphia (afterwards the University of Pennsylvania) vied with those of Princeton in bringing education to the frontiers of Pennsylvania and Virginia. The College of Pennsylvania adopted a liberal arts curriculum that included training in logic and metaphysics, ethics, civil and natural law, civil history, government, and commerce. These courses were offered in response to an unprecedented demand for training in practical professions, especially surveying and the law, which gained popularity with both parents and students as the 18th century proceeded. "Very little" is known of the extent to which these novel courses of study were pursued, but documentary and anecdotal evidence suggests that these innovations were at least "partially carried out." The more conservative Pennsylvania authorities, among them the Quakers, soon fell into animated disagreement with one another over whether such programs of study were appropriate.[27]

Although generally applauded, colleges were not viewed with universal satisfaction. A leading Puritan intellectual noted a common objection: "There is no necessity of Schools and Universities, or any humane learning [the study of humanities] to teach Divinity, or to make able preachers of the Gospel."[28] Southern parents, in particular, did not stop the practice of sending their children to England simply because a few colleges were

available in the colonies. Hundreds of children from southern plantations continued to be educated abroad, but the absolute number cannot
be estimated from the available records. Robert Carter of Williamsburg,
Virginia, wrote in 1702 concerning the education of his two nephews in
London rather than at William and Mary, "No doubt the continuance of
careful education will render them accomplished men qualified to preserve the character of their father [his brother], and fit for the service of
their country, which, to my sorrow ... does at this time labor under a very
thick cloud of ignorance. Pray God in the next generation it may flourish
under a set of better polished patriots."[29]

Many parents suspected that college professors were "not sufficiently
wise or holy" and that the schools were not always temples of learning
but sometimes served as dens of iniquity and debauchery. Such ideas
were not limited to Southern parents. College students, then and now,
tend sometimes to drink too much, to be rowdy, and to behave outside the bounds of propriety or the law. Individual students were often
expelled from college, and whole classes were sometimes dismissed for
the remainder of the term because of riots, demonstrations, and abuses
visited on the faculty, the buildings, or the grounds. The all-male student
body—females did not attend—was often condemned for harassing the
local population of young women and for supporting a large cadre of local
prostitutes and women of loose morals. The Reverend Solomon Stoddard

Young men sent to the city for an education were often sidetracked by the denizens of the local tavern. Then, as now, many students came away from college
with evil ways.

of Northampton, Massachusetts, noted, "Places of learning should not be places of riot and pride. Ways of profuseness and prodigality in such a society lay a foundation of a great deal of sorrow. Fond and proud parents should not be [made to] suffer [the] introduction of evil customs. 'Tis not worth the while for persons to be sent to college to learn to compliment men and court women."[30]

NOTES

1. Gerald N. Grob and Robert N. Beck, eds., *American Ideas: Source Readings in the Intellectual History of the United States: Foundations, 1629–1865* (New York: Free Press, 1963), 76.

2. Alvin E. Conner, *Sectarian Childrearing: The Dunkers, 1708–1900* (Gettysburg, PA: Brethren Heritage, 2000), 93.

3. Ibid., 173.

4. Louis B. Wright, *The Cultural Life of the American Colonies* (Minneola, NY: Dover Publications, 2002), 105.

5. Solomon Williams (1776), quoted in Lisa Wilson, *Ye Heart of a Man: The Domestic Life of Men in Colonial New England* (New Haven: Yale University Press, 1999), 129.

6. Phillip Fithian to his father Joseph, 28 September 1769, http://www.indiana.edu/~jah/teaching/2003_09/sources/ex2_father.shtml (accessed March 2005).

7. Grob and Beck, *American Ideas*, 74.

8. Wright, *Cultural Life*, 100–101.

9. Ibid., 98.

10. Fithian to his father.

11. Timothy 2:2, quoted by Charles Chauncy in Grob and Beck, *American Ideas*, 76.

12. Quoted in Grob and Beck, 79.

13. Wright, *Cultural Life*, 106.

14. Lyon Gardiner Tyler, "Education in Colonial Virginia" part 4, "The Higher Education," *William and Mary College Quarterly* 6 (January 1898), 172.

15. Ibid., 175.

16. Alexis de Tocqueville, *Journey to America*, ed. J. P. Mayer, trans. George Lawrence (New Haven: Yale University Press, 1960), 78.

17. Wright, *Cultural Life*, 108–9.

18. Conner, *Sectarian Childrearing*, 161.

19. Wilson, *Ye Heart of a Man*, 128.

20. Wright, *Cultural Life*, 118.

21. Quoted in ibid., 116.

22. Ibid., 118.

23. Quoted in ibid., 110.

24. Ibid., 118–19.

25. The Reverend Hugh Jones, professor of natural philosophy and mathematics at William and Mary, wrote the first recognized history of America by a college professor titled *Present State of Virginia*, in 1722. The Reverend William Smith

wrote the second such work on the same topic, titled *History of Virginia*, in 1747. See Tyler, "Education in Colonial Virginia," 179.

26. Tyler, 186–87.
27. Ibid., 180.
28. Grob and Beck, *American Ideas*, 75–76.
29. Quoted in Wright, *Cultural Life*, 112.
30. Quoted in ibid., 119.

6

Provider

Neither custom nor love doth yet teach me to maintain my wife worse then I found her except God be pleased by his Providence to call us to a lower condition then yet. He is pleased to do.[1]

—A 17th-century husband

As many as 70 percent of immigrants to New England came as members of established families with some accumulated financial resources, and their earliest settlements resembled English towns or villages in their social order, cultural prerogatives, and economic expectations. Even their legal and judicial establishments quickly came to resemble those found in London. Moreover, by the last decade of the 17th century, even the wealth-seeking adventurers who invaded the colonial Chesapeake had established family units and formed well-ordered societies, recreating many of the cultural, institutional, and economic structures they had left behind in England. The accumulated wealth brought to America during the migrations of the mid-17th century fueled trade, agricultural prices, land speculation, and manufactures. Yet no amount of wealth brought to the wilderness of colonial America could sustain a family or the larger society as a whole for very long unless it was replenished or maintained by economic activity.

In the colonial period, therefore, everyone worked to make a living, but not everyone worked in the same way. The first and second generations of New Englanders sustained themselves through mixed farming on a limited scale and some trading with the Indians along the Maine coast, but they never discovered, as did those in the Chesapeake, such major sources of wealth as export tobacco, rice, and indigo. Although a small tobacco industry appeared in the Connecticut River Valley, tobacco cultivation was initially forbidden in much of New England. There was little else in New England to attract the more adventurous sort that had invaded Virginia, and even less to create a vast demand for indentured laborers or slaves. Consequently, the standard of living in New England was somewhat parsimonious when compared to that in the Chesapeake. Yet, the concentration of wealth everywhere in the colonies was slow, and the economic ambitions of most men in the first generations remained modest.

The inheritance of traditional social ideals and conservative business practices greatly influenced subsequent generations of American-born Anglo-colonials. When a man married, his wife brought a marriage portion or a dower to the union, but he was expected to provide for her and their children for the rest of his life. Moreover, the form of a man's economic endeavor had to be appropriate to his station in life and adequate enough to provide some "ease and affluence" in his old age or for his widow. Although material wealth motivated many men to work hard, the pursuit of money for its own sake was viewed with some suspicion. Men looked for work that would provide their families with a "comfortable subsistence" and a "maintenance" of social standing. Beyond this minimum level was an income that was often termed "a certain competency of means" that allowed for comfort and security if not wealth.[2]

While he might find both profit and pleasure in his chosen occupation, a father was expected to strive to earn a living for himself and his family even if his employment was onerous or otherwise not to his liking. Those who failed to meet the minimum standards of the community in terms of supporting a family met with little regard, and those who relied only on an allowance or inheritance from their forbearers or in a sudden windfall were viewed with suspicion. A man was expected to provide for his wife and children "as any other man thereabouts" and maintain them "as well as most." He was expected to keep his wife in at least the same circumstances that she had known in her father's house—"be they high or low." One husband noted, "[N]either custom nor love doth yet teach me to maintain her [my wife] worse then I found her except God be pleased by his Providence to call us to a lower condition then yet He is pleased to do."[3]

The necessary support of a family increased as the number of a man's children inevitably grew and his circumstances changed over time. Nonetheless, a colonial father was expected to maintain the level of support for his wife during her lifetime and to provide for even the youngest of his minor children as long as they lived under his roof in most communities.

When his children were set free, or formed a household of their own, they were no longer obliged to render service to their parents, either in labor or in money. The parents were no longer responsible for the child's room and board, and if adult children elected to stay in their parents' home, they usually paid for their place. The measures taken with respect to adult daughters are not well documented, but they probably earned their place by sewing, doing laundry, or performing other household duties for their mothers.[4]

The burden of providing for a family was more than a personal duty, and the community, particularly the extended family, often monitored and judged a man's efforts in this regard, to the point of taking legal action against him if he failed. Every man, therefore, needed to choose a form of work or a settled career to be considered a proper part of the social fabric of the community.

The ministry, law, or teaching might provide a profession for those with an opportunity at an advanced education, and there is much known about the condition of these colonial men of letters. However, many of those following the professions in the colonies attest to a constant struggle to extract their pay from frugal congregations, reluctant clients, or penurious students. Ebenezeer Parkman, a minister in Westborough, Massachusetts in 1740, wrote that his flock could only provide him with a living that would "barely do" much less leave his family with a life-style having "some Handsomeness and Decency." Philemon Robbins, a minister in Branford, Connecticut in 1754, understood that men of God might expect to live in a Spartan manner. "Those that preach the Gospel should live of the Gospel," he wrote. However, he also noted that his salary of £140 a year would "not maintain my present family," and he asked the congregation for the incredible sum of £800 annually, which was denied him.[5]

Teaching could bring a salary ranging from approximately £75 to £150 annually depending on the level of instruction demanded. The particular curriculum was fashioned through a compromise between the parents' wishes and the teacher's ability. The total income realized by a teacher might be enhanced by a fee charge against each student. According to one source in the historical record a "grammar master was paid £ 150, and received fifteen shillings from each scholar" in 1770. Another teacher had "£ 80 sterling, and twenty shillings sterling a year from each scholar, except the scholarship students who were taught gratis."[6] Nonetheless, Joseph Cotton, living in Sandwich, Massachusetts, at the end of the 17th century, initially intended to give up teaching in town to return to his farm where he "could raise much of [his] own provisions." In town he "had a consider-able income," yet inflation, "a necessity of buying so much," and the other needs of his family "[ate] up all our gains." Dwight Foster, a teacher and aspiring lawyer from Northampton, Massachusetts, wrote in 1777 to his sister, "These are hard times—I find I cannot support myself by my school and indeed have not done it for some months." Nonetheless, Philip Fithian, a young divinity student from Princeton, New Jersey was pleased to accept the offer of a position as tutor made by Robert Carter of Virginia in 1773. "To teach his children, five daughters and three sons, who are from five to seventeen years old. The young ladies to be taught the English language. And the boys ... to be instructed in Latin and Greek. And he proposes to give thirty-five pounds sterling, which is about sixty pounds currency, provide all accommodations, allow [me] the undisturbed use of a room and of his own library, find provender for a horse, and a servant to wait [on me].... I accepted the offer and agreed to go in the fall into Virginia."[7]

Future president of the United States John Adams, then a lawyer in Braintree, Massachusetts, wrote in the 1770s that as a youth he had been forced "to consider of ways and means of raising a subsistence, food and raiment [clothing], and books and money to pay for my education to the bar.... I must have sunk into total contempt and obscurity, if not perished for want, if I had not planned for futurity."[8] Finally William Smith, himself a lawyer, advised prospective attorneys, "The practice [of law] in this province will keep you from poverty, that great evil ... but some lawyers have not their religion."[9]

Young men preparing for life in one of the professions expected to maintain a standard of living and social status commensurate with their services to the community. Churchmen, lawyers, and teachers from colonial times to the present have resented the parsimony of the communities in which they lived and worked, expecting a salary that reflected their educational qualifications and their place in the scheme of the social hierarchy. Those born to wealth, on the other hand, might work at managing the family business or running the plantation without regard to the willingness of their neighbors to provide them an income. Such persons directed the labor of others and formed the highest rungs of the social ladder, but almost everyone else in colonial society needed to earn a living through the application of their own physical labor.

The acquisition of manufactured goods, store-bought items, and finely tailored clothing signaled to colonials much about the purchaser and his family including their class, the degree of their success, and even their moral character. While it surely serves no constructive purpose to try to pin down with great precision the definition of luxury in the 17th or 18th century, the challenge for the modern historian is to work through the meaning of the colonial vocabulary in order to separate extravagance from necessity. Colonials, unlike us, saw no moral dilemma in keeping servants and laborers in their place by denying them the right to wear certain types of clothing or to own certain possessions. Nonetheless, the ability of all colonials to choose freely in the consumer marketplace gradually merged in the public mind with the right to certain basic human freedoms.[10]

THE NATURE OF WORK

There is presently no single, all-encompassing word to cover the world of work experienced by men in the colonial period. The concept of a distinct "working class" was an intellectual construct of the 19th century that generally isolated factory workers from farm workers, tradesmen, craftsmen, and artists. A contemporary observer noted of American colonials that "the same individual tills his fields, builds his dwelling, contrives his tools, makes his shoes, and weaves the coarse stuff of which his dress is composed."[11] Certainly this writer's views were reflected in the work of the historians of a more romantic era many decades after the end of the colonial period. They generally endowed Americans with greater abilities and more comprehensive skills than most actually possessed. Modern research suggests that rather than every man being a "jack of all trades" there seems to have been a good deal of differentiation and craft specialization among colonial working occupations.

The world of work in British North America was considerably different from that found in a large European city like London. For one thing, the colonial workmen commanded real wages that generally exceeded the wages of their contemporaries in Britain. Most colonists were more involved in farming and seamanship than in the manufacturing trades or handicrafts, creating a demand for persons in the latter occupations. Nonetheless, as the agricultural production of a colony became large enough to support an export trade, a whole new network of nonfarming occupations began to appear in the colonial economy. The expanding export trade, centered in the various colonial seaports, "necessitated the presence there of a population of sailors, shipwrights, ship chandlers, and the like, as well as specialist brokers, insurance underwriters, and often a manufacturing population to process goods in transit."[12]

Moreover, there was in colonial America a vast unconsolidated workforce of seasonal laborers (mostly farmers and seamen) dealing in furs and woodland products including lumber, shingles, barrel staves, tanning bark, charcoal, and wood ash. In slack times many farmers took up the axe or the pick and shovel, and many fishermen set their course along the coastline to participate in a little intercolonial trade by shipping tanning bark to the southern leather making industry or taking bushels of potash to seaports where it was used to make soap and glass. There were also a number of persons involved part-time in the extraction trades. The South had the potential to produce a wide range of raw materials. These included wool, hides, leather, feathers, beeswax, lime, guano, salt, coal, copper, gold, and iron ore. Other colonies provided horn, bone ivory, and shell. Forest products such as lumber, paper, firewood, and charcoal made up the bulk of the raw materials produced in the South.

Virginia and Maryland had more facilities for the production of naval stores than any combination of two Northern colonies that normally prided themselves on their production. Hemp, the basic ingredient in cables and cordage for use on sailing ships, could be grown as a cash crop. Georgia and the Carolinas supplied excellent naval materials for building ships. Cedar, pine, and live oak grew in abundance. Turpentine, tar, and pine pitch could be extracted in large quantities. However, the lack of good harbors and trained shipwrights hampered the development of the shipbuilding industry in much of the South.

The colonies were an important component of the British Empire. It is not certain that transoceanic trade with Britain is the most appropriate place to start an analysis of domestic family income. However, 19 of the 20 largest cities in British North America at the end of the colonial period were seaports, and most urban dwellers were intimately familiar with overseas trade, trade regulations, and the merchandise made available by ships and shipping.

The British trading empire was founded on the principle of mercantilism. Formulated in the 17th century, mercantilism theorized that colonies existed chiefly to benefit the parent state. This benefit was realized in two ways. First, real wealth was to be measured by the store of precious metals a nation held, and the state that accumulated the greatest store of silver and gold was thought to be the richest. Second, any nation that could maintain a favorable trade balance with its neighbors and colonies could always settle the difference by demanding payments in gold. Freedom from foreign trade deficits, therefore, was considered a measure of commercial strength and economic health. In this regard, the British were monumentally successful.

The vitality of the British economy and the Empire itself had initially been founded on the monopolies granted in the 17th century to chartered trading companies, which brought wealth into the empire through their operations. The Honourable East India Company was unquestionably the most successful of these being valued at £21 million in 1775. However, as the Industrial Revolution dawned in Britain, a highly self-contained and independent manufacturing economy evolved, and this came to better characterize the quintessential mercantile state of the 18th century. Both the raw materials and the markets for all of the finished products of a robust manufacturing economy had to remain inside the empire for the state to be successful, however. Accordingly, Britain sought to remain the center of manufacturing, banking, and military resources, while the colonials were confined by law to the dual role of providers of raw materials and consumers of manufactured goods.[13]

In 17th-century Britain, government regulation, insofar as it was enforced, recognized the rights of an incredible number of trade monopolies and working men's guilds that made the economy generally inflexible, and any upward movement through the job market was all but impossible. There was no sense at the time that this system was wrong. A minister to Parliament proudly proclaimed that more than 700 monopolies had been granted during the first four decades of the 17th century. Foreign trade was less spurred by individual initiative than by powerful companies composed of groups of merchants who received special privileges from their ruler. Thus, small groups of men personally controlled whole industries, or, if they were willing to risk their wealth, they could subscribe to the stock of a chartered trading company. Here, they were given an attentive royal ear when they begged the privilege of exploiting the potentially profitable new fields of commerce in the name of their monarch.

The value of products from the East Indies and the Indian subcontinent was well known, and the profits from trade in these items were high. However, the profits from American trade could be precarious. Initially, the New World traders relied almost entirely on unprecedented agreements with generally unsophisticated native populations who might or might not honor their compacts. Moreover, many of the unfamiliar trade goods available from these novel trading partners, such as tobacco, potatoes, or corn, initially had no established European market. When the English Crown chartered the London Company of Virginia to trade in America, it initially charged the employees to look for more readily accepted items like gold, silver, and furs. In many of these quests, the colonists were disappointed, but the European rulers who granted such charters were nonetheless able to establish colonies and secure property rights in undeveloped and unexplored places without risking their personal or royal wealth.

To better maintain its overall economic strategy, the British trading empire was ruled by a whole series of maritime regulations called Navigation Acts. First passed during the Commonwealth and renewed in 1660 during the reign of Charles II, such regulations initially allowed a good deal of trade to take place between the individual colonies and foreign markets under the watchful eyes of their colonial governors and later by the Board of Trade (established in 1696). Admitting that any system, poised to control economic affairs, would inevitably be highly complicated, the colonies were actually affected by only a handful of regulations. In the 17th century the basic navigation acts were designed to protect British shipping from competition. This protection was extended to ships built or owned by colonial merchants. Additional policies were adopted to funnel enumerated colonial products through British ports; to encourage specific industries by the use of bounties; to promote the production of certain raw materials; and, finally, to directly prohibit new industrial endeavors that would compete with those already established or promoted by other legislation.[14]

While the granting of monopolies to charter companies and individual industries was often viewed as a means to support the colonial economy, most workers found themselves entangled in perplexing and sometimes contradictory legal situations involving apprenticeships, trade organizations, shipping regulations, and monopoly prerogatives. In 1563, during the reign of Elizabeth I, a statute governing the employment of artificers and apprentices had been instituted, stating, "It shall not be lawful to any person ... to exercise any craft now used within the realm ... except he shall have been brought up therein seven years at the least as apprentice." This legislation remained in force throughout the British Empire until 1814.[15] Among those industries controlled by such regulations were the manufacture of iron, steel, copper, tin, bricks, soap, glass, dye stuffs, cloth, salt, and beer. Apart from the monopolies granted to beer, cloth, and salt producers, most products affected by these grants were considered luxuries rather than the necessities of life.

In the rural and underdeveloped atmosphere of the colonies, these monopolies and regulations had little effect on day-to-day business and commerce, but they could and did affect the ability of many men to follow a particular trade or occupation, especially as the colonial economy matured. "No freeman," pointed out a period pamphlet, "after he hath served his years [of apprenticeship] and set up his trade, can be sure long to enjoy the labor of his trade, but he is either forbidden longer to use it, or is forced at length with the rest of his trade to purchase it as a monopoly." Only the relatively remote nature of British North America kept colonial workmen from having to contend with the most objectionable regulations and changes in policy drawn up in London. Nonetheless, as the character of work in colonial America changed from agriculture to manufacturing and shipping, enforcement of the laws and regulations became more common and more rigorous. The Iron Act of 1710, for instance, fostered the erection of furnaces for the production of pig iron because it was an essential raw material used in English manufacturing, but it forbade the making of iron plate or the rolling and slitting of iron bar stock, as well as the production of any steel, in order to protect the homeland industry from colonial competition. Although master iron founders were always in demand in the colonies, the act almost certainly prevented colonial workers from developing any of the advanced skills associated with the industry. By 1763, it had become obvious that the Crown planned to restrain all future development of the colonial industrial economy, and colonial sensitivities were so assaulted by the impositions placed on domestic manufacturing and trade that they came to the point of revolution.[16]

TOWN FAMILIES

Craftsmen and Workers   Colonial society, like that of England, was generally stratified into levels, or *sorts*, and the world of work was similarly stratified along hierarchical lines. The great and the rich occupied the upper levels. Tradesmen, handicraft workers, and freehold farmers were of the middling sort; and the rest of society was composed of the laboring poor, who barely made ends meet, and the miserable poor, who were constantly in want. The different types of work were likewise sorted out. The great dealt in politics and government at the highest levels. The rich, many of whom inherited their wealth, owned the plantations, the estates, and the stock in the trading companies, and it was said that many of these men could buy a peer of the realm three times over. The upper classes, be they powerful, wealthy, or both, had people working for them and no need to indulge in physical labor. They often dabbled in the professions or in politics as magistrates and justices. This class also hired factors, agents, and managers to represent them in the colonies.

The tradesmen, artisans, and craftsmen occupied the middle levels that have come to represent American colonial society at many historic museums and village recreations. These could be identified by their work product—silversmiths made items of silver, cartwrights and wainwrights built carts and wagons, and joiners of all kinds put boards together to fashion floors, houses, or ships. Yet many of the middling class in the American colonies, probably the majority, were farmers. Quite the opposite to the thinking of some today, farming in colonial America was a generally profitable enterprise insuring a roof over a man's head, sufficient food for his family, and a modicum of personal independence. However, it would be difficult to discriminate between hired agricultural workers of the lower class and farm owners (sometimes called freeholders) of the middle class by watching them work as they generally did the same type of labor. Freeholders found that they could maintain their middle-class status even while producing their own food and clothing, but the tenant farmer or indentured husbandman lived at the whim of his landlord regardless of how hard he labored. Freeholders and middle-class master craftsmen were also often involved in building and construction of all kinds, and even the owner of a small cargo vessel might claim middle-class status as a shipper.

The common workers of the lower classes did a great deal of labor for a very small amount of money. Although generally unskilled, common laborers were, nonetheless, an important part of the labor force. Among other things they rolled wheelbarrows, carried timbers, dug ditches, and pitched manure and hay. Anywhere that a strong back or arm was needed, a common laborer could be found. The manufacture of products associated with the sea employed large numbers of common laborers, haulers, sailors, and fishermen who were generally considered members of the lower classes. Those who worked along the rivers or in the seaports doing the heavy moving and hauling associated with shipping and shipbuilding might be designated as porters, stevedores, draymen, or lightermen.

Common laborers should not to be confused, however, with the miserable poor (the unemployed), who were doomed to scrape out a living at the base of the economic pyramid. The permanent plight of these wretched people often led to vagrancy, indolence, crime, and prostitution, especially in the seaport cities. Author Herman Melville summed up the hazards posed by these denizens of the waterfront. He wrote of "the variety of land sharks, land rats, and other vermin which make the helpless mariner their prey. In the shape of landlords, clothiers, barkeepers, crimps and boarding house loungers, the land-sharks devour him limb by limb; while the land-rats and mice constantly nibble at his purse." [17]

There was an entire group of untrained and unskilled men outside the realm of agriculture who were considered simple laborers. Many of these had no specific expertise, but they regularly applied the sweat of their brow and the strength of their arms or backs to all kinds of tasks and building projects. Drovers and husbandmen controlled, fed, or drove livestock. Work could also be found collecting hay, straw, and firewood, and carting, hauling, or freighting of all kinds of materials, including timber, lumber, bricks, stone, firewood, limestone, charcoal, tanning bark, potash, provisions, farm produce, animal skins, bone, fish, seashells, seaweed, and manure.

There were also those skilled persons associated with manufacturing who might be categorized as mechanics or those with some specific knowledge who worked with their hands. This category of work, which produced goods that were commonly used by most persons, had several distinct subdivisions. Artificers were laborers who applied a minimum of skill under the supervision of a more knowledgeable overseer. They sometimes assembled finished products from pieces formed by more skilled workers. The term *artificer* was used extensively in the shoreline communities of colonial America for persons who fixed fishing nets, made rope, repaired sails, sawed planks, or caulked the seams of ships. Plankers and caulkers were some of the highest paid artificers in the shipyard, and shipbuilders sometimes hired a entire planker's gang rather than individuals. The term artificer might also apply to the persons who did the heavy work at iron foundries, brickyards, mills, tanneries, and charcoal, potash or salt works under the supervision of a master of the trade or his subordinates.[18]

The term *artisan* conveyed a greater notion among workers of artistic talent and independence from an employer. It was used to describe those skilled craftsmen and handcrafters who, usually through serving an apprenticeship of some kind, had the right to view their skill as a kind of "intellectual property" to be used by themselves to make a profit. Artisans could work in their own shop or "put out" their skill to an employer. They were often formed up into guilds or trade organizations that policed their members as to their level of skill or their "right" to practice their trade. An additional distinction among these craftsmen—although not a universally applied one—was the use of the terms *"wright"* and *"smith."* Wrights, as in wheelwrights, cartwrights, housewrights, or shipwrights, usually worked in wood, while smiths were hammermen who formed and worked metal, as in silversmiths, blacksmiths, or gunsmiths.

Finally there were the *tradesmen* who were generally persons who dealt directly with the public and actively engaged in commerce. Storekeepers, merchants, printers, clothiers, shoemakers, hatters, wigmakers, and all those who maintained a shop were considered tradesmen. They were required by the demands of the colonial economy to build a following among the townspeople who sought out the products of their trade. In all but the largest colonial cities, such men had little competition. There might be a single shoemaker or a single blacksmith in a small town, and there might not be any tailors or coopers at all, forcing residents to travel to larger population centers or do business with itinerant craftspersons.

The ambiguity among the terms used to describe workers in this period was no less confusing to colonial contemporaries who used them in their writings, letters, and journals than they are for us today. In hundreds of American schools children are taught the term *Journeyman* to describe a skilled man working for wages—an intermediary step between *Apprentice* and *Master*. Yet such a differentiation in terms or a stratification of station in the workforce seems overly simplified when even during the colonial period the terms *"master"* and *"laborer"* were filled with ambiguity. "[*Master*] could simply mean the mastering of a trade through apprenticeship and the legal right thereby to exercise it, or it could apply only to those who were, even if only on a very small scale, employers of labor."[19]

The author Daniel DeFoe wrote in 1728 with respect to this complexity of terms:

Those concerned in the meaner and first employments are called ... working men or labourers [sic], and the labouring poor such as the mere husbandman, miners, diggers, fisher[men] and in short, all the drudges and labourers in the several productions of nature or of art. Next to them, are those who, though labouring perhaps equally with the other, have yet some art mingled with their industry, and are to be particularly instructed and taught how to perform their part, and those are called workmen or handicrafts. Superior to these are the [guilds] or masters, in such works or employments, and those are called artists, mechanics, or craftsmen; and in general, all are understood in this one word *mechanics*; such are clothiers, weavers, etc. handicrafts in hardware, brass, iron, steel, copper, etc.[20]

Traveling from Maine to Maryland in 1744, Dr. Alexander Hamilton recorded the following odd anecdote related by a "comical fellow" that he met: "He gave us the story of one De Witt, a doctor at Philadelphia, who he said had begun in the world in the honorable station of porter and used to drive a turnip cart or wheel barrow through the streets." This story suggests that there was more upward mobility for the working classes than is usually thought. In fact, the doctor described was an actual person, Christopher De Witt, who, although from modest origins and poor family, trained himself as a naturalist and ultimately became a skilled and respected physician. He lived in Germantown, Pennsylvania, where he kept one of the first botanical gardens in the English colonies and dabbled in astronomy and astrology.[21]

FARM FAMILIES

The Pattern of Farm Life
Almost all white colonials involved in agriculture worked their own land and planned their lives around rural activities and seasonal chores. Regardless of their status as slave, indentured, or free, all those who made a living in the colonies by farming did the same things: clearing, plowing, hoeing, reaping, threshing, and caring for their livestock. They produced what they consumed and consumed almost all that they produced—leaving little for a cash profit. They raised a variety of edible crops, including several types of grain and vegetables, but much of their land was in pasturage or in the production of hay used to winter their animals. Their livestock commonly included chickens, hogs, oxen, sheep, goats, milk cows, and a horse or two. If the climate and soil allowed, they might put in a few acres of low-grade tobacco as a cash crop.

On small farms in the northeastern and middle colonies, family members usually cooperated in completing the chores, and parents worked beside their children and grandchildren in an idyllic, if not mechanically efficient, simplicity. We do not know to what degree these family members possessed the skills needed to make their farming endeavors commercially successful, but the desire to provide for their children caused most men to value the self-sufficiency of their families in the present and the development of their farmlands in the long run over high profits in the short run. Historians seem to have spent too little time investigating the business end of colonial farming. "Conventional wisdom suggests that high transportation costs severely limited farmers' access to markets [and] forced them into a subsistence mode of production."[22]

Deeper investigation suggests that the modes of transportation available to colonial farmers and their willingness to haul their products to market may have been underestimated. The urban population needed to be fed, and raw materials and fuel were needed in the towns to support the trades and crafts. A visitor to Boston in 1709 noted that the city was "plentifully supplied with good and wholesome provisions of all sorts" by the "country people" who if they had all come to the city at the same time "would glut it."[23] Moreover, when the demand was high, merchants from the towns often sent their own buyers into the farm districts, and the "country stores" that began to appear in rural areas often acted as important collection centers for produce. Important relationships may have formed between farmers and traders that are "too often ignored altogether or taken for granted" by historians. The surplus that farmers produced beyond their subsistence needs may have played a large part

A typical colonial farm of the 18th century had a small house, fenced pastures, orchards, and fields. The split-rail fence was an 18th-century improvement over communal pastures known as commons.

in local manufacturing and commercial enterprise. With the exception of those on the frontier, Anglo-American farmers enjoyed general agricultural success, substantial markets, and a considerable profit from their labors throughout the century between 1675 and 1775.[24]

Nonetheless, shortages of food did exist on frontier farms. In one reported instance, in order to make a limited supply of food last throughout the winter months, the father of the family decreed that there should be only two meals a day. The mother fed the children more often giving them each an extra ration of cereal daily. The account noted that the woman was fearful lest the father note the quickly diminishing stock of food; however the disappearance of grain seemingly escaped his attention. The story is probably apocryphal, but it does serve to demonstrate the subtle relationships among family members, especially those between husband and wife.[25] "The child has been the lowest rung on the economic ladder, and, therefore, has been shamefully treated in times of famine or low food production. Maternal influence, where present, has offered [the only] protection to the child."[26]

Colonials farmers in Pennsylvania, New York, or New Jersey rarely lacked the basic necessities of life. Pastures and fields were initially enclosed, with the rooted ends of tree stumps or split-rail fences to control the livestock, but the hogs and chickens were generally allowed to run free in the brush, to be harvested as the need arose. Hogs proved particularly capable of fending for themselves against wolves and other predators, and other livestock could subsist through the winter on a diet of corn, hay, and turnips. The average farmer devoted most of his fields to hay, which could be planted among the stumps because it was gathered with the use of a hand sickle. Making hay was a difficult and time-consuming task. The hayfield was cut, dried in the sun, turned to dry the reverse side, and then gathered for storage. Hay could be stored in a barn or loft for winter feeding, or it could be gathered up into a stack or mound. The shape and structure of these haystacks differed from one community to another and seems to have been dictated by the country of origin of the local settlers. Hay could usually be made from the same field twice a year. It required one cleared acre to produce the hay needed to winter a cow or an ox, and a little more, plus some grain, to winter a horse. Cows provided dairy products and horses transportation in return for their subsistence, but the hard labor required to put up hay insured the slaughter of any male calves in their first year unless they were to be neutered and trained as oxen.

The Indians had no need for hay fields because they kept no livestock except dogs, but their abandoned fields quickly became overgrown with grasses and brush. Early settlers often loosed their livestock to graze in these fields, but the native grasses provided less nutrition than European varieties. However, the animals imported from Europe often brought with them as part of their manure common European grass seeds from their shipboard fodder. These grasses, spreading naturally in the older settlements, were obviously superior to native grasses. This led colonial farmers to import English grass seeds such as bluegrass or white clover, and to actively seek their propagation.

The farm and its economic system demanded hard work, punctuality, frugality, and a composed character in the face of trouble. These important life concepts were often learned or reinforced on the farm, and children were provided with an excellent environment for the childrearing methods of that day to take effect. To that extent many colonial Americans considered farm work superior to other occupations. The agricultural duties assigned to family members were rarely perfectly matched to their talents, but parents quickly discovered that children did more work if they did not find the task distasteful.

[A child] was required to gather eggs when he was big enough and, when older, he graduated to feeding the cows and the pigs. He could milk a cow at age seven and occasionally drove a team of horses at that age. Several years older, a boy rode the horse to guide it along a row of corn which allowed the father the free use of both hands to handle the ... plow.[27]

With a limited number of hands, family members often had to perform tasks they disliked. Of course farm families worked closely together, and this mitigated much of the aversion to many of the most onerous tasks. Working besides their parents and grandparents, uncles, aunts, and cousins, children were open to their immediate instruction and profited from their example. Such experiences were significant, profound, and frequent, and the expectations of the parents were positive and attainable. These features of rural living helped the child to make the transition from play and adolescent chores to responsibility and the world of adult work.[28]

THE PLANTATION FAMILY

Southern agriculture in the tidewater region revolved around the largely autonomous plantation, which came to depend on race-based slavery to provide the manpower to clear and place into production hundreds of acres in a single decade. Sugar was the single most profitable export crop, but **The Grand Southern Lifestyle** its cultivation was almost exclusively restricted to the Caribbean Islands until late in the 18th century. Nonetheless, the profits to be realized from the mass production of tobacco, rice, and indigo on the mainland were enormous. Tobacco and rice were the most important export crops in 17th-century America. The production of lumber and indigo helped to supplement plantation income. Very little of the valuable long-staple cotton was grown in this early period except in the Sea Islands region of South Carolina, and the more common short-staple variety was used domestically to make underclothing and fine garments. Linen from the flax plant and wool were used to make most domestically produced cloth. The most abundant crop grown in the South was corn (maize), which was used almost exclusively as food for humans and feed for livestock

Plantation agriculture could produce enormous wealth. Sugar added about £3 million to the wealth of Britain annually, rice about £1 million, and tobacco about as much again. By comparison, the total value of all other exported commodities in the same period was under £1 million. These included a diversity of grain products (probably wheat, rye, and corn), wood products (barrel staves, hoops. and shingles), preserved beef and pork, and naval stores (masts, planks, beams, hemp, rope, tar, and turpentine).

The owners of large plantations maintained an aristocracy of their own devising by applying their wealth and social status to the wheels of colonial government. Yet most plantation owners were cash poor and constantly in debt. They could, however, support themselves through the annual agricultural cycle with the products of their own plantations. When their crops were sold, they experienced a glut of money with which to pay their debts or buy luxury goods brought in by New England shippers, who also carried the exported produce to foreign markets. Thus, the agricultural cycle drove much of the business cycle in the colonies.[29]

The working population of North Carolina in the early colonial period was almost entirely composed of white workers, many of them indentures. In the early years, livestock grazing and mixed subsistence farming were the major agricultural activities, and neither required the large number of enslaved field hands characteristic of the later plantation economy. From the founding of South Carolina, however, experienced planters and seasoned slaves from the Caribbean islands were the main components of the workforce. Around 1700, rice was introduced and was successfully grown on the mainland. In less than a decade, a number of large estates were established, and shiploads of black slaves were introduced to the region in response to the demand for labor. By 1708, blacks had become the majority of the population.

Many characteristics of plantation slave labor have been attributed to the growth of an export economy that focused southern agricultural enterprise on cash crops, such as tobacco, rice, and indigo. However, these same export items had been grown successfully elsewhere on a smaller scale without slave labor for many decades. It may not be appropriate to simply assign the absence of white labor, the lack of town development, the poor skill levels found among the local population or the unequal distribution of wealth in the Southern colonies to a widespread reliance on slavery. Many of these critical characteristics are based on the criteria of 19th-century economic analysts with regard to the American Civil War, not those of the colonial period. The demands of a wartime economy from 1860 to 1865 may have blurred a true measure of the extent of the South's industrial system in the colonial period, while immediate postwar analyses by Northern observers may have been prejudiced against any positive findings. Such conclusions are shallow and generally ignore the fact that many slaves worked successfully as skilled craftsmen at ancillary trades associated with an export economy. Boat building, coopering, carpentry, tanning, spinning, weaving, sewing, animal husbandry, many forms of transportation, and the production of almost all the subsistence needs for the entire population of a great plantation were practiced by the slaves on most plantations, just as they were by the communities of free laborers elsewhere.

Reliable statistics concerning southern industry and manufacturing are rare and difficult to assess from the distance of centuries. The generally accepted view of the industrial capacity of the South may need revision, and the generalizations made by economic historians of the past may require revision. Much of the industrial capability of the southern states "perished in the holocaust of the war," along with any documentation that would have recorded its extent. Many generalizations about the colonial South may have been made by well-meaning historians through the distorting lens of the Civil War. Moreover, social historians may be predisposed to finding structural flaws in a society that would go to war to defend an institution as shockingly repellent as slavery.[30]

Evidence suggests, however, that many white indentured servants came to work among the southern plantations in the 17th century. These were bound to other white men for a fixed number of years, after which they were free to take up a piece of land of their own. Colonial proprietors set aside whole areas as townships in which white freeholders and their families, who owned no slaves, might settle in the hope that a stable and diverse society much like that in rural England might be formed. These schemes generally failed in regions where cheap slave labor was common because they interfered with the ability of free whites to make a reasonable living from ordinary work. However, in western Virginia and the backcountry of North Carolina, entire counties had no slaves whatsoever in the colonial period. Neither did they support any free black population, which suggests that racial prejudice was indeed at work. The western frontier of the colonies had few slaves largely because they were too mountainous to grow tobacco, rice, or cotton economically. One county in western Virginia was so removed from slavery that not a single black person, slave or free, lived within its bounds as late as 1860. In Maryland and Delaware, slaves were found mostly in the cities, serving as tradesmen, artisans, and household help.

ON THE WATERFRONT

The Board of Trade, which controlled the economic life of the colonies from London throughout the 18th century, made few prohibitions against the development of colonial maritime industries because they were thought to **Down to the Sea in Ships** strengthen the trading empire. Soon New England was providing almost half of British shipbuilding capacity worldwide. There was an appreciable shipbuilding industry in New Hampshire, Massachusetts (including Maine), Connecticut, and New York, but nothing warranting mention in the colonies south of Baltimore.

Colonial vessels were built largely for the Caribbean and coasting trades, or for fishing. In New Hampshire, there were more people engaged in shipbuilding than in agriculture, and in Massachusetts (including Maine), it was estimated that there was one ship for every hundred inhabitants before the Revolution. Colonial shippers and merchants made their profits by moving raw materials to England and returning finished goods to the colonial markets. The government took its share of the wealth generated by this activity in the form of taxes, port fees, and customs duties.[31]

The fields along the water's edge were dotted with simple sheds that served as offices, warehouses, and shelters to many of the mercantile establishments of any port town. The blacksmith's hammer chimed rhythmically as he beat out bolts, plates, chains, tools, block sheaves, rudder irons, harpoons, and other nautical ironwork in his waterside shop.[32] Although the blacksmiths' sheds were usually placed some distance from the highly flammable hemp and flax that could cause a general fire along the waterfront, the smell of burning soft coal or charcoal still permeated the air when the wind blew from certain quarters. Apprentices tended the huge bellows, feeding air to the fires, which glowed like mythical serpent's eyes amid the blackened recesses of the ironworks, an image reinforced by the hiss of red-hot metal being plunged into cold water to temper and strengthen it.

Shipwrights were more than mere carpenters or woodworkers. They expertly sorted through the collected stores of odd-shaped wood stored in protective sheds to find the right piece to saw, carve, and shape into watertight and seaworthy vessels. Each was expert in a particular trade, such as caulking, planking, joinery, and rigging. The shipyards, always near the water's edge, were the workplace of the shipwright and his men. Large vessels were built on and launched from slipways made of massive timbers smoothed on top and laid perpendicular to the shoreline about eight to ten feet apart. Shipwrights, who were experts at marine joinery, received a different apprenticeship than simple house joiners and were highly esteemed for their specific skills.[33]

Ropemaking was also considered a maritime employment. Low, narrow buildings several hundred feet long housed the ropewalks. Here long hemp fibers were cleaned and combed through rows of iron spikes. A man called a spinner would coil the fibers around his waist and walk

Colonial Americans were a seafaring people, and maritime interests made up a large portion of the colonial economy, especially in New England.

backwards drawing the fiber taut while a boy at a wheel twisted the ends round into yarns. Combinations of the strands would then be parted out full length and twisted again into the desired size of rope or cable.

Sailmaking was an important maritime trade. The sailmaker often planned and manufactured the sails on the second floor, or loft, of his place of business. Tucked in the raftered upper floors of warehouses or in large open buildings, with stoves suspended from above to optimize floor space, sailmakers sketched patterns on the floors whereupon they laid out the canvas, cut it and sewed it to size before attaching the bolt rope around the outer edges. The genius of the sailmaker lay in his ability to design sails that would catch the wind from behind as well as when the wind was from the side. Sails in the colonial period had greater hoist than spread unlike those of later periods.

The cooper's shop was littered with wood shavings and staves. Coopers spent much of their time making open containers such as buckets and pails, but they were expert in fashioning a whole series of containers loosely categorized as kegs, barrels, and hogsheads. The epitome of the cooper's art was the watertight container, or cask. The shape of the barrel was unique in its design from simple crates and boxes. Not only was a barrel stable on its flat ends, but it could be rolled efficiently for short distances on its curved sides without needing a separate wheeled truck or cart.

Blockmakers carved the large wooden pulleys needed to haul supplies and cargo aboard the ships. Woodcarvers made ornamental work, railings, and figureheads to adorn the ships' bows. The ornamentation of 17th and 18th-century vessels was often extravagant. The figureheads could be extremely elaborate and often took the form of generals, statesmen, ladies, animals, and Indians.

From Newfoundland to southern New England was a shallow area of the ocean called the banks. The southernmost of these areas, opposite the colony of Massachusetts, were called the Georges Banks. Those off the coast of Labrador and Newfoundland were called the Grand Banks. These huge shoals on the edge of North America had attracted fishermen for centuries because they were the waters from which fishermen could catch cod. This singularly valuable cold-water fish could be found in no greater density than on the banks of the North American continent.[34] The Atlantic cod was the largest species among five related fish: cod, haddock, pollock, whiting, and hake. Cod has the whitest meat of the five types. It has virtually no fat and is more than 18 percent protein. Air-dried, sun-dried, smoked, or salted, cod was for many generations a staple foodstuff of Mediterranean nations and a leading export of British North America.[35]

From the 17th century onward, the common way to fish for cod was to go to the banks in a ship and then drop off a number of dories, twenty-foot open boats with two-man crews. Dories could be propelled by a single sail but were most often rowed. The fishing was usually done with a hand line. Traditionally, the fishermen landed their catch on the nearby shores of Newfoundland or Nova Scotia and dried or salted it themselves. New Englanders of the 18th century went out in schooners that could race back and forth to the shore with the catch, which could be processed in port. The fishermen of Gloucester, Massachusetts developed a unique type of schooner that became characteristic of the fishing fleets on the banks. They were also used to make fast runs to the French islands of the West Indies where the cod-molasses and cod-Madeira (wine) trades grew steadily until the American Revolution.[36]

Many historians remain fascinated by the three-way traffic in molasses, rum, and slaves known as the Triangular Trade. Nonetheless, the Triangular Trade was fundamentally supported by the fisheries of the Grand Banks that provided the dried, salted cod used to feed the slaves on the sugar plantations. Without the cod, the islands would have been unable to support the large number of slaves needed to produce sugar and molasses. Nonetheless, profits were to be had with every exchange made on the trading triangle. Englishmen who never saw their sugar plantations in the Caribbean made great fortunes during the 17th and 18th centuries on the molasses carried to New England by American skippers. Rum distillers in New England made tidy profits changing the molasses into liquor, and the indigenous slave traders of Africa either consumed the rum or used it as an item for further trade. The ubiquitous New England shipowners took their share of the profits by carrying the cargoes, including human ones, on each leg of the trading triangle. Profits from this business helped New England to offset its considerable deficit in commodity trading with Britain, which amounted to nearly £1.5 million in the decade before the outbreak of the Revolution.[37]

Anglo-Americans were also the unchallenged masters of whaling throughout the world. In the 17th century, lookouts stationed on high cliffs or other vantage points among the coastal islands of New England and Long Island, would signal the appearance of whales to the waiting hunters, who would launch their boats and follow the lookout signals to the pod (a group of whales). The whale would be struck with a harpoon attached by a line to drogues, huge pieces of wood two feet square. With the harpoon firmly embedded in its flesh, the animal was forced to expend its energy pulling the drogue through the water. The whalers followed, either under oar power or sail, until they could kill the exhausted animal with lances. They then towed the carcass back to the beach for processing (flensing). Heavier whaleboats, better harpoons with a metal head that secured itself in the flesh, and more serviceable lines led to the development of "fastening on" to the harpoon line and having the whale pull the boat.[38] Known as a "Nantucket sleigh ride," the practice was dangerous, but it enabled the hunters to keep closer to the whale and make an earlier kill.[39]

The advantage of a whaling station on shore was that while some of the men hunted from the boats, others did the chopping and cutting of the flesh and operated the cookeries that extracted the whale oil on shore. The crude whale oil recovered was used as a fuel for lighting in many colonial homes, and the whale bone was used as a stiffener in corsets and buggy whips. A specially refined whale oil was used as a high-grade lubricant into the 20th century, and a waxy material known as ambergris was used to make scents and perfumes.

New England whalers, especially those from Nantucket and New Bedford, adapted the square-rigged windship for whaling away from the coast in the 18th century. If the blubber could reach the home port in reasonable condition, the whalers flensed the whale along side the ship and stored the blubber in casks. If the distance was too great, they processed the blubber into oil at sea in large cookers called try-works, large metal containers placed over a fire on shipboard. The oil was ladled out of the pot directly into the oil barrels, and the remnants of fat were fed to the fire as fuel. The plume of black smoke from the fires could be seen from over the horizon. In later years, whaleships tied up to ice flows on which the flensing was done as both ship and iceberg drifted through the whaling grounds on the currents. The dual methods of processing whales on land and at sea remained characteristic of the industry for centuries.

Once the whaling industry was established, it affected the lives of all the people of coastal New England, and even inspired a small whaling industry along New York's Hudson River. To make the whaling voyages even more profitable, larger ships were constructed. These crowded the harbors, and the wharves were lined with casks of whale oil covered with seaweed for protection from the hot sun. Young men were eager to serve on the whalers, and if unable or too old to go to sea they turned their efforts to associated trades such as shipbuilding, sailmaking, or coopering. Whale-oil buyers and oil gaugers trod across the oil-soaked ground to test the quality and measure the quantity of the oil. Craftsmen in supporting trades were also kept very busy. On the cobblestone streets leading down to the waterfront, brick buildings were constructed to house the merchant offices and counting rooms. Warehouses, oil refineries, and shops were built. Bakeries specializing in dry ship's bread sprung up. Banks, marine insurance underwriters, and law offices were established in the heart of the waterfront business district.

As the New England industry expanded, Anglo-Americans found that they were producing oil and whale by-products beyond their own needs, but they found a ready market in England, where the whaling industry had come to a standstill. Nonetheless, colonial whalers were encouraged by the British colonial government, which passed major bounty acts in 1733 and 1749 for the building of whaleships of more than 200 tons. New England whalers began to range beyond the traditional whale fisheries, preferring the warmer and less risky waters of the South Seas inhabited by the sperm whale. The voyages were also taking the whalers to the Arctic to hunt the right and humpback whales. "Up to the outbreak of the American War of Independence in 1775, the story of whaling in the colonies [was] one of expansion and seizure of opportunity." In 1774, the American whaling fleet numbered more than 360 vessels and employed almost 5000 men. The spirit exhibited by American whalemen survived into the nineteenth century to make them unrivaled around the world.[40]

Arts and Manufactures The shop was the usual place of employment for men who made things, and they labored "neither in isolation nor in large impersonal crowds, but in groups of moderate size." In London the shops might have ten to twenty men working simultaneously, but in the colonies, groups of four or five men were more common. Woolcombers, knap shearers, fullers, hatters, printers, coopers, gunsmiths, wagon- and coachmakers, wheelwrights, metal founders, blacksmiths, and hammermen of all kinds worked together in shops in an organized fashion, sharing the tasks and often sharing the tools of their trade. Not surprisingly, the largest number of persons working in the manufacturing trades produced the most commonly needed items—clothing and shoes. The single largest group of such persons was weavers, followed by stocking knitters, shoemakers, and tailors.[41] Economist Adam Smith, writing in 1776, recognized the many difficulties facing independent businessman: "In all arts and manufactures the greater part of the workmen stand in need of a master to advance them the materials of their work, and their wages and maintenance till it be completed."[42]

The manufacturing environment in colonial America was vastly different from that found in the urban districts of most industrialized European countries, but even in the midst of the Industrial Revolution, it was not radically different from that found in the rural regions of the Old World. Many colonial tradespersons worked at home or in small individual shops attached to their family dwellings. Their customers and suppliers lived in the same town as they did, and they often relied on one another economically. Oddly the spinning of yarn was not generally considered a fulltime occupation in colonial America. It was thought to be a "by-industry," one that was chiefly done by women at odd moments in what was otherwise a busy day. The output of ten such spinners was thought to be needed to maintain the industry of one weaver, who had to hunt about the country for several days a week for a constant source of yarn. The dearth of yarn for weaving created a shortage of domestically produced broadcloth that tailors might fashion into clothing. This facet of domestic industry made tailors almost completely dependent on woolens imported from England.[43] The shoemaker patronized the cabinetmaker, the cabinetmaker the blacksmith, and the blacksmith the shoemaker. The close proximity of a man's workplace and his family also tended to create a bond between parents and children and between grandparents and grandchildren that would be severely challenged by the immense factories and impersonalized cities of a more industrialized 19th-century America.

In England, men completing their apprenticeships might have been fixed in their place of employment for all their lives, but in the colonies they had some chance of improving their condition. These craftsmen had the advantage of becoming masters of their own shops more quickly and with less competition than they would have found in Europe. They generally practiced their trades in the more recently settled towns and within a few decades had apprentices of their own.

Craftsmen such as tailors and shoemakers worked at making and mending clothes and shoes in all towns and in many villages, but large-scale manufacturing of these items was largely absent from British North America. Hatters and wigmakers had higher status in the colonies than in London because their work was more specialized, and there were fewer of them in the colonies. Bookbinders (an extension of the printing trade), saddle makers, cabinet-makers, wheelwrights, and coach makers enjoyed both the common trade and the patronage of the wealthy. A very small number of highly specialized tradespersons, such as engravers, locksmiths, goldsmiths, and musical instrument makers, survived economically only in the important towns and cities. The building trades did well everywhere because of the expanding nature of colonial settlement, but master house builders, stone masons, plumbers, tilers, and painters were most in demand in the aristocratic South. Skilled tradesmen were all ascending the economic ladder to prosperity and financial security in a manner undreamed of by their counterparts in Britain. Skilled trades, craftsmanship, and shipbuilding actually surpassed agriculture as the leading commercial activities in terms of the value of their annual production by 1775.

William Penn noted in his first plan of government for his colony that all children be taught some useful trade or **Wage Labor** skill so that "the poor may work to live, and the rich, if they become poor, may not want." It has also been said in counterpoint that an educated man always had his living, but a laborer had only his day's pay. In the British trading empire, wages varied between 9s (shillings) and 12s per week, with 10s being one of the most common rates found in business records from the latter part of the period. For the sixty year period from 1729 to 1789 annual income for artisans in London hovered around £44. This was equivalent to approximate 20s weekly. By way of comparison the wages of textile workers were 10s to 13s per week, but this was actually below that of other laborers because they were often charged as much as 4s weekly for the use of the employer's looms or stocking frames. This may help to account for the large number of unemployed workers who identified themselves as weavers during manufacturing downturns. Those workers with special skills such as masons, or those who provided their own specialized tools such as leather workers or joiners, may have made as much as 15s per week.[44]

Although the documentary record for wages in British North America is less complete than that for wages in London, it seems certain that colonial wages outstripped those in Britain. In 1649, an observer noted, "The poor ploughman, day laborer, and poor artificer ... laboring and sweating all the days of their lives; some for fourteen pence, others for sixteen, eighteen, twenty pence or two shilling[s] a day; which is the highest of wages to such kind of people, and the most of them to the end of their days in sorrow, not having purchased so much by their lives of labor as will scarce preserve them in their old days from beggary."[45]

Hard evidence for the wages in the colonies remains obscure, but wage levels seemingly varied from region to region depending on the demand for slaves and the availability of indentured servants or seasonal workers. Records for the wages earned in the Chesapeake region are confounded by the inclusion of wages paid to masters for the labor of their slaves. Records for the wages of mariners in Boston and of laborers, tradesmen, and tailors in Philadelphia begin in 1720 and end in 1750, but they do not include any other categories of workers. Moreover, there was a great disparity between the value of English coin and colonial paper currency of the same denominations—the former being more valuable sometimes by half. Not all available records specify in which form the wage was paid.

The income for free workers who carved out a farmstead and tried their luck at growing tobacco or raising hogs is even more difficult to determine since such men often left no record of their income at all. In the middle of the colonial period "the smallest sum upon which a family could be maintained during a period of twelve months was £20 11s, including the cost of renting a cottage and the price of the necessary amount of bread, meat, fuel, and clothing." The average income for agricultural workers rose between 1618 and 1700 from £8 8s 9d (pence) to £15 19s, but this amount remained hardly enough to make ends meet.[46]

The availability of inexpensive land and the demand for laborers kept wages in the colonies relatively high, but the effect of the influx of immigrant populations on wages is unclear except in the urban port cities. Approximately 9 percent of the colonial population lived in the five largest cities in British North America in 1690, and only 4 percent lived there in 1775. Only the constant influx of immigrants seems to have kept the urban labor market from collapsing.[47] Even here a greater emphasis on the study of migration into and out of the cities is needed to effect a more precise understanding of a dynamic quantity like wages.[48] "The traditional picture of comfortable living standards, steady work at very high wages, general prosperity, and abundance for the common man [in America] is too optimistic."[49]

Nonetheless, a good deal can be surmised from the available data. Evidence submitted to British authorities in London in the mid-18th century suggests that an average day laborer could expect to earn between

£25 and £40 annually if fully employed. However, determined and skill-ful employees doing piecework in London might briefly increase their weekly earnings to £1 or even £2. By comparison, an unmarried clerk had a reasonable expectation of earning a steady living amounting to £50 annually without regard to the season of the year. Particularly well-to-do artisans, such as the makers of jewelry, optical and musical instruments, clocks and carriages, or fine furniture, might increase their annual earn-ings to over £100 by employing apprentices and journeymen.[50]

Colonial income can be estimated by applying the proportional value of English and colonial money, but absolute wage levels were difficult to sustain in a colonial economy driven by seasonal spurts of agricultural productivity and inconsistent levels of supply and demand than in the more stable business atmosphere of London. Reports of middle-class family members working together to attain annual incomes between £200 and £600 during the 1760s and 1770s may be unreliable because they often extrapolate annual incomes from unusually high seasonal or temporary earnings.[51]

NOTES

1. Lisa Wilson, *Ye Heart of a Man: The Domestic Life of Men in Colonial New England* (New Haven: Yale University Press, 1999), 106.

2. Ibid., 23.

3. Ibid., 106.

4. Alvin E. Conner, *Sectarian Childrearing: The Dunkers, 1708–1900* (Gettysburg: Brethren Heritage Press, 2000), 91.

5. Wilson, *Ye Heart of a Man*, 109.

6. Lyon Gardiner Tyler, "Education in Colonial Virginia," part 4, "The Higher Education" *William and Mary College Quarterly* 6 (January 1898): 177.

7. Quoted in Louis B. Wright, *The Cultural Life of the American Colonies* (Mineola, NY: Dover Publications, 2002), 112–13.

8. Wilson, *Ye Heart of a Man*, 111.

9. Quoted in ibid., 25.

10. T. H. Breen, *The Marketplace of Revolution: How Consumer Politics Shaped American Independence* (New York: Oxford University Press, 2004), 150–51.

11. Quoted in Peter Padfield, *Maritime Supremacy and the Opening of the Western Mind* (New York: Overlook Press, 2002), 217.

12. John J. McCusker and Russell R. Menard, *The Economy of British America, 1607–1789* (Chapel Hill: University of North Carolina Press, 1991), 26.

13. Lucy M. Salmon, *The Dutch West India Company on the Hudson* (Poughkeepsie, NY: privately published, 1915), 15–20.

14. Oliver M. Dickerson, *The Navigation Acts and the American Revolution* (New York: A. S. Barnes, 1963), 6–7.

15. John Rule, *The Experience of Labour in Eighteenth-Century English Industry,* (New York: St. Martin's Press, 1981) 95.

16. Christopher Hill, *The Century of Revolution, 1603–1714* (New York: W.W. Norton, 1961), 34.

17. Herman Melville, *Redburn* (Originally printed in 1849. New York: Penguin Putnam, 1986), 152.

18. William Hutchinson Rowe, *The Maritime History of Maine: Three Centuries of Shipbuilding and Seafaring* (Freeport, ME: Bond Wheelwright, n.d.), 135–36.

19. Rule, *The Experience of Labour*, 23.

20. Ibid., 23.

21. Carl Bridenbaugh, ed., *Gentlemen's Progress: The Itinerarium of Dr. Alexander Hamilton, 1744* (Chapel Hill: University of North Carolina Press, 1948), 196.

22. McCusker and Menard, *The Economy of British America*, 302.

23. Quoted in Howard S. Russell, *A Long Deep Furrow, Three Centuries of Farming in New England* (Lebanon, New Hampshire: University Press of New England, 1976) 63.

24. Ibid., 65.

25. Conner, *Sectarian Childrearing*, 106.

26. Ibid., 15.

27. Quoted in ibid., 145.

28. Ibid., 145.

29. McCusker and Menard, *The Economy of British America*, 174.

30. Harold S. Wilson, *Confederate Industry, Manufacturers and Quartermasters in the Civil War* (Jackson: University Press of Mississippi, 2002), ix.

31. Marjorie Hubbell Gibson, H.M.S. Somerset, *1746–1778: The Life and Times of an Eighteenth Century British Man-o-War and Her Impact on North America* (Cotuit, MA: Abbey Gate House, 1992), 2.

32. Blacksmith James Durfee of New Bedford made 58,517 harpoons during his lifetime.

33. Robert Carse, *Ports of Call* (New York: Scribner's, 1967), 46.

34. Mark Kurlansky, *Cod: A Biography of the Fish That Changed the World* (New York: Penguin, 1997), 44.

35. Ibid., 37.

36. Ibid., 95.

37. McCusker and Menard, *The Economy of British America*, 82.

38. An African-American blacksmith, Lewis Temple, invented a harpoon head which, once inside the whale, turned at right angles to the shaft so that it would hold fast. Known as the "Temple Toggle Iron," it was used by virtually every whaler.

39. American whalers became so adept at this form of whaling that the phrase "Nantucket sleigh ride" was coined to describe it. Bill Spense, *Harpooned: The Story of Whaling* (New York: Crescent Books, 1980), 35.

40. Ibid., 44, 53.

41. John Rule, *The Experience of Labour*, 31.

42. Quoted in ibid., 31.

43. Alice Morse Earle, *Homelife in Colonial Days* (Stockbridge, MA: Berkshire House, 1993) 228.

44. Quoted in Wright, *Cultural Life of the American Colonies*, 108.

45. Quoted in Philip A. Bruce, *Economic History of Virginia in the Seventeenth Century: An Inquiry into the Material Condition of the People, Based on Original and Contemporaneous Records* (New York: Macmillan, 1896), 581.

46. Ibid., 580.

47. McCusker and Menard, *The Economy of British America*, 250.

48. Ibid., 135.

49. Ibid., 245.

50. M. Dorothy George, *London Life in the Eighteenth Century* (Chicago: Academy Chicago Publishers, 1999), 167.

51. Breen, *The Marketplace of Revolution*, 208. Such data were also reported in propaganda pieces written by semianonymous radical agitators apparently railing against the "luxury and extravagance" of the pro-British upper classes. "Save your money and save your country," wrote an author who signed as "A Pennsylvania Farmer" in 1764.

7

Protector

Blockhouses and a trembling defensive encourage the meanest scoundrels to attack us.

—British general James Wolfe[1]

Community life in British North America was by no means secure. Indians lurked around the fringes of even the largest settlements along the seacoast. As early as 1607, the English settlers of Jamestown, Virginia, understood the need to create a fortified village for protection against possible attack. Yet with their initial fear of the Indians allayed by the establishment of trade with the local chieftains, the colonists seem to have willingly invited the Native Americans into their compounds and even into their homes. They never expected that the Indians would challenge the advantages provided by European goods, firearms, and advanced technology by attacking them as happened in 1622 and again in 1644.

The greatest anxiety shared by English colonials of the 17th century was that the Spanish would attack their coastal settlements from the sea. This fear was not unfounded. The Spanish had destroyed a French Huguenot settlement on the St. John's River in Florida in 1565, showing the heretics no mercy and killing all whom they found. Moreover, in 1570, the Spanish Jesuits had established a mission in the Chesapeake Bay area very near the site of Jamestown, Virginia. Although the mission had failed, the Spanish Crown still claimed much of that land. As late as 1740, Spanish privateers could be found stalking the Atlantic coast from Florida to the Delaware Bay.[2]

The Spanish threat led the Jamestown settlers to construct a stout triangular defensive wall with a palisade of pointed tree trunks, and with far-reaching cannon mounted on the parapet—generally facing down the James River to fend off Spanish ships. Within the defensive structure were nestled all the dwellings of the inhabitants, the church, the armory, and ancillary buildings. Outside the walls were the fields in which staple crops were grown, and beyond them, the almost impenetrable woodlands.

The English in the northeastern colonies responded to a French threat from the sea by constructing strong forts, some of stone and others of wood and soil embankments, at strategic points along the coast. Fort William Henry on the Maine coast, for instance, had an overall perimeter of more than 700 English feet, with embrasures for 28 cannon. Eighteen of these heavy guns were placed on its seaward wall, which was 22 feet high and 6 feet thick. The permanent garrison consisted of between 60 and 100 soldiers. The colonials also built forts on their frontiers, both to cut off enemy incursions and to create bases for expeditions into enemy territory. Fortifications had one disadvantage: They attracted the attention of European enemies. Indeed, when the governor of New France learned that Fort William Henry had been erected in Maine in 1692, he immediately instigated an attack on it.

Forts on the frontiers never truly sealed the wilderness boundaries of the colonies, and without a large number of defenders to actively patrol the border regions, they remained porous to enemy troops. English colonists seem to have become somewhat complacent about their personal defenses with time, spreading out beyond the reach of aid from settlements and the frontier strongholds. Because the waterways were the only efficient means of transporting goods and crops and the needs of commerce quickly supplanted those of defense, the number of settlements along the rivers increased, reflecting a repetitive phenomenon in the development of frontier communities. Initial fear supports community action and substantive defenses. Growing familiarity with the surroundings leads to expansion and personal complacency, which ends in unexpected tragedy, panic, and renewed calls for community action and additional defenses.

TO PROVIDE FOR THE COMMON DEFENSE

No formal establishment of regular troops was used in America for defense for almost a century and half after the founding of the first English colony, in part because the colonists were religious dissenters or political outsiders and consequently distrustful of professional military forces. Moreover, the home government itself was in turmoil during the English Civil War (1640 to 1660) and again beginning in 1688 with the Glorious Revolution. Even if the colonists in America had wanted a regular army, there was no force available in England to send.

Unlike the French, who were ruled by a single royal family with four monarchs (the Bourbons), the British government or ruling royal houses changed six times and had twelve separate heads of state during the colonial period.[3] These continual political and social upheavals figured prominently in the history of all the English colonies. Without a consensus as to which government in England was lawful during the periods of unrest, the colonies generally reverted to the last form of legitimate governance that they knew until such time as the political questions had been resolved in England. With royalist planters controlling the southern colonies and pro-republican Puritans predominating in New England, both public and military leaders took sides in these disputes, and many soldiers deserted their posts in frustration.[4]

During the Glorious Revolution of 1688, the governor of New York, Sir Edmund Andros, considered the colonists "little better than rebels and traitors" because they generally believed the king (James II) to be a tyrant who deserved to be overthrown. They proved to be "disconcerted, angry, and stubborn—by no means the best frame of mind for facing a great public danger."[5] The unrest among the colonies continued until word came that James II had been overthrown and the new monarchs, William and Mary, appointed new governors for all the colonies.[6]

The colonists in Virginia and New England were remarkably dissimilar in their political, economic, social, and religious attitudes, yet their beliefs concerning local defense were very similar, possibly because they shared the same English military traditions. Surprisingly, most Englishmen came to America armed to the teeth. "The story of the military institutions of the American colonies is an account of efforts to keep as much of the population as possible armed and prepared to fight on short notice." Evidence of lances, crossbows, firelocks, body armor, and steel helmets reminiscent of the Middle Ages have been found in even remote colonial settlements.[7]

Each English colony designed its own systems of defense, generally fashioned around a militia formed of its male citizens. Men with European military experience, such as John Smith, Miles Standish, John Underhill, or Lion Gardiner, were engaged by the earliest colonists to provide military leadership, yet the colonial militia companies that they commanded were largely administrative rather than tactical units. Inadequate supply systems and a lack of strategic planning often reflected poorly on the colonial military leaders. After the first generation of professional military leaders had passed away, they were replaced for the most part by rank military novices. Even when they were successful in defeating their enemies, the colonists displayed a shocking degree of artlessness in their military manner and of unpreparedness in dealing with the problems of tactical coordination and logistics. More than once they failed to provide sufficient supplies in terms of food, blankets, and clothing for even short campaigns.[8] Poorly trained, infrequently drilled, or with no knowledge of military discipline at all, the new recruits that filled the ranks of the local militia companies were unaccustomed to combat and to working together. The very discontinuity of their service during sporadic outbreaks of violence or during periods of impending crisis made them amateurish, inept, and largely unreliable as soldiers.[9]

The divergent strategic imperatives among the colonies and among the settlements within each colony caused no end of confusion. Nonetheless, coastal communities and frontier settlements had similar defensive needs. Inland frontier communities such as Northampton, Hadley, Hatfield, Deerfield, Springfield, and Schenectady suffered devastating and recurring attacks, but so did the string of coastal towns of Maine from Kittery to Casco. Therefore, the quasi-military organizations fashioned to provide security to each settlement were remarkably similar in structure considering the number of individual colonial governments involved in their creation. Any differences are more easily ascribed to regional characteristics rather than any genuine inconsistency.[10]

The New England settlements bore the brunt of the French and Indian Wars of the 18th century. Neither New York nor Pennsylvania had a large militia beyond local companies. While New Yorkers followed the lead of the original Dutch founders of their colony by relying almost entirely on the good will of the Iroquois for defense, the peace-loving English Quakers and German Pietists of Pennsylvania uniformly resisted raising any local

This group of New England citizen soldiers has turned out for its monthly militia day to practice their marching and marksmanship. Americans relied on the militia for its local defense until the middle of the 18th century.

armed forces. Pennsylvania's fortunate geographic position at the center
of the English colonies allowed the antiwar majority to pursue their
pacifism into the middle of the 18th century, with the northern colonies
fighting the French on one hand and the southern colonies keeping the
Spanish at a distance on the other. Those English who settled in Virginia,
Maryland, or the Carolinas came armed and expected to fight off both the
native population and any incursions by the Spanish. The Germans and
Scotch-Irish who settled in the backcountry found that there was simply
no adequate defense for their isolated habitations. A lone defense against
the attack of even a small enemy force had no practical chance of success,
and frontier colonists resorted to the expedient of forting up during times
of unrest. A chain of log forts and solid garrison houses was established
along the colonial frontier in which local families could take refuge and
pool the strength of their defense. The need to link these outposts led to
the development of rangers, who scouted the gaps between forts looking
for signs of impending trouble.[11]

From the very beginning of the colonial period it was clear that the
native inhabitants of America were being dispossessed of their land and
that they would resist further incursions by the whites. Europeans who
arrived in the late 17th century had been favored, nonetheless, with an
unanticipated stroke of good fortune. Many of the native coastal settlements were found to be abandoned, and the fields surrounding them
were relatively clear of trees and brush and still retained a great deal of
the natural qualities of good soil. Many coastal tribes had been decimated
by disease. Moreover, migrating tribes driven into the interior by appre-
hension of the Europeans in coastal settlements established hunting trails,
cleared new lands, and settled villages near water transportation in the
wilderness. When German and Scotch-Irish settlers pushed into these
areas a few decades later they reaped the advantages of this preparatory
work in much the same way as the Pilgrims had occupied the abandoned
fields of coastal New England.[12]

The first impulse of the natives had been to avoid the newcomers,
but within a decade of the earliest settlements colonists to British North
America were being attacked by Native American tribes. For example, in
1622, a concerted effort among the native populations of the Chesapeake
Bay area—a well-thought-out conspiracy among several tribes—resulted
in the simultaneous destruction of several Virginia settlements and the
murder of 375 colonists in a single day. Many of these were killed without warning in their own homes. Only the loyalty of a few Indians, who
warned their friends among the English of the coming cataclysm, kept the
English settlement at Jamestown from being annihilated.[13]

Lacking large standing armies, colonials relied heavily on provincial
forces or local militias for protection against attack or for prosecuting war
with others. The year 1689 seems to have been a watershed in this regard
with military operations by militias against the Native Americans taking

precedence before this date and conflicts with the French undertaken by better-organized provincial forces taking precedence thereafter. From the distance of time most colonial military organizations appear the same, and it has been difficult for historians to separate out any differences or discernible peculiarities in the provincial forces that evolved from them.

In the 17th century, militias often reflected the social pecking order of the community with the regimental or battalion level officers chosen and arranged "according to a punctilious ranking." The officers in charge of brigades and the local companies that made them up were dressed in colored sashes, waistcoats, or doublets; lieutenants and sergeants carried imposing, if impractical polearms called halbreds; and the "young bachelor ensigns" stood proudly to the company banners. As a practical matter most of the able-bodied male members of the community (including servants) were included in this flamboyant display. There was also a concern that this fraternity be balanced by an equally important respect for social station with rich and distinguished men commanding less fortunate freemen and servants. Moreover, flamboyance and martial trappings alone were no substitute for military proficiency, and mandatory Sunday parade and drill were instituted in most localities. The monthly beating of drums, the squealing of fifes, the unfurling of banners, the rapid marches about the common, and the few shots taken at stationary wooden targets concealed a serious military purpose, the very survival of the colonists.[14]

Nonetheless, there was one undeniable unifying characteristic of all colonial forces during the period. Whether against natives or other Europeans, the respective colonial governments attempted to defend themselves by using the temporary volunteers that they had at hand. "Border warfare was the only school in which the [colonials] had been trained up, and as soon as the exigency was over they returned to their farms or workshops."[15]

The Burgher militias of the Dutch at Albany, New York (Fort Orange) initially found it necessary to maintain an alliance with the local Native American tribes particularly the powerful Mohawks who acted as brokers for furs coming from the more remote tribes in the interior. Initially joining in an unfortunate alliance with the Mohican people against the Mohawks, after 1630 the Dutch realized that they had more to lose than would be gained by any continued hostility. Their new alliance quickly became the standard for the New York colony with the Mohawks and their relatives among the Iroquois serving as hired mercenaries providing for defense in place of a "burgher militia."[16]

On the other hand, the Dutch around Manhattan Island (New Amsterdam) had initially been happy to trade peacefully with the local natives but ultimately became more aggressive toward them. Stripped of their economic usefulness by overtrapping the local fur-bearing animals, the indigenous people were required to submit to a haughty and arrogant colonial rule and were treated by the Dutch as an ignorant and brutish people. Dutch-Indian relations consequently deteriorated as the autonomous local tribes continued to resist colonial authority. Finally, in 1642, a group of 80 armed settlers fell upon two encampments of Indians near Hackensack, New Jersey, indiscriminately killing men, women, and children. However, this force lacked the order and structure of a true militia. The only body of militia of respectable size raised by the Dutch during the period was sent to seize the colony of New Sweden in Delaware in 1655 after the Swedes had given firearms and cannon to the local natives. The Dutch operation was successful in dispossessing the Swedish colonists of their settlement, yet less than a decade later, when a small English force seized all the Dutch possessions in North America, only a tiny garrison of Dutch soldiers stood in the way.[17] "When the time came for [the Dutch militia] to participate in [their] nation's defense [against the English], the inadequacy of their preparation was all too nakedly revealed."[18]

The New England colonies ultimately joined together under the Dominion of New England (the General Courts) in the middle of the 17th century to wage a series of wars of annihilation on particular tribes deemed unfriendly to the colonists, such as the Pequots (1637) and the Wampanoags (1675). Similar developments took place in the colonial South, resulting in wars with the Powhattan (1622), the Tuscarora (1711), the Yamasee (1715), and the Creeks (1717). These wars of extermination

The violent manner used by the militia armies of New England versus the Native American population in the 17th century unfortunately set the standard for colonial relations with the tribes thereafter.

carried out by combined forces from Virginia, Maryland, and the Carolinas were often supported by rival Native American tribes from the region.

Unlike other parts of British North America with their mountain barriers to the west, the whole extent of the New England frontier was open to the sudden descent of an enemy by canoe from the north. Rivers flowed to the sea from the interior and through most of the English settlements that made up Massachusetts, Connecticut, and New Hampshire. These rivers were highways into the wilderness for the colonists, but they were also avenues of danger to be watched lest their enemies descend upon them suddenly.[19] It was almost impossible to efficiently defend this frontier. "To block up the mouths of the rivers with forts, isolated from all support, was equally idle, as was proved by the utter failure of every such attempt."[20]

Moreover, because frontier settlements served as early warning outposts for the more settled communities, the General Courts prohibited the evacuation of those communities in times of crisis. Any family that left its home without the permission of a colonial assembly risked the forfeiture of its property. However, each settlement was promised a garrison of troops in times of danger and was encouraged to maintain itself through tax deductions and other incentives. Among these incentives were the establishment at colonial expense of units of mounted and dismounted rangers assigned to patrol the wilderness and flying squadrons of mounted dragoons, which could respond quickly to points of attack. Unfortunately, false alarms, multiple alarms, and the isolation of many communities hampered the effectiveness of the flying squadrons as a defensive force. As long as the settlements were not to be provided with permanent garrisons, they were forced to rely on the static defense provided by forting up in garrison houses, blockhouses, and small refuge forts.

The English colonial militia was characterized by a unique regional flavor even to the type and quality of the soldiers each produced. The Southern colonies preferred to raise more cavalry units than did the colonies of New England, possibly because the far-flung and widely placed plantations could be reached swiftly only on horseback. As early as 1672, the Virginia colony claimed to be able to field 20 troops of horse (30 mounted men each) and an equal number of infantry companies composed of 60 men (30 musketmen and 30 pikemen). Neither Massachusetts nor Connecticut, with populations equal to or larger than Virginia's, could field such a number or proportion of horsemen at that period.

In lightly populated areas, the militia system was an immediate and practical measure for public safety largely necessitated by an ever-shifting string of frontier villages. Yet there remains in America the cherished romantic concept of the militia as "minutemen," a mythical army of self-trained and self-armed warriors springing from the colonial soil in times of trouble. While this may seem a natural and sensible means of having,

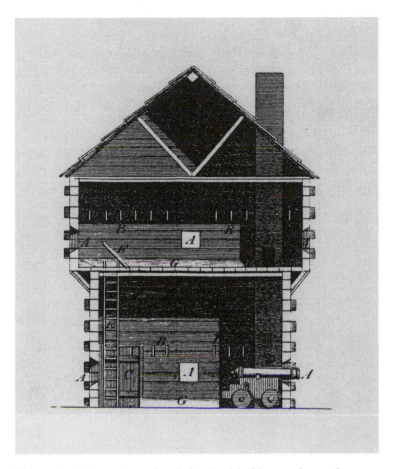

This period illustration of a defensive blockhouse shows the gun-ports for the cannon (A) and the arrangement of firing loops for muskets (B). The overhanging second floor allowed water to be dropped down, preventing fires from being set against the walls.

near at hand, contingents of men familiar with the use of weapons, the reality of relying on such a makeshift system for defense could prove a disastrous illusion.

The earliest settlers were seldom effectively organized for warfare when simply formed in hastily assembled and informally constructed groups. It was found that only with training was the colonial soldiery effective. Therefore, periodic training days were instituted, and a cadre of elected or appointed officers was formed. A local stockpile of gunpowder and a few artillery pieces were provided along with armor, pikes, and other items not commonly available to the settlers. These improvements became characteristic of most militia systems.[21]

THE LOCAL COMPANY

The structure of the local militia companies in New England has been very well documented.[22] Company strength ranged from 65 to 200 men but often fell below 65, at which time units might be combined from neighboring communities. Local command was invested in a captain, subalterns, and sergeants. These officers were usually elected by the men who were often their friends and relations. It was not uncommon for grandfathers, fathers, and grandsons to service in the same unit simultaneously. After the middle of the seventeenth century, the nomination and commissioning of officers was being approved by the General Court in New England and by colonial governors elsewhere in British North America. While military authority generally came from a legislative body or the Crown, the actual management and strategy employed any war was left to the colonial governors. The overall command structure and the level of authority of individual leaders generally lacked clear definition and varied in form from province to province. Various colonies resorted to the mode of military organization that most closely paralleled their experience and resources; others were geographically organized and administered on the town or county level.

When settlement began, every able-bodied man was a potential soldier and had a legal obligation to serve. For frontier settlers, it was often impossible to separate defense from the other tasks of daily living, such as clearing land, growing food, and building shelters. Men went to church muskets in hand, and set them down nearby in the pew or along the wall. As the character of a village or town became more settled, the nature of the military service changed; but the universal obligation of all able-bodied freemen (including servants) to serve seems to have remained in force throughout most of the colonial period.[23]

Newly settled villages found it difficult to fulfill their manpower needs, and often, several local militias needed to combine to attain sufficient unit strength to ward off determined attacks. As towns became more settled, militia membership became more social—a mark of full citizenship among the males in the community; but certain minimum property qualifications could exempt those who were wealthy in terms of land and livestock. Men on the frontier remained reluctant to leave their homes in time of danger to fight in other localities. This reluctance was somewhat allayed because the laws governing the militia usually prohibited men from serving for long periods far from home or outside their own province or colony.

Slaves were often enlisted into the militia to defend the colony, and blacks played a significant if unheralded role in the defense of many settlements. The longstanding involvement of blacks in defense was acknowledged in the statutes of many colonies. In 1652, Massachusetts required that all free Negroes and Indians living in the colony train as

This chalk-and-pencil sketch shows how settlers in frontier communities needed to cooperate to insure their security.

part of the militia, but by the end of the 17th century, the same persons were legally prohibited from serving. Nonetheless, in times of military emergency, every man, able bodied or not, became a frontline soldier.[24] In 1704, the Carolinas passed a law that specifically called for the raising and arming of slaves in times of crisis: "For the defense of the colony, our laws oblige every male person from 16 to 60 years of age to bear arms. There are likewise enrolled in our militia a considerable number of active, able Negro slaves." If such a slave killed "an enemy," the law stated, he would be granted his freedom and his master would be recompensed.

In 1708 the governor of the Carolinas reported the following:

The whole number of the militia of this province, 950 white men, fit to bear arms, viz. 2 regiments of foot, both making up 16 companies, 50 men, one with another, in a company; to which might be added a like number of Negro slaves, the captain of each company being obliged by an act of Assembly, to enlist, train up, and bring into the field for each white, one able slave armed with a gun or lance, for each man in his company.[25]

Before the slave rebellion scare of 1712, which tightened the limitations on blacks possessing arms, slaves often hunted for themselves or their masters on the plantations. Few were permitted firearms off the limits of their owner's property, however. Many blacks were familiar with weapons such as the lance, which may have been a common weapon in a former life in West Africa. During the Yamasee War of 1715, the Carolina Assembly adopted a resolution "that a sufficient number of lances be made immediately, to arm the Negroes who can not be supplied with guns." Large parties of whites, blacks, and allied native Americans fought the Yamasee on and off in the Carolina wilderness for more than four years. Oddly the white militia officers were highly suspicious of their Indian allies and depended rather on their Negro slaves in times of crisis. "600 whites ... and 400 Negroes" were used "to protect the settlements till the crops [were] all got in [and] then march[ed] to fight the enemy where they [could] find him."[26] Nonetheless, blacks slaves readily joined any opposition movement that might gain them freedom, and individual blacks could be found on both sides of many conflicts. Both slaves and free blacks served in every colonial conflict in the 18th century, including the American Revolution, with distinction and honor.[27]

PROVINCIAL FORCES

Most of the soldiers who fought for the English colonies prior to the final cataclysm of the French and Indian War were colonials. Only after 1754 were large numbers of regulars sent to the English colonies. However, these colonials were not formed into a simple citizen army but rather as regular provincial troops—enlisted for a term, formed into permanent regiments, and paid by the colony. These regiments were in some measure bound by kinship ties with fathers, sons, brothers, and cousins all serving in the same unit.

After the Pequot War of 1637, the Puritans overhauled their militia system to provide for a quick reaction force called a trained band, something like the schoolroom concept of a minuteman. They also began to fill their overall manpower needs by imposing quotas on the individual towns.[28] After the Indian wars of 1675, men were recruited to serve for longer periods in provincial regiments. After the French attack on the New York settlement at Schenectady in 1690, the English colonies continued in an almost constant state of war with their European neighbors and their Indian allies, yet not until the 1750s did armies from Europe join the fray.

The numerous appeals from the English colonies for military aid during Queen Anne's War (1702–1713) and Britain's constant need to maintain a war footing in British North America during the previous two decades provoked a formal reassessment of colonial policy early in the second decade of the 18th century. The Board of Trade in London began to consider placing the individual colonies on a more secure imperial footing by placing the frontier settlements under the strictures of martial law during times of crisis. From this point, provincial regiments replaced the less formal local militia units in major operations. In many colonies, they became permanent organizations known as the Governor's Foot Guard or Horse Guard. In later decades, they became the Royal Americans, the Queen's Rangers, or (Major Robert) Roger's Rangers. These organizations, under command of provincial officers, became adept at frontier warfare.[29]

FIGHTING AGE

Massachusetts and Virginia laws generally agreed that those men between the ages of 16 and 60 would be formed into militia units for training. This age range is generally undisputed by historical authorities, but it may suggest an incorrect picture of what a provincial army looked like. Exhaustive studies of provincial forces from the 1750s, when records were scrupulously kept, suggest that the average age of men under arms was just under 26, with 80 percent under 35 and less than 2 percent over 55 (many of them officers). Rather than a conglomerate group composed of a broad spectrum of men of many ages, as in the local militias, the ranks of the provincial regiments were peppered by only a few boys and older men. Much like armies of today, colonial armies were pragmatically composed of adult males in the prime of life. Almost 90 percent of these men were volunteers, and, unlike the soldiers of Europe, most of them were literate—able to read the Bible, sign their names, and write short letters.[30]

APPEARANCE

In the 17th century, militiamen looked very much like the heavily armored soldiers of the 16th century mostly because they were supplied with cast-off armor and weapons from the Elizabethan period by a government in London that cared little whether they survived. Many questions remain about the effectiveness of such equipment (particularly the body armor) in the American wilderness. By 1658, the New England Confederation's standing orders to its militia members no longer called for any plate armor other than the gorget—a protective iron collar worn about the neck and shoulders. After King Philip's War (1675), the pike, crossbow, and most of the metal armor all but disappeared, mirroring similar developments in Europe. By the 18th century, all semblances of armor, including heavy leather coats and quilted protective jackets, had given way to garments much closer in design and material to ordinary clothing, and militiamen were using flintlock firearms almost exclusively.[31]

In the 18th century, colonial governors expected their militiamen to supply most of their own arms, accoutrements, and clothing. The colonial governments generally supplied cannon, replacement ammunition, and provisions. Evidence suggests that there was a little uniformity of dress, each man wearing what he thought best for his own comfort and circumstance. The backcountry militia companies commonly wore the same garments in which they pursued their daily livings on the frontier. This would include a linen shirt in summer and one of deerskin or wool in winter. This was covered with an outer garment known as a hunting shirt, "a kind of loose frock, reaching halfway down the thigh, with large sleeves, open before [in front] and so wide as to lap over a foot or more when belted." Made of heavy linen with a shoulder cape of the same material, the hunting shirt was usually trimmed with a fringe of unraveled cloth and was held closed with the same belt that held a knife and hatchet.[32]

An ammunition pouch, powder horn, canteen, and haversack were usually worn on straps which crossed the chest. A wide variety of caps, hats, and kerchiefs were used to cover the head. Most men wore broad-brimmed felt hats and stocking caps. The men wore loose trousers or more tightly fitted breeches of wool or linen, moccasins or shoes with thread stockings on their feet, and their lower legs were often covered with Indian leggings of wool broadcloth or leather. These last were called leather stockings.[33]

Although local authorities kept a supply of weapons and gunpowder on hand for emergencies, every colony required that each householder provide himself and his family with specific weapons and equipment. In most colonies, each militiaman was required to bring his own musket (or rifle); one pound of lead balls "fitted" to his weapon; powder in proper

Ultimately, a father was personally responsible for the protection of his family—an idea almost perfectly captured in this early-19th-century print.

proportion to the balls; a haversack; a one-quart canteen or water bottle; and a hatchet, tomahawk, or hunting knife. Because it was not practical to load muskets directly from powder horns, ammunition was made up ahead of time in paper rolls containing both a measure of powder and leaden ball, which were kept in a cartridge box or bag. The powder horn was generally used only for priming or by riflemen who might alter their measure of powder depending on range.

A well-regulated and moderately trained local militia composed of the men of the community provided a practical solution to the defense needs of most settlements. The militia system was tested and employed successfully against the Indians in limited operations. Consequently, militias were established throughout the English colonies by the final decades of the 17th century. While their ancient armor, padded coats, crossbows, obsolete firearms, and small numbers made them less than adequate to substitute for a regular army, such local organizations were ultimately able to defend the settlements, drive back the Indians, and hold open the newly abandoned lands for European acquisition. Although more professionally trained forces would be needed to fight the French in the 18th century, the militia continued to be an important part of colonial defense, and it served as the nucleus of the army that fought the American Revolution.

NOTES

1. Francis Parkman, *Montcalm and Wolfe* (New York: Atheneum, 1984), 350.

2. David J. Weber, *The Spanish Frontier in North America* (New Haven: Yale University Press, 1992), 6, 60–61.

3. The English dynasties or ruling bodies during the colonial period are as follows: Tudor, Stuart, Puritan Republic, Stuart, Orange, Stuart, and Hanover. The heads of state were Elizabeth I, James I, Charles I, Oliver Cromwell, Richard Cromwell, Charles II, James II, William III, Anne, George I, George II, and George III. In the same period, the French Bourbon dynasty featured an uninterrupted succession: Henry IV, Louis XIII, Louis XIV, and Louis XV.

4. Samuel Adams Drake, *The Border Wars of New England, Commonly Called King William's and Queen Anne's Wars* (Williamstown, MA: Corner House, 1973), 13.

5. Ibid., 10.

6. Leisler served as interim governor but was later hanged for plotting treason.

7. Daniel J. Boorstin, *The Americans: The Colonial Experience* (New York: Vantage, 1958), 353.

8. Guy Chet, *Conquering the American Wilderness: The Triumph of European Warfare in the Colonial Northeast* (Amherst: University of Massachusetts Press, 2003), 52.

9. Ibid., 62.

10. John W. Shy, "A New Look at Colonial Militia," *William and Mary Quarterly* 35 (1963): 176.

11. Boorstin, *The Americans*, 50–53.

12. Gary B. Nash, *Red, White, and Black: The Peoples of Early America* (Englewood Cliffs, NJ: Prentice-Hall, 1982), 99.

13. One of the more unfortunate English villages Martin's Hundred. So devasting was the attack here that the few survivors hastily buried their dead and abandoned the site, which was not uncovered by archaeologists until 1969.

14. Simon Schama, *The Embarrassment of Riches, An Interpretation of Dutch Culture in the Golden Age* (New York: Vintage Books, 1997), 182.

15. Drake, *The Border Wars of New England*, 15.

16. Ian K. Steele, *Warpaths: Invasions of North America* (New York: Oxford University Press, 1994), 130.

17. Nash, *Red, White, and Black*, 92–93.

18. Schama, *The Emabarrassment of Riches*, 181–82.

19. At this time, Maine was a part of Massachusetts, and Vermont was claimed by New York.

20. Drake, *The Border Wars of New England*, 2.

21. John K. Mahon, "Anglo-American Methods of Indian Warfare, 1676–1794." *Mississippi Valley Historical Review* 45 (1958): 254.

22. See Fred W. Anderson, *A People's Army: Massachusetts Soldiers and Society in the Seven Years' War* (Chapel Hill: University of North Carolina Press, 1984); Fred W. Anderson, "Why Did Colonial New Englanders Make Bad Soldiers? Contractual Principles and Military Conduct during the Seven Years' War," *William and Mary Quarterly* 3d ser., 38 (1981): 395–417; Adam J. Hirsch, "The Collision of Military Cultures in Seventeenth-Century New England," *The Journal of American History* 26 (March 1988): 1187–1212; John K. Mahon, 254–75; Louis Morton, "The Origins of American Military Policy," *Military Affairs* 22 (1958): 75–82; and Shy, "A New Look at Colonial Militia," 175–85:

23. Lorenzo Johnson Greene, *The Negro in Colonial New England, 1620–1776* (New York: Columbia University Press, 1942), 126–27.

24. Ibid.

25. Peter H. Wood, *Black Majority, Negroes in Colonial South Carolina from 1670 through the Stono Rebellion* (New York: W. W. Norton, 1996), 126–27.

26. Ibid., 127.

27. See Dorothy Denneen Volo and James M. Volo, *Daily Life during the American Revolution* (Westport, CT: Greenwood Press, 2003), 102–3 and 110–13.

28. Morton, "The Origins of American Military Policy," 75, 80.

29. The military precepts set down by Robert Rogers in this period are now the basis for U.S. Special Forces training.

30. Anderson, *A People's Army*, 231, 44.

31. Heavy leather coats of this sort are on display at the state museum in Hartford, Connecticut.

32. David Hackett Fischer, *Albion's Seed: Four British Folkways in America* (New York : Oxford University Press, 1989), 732–33.

33. James M. Volo and Dorothy Denneen Volo, *Daily Life on the Old Colonial Frontier* (Westport, CT: Greenwood Press, 2002), 201.

8

Estate Builder

The concentration of land in the hands of a few of the better sort and the presence of a large body of white bonded servants, transported convicts, and Negro slaves in the Chesapeake tidewater … combined to buttress the barriers between classes to greater degree than in the large commercial cities or the small farm regions to the northward.

—Historian Carl Bridenbaugh

Most immigrants to America had among their ultimate goals the acquisition of land, social position, and other forms of wealth that could be devolved upon their children and grandchildren during their lifetimes or after their deaths. In colonial times, there were no 401k's, stock portfolios, or savings bonds, and the colonies were always short of cash. Of necessity, wealth consisted of tangible assets, such as farm fields, houses, ships, or slaves. Nonetheless, the earliest European settlers do not seem to have highly rated the creation of wealth or the development of great estates among their initial expectations for life in the colonies. Nonetheless, a family's increase in wealth was not a guarantee of permanent and continuing affluence. Many colonial parents believed that strength of character and purity of soul were a more lasting portion for their children than a few dozen pounds sterling or an uncleared woodlot.

The family of William Biddle, fourth-generation ancestor of Nicholas Biddle, a naval hero of the American Revolution, can be used as an example. William Biddle embarked with his wife and two small children for the colonies in 1680. As a Quaker, Biddle had suffered religious persecution, spending a short time in prison for his beliefs before deciding to settle in west New Jersey. Here he purchased about 500 acres along the banks of the Delaware River and an island in the river about half again that size. Before his death in 1712, he became involved in provincial government and was highly regarded in local society. His sole surviving child, also named William, improved and expanded on all that had been his father's. When the second William died in 1743, he had by his own efforts greatly increased the family's wealth, which was divided equally among six children. The eldest of these, a third William, divested himself of his portion of the property in lieu of cash and moved to Philadelphia to gain an education as a merchant and shipper.

In Philadelphia, young William III purchased a house and found a wife, Mary Scull. Their marriage was nearly perfect, but William's business acumen was inadequate to the trials of trade. The family, now including nine children (among them the future naval hero), would have been forced to live as paupers had it not been for the £2000 sterling that William had inherited.

A few years of carefully abstemious living ended in 1752 with William's death and the birth of a tenth and final child. Mary and the minor children had the roof over their heads and were debt free, but they were essentially penniless. Three of the ten children were provided for—the two eldest sons through their education at law and the eldest daughter through her recent marriage. Two more sons found commissions in 1754 in the provincial forces that fought during the French and Indian War, and both were awarded frontier land grants in 1757. Meanwhile, Mary Biddle struggled to support the remaining five children with the help of her adult offspring by selling maps and prints in Philadelphia. It is difficult from the perspective of two centuries to say how lucrative such a business might have been, but it seems probable that the family was largely dependent on help from the elder children, who "were [all] happy in rendering every assistance in their power." Through the influence of his eldest brother, Edward, young Nicholas found a place as midshipman in the Royal Navy although the relative peace that reigned in Europe at the beginning of the 1770s failed to satisfy his desire for action.[1]

So went the wheel of changing colonial fortunes for many families, spinning through joy and sadness, wealth and poverty, birth and death, war and peace. Because there was no life insurance or Social Security to provide a safety net, colonial men were burdened with the responsibility of providing an estate and accumulating sufficient wealth for the protection of their wives and children.

WEALTH

Almost all the wealth accumulated by years of labor on a farm consisted of livestock, cleared fields, and the improvements to the land such as buildings and fences. While raw land remained cheap in America, cleared land ready for sowing was held at a premium. The wealth of fishermen, hunters, and craftsmen was in their nets and boats, their traps and guns, or the tools of their trade. Their ships, piers, and warehouses often represented the wealth of colonial shippers. Regardless of its source, almost all the wealth of colonial America resided in objects and places rather than in cash money.

Moreover, the wealth generated by trade, merchandising, farming, and handicrafts was not evenly distributed among all Americans. It has been estimated that the average free white person in British North America in 1770 had a net wealth of £74 (sterling). This figure represented only an average distribution across the entire population of 2 million persons of a total value of assets (buildings, farmlands, slaves, livestock, raw materials, ships, cash, and personal belongings) in all the colonies estimated at £150 million. New England residents averaged a mere £33 in personal wealth, those of the middle colonies £51, and those from the agricultural plantations of the south £132. By comparison the far less numerous whites living on the fabulously wealthy sugar plantations of the West Indies averaged £1200 each.[2]

More important, the total wealth of the southern plantations (estimated at £86 million) was four times greater than that of New England (£19 million) and two and half times that of the middle colonies (£30 million). While most of the labor force of the south was composed of slaves, whose value was added to the value of Southern plantations, a much greater proportion of the labor force in the colonies outside the South was composed of free whites whose skills were valuable but unrecorded as assets to the colonial economy. Moreover, much of the tangible wealth in the northern colonies was held by a few fortunate colonial landowners, tradesmen, and shippers, making the average colonial householder a good deal less wealthy than the division of the total wealth in a region by the number of residents would suggest.[3]

Unlike the documentary evidence contained in probate inventories, which largely record the wealth of older white males in the middle and upper classes, excavations of trash pits and dirt-filled cellars in more socially diverse sites from Georgia to New England have produced remarkably parallel results. These investigations suggest that a well-developed consumer economy may have flourished across a wider range of the social spectrum than was formally thought to be the case. For instance, virtually all the pottery fragments, tea sets, chocolate pots, and broken glass bottles uncovered by archaeologists from middle-class privy pits were of either English or German origin, suggesting a vigorous and widespread import economy. Such evidence, if supported by further finds, may force a change in the historical view of colonial economic life.

NEW ENGLAND

From the beginning to the end of the colonial period, the most common occupation for men in British North America was farming. In 1620, the

Pilgrims entered upon an Atlantic shore almost devoid of native inhabitants and dotted with abandoned fields that provided substantial areas for cultivation and grazing without the need to first clear the land of the primeval forest. During the previous decade, epidemic disease had all but eradicated many Native American populations before they had an opportunity to deplete the fields and pastures of their natural fertility. The Pilgrims initially worked this soil in a communal fashion. In the first year of settlement, twenty men and six adolescent boys—using only hoes and shovels—were able to plant enough Indian corn, English peas, and barley to feed the community of approximately one hundred. However, two additional shiploads of colonists arrived from England before the onset of winter with few provisions of their own. This circumstance and a poor harvest of peas and barley caused the entire community to face starvation during the following spring.

Two years of discontent over the continuation of communal farming at Plymouth (the first failure of communal socialism in America) caused the survivors to parcel out the land thereafter in lots of twenty acres. Each person in a family received an allotment, with no family being given more than one hundred acres. The parcels were randomly distributed among the existing fields in long strips, much as yardlands had been assigned in Medieval English villages. Each allotted family tract was assured a frontage on the ocean or on a navigable stream so that small boats and barges could provide transportation. The community livestock (cattle, hogs, chickens, and goats) also was divided, but the pastureland and marshes were kept in common, with sections allotted to individuals for the production of sweet and salt hay.

The modified plan was "hailed as fair by all, and for some time content reigned." Ultimately, the long discontinuous strips of farmland were sold, exchanged, and consolidated into family fields, and the new system of family farming increased productivity. "All hands ... [became] very industrious, so as much more corn was planted than otherwise would have been." Even the women now went willingly into the fields to plant the corn and hoe out the weeds, and they took their little ones with them. The colony's General Court noted that if these women had been compelled to work in the fields, it "would have been thought [a] great tyranny and oppression." As a result of these changes, in 1625 a small amount of excess corn was available to trade for furs with the Indians of Maine. This exchange marked the birth of commercial agriculture in New England, as well as the initiation of an agricultural export trade from the region. Soon the colony was producing enough excess corn not only to trade with the Indians, but also to initiate trade with the Dutch in New Netherlands in exchange for manufactured goods.[4]

The division of land among families and the establishment of a practicable pattern of family farmsteads during the first decades of Puritan colonization set the standard for New England farming thereafter. Herein lay the seeds of wealth accumulation for future generations. By 1638, there were 356 separate fields under cultivation in the Plymouth Colony covering the five square miles between the Kingston River on the north and the Eel River on the south. Yet after ten years of farming experience, the Puritans of Plymouth were still following the Native American system of agriculture, which relied on small hillocks of soil scraped together with a hoe rather than long furrows turned with a plough. "No plow had turned a single furrow … . No power mill had yet sawed a board or ground a grist … . Not a sheep had been shorn, if indeed any had yet arrived."[5]

Few of the initial settlers of Plymouth were seasoned farmers, and the agricultural practices that they followed and farming traditions that they created in this period were shaped largely by practical necessity and by a wholesale adoption of successful Native American techniques. Moreover, they put almost all of their effort into the production of corn, beans, and squash—the "three sisters" of Native American agriculture. The planting of peas continued as did that of barley and hops, which were necessary for making English beer, but other European varieties were largely ignored as native crops displaced them.

During this same period of development, more than 20,000 Puritans—men, women, and children—arrived in New England in one of the great mass migrations of colonial history. All these people needed to be fed either by the work of their own hands or by labor of the existing community of farmers. A few of these new immigrants left the original Plymouth community to form new settlements on the Shawmut Peninsula near Boston, on the open hillsides of Quincy, or on the shore at Salem. To the north, in the region then known as Maine, settlements had expanded to include those at Portsmouth, York, Saco, and Pemaquid. New England with its rocky soil, variable weather, and short growing season proved able, nonetheless, to sustain the needs of this influx of humans. The soil around Boston, in particular, was found to be "kindly, producing every European grain and roots in plenty and perfection besides Indian corn."[6]

Also arriving in great numbers at this time were English varieties of livestock, particularly a large number of hogs, chickens, and goats. The few beef cattle, without good hay being generally available, required much more time and trouble to maintain than the porkers and hens, who could be left to range in the scrub on the margins of the fields. Nonetheless, most families attempted to keep a couple of goats to provide dairy products. Hogs could survive on acorns, nuts, and roots, and would come home to shelter in bad weather to find any feed put out for them. Many families sent their children out in autumn to gather baskets of nuts and acorns to serve as winter feed for their porkers. Moreover, the old boars with their tusks were more than a match for most woodland predators.

Ironically, when Europeans appeared with their cattle, goats, and poultry, the inevitable production of generally defenseless calves, kids, and chicks attracted wolves, bears, and birds of prey from the forests and the skies. Bounties, to be paid by the towns upon presentation of the carcass, were placed on wolves, coyotes, crows, ravens, hawks, and other predators. Israel Putnam, famed as a military leader in the French and Indian Wars and later as a general in the American Revolution, became a local legend in his youth because he killed a particularly bothersome wolf in the colony of Connecticut. From the earliest settlements, a few herds of sheep and goats were kept on deforested islands or other places surrounded by water like long peninsulas where a short section of fencing across the neck could keep them safe. Every shepherd and goatherd was made responsible by law to keep his section of fence in repair.

While goats seem to have been plentiful in the early colonies, for half a century only a minority of the available farm inventories list any sheep at all—an oddity when one considers the usefulness of wool in the cold New England climate. By the 1750s, however, many landowners were counting their herds of sheep in the thousands. Nonetheless, a minister from Rhode Island wrote in 1753, " Wool ... is pretty plentiful where I live ... [but] there is not near enough to make stockings for the inhabitants."[7]

Milk cows and oxen ultimately followed the immigrating throngs with a proportion of two milk cows to every five persons. In the 1740s and 1750s, the number of cattle in New England had also risen appreciably. By the time of the Revolution, the colony of Connecticut had so developed its livestock industry that it was viewed as a major source of beef cattle and hogs for feeding the Continental Army. Thousands of beef cattle and hogs were slaughtered and the meat salted for transportation in barrels to feed Washington's army in Pennsylvania in 1777 and 1778. Many more thousands of animals were driven from New England to the Middle colonies thereafter to make the processing more efficient.[8]

VIRGINIA

In the colonies of the Chesapeake—a generation older than those in New England—a form of English society, drastically simplified and considerably distorted from that to be found across the Atlantic, had become established. Here land took on a wildly inflated value while some human beings were viewed as disposable commodities. Basic political, religious, and cultural institutions so important in England were thoroughly overridden by the promise of quick profits. Nowhere else in the colonies was the rapid accumulation of riches held in such high regard.

In England at the beginning of the 17th century, the labor pool, whether free, slave, or indentured, came from a broad cross section of society, including skilled and unskilled agricultural workers, the old and the young, and men and women. In the Chesapeake of the 1600s, however, white immigrants were predominantly young, male, unskilled, and untrained in farming practices. Immediately upon landing, many of these young men, without the advantage of a supportive family like their counterparts in New England, attempted a reckless and single-minded pursuit of riches, first by scratching about in a vain attempt to find gold and then by undertaking the extensive cultivation of tobacco, for which task they were decidedly ill prepared. Moreover, their relations with the local native nations were contentious to say the least. The Indians might have provided advice and training in effective methods for the production of food, the lack of which caused many early immigrants in Virginia to starve to death. In general it is safe to say that the Virginia colonists, initially fearful of the Indians, ultimately treated the local natives poorly, distrusting them, and behaving in an arrogant and cruel manner toward them. English settlement quickly spread out along the numerous rivers of the region. In response the Powhattan Confederacy launched two massive and devastating attacks in 1622 and 1644 respectively in an attempt to drive the Anglo-Americans from their country. Each raid killed hundreds of colonists and caused many of the English to completely abandon some of their communities.[9]

The short-term subsistence economies of the South were severely challenged under these circumstances. Of the 7,000 English settlers who came to the Chesapeake in the two decades after its founding, only about 1,200 survived their first two years in the region. Many were killed fighting the natives, but most died of disease and starvation. The settlements, unlike those in New England, remained largely dependent on resupply by ships from England, and the time between these voyages could vary from two to six months or more. Only after half a century of less exploitive development did conditions for the English improve substantially. By 1650, the growing population of English in the region made any further attempt by the natives toward their elimination impractical, and the Indians generally retreated to more remote areas to live their lives away from the whites. This circumstance and the increase fostered by the natural abundance of the region initiated the growth of an agricultural export economy and promoted the development of a plantation culture that did not reach its pinnacle until the 19th century. Yet, only small numbers of colonists, possibly less than 10 percent, had a significant financial stake in the plantation economy, with its vast pool of slave laborers. The majority of southern farmers worked their own land and planned their lives around rural activities and seasonal chores. Family members usually cooperated in completing these chores, and this togetherness was thought to foster feelings of kinship and traditional family values. Fathers and mothers worked beside their children and grandchildren in an idyllic, if not a mechanically efficient, simplicity. This situation tended to isolate the wealth of the South in a few hands leaving most southerners less wealthy than the average New Englander.

MIDDLE COLONIES

In the 1680s, William Penn recruited his Quaker population for Pennsylvania with great care, choosing prospective colonists disproportionately from among the Cheshire and Welsh farmsteads of Britain. He could not have found a better group to settle the Pennsylvania frontier than these Quaker farmers. For generations they had successfully carved a living in a difficult foothill environment with windswept, rocky soil and a short growing season. This farming expertise served well in the conditions of Pennsylvania, where the soil was rich and dark, the water clear, the rainfall plentiful, and the growing season ample. The subsequent settlement pattern, agricultural policy, and behavior toward the native population largely reflected the religion, previous training, and experience in agriculture of these settlers. These factors led to the economic dominance of their colony in the 18th century.

The German immigrants to British North America were praised by their 18th-century contemporaries for their "indomitable industry … earnestness … frugality and … consummate agricultural skill" in putting land into commercial production, a tradition believed to be inherited "from thirty generations" of land-cultivators in the Rhineland. In both New York and Pennsylvania, "the soil, though heavily timbered, was fertile and only needed the hand of the patient husbandman in order to bloom as the rose." The Germans certainly seem to have fulfilled this condition admirably. "While their English and Scotch-Irish neighbors usually followed the course of rivers and large streams, thus lessening the labor of clearing, the Germans … would plunge boldly into an unbroken wilderness, often fifty or sixty miles from the nearest habitation, knowing well that where the heaviest forest growth was, there the soil must be good."[10]

Economic, social, and political factors in Scotland created a great exodus of young men and young families to the New World. A combination of geology, marginal soil, and uncertain weather made Scotland a harsh country. Much of Scotland had shallow and acidic soil. "The rocks poke through the worn sleeve of turf; erosion gullies fan downward from the ridges … [and] is in most places—even in the more fertile south and east—a skin over bone." Certainly most Scots were in no position to accumulate wealth in their native country, and they were unusually vulnerable to the consequences of widespread crop failure. Yet most Scots initially found Ireland more convenient than America as a destination, causing the bulk of their migration to the colonies to lag behind that of the English by more than four decades.[11] Once in America, the Scots devised an interesting economic strategy that sought out opportunities on the periphery of the more established settlements where competition from commercial rivals was less intense. For example, those Scots entering the Virginia tobacco trade quickly moved into the backcountry of the Chesapeake, "away from the tidewater districts where London interests were already well entrenched."[12]

The first of two major Scottish settlements was founded in 1682 in present-day South Carolina. The second, and more successful, was founded in 1685 in east New Jersey. Within a few years, nearly 700 families had settled there, and the prosperous colony became a gateway for other Scottish immigrants to America. By the middle of the 18th century, more than 3,000 Scottish Presbyterian families had passed through east New Jersey on their way to the frontier, and they derived economic and religious sustenance from the settlement thereafter. By the time of the Revolution, Scots apparently controlled more than half of the colonial export trade in tobacco, amounting to nearly 25,000 tons annually and an enormous profit for both planters and shippers. With such a flow of capital, planters could purchase tools, slaves, and indentured workers to expand the cultivation of crops, clear virgin land, and erect fences, barns, and houses.[13]

The economic acumen of these Scottish farmers seems implausible on its face, but recent research has uncovered evidence that individual Scots gained administrative and organizational experience through employment by the Dutch East India Company, one of the most sophisticated and cosmopolitan of European economies. The success of the Scottish Livingston family of New York testifies to the strength of this Scottish-Dutch connection and may serve as an example. Robert Livingston, successful transatlantic trader, politician, and owner of vast tracts of land in the Hudson River Valley, began as a merchant in Rotterdam. By marrying into the influential Dutch Schuyler family in New York and maintaining his ties to business connections in Scotland and Holland, he founded a family dynasty that had attained great eminence by the time of the American Revolution.

THE SOUTH

Notwithstanding the successes or failures experienced by disparate ethnic and national groups, agriculture remained the foundation of wealth everywhere in British North America. It came to be practiced across a wide spectrum ranging from small subsistence farming in New England and on the frontiers to the great commercial plantations of the South, with their wealth-producing surplus of agricultural exports. Disentangling the farm labor system from this network of diverse agricultural establishments can be difficult. Some men in the Chesapeake, with superior resources or better connections, acquired substantial holdings spread over a thousand acres, but New England maintained a more settled appearance, much like that of an English country village. In any case, the agricultural skills of colonials in all regions of British North America were not highly differentiated. Farm workers were often segregated from their landowning contemporaries only by their legal status as indentured workers, hirelings, or slaves.

Nowhere was personal wealth so conspicuously portrayed or the equality between men so completely enforced than in their ability to force others to work for them. Although there were large numbers of slaves on the major plantations in the South, most farms in British North America had only a few hired laborers and no slaves at all. These farms were generally small family operations that could be cultivated by a father, a mother, and a few older children. English and Quaker farmers rarely owned slaves, and Dutch farmsteads in New York, although likely to contain a slave or an indentured servant, rarely had more than one. Small farmers seldom owned slaves, but they may have harbored a desire to accumulate enough money to buy one. The ownership of even a single slave, or the employment of hired workers or indentured servants, raised

Wealthy plantation owners did not get their hands dirty. They used hired men, indentured servants, or slaves to do their work.

a family to a new social status. Yet the price of slaves was so high that few small farmers could afford to buy one, and indentured servants and hirelings could be difficult, contrary, and demanding.

While the sugar plantations of the Caribbean used hundreds of slaves during the 18th century, fewer than 10 percent of the plantations on the mainland in the same period had more than a few dozen slaves. Such establishments were rather the product of the 19th century when the extensive cultivation of cotton dominated southern agriculture. In the colonial era, slave owners in British North America represented as little as 6 percent of the total white population. Half of these were small freeholders who had fewer than five slaves and labored in the fields beside them.[14]

REAL ESTATE

One objective of most colonial fathers was to establish their families as landowners by building up their farms and endowing land to their children during their lifetimes. A free white immigrant with little money could obtain a good deal of land in British North America through the *headright,* an allotment of land based on the number of people in a household, including slaves and servants. This system was usually sponsored either by the colonial governments themselves to increase settlement or by agents of the land speculation companies to which land had been granted. Under the concept of headright, some colonies allowed a freeholder to claim up to 150 acres of land for himself, a similar amount for his wife and children, 20 acres for each male slave, and 10 acres for each female slave in his household. Headrights were often extended to indentured servants after they had served their time. The limits of these allowances seem to have become smaller as the 18th century progressed. Although historians are unsure how the headright system operated, it seems to have been effective—despite a good deal of corruption—in getting land into private hands.[15]

While a handful of Quaker and German farms reached 1,000 acres, the majority were between 100 and 400 acres. A good 100-acre farmstead with dark rich soil could be had for £10 in 1730 and was worth approximately £120 three decades later. Importantly, the tax paid to the colony remained as little as 1 percent of the land value. Most German fathers divested their land during their lifetimes on their children when they married or when they reached their majority; but they tried to maintain a "home place" within the family by acquiring land for divestiture to their sons and daughters in the vicinity of their own farmsteads. All deeds for land ownership were in the name of the husband. Most German men devolved the "home place" into the hands of a son—often the youngest son—on the event of their own death. This was a throwback to European inheritance practices that were especially common among those landholders living on the margins of the Alpine foothills. German fathers also partitioned land for their daughters (in their husband's name) and sometimes for their male grandchildren, often on condition that the children would care for their parents or their wives in their old age.

Durs Thommen, having immigrated to Pennsylvania in 1736, wrote home to the villagers of Niederdorf, commending the abundant, affordable, and fertile land, praising the low taxes and rents, and generally describing how well Germans were doing in the colony. His description suggests why so many of his fellows took the risk of coming to America.

I took a [farmstead] with about 435 acres, two houses and barns, and have, believe it or not, 6 horses, 2 colts, 15 cattle, and about 35 sacks of oats, 46 sacks of wheat, 25 sacks of rye, and 23 sacks of corn. For all this land I have to pay no more than 7 shillings ... for tithes, quitrents, and other dues. In this country there are abundant liberties in just about all matters.[16]

Free landowners in the southern colonies at the beginning of the 18th century made up 11 percent of the population. One third of these held more than 350 acres of land, and a mere handful of great landowners controlled more than 1,000 acres each. Two-thirds of all farms were less than 350 acres before 1750. Many of these small landowners aspired to raise their standard of living at the expense of black labor, and all free white southerners were reared in an atmosphere that supported a reasonable expectation that they could themselves become substantial slave owners. By draining swamps, manuring their fields, and planting cash crops they hoped to increase their incomes to the point that might afford the purchase of a slave or two. Thereafter the yeoman farmer hoped to capitalize on his newfound status as part of the slaveholding gentry and he hoped to stabilize his family's social position by marrying his daughters above their former social station.

New England farmers found it difficult to add to their acreage, especially in the coastal regions. The rocky soil and broken terrain made the development of new acreage suitable for farming very difficult. This forced families to seek additional land to disperse to their children many days' journey away from their initial holdings. Although coastal cities grew during the 18th century, it may have been for this reason that the proportion of the colonial population that lived in rural areas actually increased from 1700 to 1775. The maintenance of this movement from urban areas to rural ones can also be attributed in part to the regular migration of recently arrived Europeans to the agricultural frontier.[17]

Settlers in the backcountry added new acreage to their farmsteads each year by clearing the land. Those considered the most able farmers cleared the land by cutting down all the trees in early summer, hauling off the valuable logs, and leaving the least valuable wood and branches on the ground until the following spring. This was scavenged for firewood

The process of surveying the land was important. Even on plantations encompassing thousands of acres, unambiguous boundaries were important in forming a peaceful and orderly society.

during the winter, and the leavings were burned in the early spring to complete the clearing. The burning left a layer of fine ash to fertilize and soften the ground between the remaining stumps. Thereafter the stumps were usually allowed to rot of their own accord, but they could be pulled after a few years with the help of a team of oxen. Once the stumps were removed the rocks and boulders could be dragged to the edges of the field on a sledge and dumped. In the winter these stones could be made up into orderly walls for the enclosure of sheep or cattle, but only on the oldest farms were stonewalls laid up in this manner. Such "sweat equity" allowed a competent farmer to add about two acres of newly cleared land each year to their family estate.

Increased ownership of property was a preliminary goal of most families, but making the land productive was the ultimate objective of most landowners. Indian corn was usually planted in a new field, which was commonly prepared by the use of a hoe alone. The hoe and the ax were the most widely used farm implements. The plow could be driven through the open ground between the stumps or in meadows, but it was not generally used until the majority of the stumps, roots, and rocks were removed. The average farmer tended about 18 acres of crops on a 100-acre farm. The acreage not put directly into crop production was used as pasture and woodlots or left as fallow ground to recuperate from several seasons of over-farming. The concept of crop rotation had not yet been recognized as a active method of improving the soil. Additionally small kitchen-garden plots, which included a variety of herbs and greens, surrounded the family home. John Sherman, an Ohio senator speaking in 1890 at a remembrance of colonial times described the lot of the frontier farmer. "The deadening of trees, their gradual falling, the logging and burning, the clearing, the rude plowing amidst the stumps and roots— what exciting, toilsome times! Custom made the solitude and independence of their life, happiness."[18]

THE AGRICULTURAL MARKET

Historians tend to speak of agriculture in the colonial period as consisting mostly of subsistence farmers living hand to mouth from year to year, but this view of the Anglo-American farm economy may be oversimplified or even distorted. A man wielding an ax on the frontier could turn trees into lumber or firewood, and a single well-aimed musketball could bring down a month's meat in the forest. In this way, a man could provide a subsistence living for himself and a small family. Yet a more enterprising farmer might make a few pounds each winter season by selling deerskins and furs at the trading post or by splitting out roofing shingles and cutting firewood for sale in the towns. From this he could clothe his family in something other than animal skins and buy improved farm implements to ease his labor during the next farming season.

A better term than subsistence farming might be self-sufficient farming. Although survival was the initial goal of all colonial farmers, had it been their sole objective, they could have stayed in Europe and dispensed with a dangerous and time-consuming ocean voyage and a dislocation from familiar surroundings, family, and friends. On the contrary, as the seasons and years passed, colonial farmers attempted to put more land under cultivation and to sell at least some of their farm produce for cash. Nonetheless, most residents of frontier communities, scraping a living from among the stumps of the newly cleared forests, would not realize a surplus of agricultural produce for decades.

Given the uncertainties of drought, frost, wind, insects, and other circumstances that could critically damage agricultural yield, colonial farmers seem to have been a conservative lot. Their farming practices, especially in the early colonial period, often came under the negative scrutiny of their contemporaries. The common colonial farmer was severely criticized for following the agricultural methods of his forefathers, especially by proponents of the novel concepts of scientific agriculture. Samuel Deane noted, "Farmers do many things for which they can assign no other reason than custom. They usually give themselves

little or no trouble in thinking, or in examining their methods of agriculture, which have been handed down from father to son, from time
immemorial." Thomas Jefferson complained, "The aim of the farmers
of this country ... is not to make the most they can from the land, which
is, or has been cheap, but the most of the labour, which is dear, the consequence of which has been, much ground has been scratched over and
none cultivated or improved as it ought to have been."[19]

A number of factors influenced farmers with regard to their choice
of what crops to grow or livestock to raise for commercial purposes.
The needs of the people in the community or nearby town were high
among these, but the farmer's estimate of what might be bought for
resale or export was equally important. The agents of merchants at a
coastal seaport, in the West Indies, or even in Europe could influence
the price paid for agricultural produce. Market prices, however, seem
to have played only a small part in the business decisions made by most
colonial farmers because it was almost impossible to pre-determine
their level at the time of planting. Most farmers hoped only that there
would be a demand for their products at the time of harvest so that
their labor would not go to waste. However, evidence suggests that
farmers often responded to the arrival of additional children by placing more land under cultivation or by investing in new equipment and
livestock.[20] These steps not only allowed the farmer to isolate himself
and his family somewhat from actual want but also from the vagarities
of the agricultural market.

We know from probate inventories that even subsistence farmers
invested heavily in agricultural equipment, but we also know that few
families achieved total self-sufficiency without requiring help from their
neighbors or the wider community. Evidence suggests that at least one
quarter of the income of the average Anglo-American farmer was spent
on goods and consumables manufactured elsewhere.[21] While a family
might spin a few fathoms of woolen yarn and turn it into still fewer
yards of broadcloth, almost all the woolen material used by American
colonists came from British mills. Governor William Tyron of New York
flatly declared that "eleven twelfths of the population ... are clothed
in British manufactures."[22] Among the farming implements listed in a
single family inventory from 1735 are two wagons, a plow with two irons,
two mauls, three iron splitting wedges, four hoes, a spade, a shovel, a
mattock, three dung forks, two broadaxes, a joiner's ax, a joiner's
adze, an undisclosed number ("sundry") of additional carpenter's and
joiner's tools, seven scythes, five sickles, two cutting knives, three fell-
ing axes, and assorted chains, hooks, and harness. All these items were
either brought to Pennsylvania from Europe or accumulated in the
colonies in the course of just twenty-five years, attesting somewhat to
the "rapidity with which the new settlers became prosperous" if they
applied themselves.[23]

THE COIN SHORTAGE

Family wealth rarely took the form of cash or currency. Children often inherited the increase provided by the investments and holdings of their parents in the form of a line of credit against which they might charge their purchases with local merchants and tradespersons. The colonies had always suffered a severe shortage of hard currency, and it affected the daily lives of the people in many ways. It would be an error to underestimate the importance of this circumstance. Even the simplest of everyday commercial transactions was made difficult by the shortage of coins. Individuals and families with good credit could run up annual accounts with local merchants, but most laborers, farm workers, and travelers were required to pay in cash.

To help relieve the coin shortage, bar silver was sometimes chopped into small wafers called cobs, which were weighed on a scale to determine their value. Silver coins were literally cut into pieces to create smaller denominations. The silver Spanish dollar, worth eight reales, was conveniently

Fathers cleared the primeval forests an acre at a time and planted crops between the tree stumps in the hope of leaving a legacy for their children

sliced into eight wedges like pieces of a pie. Half-coin pieces, quarter pieces, and one-eighth "bits" were commonly used in trade, passing at full value with little regard to any irregularities in their shape. Many shopkeepers resorted to producing wooden tokens and paper coupons, which were given in lieu of change to their customers. Cash was so scarce that the colonial legislatures regularly accepted tobacco bonds and other promissory notes, based on future agricultural production, for the payment of taxes. Furs, tobacco leaves, potash, cattle, ears of corn, and skeins of wool, known as "country money," became the equivalent of legal tender. Even the lead musket ball passed in Massachusetts for a time as the legal equivalent of a farthing (1/4 penny) "providing that no man be compelled to take more than 12 pence of them at a time."[24]

Conscious of the chronic shortage of metal coins, the Crown allowed the colonies to mint their own. Massachusetts produced two remarkable issues, one marked with "NE" and one known as the Pine Tree Shilling. Maryland issued many quality coins, including shillings, sixpence, groats, and pennies. Most other colonial coins were poorly wrought, of limited issue, and so easily counterfeited that they circulated under a cloud of suspicion.

In 1749, Parliament tried to relieve the cash shortage by granting Massachusetts a payment of more than £175 thousand in coins for its expenses in capturing the French fortress at Louisburg four years earlier. The payment came in the form of 650,000 ounces of Spanish silver coins and nine tons of copper half-penny and two-farthing pieces. The colonial office in London also introduced thousands of copper coins into the middle and southern colonies in 1754. These were sacked, boxed, and shipped at a cost to the government of six percent of their face value. The coins were immediately absorbed into the colonial economy, but like water in a sponge they disappeared with time. The excessive expense of shipping the coins prohibited further shipments. The colonials themselves were largely at fault for removing hard currency from circulation. Coins from England were hoarded, hidden behind wallboards, or buried in gardens by apprehensive and economically unsophisticated colonials.

SPOON SILVER

Metal coins meant to facilitate commerce were equally well suited for the casting of heavily taxed household items, and they could be melted down to provide metal for flatware, tea services, candlesticks, and ornaments. Craftsmen, utilizing the fiction that they were recasting scrap, charged their customers a weight of coins to be used as a raw material in manufacturing an item while keeping the excess as compensation for their labor and skill. So common was this practice that the term *spoon silver* was used to describe certain specie coins. Copper coins, melted down and alloyed with zinc, were recast as brass candlesticks, door-knockers, and other ornaments that would have required the payment of a duty if imported directly from Britain.

Silver coins were sometimes shaved, clipped, or otherwise debased. The practice of scraping precious metal from the face and reverse of specie coins was called shaving, while removing metal from the edge was called clipping. Some coins, like the Spanish dollar, had a complex face pattern in high relief and minute ridges milled on their edges to prevent shaving and clipping. The ridges also made counterfeiting particularly difficult. Nonetheless, many genuine coins were melted down, debased by adding tin or lead to the molten metal, and restruck by counterfeiters. Not all the counterfeit coins were discernible from true currency. Many Americans, especially those in the frontier regions, rarely handled hard money and had difficultly detecting fakes, especially among unfamiliar foreign coins.[25]

This photograph shows a sampling of coins (replicas) that freely circulated in colonial America.

MONEY MATTERS

The metal currency of many countries circulated in the colonies. To the standard English shillings (s) in silver, and copper pence (d), half-pence (1/2d), and farthings (1/4d) were added Irish coins of similar denominations and composition. The foreign coins in circulation included French guineas and sous, Dutch gilders, Swedish rixdalers, Venetian sequins, and Spanish dollars (pieces of eight). Silver was the standard, but coins made of gold were also available. These included English sovereigns, crowns, and Lion dollars; French Louis d'Ors and double Louis d'Ors (doubloons); Spanish pistoles; and Portuguese Johannes. "Each gold piece was weighed separately and no two of the same nominal value were [ever] rated alike."[26] The nominal value of these coins in English money varied, but the approximate values were as follows: English sovereigns (20s), crowns (10s), and Lion dollars (120s); French Louis d'Ors (24s); double Louis d'Or (48s); Spanish pistoles (12s 3d); and Portuguese Johannes (36s).

As long as silver circulated freely most other metal coins maintained their value regardless of their origin. Ironically, the value of the English shilling seems to have varied more from province to province in America than that of the Spanish dollar. Thereby the exquisitely minted silver Spanish dollar, produced in Mexico and Central America, quickly became the standard for colonial currency. The Spanish dollar was available through trade with the West Indies, and it was freely spent by pirates and privateers in New York and New England, where the merchants were all too glad to receive hard cash with no questions asked about its source.[27]

LAWFUL MONEY

In all the colonies, monetary accounts, debts, and public finances were kept in the standard English pounds (£) of 20 shillings (s) of 12 pence (d) each. Because there was no one pound coin, it remained a simple accounting unit. The constantly changing value of silver made bookkeeping difficult, and it also rewarded colonists with an increasing wealth if they hoarded silver shillings and dollars rather than spending them. The desire to accumulate silver caused the specie coins to increase in value with respect to the paper accounts. The government in London tried to solve this problem by fixing the value of silver by law. Sterling silver dollars could pass at no more than 6s, and accounts based on this value were known as *lawful money*—a term that appears in many contracts, indentures, wills, and commercial documents from the period.

Nonetheless, the value of the silver dollar continued to fluctuate in the colonies until mid-century, when it leveled off for several years at the equivalent of 4s 6d English sterling. By 1750, New England and the southern colonies were valuing their own accounts at 6s per Spanish dollar, the middle colonies of Maryland, Pennsylvania, Delaware, and New Jersey at 7s 6d, and New York at 8s. These exchange rates for the Spanish dollar continued in force until the eve of the Revolution. Thereafter the official currency became the Continental dollar, but foreign and English money continued to be widely used.[28]

Merchants, shippers, lenders, and tax officials constantly referred to vast tables of equivalents to calculate the exchange value of commercial and public accounts in English currency. These exchange tables were usually available to the public in almanacs. The value of cargoes, contracts, insurance, and such were thereby made victim to the most recent tables available, and could change from port to port. If a parent left a sum of lawful money to a child in his will, the amount awarded to the child by the probate court might be higher or lower due to fluctuations in colonial currency. A contemporary observer noted of the monetary system, "You will not wonder that there was confusion worse confounded."[29]

PAPER MONEY

The colonial governments substituted paper currency, each of their own devising, in an attempt to solve the problems caused by a lack of coins. Maryland produced the best form of paper currency before the revolution. The sterling silver conversions for a Maryland dollar were clearly printed on its reverse using symbols for crowns, shillings, and pence that aided in its circulation and helped to maintain its value. The 1767 Maryland issue, designed with the help of Benjamin Franklin, became the basis for the new Continental currency issued in 1776.

The value of paper currency varied from colony to colony. As long as the specie coins circulated freely, the paper maintained its value. As the coins disappeared from circulation, as they did during a war or other time of crisis, the paper currency depreciated. The value of the paper usually reflected that of the Spanish dollar. In mid-century, £100 sterling silver in London was worth £160 in local paper currency in New York and New Jersey, £170 in Pennsylvania, £200 in Maryland, £800 in South Carolina and Georgia, and £1,400 in North Carolina.[30]

COUNTERFEITING

Compared with coins, paper issues were easy to counterfeit. A particularly good counterfeit issue in Virginia almost brought the economy of the colony to a complete halt as apprehensive colonials refused all currency for a time and accepted only bartered items. The laws against counterfeiting varied from province to province. In New York, counterfeiting was punishable by death, while in neighboring Connecticut, the crime drew only a fine. The British authorities in London, believing that control and regulation could solve the currency problem, declared all paper currency illegal in America in 1756. This prohibition did not remove the paper currency then circulating in the colonies, however. The colony least affected by this legislation was Massachusetts, which had retired all its paper money before its passage.

CONSUMER ECONOMICS

The traditional view, espoused by 19th-century historians and well-meaning docents at historic sites, of the lower classes dressed solely in coarse homespun or animal skins and consistently eating from wooden trenchers or lead-pewter plates—the poor man's silver—may need revision. What may have been true for backwoods settlers in the early years of settlement is not necessarily accurate for the colonial family after generations of building, development, and hard work.[31]

In the decades just prior to the American Revolution, in particular, there seems to have been a great increase in consumerism among all the colonial social classes, but there also seems to have been a sharp deterioration of the standard of living among free laborers. Rising inflation, increased taxes, and stricter enforcement of labor and trade regulations caused a large number of urban workers to migrate to the agricultural frontier to find a better and richer life. This gave added importance to the role of the farmer in the colonial economy, and it slowed the development of labor-intensive colonial industries somewhat. A slower pace of wealth accumulation may have resulted, especially in urban New England. This probably contributed to the general dissatisfaction with the mercantile economy of the British Empire among many in the working class.[32]

NOTES

1. T. M. Devine, *Scotland's Empire and the Shaping of the Americas, 1600–1815* (Washington: Smithsonian Books, 2003), 33.

2. John J. McCusker and Russell R. Menard, *The Economy of British America, 1607–1789* (Chapel Hill: University of North Carolina Press, 1991), 61.

3. Ibid., 61.

4. Howard S. Russell, *A Long, Deep Furrow: Three Centuries of Farming in New England* (Hanover: University Press of New England, 1982), 8–9.

5. Ibid., 10.

6. Lord Adam Gordon, quoted in ibid., 69.

7. Quoted in Russell, *A Long, Deep Furrow*, 85.

8. Ibid., 50.

9. See Noel Ivor Hume, *Martin's Hundred* (Charlottesville: University of Virginia Press, 1979).

10. Oscar Kuhns, *The German and Swiss Settlements of Colonial Pennsylvania: A Study of the So-Called Pennsylvania Dutch* (New York: Henry Holt, 1901), 85–86.

11. Devine, *Scotland's Empire and the Shaping of the Americas*, 15.

12. Ibid., 34.

13. Ibid., 70.

14. David Brion Davis, *Slavery in the Colonial Chesapeake* (Williamsburg: Colonial Williamsburg Foundation, 1994), 5.

15. McCusker and Menard, *The Economy of British America*, 334.

16. Quoted in Aaron Spencer Fogleman, *Hopeful Journeys: German Immigration, Settlement, and Political Culture in Colonial America, 1717–1775* (Philadelphia: University of Pennsylvania Press, 1996), 33.

17. McCusker and Menard, *The Economy of British America*, 32–33.

18. Quoted in Emanuel Spenser, "Glimpses of Log-Cabin Life in Early Ohio," *Magazine of American History* 24 (August 1890): 111.

19. Quoted in McCusker and Menard, *The Economy of British America*, 305–6.

20. Ibid., 256n.

21. ibid., 301.

22. T. H. Breen, *The Marketplace of Revolution: How Consumer Politics Shaped American Independence* (New York: Oxford University Press, 2004), 37.

23. From the inventory of Andrew Ferree of Lancaster County, Pennsylvania, in Oscar Kuhns, *The German and Swiss Settlements of Colonial Pennsylvania*, 87–88n.

24. Quoted in Beth Gilgun, "Money in the Colonies," in *Tidings from the Eighteenth Century* (Texarkana, TX: Surlock, 1993), 216.

25. Ibid., 218–19.

26. Helen Evertson Smith, *Colonial Days and Ways, as Gathered from Family Papers* (New York: Century, 1901), 343.

27. The Spanish dollar remained legal tender in the United States until 1857. The dollar sign ($), an *S* crossed by two parallel vertical lines, may symbolize the two vine-covered columns that appear on the Spanish milled dollar.

28. The British pound (£) was not actually a coin but an accounting unit. Expressed in terms of pounds sterling, the exchange rates of colonial money would be £1 (240d) British = £1 6s 8d (320d) MA = £1 13s 4d (400d) PA = £1 15s 7d (427d) NY.

29. Quoted in Gilgun, "Money in the Colonies," 217.

30. Eric Robson, *The American Revolution in Its Political and Military Aspects, 1763–1783* (New York: W. W. Norton, 1966), 7.

31. Breen, *The Marketplace of Revolution*, 50–51.

32. McCusker and Menard, *The Economy of British America*, 250.

Part III
The Role of Mother

9

Women as Wives

If ever two were one, then surely we.
If ever man were lov'd by wife, then thee.
If ever wife was happy in a man.
Compare with me ye women if you can.
— Anne Bradstreet, "To My Dear and Loving Husband"

When it came to choosing a wife, a man searched for a woman with a good disposition and a virtuous demeanor. Certainly, a pretty woman was desirable, but given the demographics of the time, physical beauty was probably a secondary consideration. Men outnumbered women in 17th-century settlements, a situation that continued into the 18th century and persisted even longer on the frontier. After the death of his wife in 1732, Thomas Clap, a minister in Windham, Connecticut, recorded these thoughts about his selection of a spouse. "I thought I wanted one near friend and acquaintance, that should be another self and help-mate for me. Among all the qualifications of an agreeable consort, I seemed more especially to have in my view these two viz. a steady serene and pleasant natural temper, and true piety: For these two qualifications seemed most directly to conduce my real comfort, contentment and happiness both in this world and that which is to come."[1]

J. Hector St. John de Crevecoeur seems to have been equally fortunate in finding a wife that met his needs. Few colonial diaries reveal the personal side of a marriage relationship. Most evidence of colonial devotion and tenderness has to be gleaned from affectionate greetings or brief expressions of longing found in letters of separated couples. Fortunately, de Crevecoeur provides this brief glimpse into his relationship with his wife:

[M]y wife rendered my house all at once cheerful and pleasing; it no longer appeared gloomy and solitary as before; when I went to work ... my wife would often come with her knitting in hand and sit under the shady tree, praising the straightness of my furrows and the docility of my horses; this swelled my heart and made everything light and pleasant, and I regretted that I had not married before.... [W]hen I contemplate my wife, by my fireside, while she either spins, knits darns or suckles our child, I cannot describe the various emotions of love, of gratitude, of conscious pride, which thrill my heart.[2]

Naturally, some men sought a woman who came with a dowry or an annual allowance. Such a quest might even be inspired by a young man's family hoping to improve its own situation with a judicious union. Generally, once a woman married all of her property and money came under the control of her husband. Under English law marriage converted a woman to a *femme covert* or "woman covered." As such she was denied the right to make decisions regarding her economic situation, restricted in the dispersal of material wealth and lost control of all her possessions, including her clothing, and person to her husband. The realities of colonial law in most places permitted women more freedom than the common law of England. While a husband may have controlled all of the financial assets of the family, a wife was expected to manage the household and to care for the children within the bounds that he set.

A good wife was expected to provide her mate with material, spiritual, emotional, and sexual comforts. She was expected to obey her husband, but the obedience was not the same as that expected of a child to a parent or of a servant to a master. Affection and mutual respect tempered obedience into support. Minister, Samuel Willard explained the unique relationship between husband and wife saying, "[O]f all the orders which are unequal, these do come nearest to equality, and in several respects they stand upon even ground. These do make a pair, which infers ... a parity. They are, in the word of God, called yoke fellows and so are drawn together in the yoke. Nevertheless, God hath also made an imparity between them ... and for that reason there is a subordination and they are ranked among unequals."[3] He later explains, "The submission ... is not to be measured by the notation or import of the word itself but by the quality of the relation to which it is applied."[4] Similarly, Benjamin Wadsworth, in detailing the duties of husbands and wives, wrote, "Wives are part of the house and family and ought to be under a husband's government .... [T]hough he governs her he must not treat her as a servant, but as his own flesh, he must love her as himself."[5]

Men and women in colonial times spent most of their time living and working side by side. In the close quarters of New England homes men

Outdoor markets were much more common in colonial times than they are today. Many women and young girls worked in the market stalls to earn a little more money for the family. For the customers like those pictured here, market days could be turned into family outings.

directed hired help, made deals with neighbors and entered into many business dealings amid the bustle of daily home life. Wives and even older daughters were often present for these transactions and gained a great deal of knowledge of the family's business dealings. Wives were called upon to testify in court to debts that were owed their husbands. In many cases they became a living record of a family's economic history. Salem court records identify one wife as not only present for a land deal but as actually "furthering the sale."[6] Wives were expected to help in the economic affairs of her husband, acting as his representative or even his surrogate, if a situation warranted it. Wadsworth advised spouses to "unite their prudent counsels and endeavors comfortably to maintain themselves and family under their joint care."[7] Ben Franklin wrote to his wife as he set sail for England, "I leave home and undertake this long voyage more cheerful, as I can rely on your prudence in the management of my affairs; and education of my dear child."[8]

Since the wife was the one to almost always be at home, she often had to direct workers or settle with creditors. She could cross over into her husband's world without staking claim to it. She was merely acting on his behalf. Moses Gillman of New Hampshire wrote to his wife from Boston in the late 17th century:

Loving wife Elizabeth Gillman these are to desire you to speak to John Gillman and James Perkins and so order the matter that Mr. Tho. Woodbridge may have twelve thousand feet of merchantable boards rafted by Thursday night or sooner if possible they can for I have absolutely sold them to him and if John Clough['s] son or any other do deliver boards to make up the sum give receipts of what you receive of him or any other man and let nobody be pressed or other ways disposed of until I return.[9]

In 1674, Henry Dering of New Jersey was given a letter in which he was given the power of attorney to collect the debts due Peter Lidget of Boston. On the reverse of the document Dering wrote, " I Henry Dering , have and do hereby constitute, ordain and appoint my loving wife, Anne Dering, my lawful attorney" to collect and sue for Lidget's debts.[10] Anne Devorix supervised spring planting of the family corn and protected the hogsheads, barrels, and flakes at the shore from the encroachment of a neighbor while her fisherman husband was at sea. In coastal communities where fishing and shipping kept husbands away from home for extended periods of time, it was quite commonplace for wives to transact much of the family's business. This sometimes led to odd situations such as when Elizabeth Holmes and Patience Marston, both acting as attorneys for their husbands, the commander and owner of a ship, respectively, settled the accounts between the men related to the voyage.[11] An 18th century journalist wrote of the Nantucket whaling community:

As the sea excursions are often very long, [the] wives in their [husbands'] absence are necessarily obliged to transact business, to settle accounts, and in short, to rule and provide for their families. These circumstances, being often repeated, give women the ability as well as a taste for that kind of superintendency, to which, by their prudence and good management, they seem to be in general very equal. This employment ripens their judgment and justly entitles them to a rank superior to that of other wives.[12]

Many husbands came to rely on their wives' skills. Sewall reported in his diary "gave my Wife the rest of my cash £4 3s 8s and tell her she shall now keep the cash; if I want I will borrow of her. She has a better faculty than I at managing affairs: I will assist her."[13] The daily routines and tasks of a husband and a wife may have been distinct, but they worked toward a common goal, the well-being of the family. A husband and wife, and in fact all family members, were interdependent.

While the primary obligation of the wife was to the household, she was expected to do whatever was needed. It was common for the wife of a shopkeeper or tradesman to work side by side with her spouse in the retail establishment. The wife of a weaver might wind the quills for him.

A farmer's wife worked in the fields at critical times, such as planting or harvesting. Salem court records attest to wives winnowing corn, branding steers, and tending cattle.[14] John Gow and his wife practiced a trade together, announcing in the *South Carolina Gazette* their services as stay-makers and mantua makers.[15] Some women ran businesses in their own right, often adding their advertisements as postscripts to notices posted for their husband's businesses. George Charleton advertised in a 1738 edition of the *Virginia Gazette* that "gentlemen may have clothes made, after the newest and most fashionable manner." Beneath this advertisement ran, "N.B. His wife is a mantua-maker, and offers her service, in that way of business, to the ladies, whom she will undertake to oblige, with the newest and genteelest fashions now wore in England, and at reasonable rates." John Thompson gave notice in a 1776 edition of the *South Carolina and American General Gazette* of his service as umbrella maker and of his wife's as milliner and mantua maker. Not all couples were in complementary businesses, however. Following the advertisement in a 1747 edition of the *South Carolina Gazette* for his "school for young gentlemen," Charles Walker Fortescue announced, "All gentlewomen who may be pleased to employ the above subscriber's wife, in the business of mantua-making, etc. shall be served in the most elegant, new and modish manner." William Trueman tendered his services to write deeds, settle accounts, and sell goods on commission and announced that his wife, Elizabeth, was available to make "mantuas, mantulets, velvet hoods, caps and hats."[16]

Some women built a reputation for quality merchandise through their own efforts. Frances Swallow's advertisements in the *South Carolina Gazette* for her millinery shop featured her name in large type while that of her merchant husband, Newman Swallow, appeared as a small postscript to her notice. Two years later, she proclaimed herself "a sole dealer." In 1770, she announced the opening of a boarding school but promised that she would continue her millinery services. Despite all this business activity, Frances was the mother of six children.[17] Sarah Pitt, the wife of Dr. George Pitt, kept a stylish shop in Williamsburg. On her death in 1772, the *Virginia Gazette* eulogized her as "a lady whose virtues through every varied scene of private life did honor to the principles she professed ... whose bosom was tremblingly alive to every tender sentiment of connubial and maternal affection [and who] discharged the duties of wife and mother in such a distinguished manner as must make her revered, and her loss forever regretted."[18]

An 18th-century diarist wrote glowingly of the accomplishments of one Nantucket wife:

The richest person now in the island owes all his present prosperity and success to the ingenuity of his wife; this is a well known fact which is well recorded, for while he was performing his first cruises, she traded pins and needles and kept a school. Afterward she purchased more considerable articles, which she sold with so much judgment that she laid the foundation of a system of business that she has ever since prosecuted with equal dexterity and success. She wrote to London, formed connections, and, in short, became the only ostensible instrument of that house.[19]

During the American Revolution, many wives had to take over the management of family affairs and businesses when their husbands went to fight. Lois Peters and her husband, Nathan, corresponded while Nathan served. Lois did whatever she could to continue Nathan's leather business while caring for their child and maintaining the household. Nathan attempted to direct Lois through his letters but with the inefficient way mail was transported, his counsel did not always reach her in a timely fashion, leaving Lois to do her best.

Although many colonial women appear to be independent, under English law, their status and authority was derived solely from their husbands. In an argument with her second husband, Henry Shelborne, Sarah Shelborne demanded to know why he "trod upon Walter Abbott's floor" and bid him "get out." The home in which they resided had come to them following the death of her first husband, Walter Abbott. Despite his passing, she still considered the home his, not hers.[20]

Many residents of the middle colonies came from Germany, Holland, or Sweden rather than a culture governed by English custom. Under Dutch law a woman maintained both legal identity and financial control in marriage. Marriage was a partnership of equals and as such the two were equally responsible guardians of the family wealth. Dutch spouses had equal claim to their initial combined wealth as well as to any wealth amassed during the marriage.

Margaret Hardenbroeck was an established merchant of New Netherlands who traded pins, cooking oil, and vinegar for furs when she met and married her husband, Peter DeVries, who dealt in lumber, paper, bricks, tobacco, sugar, wine and prunes. Margaret continued her business dealings after her marriage and even after the birth of her daughter. When her husband died, Margaret inherited his property and business. She remarried within two years to Frederick Philipsen, a carpenter. The Philipsens, husband and wife, became business partners expanding their enterprises to include property acquisition and the establishment of a transatlantic packet line. When the English took control of the colony in 1664, Frederick Philipsen swore allegiance to the English king and anglicized his name to Philipse. Margaret, however, felt the change more deeply. She became subject to the limitations English law placed upon married women. Margaret could continue to act as an agent for Frederick, but she could no longer give him her power of attorney because she had no power to give. She was no longer able to own property in her own name. Margaret and Frederick continued to prosper, but Margaret was no longer his equal under the law. She continued her business dealings in the name of her husband as his agent rather than as his partner.

On the death of a spouse, the surviving partner in a Dutch marriage inherited half the entire estate and had the right to administer the other half for the heirs. Dutch widows were not simply custodians of their husband's estate, they were heirs. As in marriage, Dutch widows could conduct all kinds of business transactions, buying and selling their property. They were free to determine their heirs and dispose of their property as they saw fit.

Quaker women enjoyed a unique kind of autonomy in their community. Quaker men and women organized themselves separately in monthly meetings. The men discussed land purchases, legal matters, business ventures and male conduct. Women did not deal with such worldly matters but they did serve as a vehicle for training and if necessary, disciplining wives and mothers. Women's groups were responsible for approving the applications for marriage within their community. Quaker wives rarely handled money or managed the revenue their home manufacturers brought to their family and were generally removed from economic concerns. In widowhood, Quaker women had less autonomy than either their

Both mother and father took responsibility for the formation of their children's character. It was often the mother who tempered the harsher realities of life for her brood.

Dutch or English counterparts. Male co-executors limited the widow's actions and male trustees guided the administration of the estate. Even the widow's guardianship of her own minor children was supervised. She was expected to submit a complete and detailed accounting for all money spent on basic necessities as well as education. Quaker widows could not sell any land without convincing the court that the estate or revenue generated from the estate were insufficient to pay their debts or support the family.

In English law, the death of the male head of the household legally meant the dissolution of the family. The archaic term, *relict*, used in reference to his survivor, paints a very accurate picture of the widow in colonial times. The widow was simply a remnant, a leftover from a relationship that no longer existed. Following the husband's death, household inventories were taken in preparation for the redistribution of resources which would inevitably take place. While a woman's rights might have been diminished by marriage, in widowhood the law became her advocate. Communities did not want the burden of having to support a man's widow. A husband was expected to continue to provide for his widow even in death, and was legally required to apportion part of his estate to her.

Some husbands made explicit pleas in behalf of their wives in their wills. Tristram Coffin directed his son, Nathaniel, to "take special care [of his mother and] provide for her in all respects." Nathaniel and his brothers each contributed a fixed sum annually to help support their mother.[21] Henry Clarke gave his wife a life interest in property that would ultimately pass to his son, Samson, who was required to "keep and maintain his mother" under penalty of losing his inheritance.[22] Laurence Simpson insisted, "Sons Michael, Rupert and Matthew are to obey their mother, follow her orders, or they are not to get their land."[23]

If she had minor children, a widow might be permitted to retain control of the entire estate until her sons came of age. The courts routinely granted the widow administration of the husband's estate in such circumstances. A study of 93 New Hampshire widows between 1650 and 1730 found that 75 to 80 percent of the women were given joint administration of their family estate even in the face of having grown sons.[24] In two Maryland counties, 75 percent of men who left wills gave their wives more than the dower third and most named their wives as executors of their estate.[25] John Smithson proclaimed, "All I have I leave her, and if I had more she should enjoy it."[26] Similarly, William Berkeley of Virginia left his wife his entire estate, professing that "if God had blest me with a far greater estate, I would have given it all to my most dearly beloved wife."[27] John Rutledge proclaimed his gratitude for his wife's understanding and tenderness to his seven young children by leaving her his entire estate and even permitting her the right to use or dispose of the estate as she saw fit.

On some occasions, however, not only was the estate removed from the oversight of the wife but it was managed by a man. A male guardian was appointed for her children. By leaving the house and lands to his widow and giving her control of the family resources, a man was able to provide for his wife and at the same time secure stability for his children. If the estate were to be divided at the time of the death, the resulting economic situation might create a drastic change of life style for the children. Widows with no resources might be more inclined to quickly find a new mate disrupting the family that a deceased man left behind.

This widow's share of the estate, or dower right, had a long-standing English tradition. Commonly, the widow inherited one-third of the household goods. She was also entitled to use or receive income from one-third of the real estate for the rest of her life or until she remarried. She was not, however, able to dispose of the property, nor could she select the ultimate owner. Upon her death the property was passed on to the husband's heirs. No matter how close the personal or business relationship between a husband and wife, it was not a blood relationship, and blood ruled under the law so that the family estate remained intact. If the wife were to inherit the property outright, she might decide to leave the property to someone outside the family. If she were to remarry, the property would go with her into her new family. Most men stipulated sentiments similar to those of Mathias Marriott, who wrote, "My wife, Alice, to have and enjoy the land I live on for her widowhood. After her death or remarriage the land is to return to my son, Wm. Marriott."[28]

The absence of a will was assumed to mean that the man accepted the normal "widow's third." In cases where a husband left less than a third, the will was usually contested and the courts tended to be sympathetic to the widow. In some cases, when a husband seemed to be recklessly disposing of the property his wife had brought to the marriage, a judge would query the woman in private to determine if she had acceded to the disposition of her property. Some fathers required prenuptial contracts that placed their daughter's inheritance in the care of third-party trustees. Certainly, such sophisticated legal undertakings were restricted to the more affluent families, but in a case where an oldest son's right was questioned by his mother in the absence of his father's unambiguous will to the contrary, the son would be upheld by the courts.

Many widows who were about to remarry entered into complex prenuptial contracts. Samuel Sewall's courtship of his third wife, the widow Mary Gibbs, was more legal negotiation than romantic flirtation. In both letters and personal conversation, the sixty-nine year old Sewall discussed the monetary affects of their potential union. In his diary, he noted, "her sons to be bound to save me harmless as to her Administration; and to pay me £100 provided their Mother died before me: I to pay her £50 per annum during her life, if I left her a Widow." Sewall was concerned because a man who married a woman before her late husband's estate was settled risked becoming liable for the previous husband's debts. Mary, naturally, was concerned about burdening her sons financially. Finally, after several letters and meetings between Sewall and Mary's sons, a prenuptial agreement was reached. Sewall agreed to forgo the £100 provided that the sons indemnified him against the debts of their father's estate, but he did reduce Mary's annual stipend to £40. The couple was married shortly thereafter.[29]

Some widows were hesitant to remarry. For the first time in their lives they found themselves in control of their finances. William Alexander, an 18th-century writer of women's history, explained that men "exercised nearly a perpetual guardianship over them [women] both in their virgin and married state, and she who, having laid a husband in the grave, enjoys an independent fortune, is almost the only woman who among us can be called free."[30]

A widow who remarried gave up all her unprotected property to her husband. She would once again have to defer to the generosity of her husband for her personal needs and those of the household. If a widow had been left in a conformable financial situation, remarriage had its risk. Widower Samuel Sewall pursued the widow Dorothy Denison asking her what financial allowance she felt he should bestow on her annually. Despite a generous offer on his part, she refused him, leaving him to note in his diary, "She answer'd she had better keep as she was, than give a certainty for an uncertainty."[31] In addition to her own security and comfort, a widow had to worry about the security of her children's inheritance. If she chose imprudently, her new mate could squander the wealth meant for the children of her previous marriage.

Naturally, many women missed the companionship and emotional support of a spouse but it was socially acceptable for them to find fulfillment with their children. It was not unusual for a widow to live with the family of one of her adult children. Even though she would have to acquiesce to her daughter or daughter-in-law as female head of the household, she held a socially acceptable place in the household.

Many widows continued to run the family businesses after their husband's passing. Colonial newspapers carried many advertisements like Hannah Lade's. "This is to give notice that Hannah Lade widow and administratrix of Mr. Nathaniel Lade deceased, continues the house and shop and keeps on the business of her late deceased husband ... and hath to sell very cheap ... all sorts of good lately advertised by Mr. Nathaniel Lade."[32] It is not difficult to imagine a woman continuing to operate her husband's dry goods shop. She probably worked in the establishment as necessary and acquired a good knowledge of the running of the business and frequently had dealings with both customers and suppliers. Some women continued less likely enterprises. When Elizabeth Timothy lost her husband, Louis, one of her first actions was to publish the following notice: "Whereas the late printer of this Gazette hath been deprived of his life by an unhappy accident, I take this opportunity of informing the public that I shall continue the said paper as usual.... Wherefore, I flatter myself, that all those persons, who by subscriptions or otherwise, assisted my late husband, in the prosecution of the said undertaking, will be kindly pleased to continue their favors and good offices to his poor afflicted widow with six children and another hourly expected."[33] Mary Stevenson advertised that she would continue the business of her husband, a glazier and painter. Jane Massey was heir to a gunsmith's shop and, with the help of an assistant, continued to operate the business for a number of years. Jane Burgess added the following postscript to the legal notice of her being executrix of her husband's will: "I still carry on the blacksmith business and shall be obliged to my friends for the continuance of their favors."[34] Mary Robinson continued her husband's tannery, advertising that she "dressed deer skins with or without the hairs, and dyed, washed and mended buck skin breeches."[35]

Some widows had to be more enterprising. They were not left sufficient funds nor did they receive an existing business. In order to continue to support herself and her children she had to use whatever resources she did have. It was not unusual for women who were left a sizable property, but not the means to continue its maintenance, to rent rooms and take in borders. In southern planter communities where transportation was difficult and homes were distant, it was common to offer hospitality for extended periods to friends, friends' acquaintances, and in some cases, even strangers. A widow, having lived such a lifestyle, would not have to make much of an adjustment to become a landlord as she already had both the physical space and servant manpower to easily undertake such an enterprise. Even in town, widows opened their homes to country folk who were visiting the city. The September 2, 1732, *South Carolina Gazette* carried an advertisements for a tavern kept by Mrs. Peach, as well as the houses of Mrs. Eldrich, Mrs. Saureau, Mrs. Delamare, Mrs. Flavel, and Mrs. Ramsey.[36] Some of these establishments were quite distinguished and appealed to members of the genteel class who preferred quiet, quality lodging to the often questionable and crowded stagecoach inn or room in a tavern garret. Some women did operate taverns and lodgings that were more liberal when it came to clientele, but others were widows of once-prominent men. Mary Luke, who ran a prominent tavern in Williamsburg was the widow of John Luke, the former collector of customs. Elizabeth Dawson, who welcomed such distinguished lodgers as the Washingtons into her home, was the widow of a past president of William and Mary College, William Dawson.[37]

While a wife may have been less than equal to her spouse in the eyes of the law, she was, in reality, a true helpmate to their husband, frequently acting as his deputy and doing whatever was necessary to help the family survive.

NOTES

1. Quoted in Lisa Wilson, *Ye Heart of a Man: The Domestic Life of Men in Colonial New England* (New Haven: Yale University Press, 1999), 47–48.

2. J. Hector St. John de Crevecoeur, Letters from an American Farmer *and* Sketches of Eighteenth-Century America (reprint, New York: Penguin, 1981), 52–53.

3. Samuel Willard, *A Complete Body of Divinity* (Boston: 1726), 609 http://www.puritiansermons.com/willard/will0178.pdf (accessed March 2005).

4. Ibid., 612.

5. See Benjamin Wadsworth, *A Well-Ordered Family* (Boston: 1712), http://personal.pitnet/primary sources/marriage.html (accessed March 2005).

6. Carol Berkin, *First Generations: Women in Colonial America* (New York: Hill and Wang, 1996), 30.

7. See Wadsworth, *A Well-Ordered Family*.

8. Quoted in Carl Holliday, *Woman's Life in Colonial Days* (Boston: Cornhill, 1922), 132.

9. Laurel Thatcher Ulrich, *Good Wives: Image and Reality in the Lives of Women in Northern New England, 1650–1750* (New York: Vintage, 1980), 39–40.

10. Ibid., 40.

11. Ibid., 40–41.

12. Crevecoeur, Letters *and* Sketches, 157.

13. M. Halsey Thomas, ed., *The Diary of Samuel Sewall, 1674—1729*, vol. 1 (New York: Farrar, Straus and Giroux, 1973), 496.

14. Berkin, *First Generations*, 27.

15. Quoted in Julia Cherry Spruill, *Women's Life and Work in the Southern Colonies* (New York: W. W. Norton, 1973), 290.

16. Ibid., 290.

17. Ibid., 290–91.

18. Ibid., 290.

19. Letters *and* Sketches, 159.

20. Ulrich, *Good Wives*, 42–43.

21. Ibid., 148.

22. Quoted in Carol Berkin, *First Generations*, 17–18.

23. Ibid., 18.

24. Ulrich, *Good Wives*, 249.

25. Berkin, *First Generations*, 17.

26. *Women's Life and Work*, 165.

27. Ibid., 165.

28. Carol Berkin, *First Generations*, 19.

29. M. Halsey Thomas, ed., *The Diary of Samuel Sewall, 1674–1729*, vol. 2 (New York: Farrar, Straus and Giroux, 1973), 908.

30. William Alexander, *The History of Women from the Earliest Antiquity to the Present Time: Giving an Account of Almost Every Interesting Particular Concerning That Sex among All Nations, Ancient and Modern*, vol. 2 (Philadelphia: J. H. Dobelbower, 1796), 338.

31. Thomas, *Diary of Samuel Sewall*, vol. 2, 908.

32. Quoted in Sprull, *Women's Life and Work*, 276.

33. Quoted in ibid., 263–64.

34. Ibid., 289.

35. Ibid.

36. Ibid., 296.

37. Ibid., 301.

10

Women as Mothers

I had eight birds hatcht in one nest
Four Cocks there were, and Hens the rest,
I nurst them up with pain and care,
Nor cost nor labor did I spare.
     —Anne Bradstreet, "In Reference to Her Children"

In marriage, a woman entered a cycle of pregnancy, birth, and nursing that set the bounds of her life for the remainder of her childbearing years. A colonial toast declared, "Our land free, our men honest and our women fruitful." For many women, twenty- to thirty-month intervals separated the birth of one child from the next. In his 1737 work, John Brickell declared, "The women are very fruitful, most houses being full of little ones, and many women from other places, who having been long married and without children, have removed to Carolina, and become joyful mothers."[1] In a letter, Rebecca Dinwittie wrote, "I do assure you will give me pleasure to hear ... Mrs. Harrison is well recovered from her lying in: tho by the time you get this she may be in that way again." Margaret Calvert wrote to her niece, "I am extremely glad to hear that ye ladies are all brought safe to bed but here you are most of you in that way again."[2] Families of ten and twelve were common. Martha Jefferson Randolph, daughter of Thomas Jefferson, bore twelve children. Molly Maury had thirteen. Martha Laurens Ramsey had eleven children in sixteen years. Mary Heathy had seven children by her first husband, seven by her second, and three by her third. David Ramsey, an early historian of South Carolina, recorded that one remarkable woman had borne 34 children.[3] Cotton Mather praised the fecundity of the colonial mother, speaking of one woman who had "no less than twenty-three children by one husband; whereof nineteen lived unto men's and women's estate [another] was mother to seven-and-twenty children: and she that was mother to Sir William Phips ... had no less than one and twenty sons and five daughters besides him."[4]

With women marrying early and bearing children well into middle age, it was not unusual for a woman to be caring for a child the same age or younger than her grandchildren. Widow Judith Somerby had three children aged eight, six, and almost three when she married Tristram Coffin. Over the next sixteen years, she gave birth to ten more children. By the time the last was born, she was already grandmother to six. Nelly Custis Lewis, mother to several children of her own, wrote a friend, "Dear mother has just recovered from her confinement with her twentieth child; it is a very fine girl, large and healthy. Mamma has suffered greatly and is extremely weak."[5]

Pregnant women carried on their normal work and social activities as their health permitted. Additionally, as a woman prepared for her confinement, she was expected to amass a set of childbed linen. As much ceremonial as pragmatic, the linens and infant wear were of the finest linen the family could afford and would be adorned with embroidery and lace. While most of this was generally the product of the woman's own needle, newspapers carried advertisements for "suits of childbed linen" and "quilted satin childbed baskets and pincushions" amid offerings of millinery and other goods.[6] A portion of this assemblage may have been handed down to a woman from her mother. It was not uncommon for these linens to be bequeathed in wills. Frederick Jones left his eldest daughter "all her mother's childbed linen with [a] white silk damask gown." Mary Atkins left "childbed linen and all other clothes belonging to a child" to a female relative.[7] To insure that a new mother would be properly prepared, sometimes these linens were given even as wedding presents.

Labor and delivery were not only momentous occasions for the family; they were community events as well. At the first stage of labor, the husband would send for the midwife, who would assist with the birth and remain with the family for a brief interval afterwards. Midwife Martha Ballard remained with one of her patients for five days awaiting the birth of her daughter. "At Mr. Parker's. His lady is about the house.... I knit while gone from home 2 pair of gloves and 5 pair & 1/2 mitts."[8] Other female friends and relatives would also attend to assist in the birth. William Byrd recorded the events surrounding the birth of his son in 1709. When his wife, Lucy, went into labor, he sent for a Mrs. Hamlin and cousin Harrison. Lucy's sister would have normally been called as well, but she, too, was in the final weeks of pregnancy. Ballard's diary frequently follows the details of her arrival to the home of a woman about to deliver with "Her women were immediately called."[9]

Often the women who were summoned to a birthing had very specific roles. One might have been a servant whose time would be spent in brewing tea, bringing cakes, and emptying chamber pots. Another would likely be a close neighbor or relative whose main job was to sit beside the woman in labor, providing comfort and conversation and noting any changes in her color or condition. There was often another woman who had some more specific knowledge of healing and delivery but was not herself a midwife. She could assist the midwife and, in the event that the midwife did not arrive in time, could deliver the child if it was a normal birth. Diarist, Samuel Sewall, registered the birth of his fourteenth child. "My Wife had some thoughts the time of her travail might come, before she went to bed; But it went over. Between 4 and 5 A.M. I go to prayer, Rise, make a fire, call Mrs. Ellis, Hawkins. Mary Hawkins calls Midwife Greenlef." Later in the day, he made a second entry: "My Wife is brought to bed of a daughter about two P.M." Mary Holyoke recorded events surrounding the birth of her twelfth child. "Sent for Mrs. Jones & Mrs. Carwick Very bad til 1/2 past 11 A.M. when I was delivered of a son. Madame Mrs. Pickman & Mrs. Derby called in."[10]

The community of women who came together at this time of "travail" was completely in control and solidly bonded. Their authority was more powerful on this occasion than at any another time during this period. It was the one time when men were kept in the shadows awaiting news while women were in the forefront managing information and activity. Byrd reported that after he had summoned the women he retired to bed leaving "the women full of expectation for my wife." He claimed that he awoke "in a blink" when the baby arrived at one o'clock. The women remained with Lucy and the baby until morning. The midwife remained for another three days.[11]

Adding to the difficulty of childbirth was the lack of anesthetics. Women were generally denied painkillers of any kind. To believers in the literal truth of the Bible, of whom there were many at the time, the pain of childbirth was the fulfillment of God's words to Eve in Genesis: "In sorrow thou shall bring forth children." Cotton Mather held that women about to give birth should have the same consciousness as anyone in danger of death. He wrote that a woman should prepare for the birth in happiness but she must also repent her sins because she might sacrifice her life in giving life to her child.[12] The woman in labor could expect, however, that the midwife would make every attempt to save the mother's life rather than the child's should such a situation arise. In fact, in his 1775 *Outlines and Theory of the Practice of Midwifery,* Dr. Alexander Hamilton stated that it was the duty of the mother's attendant to give "perfect safety to the mother, who is always justified to the first place in our intentions."[13]

A nurse often remained with the mother and child for an extended interval. The infant was often given to another woman to nurse for the first few days. Two weeks after the birth of a son, Holyoke noted,

"Nurse went to nurse Mrs. Derby."[14] The nurse was also available to help with complications following childbirth. Two days after Sewall's wife, Hannah, gave birth to their fourteenth child, she fell ill. "Sabbath-day night my wife is very ill and something delirious. Pulse swift and high." Four days later he noted, "Nurse Hill watch'd last night. Wife had a comfortable night."[15] Nine days after the birth of her ninth child, Holyoke complained of a knot in her breast. Although her husband was a physician, she recorded. "Nurse anointed it with parsley, wormwood & chamomile stewed in butter"[16] Two months after the birth of her eighth child she had also developed an infection in her breast, and her husband lanced it for her and prepared a poultice. It is likely that he attended her since by that time, the nurse would no longer be in the house.

Holyoke's diary records what seems to be a formal "sitting up week" when female friends came to visit with the mother and welcome the new babe. The day after she delivered her daughter she noted, "2 Mrs. Pinkmans, Mrs. Eppes and Mrs. Rowth here." Approximately three weeks after the birth she wrote, "Sitting up week. Mrs. Eppes, 2 Pinkmans, Mrs. Rowth and Mrs. Dowse here." Similar entries follow other births, and there are large numbers of visitors for several days during and immediately following "sitting up week." A common practice in New Amsterdam was for a pincushion to be displayed on the doorknocker to announce the birth. When the mother was strong enough, a reception was held for the mother's female friends.[17]

This population explosion in the house as labor progressed required that a large number of people be fed. One of the responsibilities of the expectant mother was to provide refreshment for those in attendance during the childbirth. "Groaning cakes," "groaning beer," and other items that would keep were made in advance of the expected event. It was also a custom to give a dinner in appreciation of those who attended the mother during the labor and delivery. Midwife Martha Ballard recorded in her diary, "At Capt. Meloy's. His lady in labor. Her women called.... My patient delivered at 8 hour 5 minutes evening of a fine daughter. Her attendants: Miss Cleark, Duttun, Sewall and myself. We had an elegant supper and I tarried all night."[18]

Samuel Sewall made note of such a meal given two weeks after the birth of one of his children: "My Wife Treats her Midwife and Women: Had a good Dinner, B'oiled [sic] Pork, Beef, Fowls; very good Roast-beef, Turkey-Pye, Tarts, Madam Usher carv'd, Mrs. Hannah Greenlef; Ellis Cowell, Wheeler, Johnson, and her daughter Cole, Mrs. Hill our Nurses Mother, Nurse Johnson, Hill, Hawkins, Mrs. Goose, Deming, Green, Smith, Hatch, Blin. Comfortable, moderate weather; and with a good fire in the stove warm'd the room."[19]

Sometimes plans were disrupted. When his wife, pregnant with their ninth child, went into labor early, Sewall wrote, "My wife was so ill could hardly get home ... at last my Wife bade me call Mrs. Ellis, then Mother Hull, then the Midwife, and through the Goodness of God was brought to

Bed of a Daughter ... Mrs. Elizabeth Weeden, Midwife. Had not Women nor other preparations as usually, being wholly supris'd, my wife expecting to have gone a Month longer."[20] Mary Holyoke had a similar experience and was unable to summon the usual attendants "Very ill. Brought to bed quite alone of a daughter child very well."[21]

The midwife was a prominent and esteemed person in every community. Midwives were called into court to testify to the age of an individual they had delivered. Sometimes their testimony was sought in bastardy cases as it was believed that a woman in labor would truthfully reveal the name of the child's father. It was also common for a midwife to sit on a jury in the case of a woman accused of infanticide. Generally, midwives did not advertise, but notices appear in newspapers announcing a change of address, and introductions were published when a midwife moved to a new community. In New Amsterdam, the midwife was a licensed professional, and she was provided with a home by the government. As an assurance that even the

Colonial women formed a society of their own that dealt with women's issues, including the birth of children. Bringing a child into the world was the province of the local midwife. Here, two very anxious young women call on the calm and self-assured midwife.

poor would have the assistance of a midwife, two women were appointed and given a monopoly unless there was an emergency.

Ministers were sometimes consulted in times of extremely difficult births. Their status as men of learning carried a certain, authority that could trump the midwife's knowledge and experience although their expertise was sometimes limited to prayer and a few medical treatises. Some men did become prominent in the field of obstetrics. Edmund Holyoke, a distinguished physician of Salem, was commonly called in to consult in cases of "hard labor." The second half of the 18th century saw the growth of the use of forceps. This technological advancement provided the physician with a tool, which gave him an advantage over the midwife. Although a rare occurrence prior to 1750, by the end of the 18th century physicians were commonly called at the time of birthing if they were available. William Buchan included the following passage in his 1769 work, *Domestic Medicine*: "We cannot help taking notice of that ridiculous custom which still prevails in some parts of the country, of collecting a number of women together on such occasions. These, instead of being useful serve only to crowd the house, and obstruct the necessary attendants. Besides they hurt the patient with their noise: and often, by their untimely and impertinent advice, do much mischief."[22]

Nevertheless, many colonists still considered the presence of a men in the birthing room a contravention of female modesty. An 18th-century manual on midwifery made further argument: "There is a tender regard one woman bears to another, and a natural sympathy in those that have gone thro' the pangs of childbearing; which, doubtless, occasion a compassion for those that labor under these circumstances, which no man can be judge of."[23] Midwives continued their dominance in rural areas, and physicians were called in only when serious complications occurred. Thomas Jefferson wrote to his daughter, "Some friend of your mamma's (I forget whom) used to say it [childbirth] was no more than a jog of the elbow. The material thing is to have scientific aid in readiness that if anything uncommon takes place it may be redressed on the spot, and not be made serious by delay. It is a case which will least of all wait for doctors to be sent for; therefore with this single precaution nothing is ever to be feared."[24] Despite this optimism, Jefferson was likely to have been deeply concerned for his daughter's health and safety. His wife had died shortly after bearing their sixth child in ten years.

Death due to childbirth was a genuine fear because it was the leading cause of mortality for women. Newspapers carried notices such as this one, which appeared in the *South Carolina Gazette* in 1776: "Of a miscarriage of twins, on the tenth instant, died here, in the 24th year of her age, one of the most pious and accomplished young women in these parts, in the person of Mrs. Calhoun, the wife of Patrick Calhoun, Esq., and daughter of the Reverend Mr. Alexander Craighead." Before the birth of one of her children, Anne Bradstreet, composed a poem to her husband, acknowledging the risk that she faced: "How soon, my Dear, death may my steps attend." She voiced her concern for the children she would leave behind and bade her husband, "These O protect from step Dames injury."[25] Husbands, too, worried. Benjamin Bang was concerned about his pregnant wife. In his diary he noted, "My dearest friend is much concerned being in and near a time of difficulty." He tried to bolster his wife and assuage her frightful dreams. Of one such night he wrote, "I put it off slightly for fear of disheartening her but directly upon it dreamed much the same myself of being bereft of her and seeing my little motherless children about me which when I awoke was cutting to think of."[26] Jefferson counseled his daughter, "Take care of yourself, my dearest Maria, have good spirits and know that courage is as essential to triumph in your case as in that of a soldier."[27]

Loss of a child was a frequent occurrence. One in ten infants did not survive the first year, and four out of ten children died before age six. Common diseases that stole away these little ones included measles, diphtheria, whooping cough, mumps, and chicken pox. Unsanitary conditions fostered epidemics, and families were often left to cope with the illnesses by themselves. Between 1767 and 1770, Oxford, Maine, experienced one of the worst diphtheria epidemics in New England's history. Twelve percent of the population died, most of them children between the ages of two and fourteen.[28] Fortunately for some families, women like Midwife Ballard were available to help. One sad story unfolds amid the pages of her diary: "Was at Mr. McMaster's. Their children two of them very ill. The other is recovering." Four days later she noted, "At Mr. McMaster's. Their son very sick. I set up all night. Mrs. Patin with me. The child is very ill indeed." The following day she write, "William McMaster expired at 3 o'clock this morn. Mrs. Patin and I laid out the child. Poor mother, how distressing her case, near the hour of labor and three children more very sick."[29] Certainly, Ballard empathized with Mrs. McMaster's anguish, as she had lost three of her own six children in ten days during the diphtheria epidemic.

Hannah and Samuel Sewall had fourteen children and one stillborn infant. Seven of the children died within 25 months of birth. Anne Lake Cotton gave birth to nine children in twenty years. She lost her first child two months before the birth of the second. The next four survived infancy but the last three died at or shortly after delivery.[30] Mary Holyoke gave birth to twelve children in twenty-two years. Although her husband was a prominent physician, only three of their children survived to adulthood. Seven Holyoke children died at birth or in infancy. One died at three years of age and another at seventeen.[31] Mather spoke of a "woman has had no less than twenty-two children: whereof she buried fourteen sons and six daughters."[32]

Accidents claimed children, too. Colonial households were bustling, cluttered places that were not always safe for children. Open fires, kettles of boiling water, privies and unfenced ponds and wells were daily dangers to a toddler or a small child. Busy adults and older children could easily

years since my daughter Martha's death (Martha was 8 years & 2 months & 28 days.)"[39]

Mary Shippen Livingston held a more modern view of her relationship with her child. One of the few diarists to record small and intimate interactions with her child, she wrote, "I have the sweetest child that was ever born—in her I shall be most blest." Later, she writes, "This morn I sent Betsy out with the child to give it an airing—sat down to work at the tambour.... When the child return'd I almost devour'd it with kisses."On another day, she notes, "I spend so much of my time caressing and playing with Peggy that I almost forget I have anything else to do—I forget to read—to write—to work—in short I neglect the business of the day."[40]

New England ministers often cautioned against such indulgence, claiming that it would bring turmoil into the family. One pastor told his congregation, "Persons are more often apt to despise a Mother, (the weaker and frequently most indulgent)." Another explained that a mother was more likely to be subjected to irreverence "by reason of her blandishments and fond indulgence."[41] William Kendrick in his *The Whole Duty of a Woman* cautioned mothers against showering their children with "an excess of thy love" as it would lead to spoiled and indulged creatures who would "bring a curse upon thee and not a blessing." Additionally, by distancing themselves from their children mothers would lessen their grief in the event of losing a child.[42]

Often a bride came to a household that already had several children. Many men who lost their wives were anxious to find a new mother for their children. John Thurston married Thomasine, a widow who had three children. She bore him sixteen children in sixteen years and died thirteen days after the birth of her nineteenth child. One month and thirteen days later, John married his second wife, with whom he had eight more children. Mather tells of a Mr. Sherman who was "twice married. By his first wife he had six children. By his next wife ... Mr. Sherman had no less than twenty children added unto the number of six he had before."[43] Naturally, by the time the youngest children were born, the eldest had moved out to establish families of their own.

Loss of a wife affected the entire household negatively. A wife provided essential services to the family, and without her it functioned poorly. Besides the emotional loss of a loving spouse and companion, a widower experienced a void in his household. On their deathbeds many young women urged their husbands to remarry. This concern for their surviving spouse was less out of regard for his happiness than for the welfare of their children. A mother knew that the vacancy she left would put tremendous strain on the family. Mary Clap told her husband to "get another Wife as soon as you can ... one that will be a good Mother to the Children."[44]

Child rearing added greatly to the burden of a woman's responsibilities. While fathers were responsible for the education of the children and were the ultimate authority in matters of discipline, mothers attended to their everyday care. This, of course, was in addition to the myriad other duties, which they had to do. After the birth of her second child, Esther Burr wrote in her 1756 journal, "When I had but one child my hands were tied, but now I am tied hand and foot. ... [H]ow shall I get along when I have got 1/2 dzn. or 10 children I can't devise."[45]

Mothering, however, was not as central to a woman's identity in this period as it would be in the 19th century when the entire household became more female centered.[46] Historian, William Alexander noted in 1796, "A father only is empowered to exercise a rightful authority over his children, and no power is conferred on the mother."[47] The mother represented the tender and affectionate side of parenting in an otherwise authoritarian system of child rearing. Additionally, in New England, the entire community of adults held an obligation to instruct and supervise the children with special attention to their religious well being. Such societal mothering led to the common practice of addressing any older women as "mother" or "gammar" (grandma).

The practice of "sending out" children in apprenticeships separated many mothers from their children at a very young age and brought into the home children of neighboring families and other relatives. Once children passed toddlerhood, they generally spent much of their time with the same gender parent as they learned the skills needed for their roles as adults. Fathers took the boys to the fields or the shop while mothers instructed the girls in housewifery. Pragmatic child rearing often replaced the romanticized tradition of mothering. Eliza Lucas Pinckney wrote to herself, "I am resolved to be a good mother to my children, to pray for them, to set them good examples, to give them good advice, to be careful both of their souls and bodies, to watch over their minds, to carefully root out the first appearing and budding vice, and to instill piety, virtue and true religion into them."[48]

Woman seldom wrote about their children. What entries were made in addition to their births and all too often of their deaths, tend to record milestones in the child's life. Holyoke's journal referenced her first daughter only three times in three years. She noted when Polly "began her shoes and stays," when she "first went to meeting" and when she "went to school."[49] Nancy Shippen Livingston was uncommonly more reflective on her role as mother. She, wrote, "I cannot have a more pleasing task than taking care of my precious child—It is an amusement to me preferable to all others."[50] Livingston also had some definite ideas about raising her daughter and she recorded them in her diary: "I thought seriously about my child's education. . . . I will insert them here that I may not forget them." The resulting list of thirty-five ideas, entitled "Some Directions Concerning a Daughter's Education," included:

> Give her a pleasing idea of good & an ugly frightful one of evil.
> Watch over her childish passions & prejudices, & labor sweetly to cure them.

Particularly inform her in the duties of a single & married state.
Let her always be employ'd about what is profitable or necessary.[51]

Anne Bradstreet expressed her feelings about motherhood in her poetry. Although written in 1656, the feelings she expressed are timeless.

I had eight birds hatched in one nest
Four cocks there were, and hens the rest
I nursed them up with pain and care,
Nor cost, nor labor did I spare,
Till at the last they felt their wing,
Mounted the trees, and learn'd to sing.

She continues, as would any mother, expressing her enduring concern for the welfare of her offspring even though they are adults and on their own.

Long did I keep you soft and warm,
And with my wings kept off all harm,
My cares are more, and fears than ever.
My throbs such now, as 'fore were never.

Bradstreet ends with the hope that she will live on in the memories of her grandchildren, fulfilling the greatest goal of motherhood, to see her family grow and continue in future generations.

When each of you shall in your nest
Among your young ones take your rest,
In chirping language oft them tell,
You had a dam that lov'd you well
That did what could be done for young.
And nurst you up till you were strong,
And fore she once would let you fly,
She shew'd you joy and misery;
Taught what was good, and what was ill,
What would save life, and what would kill.
Thus gone, amongst you I may live,
And dead, yet speak, and counsel give.[52]

As a widow with three young children, Eliza Pinckney tried to be both mother and father to her family. After a five-year visit in England, Pinckney and her husband, Thomas, returned to their home in South Carolina with their nine-year-old daughter, leaving their young sons behind to continue their education. Shortly after their arrival, Thomas contracted malaria and died. Eliza remained in South Carolina in order to settle the estate. She assumed the role of guardian of the Pinckney children and did her utmost to perpetuate the family holdings and community standing in order to provide for her sons' future. Fortunately, Pinckney had a considerable

Even today this picture speaks for itself to any busy housewife and mother. Colonial parents were not supermen and superwomen. They were people very much like us.

amount of business experience having assisted her father with the management of three plantations while still in her teens and creating a process that made the production of indigo much more profitable.

Eliza maintained a healthy correspondence with the family caring for her boys, and she directed specific activities from across the ocean. In a letter to the host family, she wrote, "[T]he children should make your servants some acknowledgment of their trouble at holi-day [*sic*] times—what you think proper. It was always what they did for our own."[53] She also wanted to ensure that her values were reinforced in the children in her absence: " [R]eprove them if ever you know them to do anything wrong—for heedlessness and inadvertence is almost inseparable from youth."[54] She counseled the boys in her letters much as their father would have done. When Charles was to be sent to university she warned him, "[Y]ou will be in a city surrounded by temptations with every youthful passion about you. It will therefore require your utmost vigilance to watch over your passions.... Be particularly watchful against the heat of temper; it makes constant work for repentance and chagrin and is often productive of the greatest mischiefs and misfortunes."[55] The pain of her separation was also obvious in letters to both the boys and their host family. "I believe indeed 'tis better for them I am at a distance, painful as it is to me, for I find such an over-flowing of tenderness for them that might degenerate into weakness had I an opportunity for such indulgence."[56] Yet she knew that the proper management of her husband's assets required her direct supervision and were essential to the future well being of her children.

Motherhood was, and still is, a complex and all consuming calling. In a tribute to his wife a colonial writer thought to be a president of Yale penned the following: "Indeed she would sometimes say to me that bearing, tending and burying children was hard work, and that she had done a great deal of it for one of her age, (she had six children, whereof she buried four, and died in the 24th year of her age) yet she would say it was the work she was made for, and what God in his providence had called her to, and she could freely do it all for Him."[57]

NOTES

1. John Brickell, quoted in Julia Cherry Spruill, *Women's Life and Work in the Southern Colonies* (New York: W.W. Norton, 1973), 46.

2. Quoted in ibid., 49.

3. Ibid., 47–48.

4. Arthur W. Calhoun, *The American Family in the Colonial Period* (Minneola, NY: Dover Publications, 2004), 88.

5. Quoted in Charles Moore, *Family Life of George Washington* (New York: Houghton Mifflin, 1926), 166–67.

6. Julia Cherry Spruill, *Women's Life and Work in the Southern Colonies*, 50. Pincushions were popular gifts for new mothers. The cushions were usually made of fine fabric and pins were inserted so that the heads, when pressed down into the fabric, spelled out a phrase. "Welcome little stranger" was a common message. More ambitious projects carried a verse from scripture.

7. Ibid.

8. Quoted in Laurel Thatcher Ulrich, *A Midwife's Tale: The Life of Martha Ballard, Based on Her Diary, 1785–1812* (New York: Vintage, 1991), 164. With a single exception, Ballard identifies the house as the husband's when she records a call upon the wife.

9. Ibid., 6.

10. George Francis Dow, ed., *The Holyoke Diaries* (Salem: Essex Institute, 1911), 107.

11. Kathleen M. Brown, *Good Wives, Nasty Wenches, and Anxious Patriarchs: Gender, Race, and Power in Colonial Virginia* (Chapel Hill: University of North Carolina Press, 1996), 302.

12. Susan Burrows Swan, *Plain and Fancy: American Women and Their Needlework, 1850-1850* (Austin, Texas: Curious Works Press, 1995), 28.

13. Ibid., 30.

14. Dow, *The Holyoke Diaries*, 107.

15. M. Halsey Thomas, ed., *The Diary of Samuel Sewall, 1674–1729,* vol. 1 (New York: Farrar, Straus and Giroux, 1973), 459.

16. Dow, *The Holyoke Diaries*, 81.

17. Ibid., 95.

18. Ulrich, *A Midwife's Tale*, 162–63.

19. Thomas, *The Diary of Samuel Sewall*, vol 1, 460–61.

20. Ibid., 264.

21. Dow, *The Holyoke Diaries*, 77.

22. Quoted in Ulrich, *A Midwife's Tale*, 66.

23. Ibid., 12.

24. Spruill, *Women's Life and Work in the Southern Colonies*, 51.

25. Joseph R. McElrath Jr. and Allan P. Robb, eds., *The Complete Works of Anne Bradstreet* (Boston: Twayne, 1981), 179–80.

26. Clifford K. Shipton, *Sibley's Harvard Graduates,* vol. 17 (Boston: Historical Society, 1975), 480.

27. Spruill, *Women's Life and Work in the Southern Colonies,* 51.

28. Ulrich, *A Midwife's Tale*, 12.

29. Ibid., 38–39.

30. Ibid., 129.

31. Dow, *The Holyoke Diaries*, 73.

32. Calhoun, *The American Family in the Colonial Period,* 88.

33. Ulrich, *A Midwife's Tale*, 157.

34. Swan, *Plain and Fancy*, 30.

35. McElrathand, *The Complete Works of Anne Bradstreet*, 188.

36. Ibid., 187.

37. Dow, *The Holyoke Diaries*, 60.

38. Ibid., 107.

39. Ulrich, *A Midwife's Tale*, 12.

40. Quoted in Margo Culley, ed. *A Day at a Time* (New York: Feminist Press, 1985), 56–62.

41. Quoted in Ulrich, *A Midwife's Tale*, 154.

42. Quoted in Swan, *Plain and Fancy*, 34.

43. Quoted in Calhoun, *The American Family in the Colonial Period*, 88.

44. Lisa Wilson, *Ye Heart of a Man: The Domestic Life of Men in Colonial New England* (New Haven, CT: Yale University Press, 1999), 161.

45. Swan, *Plain and Fancy*, 36.

46. See James M. Volo and Dorothy Denneen Volo, *Encyclopedia of the Antebellum South* (Westport: Greenwood Press, 2000), 339–40.

47. William Alexander, *The History of Women from the Earliest Antiquity to the Present Time: Giving an Account of Almost Every Interesting Particular Concerning That Sex among All Nations, Ancient and Modern,* vol. 2 (Philadelphia: J. H. Dobelbower, 1796), 343.

48. Elise Pinckney, ed. *The Letterbook of Eliza Lucas Pinckney: 1739–1762* (Charleston: University of South Carolina Press, 1997), xxi.

49. Dow, *The Holyoke Diaries*, 57–58.

50. Culley, *A Day at a Time*, 62.

51. Ibid., 60–62.

52. Anne Bradstreet, *"To My Husband" and Other Poems* (Minneola, NY: Dover Publications, 2000), 6–8.

53. Pinckney, 105.

54. Ibid., 137.

55. Ibid., 159.

56. Ibid., 121.

57. Calhoun, *The American Family in the Colonial Period*, 90.

11

Women as Housewives

[She] did the morning work of a large family, made her cheese, etc. and then rode more than two miles, and carried her own wheel, and sat down to spin at nine in the morning, and by seven in the evening spun 53 knots, and went home to milking.
—A newspaper report of a woman attending a spinning bee

A wife's domain consisted of her home and the yards surrounding it. The specifics of her environment varied as did the family's economic situation and to some extent as to whether the location was rural or urban; but, in general, inside the home, the wife's purview encompassed the kitchen and its appendages, the cellars, the pantries, the brew house, the milk house, the wash house, and the buttery. Outside, it would include the garden, the milk yard, the pigpen, the hen house, the well and (to some extent) the orchard. In season, it would reach into the woods for berrying or mushroom gathering. A woman's sphere would also extend into the home of her neighbor and into the markets of town. The fields were generally the domain of the husband, although in times of danger or hardship a wife might work at his side.

It was the woman's responsibility to manage and direct the economic productivity of her household. This included caring for the children and overseeing the servants. Certainly the scope and nature of the duties of a plantation mistresses or the lady of a town mansion differed from those of the frontier woman or a poor farmer's wife. Additionally, a wife's specific activities depended to some extent on her personal skills and propensities. Whatever her activities, a wife was expected to be a model of industry and thrift. William Byrd boasted that his daughters were "every day up to their elbows in housewifery, which will qualify them effectually for useful wives."[1] Eliza Pickney wrote to her son-in-law, "I am glad your little wife looks well to the ways of her household .... The management of a dairy is an amusement she has always been fond of."[2]

There are few records to personally illuminate a wife's routine chores. Most were so boring and repetitive, so basic to the family's survival, that they were seldom detailed in diaries and journals. The few references that have survived are daybooks that merely list the day's activity. In many cases the writer seemingly defined herself by the labor she did. Martha Ballard's diary contains entries such as, " [C]ombed 9 lbs. of flax and knit 40 purls on my stocking," or "Hetchelling flax and making soap."[3] Most surviving diaries were written by women of considerable wealth and leisure who were more interested in recording social events and visitors than detailing their housekeeping labors.

Many of a housewife's chores were governed by the seasons. In the food provision realm, dairying began the cycle with calving. Dairy cows and their calves came under the dominion of the housewife. Cows were an important economic commodity providing milk and offspring which supplied meat, tallow, horn and labor. They furnished not only the needs of the family, but they also produced a marketable commodity. Women helped with calving, tended the cows when they were sick or injured, and were intimately involved with their daily care. Cows were milked twice a day and sometimes, during periods of high production, three times daily. Milking the cows was physically demanding and time consuming. The task required strong hands, wrists and back. Some cows were easy and could be milked in ten minutes while others might require a half hour. A good dairy woman knew her cows and soon learned how, with patience and soothing manner, to cajole each one into tractability.

Most cows were bred to calve in late spring when grass was plentiful but a few would be bred to give birth in the winter in order to provide fresh supplies of milk for cheese and butter when supplies ran low. Calves born in the winter required more care than those born in spring as they had to be pail-fed warm milk twice a day. Housewives often relied on herbal supplements to prolong milk production for as long as possible. One involved a posset of anise and coriander seeds mixed in a quart of ale. It provided "plenty of milk, but gave a disagreeable flavor from the seeds." Once the concoction was terminated the taste would disappear but even unpleasant tasting milk was better than no milk at all.[4]

Many women in New England came from an English culture that placed great value on dairy production. Dairy products were a more important source of protein than beef or pork. Little of the milk was consumed as a liquid. The dairy house, where the milk was processed into butter or cheese, was exclusively the domain of the housewife. Sometimes the dairy was little more than a room off the kitchen or a stone addition to the barn. It was essential, however, that the dairy provide clean and cool storage for the dairy products. To make cheese a housewife would heat several gallons of raw milk along with rennet, which had been dried and saved from the autumn slaughtering.[5] After an hour or two, the curd would form. The housewife would break it, drain off the whey and work in some butter. The mixture would be wrapped in cheesecloth, placed in a mold and put in a press for an hour. During this time, the cheesecloth would have to be changed and washed as the whey dripped out. It would then be repacked in a dry cloth and set in a press for thirty or forty hours. After one final wash in whey, it would be dried and placed on a shelf in the dairy to age. Some women sold their surplus milk, butter and cheese at local markets or even door to door.

More often than other livestock, cows and calves were given substantial shelter in a barn. It was not unusual for a husband to create a fenced-in area next to the cow barn in order to confine them and make it easier for his wife to care for and feed them. Mucking the stall and removing the dung was generally done by the males in the household, and the manure

The round cheeses seen here are drying in a "safe." When the doors were closed, the safe protected the cheese from vermin, flies, and other pests.

was spread on the fields. The cows would have been put out to graze as soon as the spring grass was established. Cows were permitted to graze wherever they found the browse. Rather than fencing them in, areas were fenced to keep them out. In fall they were permitted to glean the fields, but in winter the women would have to haul hay to feed them. Cows that lived in towns were gathered in the morning from designated locations and taken by a cow keeper to a community pasture. It was the housewife's job to be sure that the cows were ready for pickup a half hour after sunrise and that she was ready to receive them again at a half hour after sunset. The importance of dairy cows and calves to a community can be seen in the meadow allowances granted by the town of Sudbury. Men were given six acres for the grazing of their oxen, but their wives were apportioned six and a half acres for their cows and calves.[6]

Gardening followed close behind dairying as an important task. With spring planting and summer cultivation the household garden was an important part of a family's diet. Garden produce was supplemented in summer with berry gathering. In addition to vegetables, a housewife planted a variety of herbs in her garden. Herbs were the among the first things planted. Parsley, skirret, and sorrel were harvested for "sallets." Cooked and served hot or cold with an oil and vinegar dressing, they were served as accompaniments to other dishes. Herbs also had tremendous value as seasonings for meats that had been heavily salted for preservation. Some herbs were used as pesticides to deter flies, fleas, and moths. Early records and surviving seed lists have provided insight into what colonists considered to be essential herbs. In 1631, John Winthrop Jr. ordered seeds for angelica, basil, burnett, dill, fennel, hyssop, marjoram, parsley, rosemary, savory, thyme and tansey.[7]

What was available to a family in the winter and spring depended on a wife's careful preservation of their excess produce. For many families, particularly those in the north, a woman's expertise in this area made the difference between comfort and starvation not only through the winter but well into the spring. Food preservation was an ongoing process, which responded to the seasons, but it became especially intense during harvest time. The frontier family that did not have time to plant a garden faced a winter of intense hardship. John Reynolds and his family survived such a adversity on the Pennsylvania frontier. He wrote, "Our bread was flour and water without salt or leaven, baked in the ashes in thin cakes .... Bacon was our standing dish of meat. Chocolate with sassafras or wintergreen tea was our drink at meals. Vegetables we had none."[8]

The garden's harvest was stockpiled in a variety of ways. Only in the very Deep South were fresh vegetables available in winter. As far north as Virginia, small amounts of produce could be grown in hot frames, which utilized the heat generated by rotting manure to keep temperatures warm enough to produce the year round. Vegetables such as beets, cabbage, carrots, onions, parsnips, potatoes, radishes, turnips, and winter squash

By managing the garden, a woman could provide her family with a wide variety of fresh produce. In this picture, taken in New Jersey, the herb garden is in front of the house, conveniently near the doorway into the kitchen.

were stored in root cellars, where the climate allowed. In other areas, they were packed in straw and stored in barrels. The straw acted as a barrier to prevent the spread of spoilage to the entire barrel. Carrots were often buried in sawdust or sand boxes. Other vegetables, such as corn, beans, and peas were dried and used in cooking. Green corn was preserved by turning back the husk, leaving only the last, very thin layer and then hanging the ear in the sun or a warm room to dry. When it was needed for cooking, it was parboiled and cut from the cob. Sweet corn was parboiled, cut from the cob, dried in the sun and stored in a bag, which was kept in a cool, dry place. Sweet corn was also dried in the husk and then buried in salt. String beans, squash, and pumpkins were strung on thread and hung to dry. String beans were strung whole while other produce was sliced thinly and dried in strips. Vegetables could also be preserved by making them into pureed sauces, and cabbage could be made into sauerkraut.

Fall was the time for slaughtering. To survive the winter, a family needed barrels of salted pork; crocks of corned beef; and racks of smoked or sugar-cured ham, bacon, and sausage. While the men may have dispatched the larger animals, a housewife may have slaughtered smaller pigs herself. A period observer described a woman who "took the hinder parts between her legs ... and taking the snout in her left hand,"[9] dispatched the pig. Pork was a main meat of the colonial diet. Pigs were easier to keep than other live-stock as they could be fed on most anything including leavings from food preparation. Pigs did not have to be put to pasture and consumed less feed than cattle, to add the same amount of weight. Virtually every part of the pig was used. Organ meats would have been used immediately. Intestines would have been cleaned for use as sausage casings. They would be stuffed with meat scraps and herbs and smoked. Larger cuts of meat could be roasted and eaten right away or preserved for future use. Pork could easily be preserved in a number of ways such as pickling, salting, and smoking. Much of the pork would have been soaked in a solution of brine, jarred, and stored in the dairy where the temperature was generally cool. Some of the pork was also preserved as bacon. The slabs would be salted in tubs for several weeks in early winter before being hung in the chimney for smoking.

Fall was also the time for making cider, a mildly alcoholic beverage made from the natural fermentation of apple juice. This was the most common way of preserving the majority of the apple harvest. Cider was a staple of the New England diet. Some wives also brewed a winter's supply of "strong beer" at this time and stored it in the cellar. Others brewed "small beer" on a weekly or biweekly process and consumed immediately. "Small beer" was a mild beverage made from cracked malt or grist. First the brew was slow steeped just below the boiling point in a process called *mashing*. This smelly stage was crucial to the process and care had to be taken not to let the mixture sour. In the brewing stage, herbs and hops were mixed with the malted liquid. Finally, the brew was cooled and mixed with yeast.

Making candles was another labor-intensive autumn activity. Candles could be made in molds or dipped by hand. On the frontier and in rural areas, dipping was probably the most common method. Tallow was melted in huge kettles. Wicks were attached to candle rods, which were laid across pairs of poles suspended from chairs or stools. In turn, each candle rod was dipped in the tallow and placed across the poles to harden. Skill was required to know how to dip slowly enough so that the wax did not dry too quickly and produce brittle candles which would crack. A skilled candle dipper could make two hundred candles in a day. The quality of a candle depended upon the quality of the fat that was used. On the frontier, every bit of fat from butchered meat, including deer and bear, was used for candle making. The better the quality of the fat, the firmer and less smelly was the candle.[10] New England settlers were fortunate to discover that the waxy berries from the bayberry bush made very pleasant-smelling candles. Swedish naturalist Peter Kalm wrote about them in 1748 after a trip to America. "There is a plant here from which they make a kind of wax.... Candles of this do not easily bend, nor melt in summer as common candles do; they burn better and slower, nor do they cause any smoke, but yield rather an agreeable smell when they are extinguished."[11]

Candles were stored in candle safes to protect them from being eaten by vermin. Having been made from animal fat, care also had to be taken that they would not spoil. One method was to bury them in bran to limit exposure to air. Rural families and those with limited means relied heavily on less intensive means of light production such as fat lamps and rush lights. Fat lamps were shallow metal containers with a channel to support a wick that burned liquid formed from small amounts of melting fat. Rush lights were clamp-like devices that burned rushes that had been gathered from marshes and soaked in fat.

Housewives were also kept busy with many year round chores, of which cooking was most important. Seventeenth-century writer Gervase Markham declared that a woman who could not cook could "then but perform half her vow: for she may love and obey, but she cannot cherish, serve and keep him with that true duty which is expected."[12] Maintaining the fire was an essential part of this task. Fireplace cooking was best accomplished by using the heat of hot coals produced at the back of the fireplace. Coals were produced by burning hardwoods like oak and hickory. The coals could be stirred up or pulled on to the hearth apron and used beneath Dutch ovens and three legged skillets as needed.

Boiling was the most common method of cooking. A boiling pot required little attention, allowing the busy housewife to attend to her myriad other duties. It also required only one pot that could be hung in the fireplace from a lugpole or crane. Cooking temperatures were adjusted by raising or lowering the pot through the use of pothooks, chains, or trammels. Stews, thick soups, and porridges were commonly made using this method. It would not be unusual to find a pot of dry beans soaking in warm water on the hearth at almost any time of day.

Roasting was popular for cooking meat. Because roasting meat needed almost constant attention, the task of turning the roast was sometimes given to a small child. A roast or bird could also be hung vertically from a pair of cords fastened inside the chimney. When twisted, the cords wound and unwound around each other for quite some time with amazing regularity and evenly cooked the meat. Very wealthy families sometimes had a weighted clockwork device that rotated the meat. Reflector ovens, open to the fire on one side and closed on the other to reflect the fire's heat to the back of the roast as it turned on a spit, were less expensive but not available to every housewife. Meat was also broiled on a gridiron placed over coals on the hearth apron, but this method often lost the fats and drippings of the meat to the flames. Loss of this fat seriously reduced the caloric content of meat, which was important in situations where food resources were limited.

Frying retained the juices of the meat and was commonly done in a long-handled, three-legged skillet called a *spider*. Frying pans were used to cook food other than meat in oil, fat or lard. Flat disks of cornmeal, wheat flour, bread dough, and the meats of acorns or chestnuts were sometimes prepared in this manner into hoe cakes or journey cakes. Batters of many types were dropped into boiling oil to make spoon bread.

Because the housewife was busy with milking early in the morning, breakfast was often composed of easily prepared foods like toast and

The most prominent feature in an early colonial home was the large area dedicated to the hearth. In the 18th century, fireplaces were constructed of brick or stone in an attempt to make them more efficient as heaters.

cheese, or was made from leftovers from the previous night's meal. Dinner, served at noon, was the main meal of the day. Supper, much like breakfast, was a simple meal of leftovers or the like. On southern plantations, however, breakfast could be quite an elaborate meal, including cold meats, fowl, game, hominy and hot breads. A British traveler visiting plantations in Virginia reported a breakfast replete with "roasted fowls, ham, venison, game and other dainties." Even at Williamsburg it was "the custom to have a plate of cold ham on the table; and there is scarcely a Virginia lady who breakfasts without it."[13] Menus reflected the season's bounty. Spring dinner might have been an eel pie flavored with winter savory. While spring brought reassurance of nature's renewal and promised the bounty of the harvest, it was the least generous of all the seasons. Spring provided little in the way of fresh produce and stores put away in the fall had been greatly depleted during the winter. A housewife welcomed early season greens such as wild onions, dandelions, and even skunk cabbage to supplement a dwindling supply of root crops, such as turnips, parsnips, and carrots. In summer, she served a leek soup and garden greens. A fall dinner might have included recently slaughtered pork or goose with apples. In winter, boiled meats made more appealing with a variety of sauces or vegetable and fruits preserved from the harvest would have been standard fare. The inventory taken in January 1672 following Francis Plummer's death provides insight into the resources of a family of the "middling sort." The dairy house held 4 1/2 *flitches*, or sides of bacon, a quarter of a barrel of salt pork, 28 pounds of cheese, and 4 pounds of butter. Upstairs in a chamber were more than 25 bushels of English grain—barley, oats, wheat and rye—two bushels of malt, and a bushel of peas and beans. The cellar contained a full barrel of cider. Small amounts of pickles, preserves, and dried herbs were unlikely to have been counted.[14]

Baking was traditionally done one day a week. Some homes had outdoor freestanding bake ovens protected by a small, open-sided structure with a wooden roof. Others had ovens built into the fireplace. Before baking began, a fire would be built in the oven and kept burning until the oven reached the proper temperature. The coals and ashes would then be swept out, the flue closed, and the food set inside to bake. Mrs. Smith of Sharon, Connecticut, recalled that by "five o'clock [in the morning] the bread was ready to be molded, the hickory coals were lying in great glowing mass on the oven bottom, casting a brilliant light over its vaulted top and sending such a heat into my face when I passed by the oven mouth that it caused me to think then, as it always does, of Nebuchadnezzar's fiery furnace, seven times heated."[15] If a house had no oven, baking was done in iron kettles. In New England, brown bread, made by the first settlers from a mixture of wheat and corn, became a staple. Primitive mortars used to grind corn into meal and wheat into flour were a fixture in the frontier home. Since the time of ancient Rome, rye flour had been considered of secondary quality for baking, but following an outbreak of wheat rust in the 1660s, rye flour almost completely replaced wheat for several years. The wheat flour was elevated thereafter for use on special occasions and for ornamental uses such as the top crust of a pie.

A family's clothing also depended greatly on the skill and industry of the housewife. Early in the process, men and boys were involved in the labor-intensive gathering and processing of wool and flax, but it was a woman's job to spin it, weave it, and fashion it into clothing and linens. During the initial period of settlement, colonists depended on English imports for their clothes, and spinning wheels and looms were rare. However, when trade with England was disrupted by the English Civil Wars, the spinning wheel became an increasingly common furnishing in colonial homes. In 1656, the Massachusetts General Court passed a compulsory spinning law that detailed weekly spinning quotas and fines for failing to meet assessments. By the end of the 17th century, virtually every family was involved in some small-scale textile production. A contemporary writer observed that families made "their own ordinary clothing and covering for beds."[16] Once spun, wool could easily be knitted into caps, stockings, mittens, and dishcloths.

Spinning could be done with several devices. The simplest was the drop spindle, a weighted stick that could be spun like a top. The spinner attached a leader of prepared wool, or *rolag*, to the shaft and, giving the spindle a quick turn, let it drop. As it fell, it twisted the fibers of wool into thread. When the spindle stopped, the spinner wound the newly spun yarn onto the shaft, added a new piece of wool, and repeated the process.

The spinning wheel was a mechanical device that helped to keep the spindle in motion, usually through some sort of foot-operated or hand-operated mechanism. The spindle was attached horizontally to a post and connected by a cord to a drive wheel. There were several kinds spinning wheels. The largest of these was the great wheel, or "walking wheel." It got this nickname from the fact that the spinner gave the wheel a turn with one hand and drew out the woolen fiber with the other, stepping backwards, inch by inch as the thread lengthened, as far as her arm would reach. She would then walk toward the wheel, reeling the thread on to the spindle, adding a new piece of fiber and repeating the process. At the end of a day's spinning using the great wheel, a woman would have done a good deal of walking.

The flyer wheel or foot wheel was a much smaller spinning wheel that permitted the spinner to sit as she spun. This wheel was most commonly used to spin flax into linen thread although it could be adapted to spin wool yarn. The spinner threaded the fiber through a bobbin and onto metal hooks on a U-shaped device called a flyer. As the bobbin turned, it spun the fiber on to the shaft. A foot treadle permitted the spinner to use both hands as she spun. When spinning flax, a cage like device called a distaff was used to hold the combed flax. Spun yarn was wound onto a handheld niddy-noddy, or mechanical click reel, to form skeins.[17] After winding, the skeins were washed, dyed, and placed on a swift to be wound into balls for knitting, spooled for warping, or wound onto quills for the weaver's shuttle.

Spinning was a nonseasonal activity. A woman might spin just enough yarn for a particular item, or she might spin every day. Elizabeth Wildes's daybook contained such entries as, "I spun one black stocking. Cleaned my west room and scoured the pewter." and "Wove some on the children['s] coats." Similarly, Ruth Henshaw noted that she had spun linen for curtains, carded wool for a wrapper, and woven an apron.[18] Following the imposition of the Townshend duties in 1767, the domestic production of cloth took on new significance. Women had long gathered at the minister's home to spin cloth for his personal wardrobe, but the editors of Patriot newspapers began capitalizing on these gatherings and redirecting them to the purposes of the boycott by producing cloth. In urban areas, woman began to assemble with their spinning wheels in day-long gatherings of patriotic fervor. Even women of means proudly sported garments manufactured at home.[19]

Weaving, unlike spinning, remained a predominately male occupation and virtually every community of some size had its weaver. Households would bring their spun linen and wool to the weaver to be woven into yard goods. The weaver also would have yard goods of his own production available. Housewives often had small hand or table looms known as tape looms. These were used to weave narrow strips for use as garters, shoestrings, belts, hat bands, stay laces, braces, and tapes. Tapes were essential to secure petticoats, shifts, and aprons. Simply a heddle frame, these primitively shaped boards were cut so that the center of the board had a row of narrow slats pierced by a small hole through which the warp threads passed. The board could be held at the bottom by the weaver's knees and steadied at the top by being tied to the back of a chair. The lightness of these small looms allowed them to be carried to a neighbor's house for an afternoon of work and socializing.

Southern plantation mistresses did not spin nor weave for their families. Most of their clothing, linens, and cloth was imported. A diarist noted of Virginians, "They have their clothing of all sorts from England ... yet, flax and hemp grow no where in the world better than here. Their sheep ... bear good fleeces; but they shear them only to cool them."[20] Female servants and slaves produced clothing when trade prices were depressed and import costs high.

Sewing was also an essential skill for colonial women. A housewife had to supply her household with bed linens and towels, as well as producing clothing for constantly growing children and doing everyday mending. Mastery of the needle was an essential skill for all women at this time. Wealthy women had the opportunity to spend a good deal of time doing fancywork, which demonstrated their needle skills in decorative projects, but they still needed a knowledge of plain sewing to oversee their servants and hired help. Most women engaged mainly in plain sewing.

Textiles were a large part of a family's wealth. Inventories taken for probate commonly listed textiles immediately after land holdings, money, and silver. Clothing was repaired, remodeled, and recycled. Such conservation was not done solely out of frugality. It was less time consuming than making a new garment. When a garment was no longer able to be used it would be cut down and remade for a smaller family member. Infants and toddlers were dressed in gender-neutral gowns until the age of four or sometimes older. These simple garments were easy to make and eliminated the need to engage in detailed sewing of garments, which the little ones would soon outgrow. Although sewing was a regular part of her routine chores, needlework may have been a welcome opportunity for a woman to sit down and relax while still being productive. The simplicity of the task even allowed it to be done by the limited light of the fire at night. Sewing could be brought along while visiting or employed while socializing. Such elementary sewing as mending and hemming required little attention and permitted a woman to converse or to listen to someone reading.

From time to time, clothing needed laundering. Woolen jackets and petticoats probably never got more than a good beating, a brushing, and an airing, but linen shifts, caps, fischus, aprons, shirts, and household

Women often brought small items of textile production with them when they visited. The women here can be seen sewing and knitting while carrying on a casual conversation.

linens required washing. Households almost always had a child in diapers, and women must have engaged in this activity with some regularity. Women did not write about the process of doing laundry, but period texts on housewifery provide some insight to students of the period. Stains and heavily soiled items were pretreated. One suggestion was to lay the cloth in "the juice of sorrel and salt." Other directions included rubbing butter into a stain and letting the cloth soak in scalding hot milk prior to washing or "scrape chalk thin all over." Soaking the item in urine was recommended to remove ink stains.[21]

The next step in the cleaning process was "bucking" where the linens were steeped in lye. Ash was placed at the bottom of a tub and alternate layers of ash and cloth were stacked until the tub was filled. This was then covered "with a bucking cloth" and the laundress was instructed to "then pour into all through the uppermost cloth so much warm water, till the tub can receive no more; and let it stand all night." The following morning the water was drained from the tub by means of a spigot at the bottom of the tub. The woman was instructed to let "the water therein run into another clean vessel, as the bucking tub wasteth, so shall you fill it up again with lye which cometh from the bucking tub, ever observing to make the lye hotter and hotter till it seeth, and then when it so seetheth, you shall as before apply it with boiling lye at least four hours together, which is called the driving of a buck."[22] Finer quality ashes were best for bucking, and the New England colonies were plentiful with the best trees for producing good "pot" ash, and loads of ash were sent to England as a product of the country. Linens bucked with such ashes became "more white by this means by once bucking of it, then by sundry times with ... ordinary ashes."[23] After bucking came "batting, or beating cloths to get the bucking stuff out."[24] New cloth also had to undergo bucking. Markham advises the housewife to "with your hand ... poss and labor" the cloth in a bowl or dish to get more lye and ashes into it then rinse clean to remove the ashes.[25] Both household linens and new linens were laid in the sun to bleach.

Early writings from Plymouth colony mention other materials used to launder clothing and cloth. *Mourt's Relation* states, "Here is sand, gravel, and excellent clay, no better in the world, excellent for pots and will wash like soap." Chalk, a form of clay, was used to scrub clothes during the laundering process.[26] Soap was made by boiling a mixture of animal fat and lye in a kettle for many hours. Lye was obtained by pouring water into a leach barrel filled with hardwood ashes. The water would drain through the layers of ash, and the lye trickling out a small opening at the bottom was captured in a small bucket or tub. An older recipe explains," The great Difficulty in making Soap come is the want of Judgment of the Strength of the Lye. If your Lye will bear up an Egg or a Potato so you can see a piece of the Surface as big as a Nine pence it is just strong enough."[27] Six bushels of ash and twenty-four pounds of grease rendered enough lye to make a barrel of soft-textured soap. This soap was very harsh and seldom used for personal hygiene. A hard soap made from the waxy bayberry was more desirable for toilet use.

Herbs served as both spice rack and medicine chest. The garden was also an important resource to housewives who were expected to be knowledge in making medicines and nursing the sick. The tradition of using plants as "physicks" for healing as well as seasoning came along with the settlers from Europe. When John Pynchon was suffering from a rash on his hands, his wife made an ointment of "walnut tree buds beaten and moistened with strong liquor."[28] Just as women learned to bake bread or make a pie from their mothers or kinswomen, they learned to make medicines to treat common family ailments such as coughs and weeping sores. Much of this knowledge was handed down through oral tradition but sometimes medicines were recorded along with recipes with for mushroom catsup and syllabub in notebooks called "receipt books." The mainstay of these remedies were plants such as rosemary, mint, savory, and other herbs grown in the garden. Garden herbs were likely to be the only medicines available to many colonists, especially those in rural areas. Hyssop was mixed with honey to make a cough syrup. Yarrow were placed on wounds to stop bleeding, Savory was used to treat colic. Many herbs, notably marjoram, had a variety of uses. Tea brewed from marjoram leaves was given to relieve spasms, colic, and indigestion. When chewed, marjoram eased toothaches. Mixed with honey, the leaves lessened bruising. [1]The colonists learned to use native plants from the Indians. They were introduced to bee balm, which was brewed into "Oswego tea" for relief from colic, fever, or colds. Most medicines were made by distilling. The plants were boiled in water or wine, and the condensation collected in another vessel. Some were made into a tea that was steeped in water left out in the sun. Ointments and poultices were made by mixing the herbs with lard or oil.

Family nursing was not limited to providing syrups and salves. The mistress of a house was obligated to watch over anyone in her household who was taken ill, including servants and apprentices. When someone was ill, they were never left alone. There was always someone or even a group of people "watching" over them. The watcher could be anyone in the household, but the mistress of the house was primarily responsible and probably seldom left the bedside, especially if it were a sick child. Neighbors could also serve as watchers. A woman would be expected to spend some time assisting a neighbor with watching a sick person in her household as well. Mary Holyoke, for example, traveled from Salem to Boston to attend the deathbed of a former African servant who was then working for another family.[29]

An informal hierarchy of healers formed within communities of women. Some women gained considerable expertise in tending the sick. Cotton Mather declared that it was the duty of "our gentlewomen" to care for the sick.[30] Indeed, some women in higher social classes maintained a supply of remedies that could be given to less fortunate or less knowledgeable families in need. Elizabeth Davenport, a clergyman's wife in Connecticut, maintained a supply of medicines, which she used to care for New Haven's sick.

Women not only helped one another in times of sickness, they also bargained and traded their products and skills. They joined together to accomplish time consuming activities such as candlemaking. One woman could oversee a large group of children freeing up the others to focus on the task at hand. Such communal activity also limited the number of implements that any one woman needed to own. Each member of the group might own one or more of the tools needed for the task. Evidence of such tool sharing by neighbors shows up in probate records with inventories listing "half a hetchel" or "half a dyepot."[31] This pooling of energy, skill, and apparatus proved an effective means of attacking tedious or unpleasant tasks. The work product of the activity would then be divided among the women.

While the plantation mistress did not have to toil over the hearth cooking, nor spend countless hours sewing and mending clothing for her household, she was responsible for a large number of servants and slaves and was often required to take in visitors. In a region where widely-placed and sweepingly-large plantations produced few travelers and left the countryside bereft of small villages, it became the custom for travelers to ask for lodging at any private home happened upon as night fell. Additionally, when people of the upper classes traveled in the area, they wrote to relatives, friends, and friends-of-friends seeking accommodations while in the area. Oftentimes, these visits were for a considerable number of days. The plantation mistress was expected to graciously welcome these temporary inflations of her household in stride. Philip Fithian, a tutor at Nomini Hall plantation reported, "Mrs. Carter informed me last evening that this family, one year with another, consumes 27,000 lbs. of pork and twenty beefs, 550 bushels of wheat, besides corn—4 hogsheads of rum and 150 gallons of brandy."[32]

The mistress of a plantation did not have to personally execute the often labor intensive tasks tackled by women of lesser means. She was responsible, however, for directing and supervising others who did. Fithian frequently returned to Nomini and "found Mrs. Carter seeing to the roosting of her poultry."[33] Nor was it strange that, in February, it was Mrs. Carter who "ordered the gardener to sew [*sic*] lettuce and plant peas this day in the garden."[34] The mistress of the plantation, just as a woman of lesser means, would have been responsible for the oversight of the household garden. While she had not actually toiled in the sun nor dirtied her hands working the soil, it was Mrs. Carter, nonetheless, who proudly displayed her apricot-grafts and asparagus beds to visitors later that spring.

While the work of the housewife varied in accordance with social status and location, her tasks also evolved as time progressed and communities developed. The earliest women settlers and those who lived on the frontier were mainly concerned with supplying the family's basic needs. The majority of their time was taken up with producing, cooking, and preserving food; sewing and repairing clothing; caring for the children; and assisting their spouse in any way they could. Cooking and other food-related activities probably consumed the largest portion of a housewife's time. As settlements grew into towns and cities, women had greater access to processed goods and manufactured materials. Most townswomen continued to tend gardens and care for domestic animals, but those who could afford to do so increasingly relied on servants or hired poorer women to provide some relief from the drudgery of maintaining their household and to provide the opportunity to engage in some personalized expression of the household skills in which she excelled.

This infusion of consumerism in the 18th century brought about other changes as well. For the more affluent, it meant a wide variety of luxury and decorative household items that required a whole new set of household chores. Silver had to be polished, furniture dusted, and company entertained. Women hosted teas that required a number of ancillary items in addition to the tea kettle, teapot, and tea cups. Serving required the right tea table, canisters, bowls, saucers, spoons, strainers, a milk or cream pitcher, a sugar container, sugar tongs, and a slop bowl. Custom even dictated the arrangement of the serving pieces, which varied according to the shape of the serving table. Rather than simple one-pot meals, dinners became an elaborate procession of courses that were guided by books that detailed symmetrical placement of serving pieces. All this spawned new domestic strategies and required more food preservation, careful shopping and knowledge of social etiquette.

NOTES

1. Julia Cherry Spruill, *Women's Life and Work in the Southern Colonies* (New York: W.W. Norton, 1973), 64.

2. Ibid., 65.

3. Laurel Thacher Ulrich, *The Age of Homespun: Objects and Stories in the Creation of an American Myth* (New York: Vintage, 2001), 285.

4. Pamela J. Snow, "Increase and Vantage: Women, Cows, and the Agricultural Economy of Colonial New England," 2001 Annual Proceedings Dublin Seminar for New England Folklife (Boston: Boston University Scholarly Publications, 2003), 33.

5. Rennet is an enzyme obtained from the stomachs of slaughtered newborn calves that clots or curdles milk. The dried inner membrane was kept in salt until needed, then soaked in water.

6. Snow, "Increase and Vantage," 24.

7. Richard M. Bacon, *The Forgotten Art of Growing, Gardening, and Cooking with Herbs* (Dublin, New Hampshire: Yankee, 1972), 8.

8. Quoted in Marian I. Doyle, "A Plentiful Good Table,"in *Early American Life*, (December, 2001), 46.

9. Ulrich, *The Age of Homespun*, 22.

10. Every bit of fat left over from cooking was set aside for candlemaking. Beef fat produced candles that were firmer and less unpleasant smelling than those from pork fat. Families used whatever fat was available, even that from predators or pests.

11. Quoted in Alice Morse Earle, *Home Life in Colonial Days* (1940; reprint, Stockbridge, MA: Berkshire House, 1993), 39–40.

12. Quoted in Michael R. Best, ed., *The English Housewife* (Montreal: McGill-Queens University Press, 1986), 22.

13. William Pierce Randel, *The American Revolution: Mirror of a People* (New York: Routledge, 1973), 65.

14. Ulrich, *The Age of Homespun*, 19.

15. Helen Everston Smith, *Colonial Days and Ways* (New York: Century, 1901), 229.

16. Ulrich, *The Age of Homespun*, 84.

17. Both the niddy-noddy and click reel have given rise to children's rhymes. The niddy-noddy, with its two T-shaped heads, brought about "Niddy-noddy, niddy-noddy, two heads, one boddy," and the popping sound of the click wheel or weasel was the inspiration for "Pop Goes the Weasel."

18. Ulrich, *The Age of Homespun*, 187.

19. For a more detailed examination of women's spinning as a demonstration of the patriot cause and how women were affected by the American Revolution, see Dorothy Denneen Volo and James M. Volo, *Daily Life during the American Revolution* (Westport, CT: Greenwood Press, 2003), 229–38 and 260–71.

20. Qoted in Sprull, *Women's Life and Work*, 75.

21. Maureen Richard, "Washing Household Linens and Linen Clothing in 1627 Plymouth," 13.

22. Best, *The English Housewife*, 162–64.

23. Richard, "Washing Household Linens," 16.

24. Ibid., 16.

25. Quoted in Best, *The English Housewife*, 163. To "poss" was to beat or stamp.

26. Dwight B. Heath, ed., *Mourt's Relation: A Journal of the Pilgrims at Plymouth* (Boston: Applewood Books, 1986), 39.

27. Quoted in Earle, *Home Life in Colonial Days*, 254.

28. Rebecca J. Tannenbaum, "The Housewife as Healer: Medicine as Women's Work in New England," 160.

29. Ibid., 162.

30. Ibid., 166.

31. Ulrich, *The Age of Homespun*, 288.

32. Philip Vickers Fithian, *Philip Vickers Fithian: Journals and Letters*, ed. (Princeton, New Jersey: University Library, 1900), 75.

33. Ibid., 45.

34. Ibid., 63.

Part IV
The Role of Children

12

Children as Family

How senseless is my heart and wild!
How vain are all my thoughts!
Pity the weakness of a child,
And pardon all my faults.

—Isaac Watts, Song 24
Divine and Moral Songs

During the colonial period, families generally included a large number of children. The general abundance of food and raw materials to be had in America allowed even the poor to support a larger family than would be found in Britain or other parts of Europe. The scarcity of wage laborers demanded large numbers of children. Big families meant that there would be plenty of hands to help with family productivity. It was the duty of children to contribute to the well-being of the family with their labor. A large number of progeny also increased the likelihood that parents would be provided for in their old age. Families having ten to twelve children were not uncommon. Often, these children had different mothers. When a man lost his wife, he often quickly remarried to provide a mother to an earlier brood of children.

For example, Charles Carter married twice and had 23 children. John Paige had 12 children by his first wife and 8 by his second. Thomas Smith had 20 children, 10 by each of his two wives. George Moore had 27 children. By the time the younger children were born, older sisters and brothers had often left home, married, and had children of their own.

Some children had aunts and uncles younger than themselves. Writing to his brothers in 1754, Peter Fontaine mentioned 6 grandchildren ranging in age from newborn to five years and minor children of his own ranging from four months to 12 years. Two years later, he fathered another child. When he died a year later, he left the care of his younger children to those children of his first marriage who had families of their own.[1]

Children were often given names with deep religious significance. After naming his daughter Sarah, Samuel Sewall wrote, "I was struggling whether to call her Mehetable or Sarah. But when I saw Sarah's standing in the Scripture, Peter, Galatians, Hebrews, Romans, I resolv'd on that side."[2] Sometimes parents named their children for the virtues or character traits they hoped the child would develop, such as Comfort,

Children were often dressed as miniature adults. This youngster of nine or ten has even been given a dress sword as part of his ensemble.

Deliverance, Temperance, Peace, Hope, Patience, Charity, Submit, or Silence. This tradition was a carryover from a practice in vogue among English Puritans during the late 16th and 17th centuries. Roger Clap named his children Experience, Waitstill, Preserve, Hopestill, Wait, Thanks, Desire, Unite, and Supply. Sometimes events provided the inspiration. Susanna Johnson named the child born during her Indian captivity Captive. Widow Dinely, whose husband was lost in a snowstorm, named the child Fathergone.[3]

Children were also named for deceased siblings or ancestors. Necronyms (names of the dead) were given 80 percent of the time when a child of the same sex was born after the death of a family member. Ephraim and Elizabeth Hartwell of Concord, Massachusetts, lost their five children, Ephraim, Samuel, John, Elizabeth, and Isaac to "throat Distemper" in a single month in 1740. The parents had nine more children named Elizabeth, Samuel, Abigail, Ephraim, John, Mary, Sarah, Isaac, and Jonas.[4]

In Pennsylvania and Delaware, Quaker babies underwent a ritual known as nomination. The infant's name was selected by the parents, certified by friends, witnessed by neighbors, and finally entered into the register of the meeting. Quakers tended to name their firstborn children after grandparents. They were careful to acknowledge both sides of the family, sometimes going so far as to name the first girl to commemorate the paternal line and the first boy to honor the maternal line. This tradition was particularly popular in the Delaware Valley. Other favored names came from the Bible. John, Joseph, and Samuel were popular for sons; Mary, Elizabeth, and Sarah were often chosen for daughters. Many families chose attribute names for daughters, such as Patience, Grace, Mercy, and Chastity. Double Christian names, such as John Paul or Abigail Mary, were rare until after the Revolution except in Puritan communities.

While parents surely loved their children, their demonstrations of affection, in some ways, differed from those of today. Puritan parents who hoped to bring their offspring to God had the responsibility of breaking the spirit of independence in the child. In his essay, "Children and Their Education," John Robinson wrote, "Surely there is in all children a stubbornness and stoutness of mind arising from natural pride which must in the first place be broken and beaten down so that the foundation of their education being laid in humility and tractableness other virtues may in their time be built thereon." This "breaking and beating down" was generally achieved through harsh and restrictive supervision. Puritans believed that children were born empty of both knowledge and goodness but full of willfulness.[5] Anne Bradstreet's poem "The Four Ages of Man" illustrates this attitude.

When Infancy was passed, my Childishness,
Did act all folly, that it could express ...

From birth stained, with Adam's sinful fact;
From thence I 'gan to sin as soon as act.
A perverse will, a love to what's forbid:
A serpents sting in pleasing face lay hid.
A lying tongue as soon as it could speak,
And fifth Commandment do daily break.[6]

Mary Osgood Sumner kept a *Monitor*, or diary, in which she kept a *Black Leaf*, or page of all her childish misbehaviors and omissions of duty and a *White Leaf* showing the duties she conscientiously performed. Her cited misdeeds were:

July 8	I left my stays on the bed.
9	Misplaced sister's sash.
10	Spoke in haste to my little sister, spilt the cream on the floor in the closet.
16	I left the brush on the chair; was not diligent in learning at school.
17	I left my fan on the bed.
19	I got vexed because sister was a-going to cut my frock.
22	Part of this day I did not improve my time well.
30	I was careless and lost my needle.
Aug. 5	I spilt some coffee on the table.[7]

Mary's White pages, which contain many more entries than her Black, testify to the long and busy days during which children were expected to contribute to the family's needs. A typical entry was, "I did everything before breakfast; after breakfast made some biscuits and did all my work before the sun was down."[8] Some days Mary rated herself as less industrious. "I was pretty diligent at my work to-day and made a pudding for dinner;" or "I stuck pretty close to my work to-day and did all that sister gave me and after I was done I swept out the house and put things to right"; or "I got some peaches for to stew after I was done washing up the things and got my work and was middling diligent."[9] Often she referred to her studies or to sermons that she heard.[10] "I did everything before breakfast; endeavored to improve in school; went to the funeral in the afternoon, attended to what was said, came home and wrote down as much as I could remember."[11]

Such record keeping made children very aware of both their good behavior and their shortcomings. Children were expected to be productive and to contribute to the work of the household as their age would permit. They were lectured about the sudden deaths of other children and were required to read intimidating verses from the Bible. They were taught never to be confident of their salvation. Such strain caused Sewall's daughter to break down while reading from Scripture: "Betty can hardly read her chapter for weeping; tells me that she is afraid she is gone back, does not taste that sweetness in reading the Word [scripture] which she once did; fears that what was once upon her is worn off. I said what I could to her, and in the evening pray'd with her alone."[12]

Children were corrected not only to teach them socially acceptable behavior but also because they bore the mark of original sin. Sewall recorded an incident involving his badly behaving four-year-old son and concluded with a biblical reference to Adam: "Joseph threw a knob of Brass and hit his Sister Betty on the forehead so as to make it bleed and swell; upon which, and for his playing at Prayer-time, and eating when giving Thanks, I whip'd him pretty smartly. When I first went in (call'd by his Grandmother) he sought shadow and hide himself from me behind the head of the Cradle which gave me sorrowful remembrance of Adam's carriage."[13] Ezekiel Rogers, a Puritan minister, wrote, "I find greatest trouble and grief about the rising generation. Young people are little stirred here; but they greatly strengthen one another in evil by example and counsel. Much ado have I with my own family."[14]

Ministers instructed parents on the importance of disciplining children. When it came to honor and reverence, some ministers observed that often parents seemed "not to expect or challenge it from their children, either in word or gesture."[15] Warning that such an attitude allowed children to become over familiar, as if there were "no difference twixt parent and child,"[16] these ministers feared that too many children "carry it proudly, disdainfully and scornfully towards parents."[17] It is thought by many students of the period that these fears lead Puritans to the practice of "sending out" their children to other families. Children were commonly placed with other relatives, neighbors and even strangers. With their new families, children were expected to learn life skills such as reading, housewifery, or a trade. This placement may also have made disciplining children easier. Children left home just at the age when they would begin to assert themselves and their independence. Surrogate parents were less likely to be indulgent and forgiving of their charges. This allowed parents to avoid such friction and fostered an air of parental affection.

Permissive parents were not tolerated within the Puritan community. Laws compelled parents who were remiss in this regard to do what others did of their own volition. New England laws provided that a rebellious son or any child that cursed or smote his parents deserved death. Typically, however, the courts turned to another law that stated that when a child was permitted to become "rude, stubborn and unruly" the state could remove the intractable offspring from his family home "and place them with some masters for years which will more strictly look unto, and force them to submit unto government ... if by fair means and former instructions they will not be drawn unto it."[18] A Connecticut statute stated:

> Foreasmuch as incorrigibleness is also adjudged to be a sin of death, but no law yet amongst us established for the execution thereof … it is ordered, that whatsoever child … shall be convicted of any stubborn or rebellious carriage against their parents or governors … the governor or any two magistrates have liberty and power from this court to commit such person or persons to the house of correction, and there to remain under hard labor and severe punishment, so long as the court or the major part of the magistrates shall judge meet.[19]

Some communities also took control from the parents when the behavior of children at worship fell below community standards. The "disorder and rudeness of youth in many congregations in time of the worship of God, whereby sin and profaneness is greatly increased" caused great consternation to many congregations. A Connecticut justice recorded some of the behavior. Included were "Smiling and laughing and enticing others to do the same … . Pulling the hair of his neighbor … [and] Throwing Sister Pentecost Perkins on the ice on the Sabbath day between the meeting house and his place of abode." Some communities hired a man for the express purpose of "keeping the boys in subjection." The congregation at Harwich voted "that the same course be pursued with the girls." A congregation at Farmington in 1772 passed the following resolution: "Whereas indecencies are practiced by the young people in time of public worship by frequently passing and repassing by one another in the galleries; intermingling sexes to the great disturbance of many serious and well minded people—Resolved that each of us that are heads of families will use our utmost endeavor to suppress the evils."[20]

While many parents used physical punishment to maintain discipline, not all parents condoned its use. Prominent Puritan minister Cotton Mather chose a more compassionate path. In his booklet *A Family Well-Ordered, or an Essay to Render Parents and Children Happy in One Another* he explained how he trained his children in goodness and piety.

> I first beget in them a high opinion of their father's love to them, and of his being able to judge, what shall be good for them. Then I make them sensible, tis folly for them to pretend unto any wit and will of their own … my word must be their law … I would never come to give the child a blow, except in the case of obstinacy, or some gross enormity. To be chased for a while out of my presence I would make to be looked upon as the sorest punishment in his family … The staunch way of education carried on with raving and kicking and scourging (in schools as well as in families), is abominable.[21]

In time, such progressive attitudes became more widespread, and the influence of less severe religious sects created a more moderate philosophy of child rearing. The letters between John and Abigail Adams reveal them as tender and caring parents who were aware of their responsibility to raise dutiful children. A letter from John in 1774 counsels, "from that affection for our lovely babes, [we must] apply ourselves by every way we can …. Above all cares of this life, let our ardent anxiety be to mold the minds and manners of our children …. Pray remember me to my dear little babes, whom I long to see running to me and climb up upon me …. [M]ake your children hardy, active and industrious; for strength, activity and industry will be their only resource and dependence."[22]

The Quaker attitude toward children was quite different from the Puritan outlook. Quaker households were child centered, reflecting the belief that young children should be protected from the world and nurtured within a controlled environment. Parents preferred rewards to punishments, and as children grew older, they appealed to their reason. William Penn advised parents to love their children "with wisdom, correct them with affection: never strike in passion, and suit the correction to their age as well as fault. Convince them of their error before you chastise them."[23]

Children of Dutch settlers enjoyed a carefree youth of simple pleasures, and parents openly displayed their affection for their youngsters. Traveling in colonial New York, Anne Grant reported, "You never entered a house without meeting children. Maidens, bachelors, and childless married people all adopted orphans and all treated them as if they were their own."[24] She described picnics, parties, and other fun activities for children, which took place regularly. Contrary to New England practice, she noted, "Indeed, it was the females that the task of religious instruction generally devolved. … [T]he training of children … was the female province."[25]

On southern plantations female slaves who were responsible for waking, feeding, and dressing the child in the morning and preparing the child for bed at night frequently provided the majority of childcare eclipsing somewhat the role of the mother. Children often formed very close attachments to these women. Two-year-old Thomas Jones became extremely fond of his nurse, Daphne, during his mother's absence. Young Jones affectionately called her, "Da Da" and often clung to her neck. His grandmother, Elizabeth Cooke Holloway, observed, "He kisses her and runs his head in her neck."[26] Such behavior was often tolerated in early childhood, but children were expected to distance themselves from slaves and servants as they got older. Those children who were slow to make the transition were a cause of concern to family members who worried about the child's ability to assume the proper position of the social class. Anne Blair wrote a letter expressing her relief that her niece had finally lost interest in keeping company with the slaves and as a result was beginning to break the habit of speaking like them.[27] For many young girls, such a voluntary separation signaled that they were entering womanhood and becoming aware of their position in plantation society. Nonetheless, many women maintained long-lived relationships with their nurses, which continued even after marriage.

From an early age, plantation children were well aware of the difference between a directive from their parents or guardians and one from their nurse. In a letter to her cousin, Maria Carter described a typical morning at Westover plantation in the 1750s. "I am awakened out of a sound sleep with some croaking voice either Patty's or Milly's or some other of our domestics with 'Miss Polly, Miss Polly get up, tis time to rise, Mr. Price[28] is down stairs', and tho' I hear them I lie quite snug till my Grandma raises her voice, then up I get, huddle on my clothes and down to book, then to breakfast then to school again."[29]

Except in the most elite ranks of society, colonial children were expected to contribute to the family's welfare as soon as they were able. Only in infancy were they treated simply as children with no responsibilities. As early as three years old, children were given simple chores. Not only did this help to instill a sense of responsibility, but it kept them from underfoot as well. Young children gathered goose feathers, picked berries and helped process food. Older children plaited straw, weeded the garden, or knitted stockings.

Early American attitudes toward children were reflected to a degree in their clothing. Infants and toddlers were dressed in gender-neutral gowns until the age of four or sometimes later. Thereafter, they were dressed as miniature adults. While frontier and rural children were usually dressed in clothing made by their mothers or in garments cut down from the castoffs of older siblings, portraits of children from wealthy families show the excess to which some families went in costuming their offspring. Privileged children were lavished with every fashion excess to which their parents succumbed. Staymakers advertised that they had stays for young girls "to make them appear straight"[30] Mary Holyoke noted in her diary when her child was only slightly over sixteen months old, "Poll began her shoes and stays."[31] Some children were outfitted with wigs, which were fairly expensive even for adult fashion tastes. An expense book from 1750 shows that a father not only purchased wigs for his sons, aged eleven, nine, and seven years but even paid for "shaving my three sons [heads] at sundry times."[32] George Washington's order for clothing for his six-year-old stepdaughter included such impractical items as "a coat made of fashionable silk … stays … 2 pair of satin shoes with flat ties … 12 pair of mitts … [and] 6 pair white kid gloves."[33]

Seventeenth-century settlements in Connecticut, Massachusetts, and Virginia had sumptuary laws prohibiting extravagance in dress. Despite the admonitions of ministers and threats from magistrates, children and adults were often unable to curb their passion for large sleeves and heavily laced attire. The Dutch—possibly the most sophisticated group in Europe at the time—never attempted to restrain fashion embellishments. In New York, clothing was rich and abundant, with fashionable clothing

Both children pictured here are boys. Young boys, like the one on the right, were dressed in gowns until they were breeched. Older children were often dressed as miniature adults.

making up a considerable part of estate inventories. A portrait of three-year-old Katherine Ten Broeck shows her wearing earrings.

Playthings were few and simple. Boys played with marbles, balls, whistles, tops, small boats, toy soldiers, wooden animals, and whatever else a loving father might carve from a piece of wood by a winter's fire. A book published in America near the end of the colonial period lists a number of games and pastimes for boys, including kite flying; dancing round maypoles; marbles; fishing; blind man's bluff; shuttlecock; thread the needle; hop, skip and jump; stool ball; trap ball; swimming; and leap frog. Every game is described in rhyme and accompanied with a moral lesson, illustrating that few opportunities were wasted to lecture children in proper behavior and attitude. The game of chuck-farthing is presented thus.

> Chuck—Farthing
> As you value your pence
> At the hole take your aim
> Chuck all safely in,
> And you'll win the game.
> Moral.
> Chuck-farthing like trade
> Requires great care

The more you observe
The better you'll fare.[34]

These lines describing the game of marbles conjure an image of children at play around a circle scratched in the sandy ground.

Marbles Knuckle down to your taw.
Aim well, shoot away.
Keep out of the Ring,
You'll soon learn to play.
Moral.
Time rolls like a marble,
And drives every state.
Then improve each moment,
Before it's too late.[35]

Other rhymes, such as this one for "Pitch and Hussel" depict games that have been lost over time, and the vagueness of the lines leaves little indication of how the game was played.

Poise your hand fairly
Pitch plumb your slat
Then sake for all heads
Turn down the hat.[36]

Girls mimicked their mothers' activities playing with whatever bowls and spoons were not in use. They also played with moppets, or dolls, made from scraps of fabric or pieces of wood. Many were more like a log with a face carved or drawn on it than like a make-believe baby. Both boys and girls enjoyed blowing bubbles. Outside, children used their imaginations and nature's playthings to fashion garlands of flowers, small boats of leaves and pods, and whistles from blades of grass. Winter always brought sledding, ice-skating, early forms of hockey, ice-fishing, and snowball fights. Unfortunately, not all children were careful to restrain their throws or to check the stability of the ice before venturing out on its surface.

Books specifically written for children were unavailable until the mid-18th century when English publisher John Newbery began to publish them. Just after the Revolution, American printer Isaiah Thomas began to publish children's books for the American market, most of them wholesale copies of English works. These books exhorted goodness and virtue in children and commanded obedience to parents and God. Children were taught to behave well and to fear hell. Horrible fates befell the mischievous children between the covers of these volumes and the good and virtuous were well rewarded by the final pages. In *The Fairchild Family*, little Lucy, a remarkably introspective child, recites the

Unlike teens today who like to sport their own style, colonial
teenagers dressed like their parents.

following prayer: "My heart is so exceedingly wicked, so vile, so full of
sin, that even when I appear to be tolerably good, even then I am sinning.
When I am praying. or reading the Bible, or hearing other people read the
Bible, even then I sin. When I speak, I sin; when I am silent, I sin." Such
was the emphasis placed on the flaws in human nature due to original sin
that even little children were taught to consider themselves innately evil,
requiring them to constantly struggle against their sinful tendencies.[37]

Childhood in the 17th and 18th century was often tenuous and harsh.
Illness and accidents claimed many children. Discipline was sometimes
harsh and idleness was unacceptable. Children put in long days to help
the family meet its needs. Yet families were strongly bound together
by respect, love, and honor. Isaac Norris wrote of his two daughters,
"They are a constant care as well as great amusement and diversion to

me to direct their education aright and enjoy them truly in the virtuous improvement of their tender minds."[38]

NOTES

1. Julia Cherry Spruill, *Women's Life and Work in the Southern Colonies* (New York: W. W. Norton, 1973), 48–49.

2. M. Halsey Thomas, ed., *The Diary of Samuel Sewall, 1674–1629*, vol. 1 (New York: Farrar, Straus, and Giroux, 1973), 324.

3. Alice Morse Earle, *Child Life in Colonial Days* (New York: Macmillan, 1940), 15.

4. David Hackett Fischer, *Albion's Seed: Four British Folkways in America* (New York: Oxford University Press, 1989), 96.

5. Earle, *Child Life in Colonial Days*, 191–92.

6. Joseph R. McElrath Jr. and Allan P. Robb, eds., *The Complete Works of Anne Bradstreet* (Boston: Twayne, 1981), 37–38.

7. Quoted in Earle, *Child Life in Colonial Days*, 167.

8. Quoted in ibid., 168.

9. Quoted in ibid., 168–69.

10. It was common practice for both children and adults to maintain a book with notes from sermons they had heard.

11. Quoted in Earle, *Child Life in Colonial Days*, 168.

12. Thomas, *The Diary of Samuel Sewall*, 300.

13. Ibid.

14. Quoted in Arthur W. Calhoun, *The American Family in the Colonial Period* (Minneola, NY: Dover, 2004), 118–19.

15. Quoted in Edmund S. Morgan, *The Puritan Family Religion and Domestic Relations in Seventeenth-Century New England* (New York: Harper and Row, 1966), 77.

16. Ibid., 77–78.

17. Ibid., 78.

18. Ibid., 78.

19. Arthur W. Calhoun, *The American Family in the Colonial Period*, 120.

20. Ibid., 117.

21. Ibid., 113–14.

22. Ibid., 115.

23. Fischer, *Albion's Seed*, 509.

24. Anne Grant, *Memoirs of an American Lady, with Sketches of Manners and Scenery in America as They Existed Previous to the Revolution* (New York: Samuel Campbell, 1805), 62.

25. Ibid., 29.

26. Quoted in Kathleen M. Brown, *Good Wives, Nasty Wenches, and Anxious Patriarchs: Gender, Race, and Power in Colonial Virginia* (Chapel Hill: University of North Carolina Press, 1996), 300.

27. Ibid., 300.

28. Mr. Price was most likely Maria's tutor.

29. Quoted in Brown, *Good Wives*, 299.

30. Earle, *Child Life in Colonial Days*, 58.

31. George Francis Dow, ed., *The Holyoke Diaries* (Salem: Essex Institute, 1911), 54.

32. To ensure a good fit and increase comfort, many wig wearers shaved their heads. See Earle, *Child Life in Colonial Days*, 50.

33. Quoted in ibid., 66–67.

34. Quoted in ibid., 347.

35. Quoted in ibid., 375.

36. Quoted in ibid., 347.

37. Quoted in ibid., 297.

38. Fischer, *Albion's Seed*, 508.

13

Children as Learners

I quickly learned to read without going to any school I remember.
—Josiah Cotton, his diary

Colonists in America retained the Old World tradition that stressed the centrality of the household as the primary place of education. This was reinforced by the reality that many settlers had limited access to formal institutions of learning. Believing that the inability to read was an attempt by Satan to keep people from the Scriptures, the Puritans of Massachusetts passed a law in 1642 requiring that all children should be taught to read. Parents were required to instruct their own offspring and any children placed in their care to "read and understand the principles of religion and the capital laws of the country" and to provide them with skills for employment.[1] Other colonies enacted similar statutes, with Connecticut following in 1650 and New York in 1665. A Pennsylvania ordinance of 1683 asserted that all parents and guardians should instruct their children "in reading and writing, so that they may be able to read the Scriptures and to write by the time they attain twelve years of age; and that they be taught some useful trade or skill."[2] Fines were established for violators of these laws although records are unclear as to whether or not they were actually levied. The widely scattered homesteads of the American South dictated educational self-sufficiency but even in the more densely settled New England villages with established churches and schools, Puritans considered the family the most important agent of education.

Virginia required that both children and servants be provided with weekly religious instruction. An act of 1705 provided that the master of every orphan bound as an apprentice be "obliged to teach him to read and write"[3] in addition to teaching him a trade. Orphaned children of free parents were generally apprenticed. In some localities, this process was overseen by the church, but the ultimate jurisdiction over such matters rested with the courts. Some indentures were quite specific. Richard Allen was promised "three year's [*sic*] schooling, and ... to be sent to school at the [age] of twelve or thereabouts." Sarah Allen's master was required "to instruct her in the rudiments of the Christian religion, [and] to learn or cause her to learn to read perfectly." Ann Chandler's apprentice indenture required that she be "taught to read a chapter in the Bible, the Lord's Prayer, and Ten Commandments." A 1724 order in the Petsworth Parish records stated that "all orphan children bound out by the parish hereafter, that if they cannot read at thirteen years of age that they shall be set free from their master or mistress or be taken from them."[4]

Because it provided access to the Scriptures, reading received the greatest emphasis. Common lessons included the alphabet, a few simple words, or a prayer such as the Lord's Prayer or the Apostle's Creed. Affluent families may have bought an instruction manual, such as Edmund Coote's *The English Schoole-Maister* Designed for "the unskillful ... as have undertaken the charge of teaching others," this book specifically identified tailors, weavers, shopkeepers, and seamstresses, among other skilled persons, as potential purchasers. With or without a textbook, children were taught to read using passages with which they were already familiar. The Bible was often the most common source, but devotional works such as *The Book of Martyrs* and *Pilgrim's Progress* also provided material. Parents had the responsibility to educate their children in the manners and morals of the community. *The Practice of Piety*, *The Way of Duty* and *The Poor Man's Family Book* and other such works of faith, which dealt with cardinal virtues and their application in human affairs, were also employed. Polly Wharton wrote to her cousin, Mary, on Christmas day in 1778, "After my embroidery, I read from the Bible and then from my father's copy of Mr. Foxe's *Book of Martyer's* [*sic*]. I also read from Mr. Janeway's *A Token for Children*. He teaches us that laziness is the worst form of sin; that good children must rise early and be useful before going to school, and do their chores at evening. He tells us to love the Lord and to serve our elders."[5] Some families drew selections from books on proper deportment and demeanor, such as *The Schoole of Virtue* or *The First Schoole of Good Manners at the Academy of Complements*, which purported to instruct the reader in appropriate language for every occasion from a lover's tryst to a long trip requiring small talk. Isaac Watt's *Divine and Moral Songs* was a collection of rhymes for children intended to lay a foundation for virtue and industry. The rhymes addressed such topics as lying, quarreling, and fighting; scoffing and calling names; pride in clothes; and obedience to parents. They were rife with threats of terrible fates for children who failed to live a live of virtue. Song 23 began:

> Let children that would fear the Lord
> Hear what their teachers say;
> With reverence meet their parents' word,
> And with delight obey.
> Have you not heard what dreadful plagues
> Are threatened by the Lord,
> To him that breaks his father's law,
> Or mocks his mother's word?
> What heavy guilt upon him lies!
> How cursed is his name!
> The ravens shall pick out his eyes,
> And eagles eat the same.[6]

Guardians were also responsible for training children "in some honest lawful calling, labor, or employment."[7] At the very least, boys would be instructed in how to manage a household, farm, or shop. Instruction was commonly done through a family business or an apprenticeship. Benjamin Franklin began working in his father's business as tallow-chandler at age 10. By 12, he believed that he was "destined" to that profession. He recalled, "[M]y dislike to the trade continuing, my father was under apprehensions that if he did not find one more agreeable, I should break away and get to the sea. ... He therefore sometimes took me to walk with him, and see joiners, bricklayers, turners, braziers, etc. at their work, that he might observe my inclination, and endeavor to fix it on some trade or other on land." Franklin was ultimately apprenticed to his older brother James, a printer.[8]

A single trade or business, such as lumbering, ironmaking, or fishing, dominated certain communities. It followed that the residents had a narrow focus of education and training, and the opportunities for young men were limited. For island communities, the sea was their lifeblood and those who would live and prosper there needed to understand all aspects of its commerce. Teamsters drove wagons to and from the wharf. Sailmakers made and repaired sails in their sail lofts. Rope makers were busy twisting rope of all sizes. Blacksmiths forged harpoons and lances. Coopers made oil and water casks while carpenters fashioned masts, spars, and other ship's fittings from wood. Chandlers provided the ships with provisions and supplies. Wealthy whaling merchants and captains had stylish houses designed and built for them.

In his description of 18th-century Nantucket, J. Hector St. John de Crevecoeur described how boys were trained to become productive members of a whaling community.

This illustration from an antique linen postcard shows a young apprentice blacksmith hard at work. Apprenticeships at a trade or craft usually began at the onset of adolescence and lasted for seven years.

At schools they learn to read and write a good hand, until they are twelve years old; they are then in general put apprentices to the cooper's trade, which is the second essential branch of business followed here; at fourteen they are sent to sea, where in their leisure hours their companions teach them the art of navigation, which they have an opportunity of practicing on the spot. They learn the great and useful art of working a ship in all the different situations which the sea and wind so often require, and surely there cannot be better or more useful a school of that kind in the world. They then go gradually through every station of rowers, steersmen, and harpooners; thus they learn to attack, to pursue, to overtake, to cut, to dress their huge game; and after having performed several such voyages and perfected themselves in this business, they are fit either for the counting-house or the chase.[9]

Most girls were taught by their mothers to manage a household using example and participation as a means of instruction. From as early as three years of age, girls were expected to assist their mothers in caring for the household. Tasks assigned were appropriate to the child's age and increased in number and difficulty as she grew. Mothers passed on generations of advice and custom through conversation and demonstration. Much the same means were used to teach the boys who learned husbandry from their fathers. Additional pedagogical instruction may have come from such popular books as *Five Hundred Points of Good Husbandry*. A farmer's son or young man apprenticed to agriculture might have learned a rhyme such as this one:

> Banks newly quick settled, some weeding do
> The kindlier nourishment thereby to have.
> Then after a shower to weeding a snatch
> more easily weed with the root to dispatch.

A young woman may have recited:

> Good flax and good hemp for to have her own,
> in May a good housewife will see it be sown.
> And afterward trim it, to serve at a need,
> the fimble to spin and the carl for her seed.[10]

Peter and Margarite Schuyler adopted and educated in their well-to-do household a number of nieces and nephews. Their instructional routines included the reading of Scriptures at breakfast. This was followed by directives to the domestic servants as part of an apprenticeship in the value of good housewifery. At dinner and tea, there was pleasant and edifying conversation. Madame Schuyler's perpetual knitting was said to set an example of humble diligence for all. The girls would have been taught plain sewing, which included knitting, mending, and simple stitching. The simplicity and repetitiveness of plain sewing lent itself to conversation. Women sewed as they visited and caught up on news. Sometimes one person read aloud while the others worked. Even very young girls who sat and worked as the elders chatted learned the attitudes and expectations society had for them as adults. The Schuylers, like many others, provided a education in social cultivation and useful knowledge for the children of their household.

Such deliberate yet casual instruction was not uncommon. Recalling his boyhood, Franklin wrote, "At his table [my father] liked to have, as often as he could, some sensible friend or neighbor to converse with, and always took care to start some ingenious or useful topic for discourse, which might tend to improve the minds of his children. By this means he turned our attention to what was good, just and prudent in the conduct of life; and little or no notice was ever taken of what related to the victuals on the table."[11]

The Carters of Virginia provided a similar kind of household education. Additionally, they retained a number of music and dancing masters, governesses, and tutors, including Philip Fithian, who worked for the household during 1773 and 1774. Like many Virginia tutors of the day, he was from Scotland. Commenting on this practice, he wrote, "[I]t has been the custom heretofore to have all their tutors, and schoolmasters from Scotland, tho' they begin to be willing to employ their own countrymen."[12] Because Fithian was engaged to teach eight children ranging in age from 17-year-old Benjamin to 5-year-old Lucy, he was required to individualize instruction over a wide range of skill levels. Fithian recorded the following entry in his journal after his first day of tutoring: "The school consists of eight—two of Mr. Carter's sons—one nephew—and five daughters. The eldest son is reading Salust: Grammatical Exercises and Latin Grammar—The second son is reading English Grammar and reading English: Writing and ciphering in subtraction. The nephew is reading and writing as above and ciphering in reduction. The eldest daughter is reading The Spectator;[13] writing and beginning to cipher. The second is reading next out of the spelling book[14] and beginning to write. The rest is reading in the spelling book. The fourth is spelling in the beginning of the spelling book and the last is beginning her letters."[15] In addition to providing instruction to the children, he mediated their arguments and escorted them to neighboring plantations for dances.

Daughters of southern planters often benefited from the fact that when tutors were engaged to teach the boys in the family, the girls were often sent as well. At age fifteen, Mary Ball, later to become the mother of George Washington, wrote of her Virginia education: "We have not had a schoolmaster in our neighborhood till now in nearly four years. We have now a young minister living with us who was educated at Oxford, took orders and came over to assist Rev. Kemp. The parish is too poor to keep both, and he teaches school for his board. He teachers Sister Susie and me and Madam Carter's boy and two girls. I am now learning pretty fast."[16]

Long school days were the norm on plantations. Fithian provides some insight: "[I]n the morning so soon as it is light, a boy knocks at my door to make a fire; after the fire is kindled I rise which is now in the winter commonly by seven, or a little after. By the time I am dressed, the children commonly enter the school room, which is under the room I sleep in; I hear them round one lesson when the bell rings for eight o'clock.... The children then go out; and at half after eight the bell rings for breakfast ... after breakfast, which is generally about half after nine, we go into school, and sit 'til twelve, when the bell rings and they go out for noon; the dinner bell rings commonly about half after two, often at three, but never before two. After dinner is over, which ... is about half after three we go into school, and sit till the bell rings at five, when they separate 'til the next morning."[17] John Harrower reported similarly long days: "My school hours [are] from 6 to 8 in the morning, in the forenoon from 9 to 12 and from 3 to 6 in the afternoon."[18]

Many Virginia tutors were indentured servants. Colonel Daingerfield hired John Harrower for a four-year indenture. On his first day as tutor, Harrower wrote, "[T]he Colonel delivered his three sons to my charge to teach them to read, write and figure. [H]is eldest son, Edwin, 10 years of age, entered into two syllables in the spelling book. Bathurst, his second son, six years of age, in the alphabet and William, his third son, 4 years of age does not know the letters."[19] Harrower received excellent treatment, taking meals at his master's table, sharing the company of visitors, and accompanying the family to church, barbecues, and fishing parties. Such privileges reflected Harrower's personal traits and the value which Daingerfield placed on education. Like other tutors, Harrower was encouraged to take on additional pupils from neighboring plantations and permitted to keep any fees he charged, providing a most welcome augmentation to his income. One of Harrower's adventitious pupils was John Edge, the deaf-mute son of a neighboring planter. After having worked with the young man for only five months, Harrower reported that "he can write mostly for anything he wants and understands the value of every figure and can work single addition a little."[20]

Virginia tutor Jonathan Boucher viewed tutors like Harrower or Fithian in a different light, complaining in 1773 that at least two-thirds of the instructors in Virginia were either indentured servants or transported felons. He alleged that every ship arrived with either redemptioners or convicts who advertised as schoolmasters, weavers, tailors, or any other trade, noting that the only difference was that the tutors fetched a lower price than the others.

Where settlements were better established, colonial communities made an organized effort to provide more formal instruction. The instigation for this came from the communities themselves rather than from the colony governments. By 1650, institutional schooling was firmly established in North America to varying degrees in different regions. Maryland had a school for teaching the humanities. Benjamin Syms endowed a free school in Virginia, bequeathing 200 acres of land and its produce, along with the increase of eight cows, for the children of Elizabeth City and Poquoson. New Netherlands had a town school in New Amsterdam, and New England had at least a dozen schools capable of providing Latin grammar instruction and numerous other dame and master schools.

Unlike New England, the middle colonies had no tradition of mandatory education. The constitution that Penn drafted in 1682 included requirements for a public school system, but no one ever saw that they were enforced. Schooling was generally left to various religious groups to handle as they saw fit. German was the predominant language in areas such as Lancaster County, and it was often the main, if not sole, language used for instruction.

Dutch settlers in New York also wanted their schools to reflect the teachings of their church. A public school was established in New Amsterdam as early as 1633, but it was only for children whose parents were members of the Dutch Reform Church. Following the English takeover of New Netherlands, Dutch parents wanted to ensure that their children retained their native tongue. As late as 1755, a group of Dutch parents in New York refused to hire a schoolmaster who spoke English. Dutch schools heavily emphasized religious teachings, stressing catechism drills and infusing daily activities with prayers. Girls attended school with boys but in different schoolrooms.

The number of schools and the extent of schooling increased tremendously during the 18th century throughout the colonies. Rapid economic growth and increased social mobility made education both necessary and attainable. The interest of individuals to enter politics spawned a profusion of newspapers and pamphlets and a widening desire to be literate. Additionally, denominational sects increasingly turned to schools as agencies of their religious message. Educational expansion was, however, by no means linear, nor was it uniform from region to region.

Educational institutions could be classified into three basic categories. The *petty* or *dame schools* initially stressed reading, but by the 18th century included writing and simple arithmetic. Latin *grammar schools* offered instruction in classical languages, literature, and mathematics. Some offered algebra, geometry, trigonometry, navigation, surveying, rhetoric, logic, and astronomy. *Academies*, the least well defined category, offered varied curricula often governed by the knowledge of the master and the interest of the sponsor.

The curriculum generally was in keeping with that found in England. Religious reading received the greatest emphasis in schools as it did in the home. The standard sequence of reading instructional materials began with the hornbook then moved to the primer, the Psalter, the New Testament, and finally the complete Bible.

Hornbooks were paddlelike boards with a thin, transparent piece of horn covering the piece of paper containing the information to be learned. The sheet of horn that gave the instrument its name protected the lesson from soiling as it was passed from child to child. The first mention of a hornbook in colonial records is a bill "for horning book" that Charles Lidgett made out to his wife in 1678.[21] Samuel Sewall noted in his diary in 1691, "This afternoon had Joseph to school to Capt. Townsend's mother's, his cousin Jane accompanying him, carried his hornbook."[22] It is not surprising that Joseph needed assistance as he was only three years old at the time. Records of the Old South Church in Boston show payments for "horns for catechizing," and throughout the 18th-century, newspapers carried advertisements offering hornbooks for sale.[23] Hornbooks

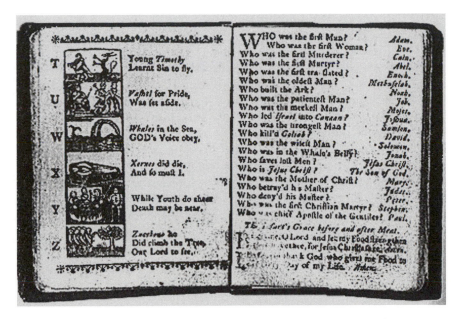

The photograph shows a surviving New England Primer from the 18th century.

were usually a child's introduction to formal learning. Gifts were made of hornbooks and some were quite fancy trimmed in gilt or ivory. Some cookie molds were made to replicate a hornbook with an alphabet lesson. It would be used to produce a kind of gingerbread hornbook treat for the good scholar. An 18th-century rhyme proclaims, "And that the child may learn the better, All he can name he eats the letter."[24]

Texts were generally few, and one book served a number of students. Arithmetic was often taught without textbooks. Teachers had manuscript sum-books from which they dictated rules and problems to their pupils. Sometimes the sums were given to pupils to be copied without any explanation. A 1773 sum-book belonging to Sarah Keeler contained multiplication examples of fifteen figures multiplied by fifteen figures and long division examples of a dividend of quintillions, mainly in sevens and nines, divided by a mixed divisor of billions in eights and fives. It would be remarkable if modern students could understand such ciphers.[25]

Rhymes were thought to be an aid to memory, and they were used as an instructional vehicle for almost any topic. *The Grammar of the English Tongue* offered this verse for the definition of a letter:

A Letter is an uncompounded Sound
Of which there no Division can be Found,
Those Sounds to Certain Characters we fix,
Which in the English Tongue are Twenty-Six.[26]

The 18th century also saw a popular trend away from the more classical content toward a more practical curriculum. A letter to the editor summed up the feelings of many people at the time, asserting that classical languages were in "no way necessary for useful knowledge. How many children have been forced to drudge several years in learning Greek and Latin, who after they left the school entirely forgot those languages, by being of no manner of use to them in the course of their life. As to these (who are likewise the most numerous) their time might be better employed in their manner of life and business."[27] A mid-18th-century chronicler of his education noted that a classmate "thought he had Latin enough, as he was not designed for a learned profession; his father thought so too, and was about taking him from school." This attitude pervaded the class. "We were all, therefore, to be merchants ... and accordingly, when the question was proposed which of us enter upon the study of Greek ... there were but two or three who declared for it."[28] Advertisements by 18th-century teachers showed a movement toward more practical studies that mirrored like changes in attitude at the college level. One such advertisement served notice that "near the sign of the Red Lion, are taught these Mathematical Sciences viz., Arithmetic, Geometry, Algebra, Fluxions, Trigonometry, Navigation, Dialing, Astronomy, Surveying, Gauging, Fortification, gunnery; the use of globes, also other mathematical instruments likewise the projecting of the sphere on any circle, etc. with other parts of Mathematics."[29]

A child's introduction to school often came in the form of a dame school. Both boys and girls were welcome, and some children began as early as three years old while others might be as old as ten. Mary Holyoke noted in her diary that her daughter, Polly, who was just 31 months old, "went to school."[30] Attendance was often haphazard, and students remained in school for a varying number of years. Classes were held in the schoolmistress' house, enabling her to attend to her household chores, as well as to her students. The mistress, though literate, generally lacked formal schooling. She heard her students recite their prayers or the alphabet while she sewed, spun, or prepared the day's meals. Elizabeth Wright ran a dame school for twenty-two weeks each summer while she cared for her four young children, sewed shirts for Indians and breeches for Englishmen, and wove fine linen.

Instruction was extremely basic. The children were taught some reading and writing and possibly some figuring (simple arithmetic). The girls would have learned simple sewing and knitting, skills they would have begun with their mothers at home. John Barnard wrote about his experience in such a school: "By that time I had a little passed my sixth year, I had left my reading school, in the latter part of which my mistress had made me a sort of usher appointing me to teach some children that were older than myself as well as some smaller ones."[31]

Swedish naturalist Peter Kalm, who traveled throughout America between 1748 and 1751, observed, "They had separate schools for small boys and girls. When a child was a little over three it was sent to school both morning and afternoon. They probably realized that such little children would not be able to read much, but they would be rid of them at home and thought it would protect them from any misbehavior. Also they would acquire a liking for being with other children."[32]

Alexander Graydon's recollections of his education. show that then, as now, the personal strengths of teachers had a great effect upon their pupils, and not all students embraced their educational opportunities with the dedication for which their parents may have hoped. When Graydon was between his sixth and seventh year, he was enrolled in a private school conducted by David James Dove. Graydon recalled, "It was his [Dove's] practice in his school to substitute disgrace for corporal punishment. His birch was rarely used in canonical method, but was generally stuck into the back part of the collar of the unfortunate culprit, who with this badge of disgrace towering from the nape ... was compelled to take his stand upon the top of the form for such a period of time as his offense was thought to deserve." When students were late, Dove would "dispatch a committee of five or six scholars ... with a bell and a lighted lantern" to collect the tardy students and escort them to class "the bell all the while ringing." Apparently, Dove was a fair man, able to take as well as give punishment. One day when he was late to class, "he found himself waited on in the usual form. He immediately admitted the justice of the procedure ... and marched with great solemnity to school, to the no small gratification of the boys."[33]

At age eight, Graydon was sent on to an academy. There "[t]he task of the younger boys, at least, consisted in learning to read and write their mother tongue grammatically; and one day a week ... was set apart for the recitation of select passages in poetry and prose ... . This speech was carefully taught him by his master, both with respect to pronunciation and the action deemed suitable to its several parts."[34] From there Graydon went to the Latin school and became a pupil of John Beveridge, whom he describes as "diligent and laborious in his attention to his school. But unfortunately, he had no dignity of character, and was no less destitute of the act of making himself respected than beloved." He made "pretty free use of the rattan and the ferule[35] but to very little purpose" and consequently was "very unequal to the management of seventy or eighty boys, many of whom were superlatively fickle and unruly. He was assisted, indeed, by two ushers who eased him in the burden of teaching, but who, in matters of discipline seemed disinclined to interfere."[36] Graydon recorded various indignities that were played on Beveridge, a diminutive man, by his students. The most vicious, perhaps, was a grand conspiracy. As he entered the door, all the window shutters were slammed shut. At once the room was plunged into "utter darkness, the most hideous yells that can be conceived, [were] sent forth from at least threescore throats; and Ovids, and Virgils, and Horaces, together with the more heavy metal of dictionaries ...

[were] hurled without remorse at the head of the astonished preceptor, who on his side, groping and crawling" made his way to the door.[37]

Students were held to a high standard. Reverend Isaac Watts ran Harrow Hall for boys. He listed the attributes cultivated at his academy in a letter to a parent considering enrolling his son. "My scholars will be Amiable, Benevolent, Conscientious, Forgiving, Grateful, Humble, Industrious, Mannerly, Punctual, Obedient, Quiet, Responsible, Studious and Truthful." He also identified vices that would not be tolerated. "They shall not be Heedless, Selfish, Disobedient, Revengeful, Unthankful, Arrogant, Slothful, Disrespectful, Thoughtless, or Lazy."[38] It was not uncommon for discipline to be served in the form of embarrassment or corporal punishment. Those who did not know their lessons might be required to wear a dunce cap. Those guilty of other acts were often singled out and required to wear a sign around their neck identifying them as a "liar," "gossip," or "idler."[39] A Connecticut schoolmaster ended his detailed description of a "bad boy" with this advice: "To avoid this end, and to make a bad boy into a good one, he should be thrashed daily for some reason or other, and locked securely in a closet. There he can meditate upon his sins and thus avoid his fate."[40]

Once the children reached an age when they were needed at home or in the fields, their education usually ceased. Benjamin Franklin was initially sent to a grammar school, but his father rethought the expense and removed his son to a school for writing and arithmetic taught by George Brownell. By his own account, Franklin "acquired fair writing pretty soon but failed in the arithmetic, and made no progress in it. At ten years old [he] was taken home to assist [his] father in his business, which was that of a tallow-chandler and soap-boiler."[41]

Education of female children was viewed as less essential compared to that of male. It was accepted that a young woman should learn to read and even, perhaps, to write. The ability to cipher a little was also within reason. In practice many women lived their entire lives never learning to do any of these. Ralph Verney was a tender and generous father who adored his little girls even to the neglect of his sons, yet he wrote to a friend, "Let not your girl learn Latin or short hand; the difficulty of the first may keep her from that vice, for so I must esteem it in a woman; but the easiness of the other may be a prejudice to her; for pride of taking sermon notes hath made multitudes of women most unfortunate."[42] An anonymous father quoted in a period newspaper surely would have concurred when he advised his wife on how to educate their daughter:

> Teach her what's useful, how to shun deluding;
> To roast, to toast, to boil and mix a pudding;
> To knit, to spin, to sew, to make or mend;
> To scrub, to rub, to earn & not to spend.[43]

Even Abigail Adams, a consummate lady of letters and wife of a president, complained of her early New England education, "I was never sent to any school.... Female education in the best families went no further than writing and arithmetic; in some few and rare instances music and dancing."[44] Girls in other parts of the country fared no better. Anne Grant wrote of her childhood in Albany in the first half of the 18th century: "[F]emale education was in consequence conducted on a very limited scale; girls learned needlework (in which they were indeed both skillful and ingenious), from their mothers and aunts; they were taught, too, at that period to read, in Dutch, the Bible and a few Calvinistic tracts of the devotional kind."[45]

Most young women who were sent to study learned needlework. A work entitled *Good Order Established in Pennsylvania and New Jersey*, written by a Quaker in 1685, encouraged the establishment of schools where girls could be instructed in "the spinning of flax, sewing, and making all sorts of useful needle work, knitting of gloves and stockings, making straw-works, as hats, baskets, etc. or any other useful art or mystery."[46] The teaching of needlework was commonplace in cities and towns throughout colonial America. Many such schools were actually no more than small classes taught by a woman in her home. Most of these classes were advertised as private tutorials rather than as schools. Students generally ranged from eight to sixteen years old and remained from one to three years with varying degrees of regularity. Girls from rural areas often stayed with a relative while they attended school in a town or city. Many gentlewomen in need of extra income took in girls to board. Period newspapers carried many advertisements offering board for young ladies. Some schools permitted students to board with the family.

Anna Green Winslow traveled from Nova Scotia in to stay with her aunt in Boston while she attended such a school. The twelve year old studied a variety of subjects at different schools. She studied needlework with Mrs. Smith, took a dancing class several days a week with Mr. Turner, and practiced writing with Mr. Holbrook. Anna's attendance was often erratic, skipping classes because of inclement weather or the promise of social engagements. Writing schools like the one Anna attended were actually schools of penmanship. Students practiced their penmanship and studied how to embellish their writing with decorative flourishes called "fine knotting" or "knot work." The journal she kept for her parents frequently contained confessions such as "I have attended all my schools this week, except one day."[47] At one point, the aunt with whom Anna boarded required her to write in her journal, "Whenever I have omitted a school my aunt has directed me to sit it down here, so when you don't see a memorandum of that kind, you may conclude that I have paid my compliments to messrs.

Holbrook & Turner ... & Mrs. Smith as usual."[48] The classes themselves were somewhat fluid. Anna wrote, "I was at sewing and writing school, this afternoon all sewing, for Master Holbrook does not in winter keep school of afternoons."[49]

In both needlework classes and in dame schools, virtually every little girl made a sampler to demonstrate her proficiency in needlework. In the 18th century, most girls from well-to-do families worked two samplers. A simple marking sampler was often done in dame school. On this piece the maker worked the alphabet and often included her name, age and date. The ability to work the alphabet was an important skill as all household linens had to be marked with the owner's initials to distinguish them in the laundry. Emily Robinson finished her alphabet sampler in 1776 with the following verse:

> When I am dead and in my grave
> This needlework will tell
> That I tried to do my very best
> And learned my lessons well.[50]

A favorite rhyme found on other samplers was

> When I was young and in my prime
> You see how well I spent my time
> And by my sampler you may see
> What care my parents took of me[51]

Thereafter, a girl would make a fancy sampler or needlework picture. These still may have contained names and dates but usually lacked alphabets. These intricate projects were prized by the families of the young women who made them. Mary Ann March proclaimed in the *Maryland Gazette* in 1751 that she and her daughter were available to "teach young misses all sorts of embroidery, turkey work, and all sorts of rich stitches learnt in sampler work."[52] Often the completed samplers were hung for display. Sally Wister recorded in her journal that a southern officer visiting her Philadelphia home during the American Revolution "observed my sampler, which was in full view. [He] wished I would teach the Virginians some of my needle wisdom; they were the laziest girls in the world."[53]

As wealth among the middle classes increased in the 18th century, so did the number of girls who were sent to sewing schools. Sewing encompassed a considerable body of skills. One sewing teacher of the period advertised that she taught "all kinds of needlework, viz.: Brussels, Dresden gold, silver and silk embroidery of every kind. Tambour, feather, India & darning, springings with a variety of open-work to each. Tapestry plain, lined, and drawn. Catgut, black and white, with a number of beautiful stitches. Diaper and plain darnings, French quiltings, knitting, various sorts of marking with embellishments of the royal cross, Queen, Irish, and tent stitches."[54]

The painter John Trumbull wrote, "My two sisters, Faith and Mary, had completed their education at an excellent school in Boston, where they both had been taught embroidery; the eldest, Faith, has acquired some knowledge of drawing, and had even painted in oil, two heads and a landscape."[55] By mid-century, many sewing schools began to offer the girls an increasing body of accomplishments. The curriculum was expanded to include skills such as drawing, painting, dancing and even French.[56] A Mrs. Duneau proclaimed that she would instruct her students in "the French and English languages grammatically—geography—history— with many instructing amusements to improve the mind with all sorts of fashionable needlework."[57] Mary Salisbury opened a school in Annapolis in 1754 at which she taught French and "tapestry, embroidery with gold and silver, and every other curious work which can be performed with a needle, and all education fit for young ladies except dancing."[58]

Running a school was often a family enterprise run by sisters, or husbands and wives. One of the first private schools to advertise in the Virginia papers was run by John Walker and his wife. It was somewhat unique in that it accepted both boys and girls. John taught the boys reading, writing and arithmetic, as well as "the most material branches of classical learning and ancient and modern geography and history" while his wife instructed the girls in needlework.[59] John and Mary Rivers offered boarding to young ladies, along with instruction in dancing, singing, French, and fancy needlework.[60]

Teachers of specialized subjects were often brought in to expand the curriculum. One of the earliest examples of this trend was Mary Hext, who advertised in 1741 that she would board "young misses," school them in fashionable needlework, and engage well-qualified masters in writing, arithmetic, dancing, and music. Anna Maria Hoyland taught young ladies to read, embroider and "flourish" and provided masters for writing, arithmetic, dancing, music, and French. M. Harward taught reading and needlework while engaging masters for writing, arithmetic, dancing, music and French.[61]

A widening variety of ladies' accomplishments was offered as the 18th century progressed. E. Armstrong advertised in the *Virginia Gazette* in 1766 that she would teach young ladies French and the latest fashions in needlework. Six years later, the course of study had been expanded to include

petite point in flowers, fruit, landscapes, and sculpture, nuns work, embroidery in silk, gold, silver pearls, or embossed, shading of all kinds, in the various works in vogue, Dresden point work, lace ditto, catgut in different modes, flourishing muslin after the latest taste, and most elegant pattern, waxwork in figure, fruit, or flowers, shell ditto, or grotesque, painting in water colors and mezzo tinto; also the art of taking off foliage, with several other embellishments for the amusement of persons of fortune who had taste.[62]

Various "ladies' arts" rose and fell in fashion during this time. Naturally, many parents wanted their daughters to be proficient in the latest and most fashionable rage. Advertisements often specifically listed the various skills. Reverse painting on glass was quite in vogue toward the end of the period. Mary M'Callister advertised in 1787 that she taught young ladies "painting on glass, Japanning with prints,[63] wax and shell work[64] in the newest and most elegant taste" in addition to needlework. She also made the unusual offer to teach pastry making one day a week.[65]

Making artificial flowers was also quite popular toward the end of the 18th century. The *Boston Evening Post* in 1767 carried the following notice: "To the young ladies of Boston: Elizabeth Courtney ... proposes to open a school and that her business may be a public good, designs to teach the making of all sorts of French trimmings, flowers, and feather muffs and tippets ... as every lady may have a power of serving herself of what she is now obliged to send to England for [sic]."[66]

By the end of the century, it became popular for parts of embroidered pictures, such as faces, to be enhanced with some painting. John Thomas advertised in the *South Carolina Gazette* in 1753 that he was willing to "teach about six young ladies to draw and shade with India ink pencil, which may not only serve as an amusement to their genius, but in some respects become serviceable to them in needlework."[67] John and Hamilton Stevenson advertised in the same publication in 1774 that they taught "painting from life in crayons and in miniature on ivory; painting on silk, satin & etc. fan painting together with the art of working designs in hair upon ivory, & etc."[68]

This trend of broadening the curriculum led to the young ladies' boarding schools that were common in the latter part of the century and flourished through the middle of the 19th century. Many offered formal boarding for their pupils, but girls who lived in town or had family in town attended as day students. Elizabeth Cassens advertised that she would teach children to "do plain work" and was willing to take two or three as boarders. Twelve years later, she indicated that she could take six more young ladies as "constant boarders" and six as "day boarders."[69] Rebecca Woodin advertised that she had relocated to "a healthful and convenient house" where she would continue to instruct young ladies "in different branches of polite education, viz. reading, English and French, writing and arithmetic, needlework; and music and dancing by proper masters.[70] Even though these institutions offered academic subjects in addition to needlework and other aesthetic accomplishments, boarding schools focused on shaping an ideal woman. They trained the girls in obedience, docility, and deportment. Teachers monitored the posture of the girls as they sewed to be sure that they sat straight-backed and held their heads high. At her "boarding and day school," Elizabeth Girardeau promised parents that she would "take the utmost care of their behavior."[71]

A few reformers advocated a more practical education for young women. Hanna More, a late-18th-century champion of women's education, wrote, "[O]rnamental accomplishments will but indifferently qualify a woman to perform the duties of life, though it is highly proper she should posses them [for a diversion]."[72] Dr. Benjamin Rush questioned the value of musical instruction, saying, "After they become mistresses of families their harpsichords serve only as side-boards for their parlors."[73]

Some private schools, such as James Whitfield's, accepted both "young masters and young misses."[74] These schools generally provided the girls with a more academic course of study than most. William Johnson offered both girls and boys schooling in reading, writing, arithmetic, English grammar, geography, and natural philosophy.[75] Another such school advertised in the *South Carolina Gazette* that its course of study included reading, writing, arithmetic, dancing, geography, French, Latin, mathematics, mechanics, and fencing.[76] The girls would not have taken classes in mechanics or fencing, however, and it is not likely that they pursued Latin or mathematics. Classes were not coeducational. Masters took care to make the point in their advertisements that the young ladies were provided with "a convenient separate room"[77] A Mr. Watson advertised in the *South Carolina Gazette* that he had a room for the young ladies "distinct from that in which the young gentlemen are to be."[78]

Rooms were not the only things that separated the young men from the young women. As young ladies were presumed to need only a passing knowledge of most subjects, textbooks were printed specifically for girls. Young ladies studied from *Newton's Ladies Philosophy*, *The Lady's Geography*, *The Female Academy*, and *The Ladies Compleat Letter Writer*. A book entitled *An Accidence to the English Tongue* was a popular grammar designed for boys who had not studied Latin, but it was also touted as being suitable "for the benefit of the female sex."[79]

By the mid-18th-century, Pennsylvania was offering more progressive opportunities to young women than other regions. Quaker schools in Philadelphia provided academic instruction in addition to fine needlework skills. The Moravian School in Bethlehem, which opened in 1740, began to admit non-Moravian girls in 1786. Daughters of many prominent families traveled from as far as South Carolina to study there. The curriculum offered was very similar to that offered at the Moravian school for boys and included reading, writing in English and German, arithmetic, geography, and music, along with some history and botany. Additionally, girls were offered music, drawing, spinning, weaving, and intensive needlework. Girls could enter as early as age five and remain until age sixteen. The needlework produced by these Moravian girls and women became so renowned that visitors to Bethlehem purchased this exceptional work as souvenirs. Of this needlework, Count Francesco del

Verme wrote, "They made very fine tambour embroidery. [It has become] the custom [to buy] something which everyone does who visits this place."[80]

The Moravian philosophy of education stressed gentleness and sensitivity, and the girls were nurtured both intellectually and spiritually in this manner. Discipline was quite progressive for its time. Students in need of discipline might be asked to sit on a bench away from the others. This was in sharp contrast to dame schools, sewing classes, and boarding schools where corporal punishment was the rule. Inattention or carelessness might be rewarded with a thump from a *thimbled digit*. More severe punishments included being blindfolded and forced to stand in the corner or having to sit on a one-legged stool. Some teachers made intemperate and excessive use of the hickory switch as their chosen method of attaining discipline.

Some fathers seem to have had an enlightened view regarding the education of their daughters. When Jonathan Edwards was away from his family, he wrote the following instructions pertaining to his eight-year-old son and five daughters: "[T]ake care that Jonathan don't lose what he hath learnt.... I would also have the girls keep what they have learnt of the Grammar, and get by heart as far as Jonathan has learnt; he can keep them as far as he had learnt. And would have both him and them keep their writing, and therefore write much oftener than they did when I was at home."[81] While Edwards was concerned about his daughters progressing in the footsteps of their brother, this practice probably would not persist as Jonathan advanced into classical studies. Girls were almost never expected to study geometry or any mathematics beyond simple arithmetic, nor would they proceed to a study of Latin or Greek. It was a generally accepted belief that such studies were beyond the capabilities of young women. If young women were to be provided with additional instruction beyond the basics it was more likely to be in performance on a musical instrument or in dancing. Philip Fithian reported that two of his female pupils were absent as they were "practicing music, one on the forte-piano, the other on the guitar. Their Papa allows them for that purpose every Tuesday and Thursday."[82] If a young woman learned any language besides English, it was likely to be French.

Dancing schools in the South were often held in pupils' homes and rotated from house to house. The schools often lasted for several days and were similar to miniature balls. Fithian described a dancing school conducted at Nomini plantation before Christmas 1773. The students, "young misses about eleven & seven young fellows," began to arrive Friday afternoon. Fithian continues:

After breakfast, we all retired to the dancing-room, & after the scholars had their lesson singly [*sic*] round Mr. Christian.... There were several minuets danced with great ease and propriety; after which the whole company joined in country dances, and it was indeed beautiful to admiration, to see such a number of young persons, set off by dress to the best advantage, moving easily to the sound of well performed music, and with perfect regularity, tho' apparently in the utmost disorder—the dance continued til two, we dined at half after three—soon after dinner we repaired to the dancing room again; I observe in the course of the lessons, that Mr. Christian is punctual, and rigid in his discipline, so strict indeed that he struck two of the young misses for a fault in the course of their perfor-mance, even in the presence of the mother of one of them! And he rebuked one of the young fellows so highly as to tell him he must alter his manner, which he had observed through the course of the dance, to be insolent and wanton, or absent himself from the school.

The dancing continued until "it grew too dark to dance," and they with-drew and conversed for a while. "When the candles were lighted we all repaired, for the last time, to the dancing room; first each couple danced the minuet; then we all joined as before in the country dances, these continued till half after seven when Mr. Christian retired." The students remained, engaging in a variety of amusements. They dined at eight thirty and retired at ten. The following morning they returned to their respective homes.[83]

The *Catechism of Health*, a standard children's book, provided the fol-lowing guidance to parents who had questions about the extent to which their daughters should be educated. "Query: Ought female children to receive the same education as boys and have the same scope of play? Answer: In their earlier years there should be no difference. But there are shades of discretion and regards to propriety which judicious and pru-dent guardians and teachers can discern and can adjust and apply."[84]

Records show that many parents made provisions in their wills for the education of their daughters. In 1657, Clement Thrash willed that his entire estate be used for the education of his thirteen-year-old stepdaughter for three years. He even specified that she study with a Mrs. Peacock. Similarly, Sarah Pigot declared that her entire estate be used for the schooling of her granddaughter. Nicholas Granger designated the profit from a number of cattle to provide for his daughter's education. Francis Page's will charged that his daughter be provided with "the best education which this country could afford," and John Russell's funded his daughter's education until she married.[85]

Some communities established schools for poor and orphaned children. In addition to being concerned about the spiritual and educational needs of the children, these institutions were careful to make sure that the chil-dren learned a trade that would permit them to make a living, and much of the children's day was spent in this pursuit. One of the most remark-able of these charitable institutions was the Orphan House at Bethseda, Georgia. Established by the Reverend George Whifield, the orphanage took in both boys and girls. A former inmate described the daily schedule, which began at 5 in the morning. Students washed and dressed, attended church and sang hymns before breakfast. After this morning meal, students worked at various "employs": "At ten they go to school, some to writing, some to reading. At present there are two masters and one mistress, who in teaching them to read the Scripture, at the same time explain it to them"[86] After lunch they again engaged in their assigned productive tasks. "From two till four they go to school as in the morning, and from four to six work at their respective (work) stations."[87] The children retired to bed at nine o'clock.

NOTES

1. Lawrence A. Cremin, *American Education: The Colonial Experience, 1607–1783* (New York: Harper and Row, 1970), 124.

2. Quoted in ibid., 125.

3. Lyon Gardiner Tyler, "Education in Colonial Virginia," part 1, "Poor Children and Orphans," *William and Mary College Quarterly* 4 (April 1897), 220.

4. Quoted in ibid., 220, 222.

5. Quoted in John L. Loeper, *Going to School in 1776* (New York: Atheneum, 1973), 69–70.

6. Isaac Watts, *Divine and Moral Songs* (New York: Hurd and Houghton, 1866), 23.

7. Quoted inCremin, *American Education*, 133.

8. Alden T. Vaughan, *America before the Revolution,1725–1775* (Englewood Cliffs, NJ: Prentice-Hall, 1967), 80.

9. J. Hector St. John de Crevecoeur, *Letters from an American Farmer and Sketches of Eighteenth-Century America* (New York: Penguin, 1981), 128–29.

10. Thomas Tusser, *Five Hundred Pointes of Good Husbandrie,* ed W. Payne and Sidney (London: Tribner, 1878), 113.

11. Quoted in Vaughan, *America before the Revolution*, 80.

12. Philip Vickers Fithian, *Philip Vickers Fithian: Journals and Letters* (Princeton, New Jersey: University Library, 1900), 58.

13. *The Spectator* was a popular newpaperlike English periodical.

14. Spelling books were introduced into the colonies around the turn of the 18th century. More than just the spellers of modern times, these books also taught reading and even morality. Before the American Revolution, spelling books, like most texts, were imported from England. In 1783, Noah Webster spent his own money to publish *A Grammatical Institute of the English Language,* a speller that he claimed would unify the young nation by introducing a uniform system of pronunciation.

15. Fithian, *Journals and Letters*, 50.

16. Quoted in Alice Morse Earle, *Child Life in Colonial Days* (New York: Macmillan, 1940), 94.

17. Fithian, *Journals and Letters*, 60.

18. Quoted in Vaughan, *America before the Revolution*, 40.

19. Ibid., 40.

20. John Harrower, (updated 25 January 1999), http://www.chatpress.com/uae-5.html (accessed).

21. M. Halsey Thomas, *The Diary of Samuel Sewall, 1674–1729* (New York: Farrar, Straus, and Giroux, 1973), 277.

22. George A. Plimpton, "The Hornbook and Its Use in America," *Proceedings of the American Antiquarian Society* 26 (1916), 269.

23. Ibid.

24. Ibid., 268.

25. Earle, *Child Life in Colonial Days*, 139.

26. Quoted in ibid., 136.

27. Quoted in Vaughan, *America before the Revolution*, 88.

28. Quoted in ibid., 78.

29. Quoted in ibid., 90.

30. George Francis Dow, ed., *The Holyoke Diaries* (Salem: Essex Institute, 1911), 58.

31. Earle, *Child Life in Colonial Days*, 97.

32. Adolph B. Benson, *Peter Kalm's Travels in North America*, vol. 1 (New York: Dover Publications, 1934), 204.

33. Quoted in Vaughan, *America before the Revolution*, 74.

34. Quoted in ibid., 76.

35. The rattan and the ferule were wooden sticks used to discipline students. The rattan was canelike and the ferule was flat, much like a ruler.

36. Quoted in Vaughan, *America before the Revolution*, 76–77.

37. Quoted in ibid., 77.

38. Quoted in John L. Loeper, *Going to School in 1776*, 33.

39. Such chastisement was similar to the mortification conferred on adults by confining them to the pillory as punishment for certain crimes. Boston had a pillory as late as 1803. Samuel Beck wrote of Boston in 1771, "A little further down the street was to be seen the pillory with three or four fellows fastened by the head and hands, and standing for an hour in that helpless posture, exposed to gross and cruel jeers from the multitude, who pelted them incessantly with rotten eggs and every repulsive kind of garbage that could be collected." Offenders wore signs identifying their crimes. Soldiers found guilty of theft or drunkenness were often marched through the camp at drumbeat wearing similar signs.

40. Quoted in Loeper, *Going to School in 1776*, 63.

41. Vaughan, *America before the Revolution*, 80.

42. Earle, *Child Life in Colonial Days*, 91.

43. Selma R. Williams, *Demeter's Daughters: The Women Who Founded America, 1587–1787* (New York: Atheneum, 1976), 111.

44. Earle, *Child Life in Colonial Days*, 94.

45. Ibid.

46. Alice Morse Earle, *Home Life in Colonial Days* (Stockbridge, MA: Berkshire House, 1993), 259.

47. Earle, ed., *Diary of Anna Green Winslow, a Boston Schoolgirl of 1771* (Bedford, MA: Applewood, 1996), 34.

48. Ibid., 70.

49. Ibid., 35.

50. Loeper, *Going to School in 1776*, 68.

51. Earle, *Home Life in Colonial Days*, 267.

52. Julia Cherry Spruill, *Woman's Life and Work in the Southern Colonies* (New York: W. W. Norton, 1972), 199.

53. Sally Wister, *Sally Wister's Journal: A True Narrative* (Bedford, MA: Applewood, 1995), 48.

54. Earle, *Diary of Anna Green Winslow*, 105.

55. Theodore Sizer, ed., *The Autobiography of Colonel John Trumbull* (New Haven, CT: Yale University Press, 1953), 5.

56. French became popular in large cities following the American Revolution because of the close relationship between the two countries. In some port towns, such as Charleston, South Carolina, French was taught earlier in the century as trade with the French West Indies brought many native speakers to the town.

57. Spruill, *Woman's Life and Work*, 199.

58. Ibid.

59. Ibid, 200.

60. Ibid., 199.

61. Ibid., 198.

62. Ibid., 200.

63. Japanning with prints is similar to modern decoupage.

64. Shell work and wax work, which involved arranging shells or small figures made from wax into decorative pictures enclosed in deep frames, were often combined with quilling, a delicate craft that involves rolling thin strips of paper into tiny coils and cones, to make intricate wall decorations. These pieces were assembled and configured to form flowers, animals, and other designs. Frequently, the completed work was sprinkled with bits of mica to catch the light of a candle. Such handiwork was especially popular from the late 17th century through the third quarter of the eighteenth century.

65. Susan Burrows Swan, *Plain and Fancy; American Women and Their Needlework, 1650–1850* (Austin: Curious Works Press, 1995), 74.

66. Alice Morse Earle,ed, *Diary of Anna Green Winslow*, 109–10.

67. Swan, *Plain and Fancy*, 75.

68. Ibid.

69. Julia Cherry Spruill, *Women's Life and Work*, 198.

70. Ibid., 198.

71. Ibid., 199.

72. Swan, *Plain and Fancy*, 77.

73. Ibid.

74. *Women's Life and Work*, 201.

75. Ibid.

76. Ibid.

77. Ibid., 202.

78. Ibid.

79. Ibid.

80. Elizabeth Cometti, ed., *Seeing America and Its Great Men: The Journal and Letters of Count del Verme, 1783–1784* (Charlottesville: University Press of Virginia, 1962), 32. Tambour work, a form of embroidery, gets its name from the tambourine-shaped frame on which the fabric was stretched. The thread was drawn through the fabric with an extremely fine hook, producing a chain stitch much more quickly than a traditional needle. Tambour work became popular in the last quarter of the 18th century and continued into the early 19th century.

81. Earle, *Child Life in Colonial Days*, 93.

82. Fithian, *Journals and Letters*, 76.

83. Ibid., 63–64.
84. Earle, *Child Life in Colonial Days*, 95.
85. Spruill, *Women's Life and Work*, 185.
86. Ibid., 192.
87. Ibid., 193.

14

Children as Workers

[L]ittle children here by setting of corn may earn much more than their maintenance.

—Reverend Francis Higginson,
Higginson's True Description, 1629

The Puritan belief in the virtue of work and the sin of idleness made a childhood of fun and play very brief indeed. In his *Well-Ordered Family,* Benjamin Wadsworth wrote, "[T]ime for lawful recreation now and then, is not altogether to be denied [to children] .... Yet for such to do little or nothing else but play in the streets, especially when almost able to earn their living is a great sin and shame."[1] This exaltation of industry was not only a matter of faith, it was also a necessity in the early days of the New England colonies. William Bradford wrote that in light of the "grim and grisly face of poverty coming upon them ... necessity was a stern task-master over them, so they were forced to be such, not only to the servants but in a sort to their dearest children."[2]

Court records throughout the 17th and 18th centuries perpetuated this concern regarding idle children. In 1640, the Great and General Court of Massachusetts required magistrates to see "what course may be taken for teaching the boys and girls in all towns the spinning of yarn." The following year, the court declared, "[I]t is desired and will be expected that all masters of families should see that their children and servants should be industriously implied so as the mornings and evenings and other seasons may not be lost as formerly they have been."[3] Concerned that some parents were too indulgent of their offspring, the court issued more specific orders in 1642 relating to children who were keeping cattle. This endeavor alone was not considered industrious enough by Puritan standards, and it was decreed that children tending livestock should "be set to some other implement withall as spinning upon the rock,[4] knitting, weaving tape,[5] etc." In 1656, in an effort to promote the manufacture of cloth an order advised that "all hands not necessarily employed on other occasions, as women, girls and boys, shall and hereby are enjoined to spin according to their skill and ability and that the selectmen in every town do consider the condition and capacity of every family and accordingly assess them as one or more spinners." Neither wealth nor position excused a family from spinning. It was considered a public duty in Massachusetts to provide for the training of children in "labor and other employments which may be profitable to the Commonwealth."[6]

Nonetheless, in a preindustrial society, there was more than enough work at home in which to employ the children. Bradford lamented, "[M]any of [the] children ... having learned to bear the yoke in their youth, and willing to bear part of their parents' burden, were, oftentimes, so oppressed with their heavy labors that though their minds were free and willing, yet their bodies bowed under the same and became decrepit in their early youth."[7]

Girls were often employed in tasks related to the production and mending of clothing. They were taught knitting as soon as they could hold and manipulate the needles. Children as young as four could knit stockings. By six, girls, and some boys as well, were making important contributions to the family's supply of stockings and mittens. Ann Winslow reported, "I have been a very good girl today about my work.... I sewed on the bosom of uncle's shirt, mended two pair of gloves, mended for wash two handkerchiefs, sewed on half a border of a lawn apron of aunt's, read part of the xxist chapter of Exodus, & a story in the Mother's gift."[8] In 1775, Abigail Foote recorded the following accomplishments in her diary:

Fixed gown for Prude—Mended Mother's riding-hood—Spun short thread—Fixed two gowns for Welsh's girls—Carded tow—Spun linen—Worked on cheese basket—Hatcheled flax with Hannah, we did 51 lbs a piece—Pleated and ironed—Read a sermon of Dodridge's—Spooled a piece—Milked the cows—Spun linen, did 50 knots[9]—Made a broom of Guinea wheat straw—Spun threat to whiten—Set a red dye—Had two scholars from Mrs. Taylor's—I carded two lbs of wool—spun harness twine—Scoured the pewter.[10]

Sally Wister, daughter of a prominent Quaker family, recorded that she "rose at half-past four this morning. Iron'd industriously till one o'clock, din'd, went upstairs, threw myself on the bed, and fell asleep."[11]

Samuel Sewall wrote a letter requesting the purchase of "white Fustain drawn, enough for curtains, woolen counterpane for a bed, and half a dozen chairs, with four threaded green worsted to work it" for his wife so that "she may set her two little daughters on work and keep them out of idleness."[12] The daughters, Elizabeth and Hannah, were aged five and seven. Mary Osgood Sumner's diary contained many entries detailing chores performed prior to breakfast. A typical entry read, "I did everything this morning same as usual, went to school and endeavored to be diligent; came home and washed the butter and assisted in getting coffee."[13] Siblings were also responsible for looking out for one another. Mary noted, "I did everything before breakfast and after breakfast got some peaches for Aunt Mell and then got my work and stuck pretty close to it and at night sat up with sister and nursed her as good as I could."[14]

Girls commonly used any spare time to weave long tapes of string or yarn. A family had an almost constant need for yards and yards of tape. Narrow tape was used to secure most children's and women's clothing, and even men's garments often had lacing in the back to adjust the fit of breeches and waistcoats. Skirts (or petticoats, as they were called), shifts, and aprons were all secured by drawstrings. Stays, which women wore to shape their upper torso, were laced with tape. Pockets, which were not sewn into women's clothing, were suspended from a tape tied around the waist. The dresses worn by very young children, both boys and girls, were tied or laced at the back. Wider tapes were used as garters to secure stockings and as suspenders for breeches. In addition to small table-top box looms or belt looms used in and around the home, girls often carried small U-shaped tools called lucets for making strong, thin cord. Although some lucets had handles, most were small enough to fit in the palm of the hand. Both girls and women often carried lucets in their pockets so that they could work on the cord whenever they found themselves idle or even when visiting another's home. Such industry was considered a sign of good upbringing.

The process of working flax into linen was a labor-intensive operation involving approximately twenty steps, half of which could safely be assigned to children. While spinning and weaving cloth at home was more necessary in the 17th century than in the 18th, homespun cloth remained popular in rural areas throughout the colonial period and enjoyed a tremendous revival immediately before and during the American Revolution.[15] Diaries kept by a pair of young sisters, Abigail and Elizabeth Foote, report that each girl spun two pounds of flax per day. When 12-year-old Anna Green Winslow became "disabled by a whitlow on [her] fourth finger" in 1771, she was advised by her aunt that "it would be a nice opportunity . . . to perfect [herself] in learning to spin flax."[16] Ann reported, "I am pleased with the proposal & am at this present, exerting myself for this purpose."[17] She later wrote, "So I will lay my hand to the distaff, as the virtuous woman of old did."[18]

Elizabeth Fuller was one of 10 children. Her diary shows that by age 15, she was intimately involved in all aspects of cloth manufacturing, including carding, picking, combing, washing, spinning, weaving, and dyeing. Often her diary entry merely records the fruits of her day's labor: "I wove three yards and a quarter," "I spun two double skeins of linen," or "I got out the piece there is sixteen yards & a half. I got in the piece for rag coverlids. I wove four yards."[19] Aside from visitors, her only contact with people outside her home seems to have come from attending church, and she always found time to be productive. "Mrs. Brooks here visiting. I wove."[20] Following two weeks of entries, excepting the Sabbath and a muster day, she simply stated "I wove today. Pleasant.... Cold. I wove." Elizabeth also wrote, "My birthday. I am sixteen years old. How many years have been past by me in thoughtlessness & vanity."[21]

Young girls were also often greatly involved with the domestic production of wool yarn. They were taught to spin at a very early age. They skeined yarn on the niddy-noddy and clock reel.[22] The children's song, "Pop Goes the Weasel," and the rhyme, "Niddy-noddy"[23] were inspired by the skeining process. Young Ann wrote, "My cousin Sally reeled off a 10 knot skein today[24] .... The yarn was of my spinning."[25] Several days later she reported, "Another ten knot skein of my yarn was reeled off today."[26]

Girls also helped to prepare and preserve food. Even very young children could snap the ends off beans or husk corn. Churning butter was another task that could be performed by girls. To help pass the time and to maintain a good rhythm, children were taught the rhyme,

> Come, Butter, Come.
> Come, Butter, Come.
> Come, Butter, Come.
> Johnny is waiting at the gate.
> He wants a piece of buttered cake.
> Come, Butter, Come.

Additionally, they helped with all kinds of housekeeping, as their age would permit, including soap making, candle dipping, and goose picking.[27]

Boys were never without work because of the endless need for firewood, buckets of water, and the regular care needed by livestock. Many of their duties were out of doors. Besides feeding and watering the animals, they often guarded the animals in the pasture. They helped with preparing the fields for planting and sowed the seeds in the furrows. At harvest, they helped gather in the crops. Boys hunted and fished, providing themselves with recreation and their families with a welcome and, sometimes, necessary addition to the table. Older boys often accompanied men on hunting trips for meat or on community wolf hunts or wolf drives. Wolves were

Young girls were an important part of the family's labor force.

considered treacherous predators of livestock, and towns offered boun-ties for every wolf head turned in.. Notices like this one from Stratford, Connecticut, drew many hunters: "It was voted and agreed upon that the next Thursday should be the day to go upon this work of killing wolves. . . . All persons to be ready by seven of the clock in the morning and meet upon the hill at the meeting house by the beat of the drum."[28] The hunters would surround a section of woods in which they thought the wolf or wolves would be found and gradually close in on the prey. Israel Putnam would become a leader in the American Revolution, but as a youth he garnered local fame when he single-handedly killed a particularly notorious wolf.

Maple sugaring heralded the arrival of spring and all hands were needed to execute this great labor. Boys joined adult males as they spent several nights in the sugar camp set up in the woods. Surely this must have been an exciting time for the boys. The boys collected sap buckets and helped to process the tremendous volume of wood needed to main-tain the fires under the huge sugar pots as they boiled off the water from the much-desired maple syrup. In a like vein, boys would often seek out the hives of bees and rescue the honey. Both maple syrup and honey were used as substitutes for expensive sugar, which could not be readily grown outside the West Indian Islands.

All children engaged in harvesting and weeding the household or kitchen garden, gathering nuts, and picking berries. Even the very young were given pails or baskets and taken by older siblings to gather berries. Some entrepreneurial youngsters would gather and sell wild cherries, known as choke cherries, which were used for making cherry rum or cherry bounce. A good-sized tree would yield approximately six bushels. Children also weeded flax plants. Only three to four inches high, the small plants were so tender that the children and young women who weeded them worked barefoot. If the area contained thistles, the weeder would work in several pair of woolen socks for protection. Children gathered rushes whose reeds were soaked in fat and used as rush lights. Young boys often used their spare time, particularly in winter, to make birch-splinter brooms that could be sold to storekeepers.

Employing the children in such laborious tasks was essential in a time when families had to be self-sufficient. It also served to teach children the skills that they would need to maintain their own families. Most children in the early colonial period, especially those living on the frontier, needed these life skills more than they needed reading and writing.

As noted earlier, Puritan families often sent out their pubescent children to other respectable homes to learn a skill or apprenticed them to a trade. Often the children were placed with a neighbor or relative and many were treated almost as equals to other children that might be in the in the household. When William Hoskine placed his daughter, Sarah, with Thomas and Winifred Whitney, the indenture stated that they were to treat "her as their child, and [be] unto her as father and mother."[29] This custom was not limited to New England. Benjamin Franklin was sent to learn the cutler's trade with cousin Samuel, but when that attempt did not work out, he was placed with his brother James to learn printing. Such arrangements were formalized with contracts, known as indentures. Samuel Sewall sent his daughters away: Hannah to learn housewifery, Elizabeth to learn needlework, and Mary to learn reading and writing. His son, Samuel Jr., was bound as an apprentice. While the parents' intentions may have been good, leaving home was sometimes a painful experience. Sewall made the following entry upon leaving Hannah: "much ado to pacify my dear daughter, she weeping and pleading to go [home] with me."[30]

A widower with no inclination to remarry might apprentice his daughter to a family that wanted a young girl to help with household chores and ask that she be taught to read. The daughter would learn the skills that her mother would have taught her and be taught to read as well. Such training was likely to be the only education that the girl would receive. Many free black women arranged to apprentice their children to protect them from unprincipled masters who might seek to enslave them. The indenture was proof of their free status. Jane Hall bound her daughter, Ann, to Ruth Sydnor in 1729. Ann was to be taught to read, sew, knit and spin.[31]

Children whose families could not support them could also be apprenticed to learn a skill. Samuel and Elizabeth Edeth bound their 7-year-old son, Zachary, John Brown to be instructed "in his employment of husbandry" until he was 21. They explained their action by saying that they had "many children and by reason of many wants lying upon them, so as they were not able to bring them up as they desire[d]."[32] Children in such a situation may not have been as well situated as those of more affluent families who were "sent out" to relatives or neighbors. Some apprenticed children were treated as servants. Francis and Christian Billington apprenticed their seven-year-old daughter to John and Mary Barnes "to do their service until she accomplish[ed] the age of twenty years."[33]

Some families came to the colonies as indentured servants, binding themselves by contract for a specified number of years, generally from four to seven, in payment for their passage. Gottlieb Mittelberger recorded

This illustration shows young cooper's apprentices. Coopers made barrels, buckets, churns, and casks of all kinds. Only a skilled cooper could make a watertight container.

the plight of some Germans who arrived in Philadelphia in 1750: "Many parents must sell and trade their children away like so many head of cattle; for if their children take the debt upon themselves, the parents can leave the ship free and unrestrained; but as the parents often do not know where and to what people their children are going, it often happens that such parents and children after leaving the ship, do not see each other again for many years, perhaps no more in all their lives." Explaining that parents cannot transfer obligation when children are under five years old, he added, "[S]uch children must be given to somebody without compensation to be brought up, and they must serve for their bringing up till they are 21 years old. Children from 5 to 10 years, who pay half price for their passage ... must likewise serve for it till they are 21 years of age; they cannot, therefore, redeem their parents by taking the debt ... upon themselves. But children above 10 years can."[34]

At least one immigrant saw such a situation more positively. John Naas, an early leader of the Dunker sect, wrote to his son in Germany in 1733:

[T]he child takes over the indenture for both his and his father's or mother's passage for four years, and is able in that time to earn all the necessary clothing and finally a handsome outfit from head to foot, a horse, a cow with a calf; small children take on one and a half's year indenture. When they are twenty-one years old they have to be taught reading and writing, and leave well-dressed and with a horse and cow .... One finds few houses in the city or country where the people are rather prosperous where there are not one or two children .... Often parents and children are ten, eleven, [or] twenty hours from each other. Often those indenturing themselves are better off than those who paid their passage, as they get their expenses paid by others and learn the peculiarities of the country.[35]

Apprenticeships were always gender specific. Orphans John Oulds and Jane Studs were bound to the same master in 1688. John was to be taught reading, writing, and the trade of tailoring, but Jane was to be taught "household work."[36] Boys were often placed to learn trades such as joyner, cooper, blacksmith, or printer. Boys could also be apprenticed to learn farming (husbandry). Seldom, however, were girls apprenticed to female professionals such as corset makers, mantua-makers, or milliners, although there are records of some. Jane Thompson of Charles Town advertised on several occasions between 1771 and 1774, seeking young girls to be apprenticed to the millinery trade. Hannah Coleman informed the public that she had been apprenticed to the prominent shopkeeper Mrs. Wish and that her services as mantua maker "in all its branches" were available to anyone who wished to employ them.[37] Generally, girls were taught to sew, card, spin, knit or other skills of housewifery. Additionally, indentures often specified that a child be taught to read, write, or cipher.

The indentures legalized the agreements, specifying what duties and behaviors were expected of the apprentice and what the master or mistress was required to provide in return. Certain social activities might be specifically prohibited. For example, an apprentice might be forbidden to "play at unlawful games or contract matrimony"[38] or to "haunt taverns."[39] The term of service could last for a specific time, such as 4 or 12 years or until the child reached a certain age. Indentures for girls usually contained a clause concerning marriage. Sarah Hoskine's contract stated, "[I]f it shall happen that said Sarah ... marry before she shall have accomplished the said age of twenty years (she being six years of age the xvth of September last past) then the said Thomas shall have such satisfaction for her time then remaining as shall be adjudged reasonable and equal by two indifferent men."[40] At the satisfactory conclusion of the indenture, the apprentice would be given certain essentials, which would allow them to go out on their own. Generally, this involved a provision of clothing and essential tools for the former servant to ply their newly learned trade.

After her father died, Rebekah Goslee was apprenticed by her guardians. The 1756 indenture stated that she would "well and faithfully serve [Timothy Hale and his wife Rebecca]. Keep his or their commandments lawful and honest ... not do hurt not damage to her ... master nor his mistress nor consent to be done of others ... not waste the goods of her ... master nor lend them to any person without his consent ... not either by day or by night absent herself from her ... master or mistress service, but in all things as a good and faithful servant demean herself towards [her master and mistress]." In return, the Hales were expected to "take reasonable pains to instruct her and also to teach her to read the English tongue." They were also required to supply Rebekah with "sufficient wholesome and complete meat, drinking, washing and clothing and lodging." Rebekah was indentured until she was 18 years old. At the end of her service, the Hales had to supply Rebekah with "double apparel," meaning that she would have clothing "to have and to ware as well as on the Lord's days as on working days." She was to have clothing of "linen and wool, shoes, stockings and all other." Additionally, Rebekah was to be given "one good cow and one English bible."[41]

In 1770, the selectmen and "overseers of the poor" in Preston, Connecticut, indentured 8-year-old Benjamin Jeffords to learn the skill of husbandry. At age 21, when Benjamin's service was to be completed, he was to receive two suits of clothing, "a bible and ten good store of sheep."[42] Placing unsupported children as indentured servants relieved the community of having to maintain the unfortunate youths and provided them with skills to enter society as productive adults.

This attitude followed in the footsteps of the poor laws of Elizabethan England, which provided for the apprenticing of pauper children, providing cheap child labor masked as philanthropy. Much the same policy was adopted in the colonies. Boston notified a number of people to "dispose of their several children ... to serve by indentures according to their ages and capacities."[43] The children involved were both male and female and as young as eight. If this directive was ignored, the selectmen were

charged to take "said children from them and place them with such masters as they shall provide accordingly as the law directs."[44]

Children were generally placed with a family until they were 14, at
which time they would be bound as apprentices to learn a useful trade
until they became free by law. Connecticut had a similar system. If parents
allowed their children "to live idly or misspend their time in loitering,"[45]
the child would be bound out, "a man child until he shall come to the age
of 21 years; and a woman child to the age of 18 years or the time of marriage."[46] The Connecticut law of 1750 provided that not only should the
children of paupers or indigent parents who could not or did not provide
competently for them be bound out, but also "any poor children in any
town, belonging to such town, that they live idly or are exposed to want
and distress, provided there are none to care for them." The Quakers also
believed that children should be taught to work. The Great Law of the
Province of Pennsylvania required that all children "of the age of twelve
years shall be taught some useful trade or skill, to the end none may be
idle, but the poor may work to live and the rich if they become poor may
not want."[47]

There is little record of the actual circumstances under which these
children lived. Doubtless, they varied as much as the masters and mistresses who took the children into their care. Unlike other indentures,
the agreements binding out pauper children did not always provide for
instructing the child in a trade. In some cases, the papers expressly state
that the person taking the child "shall have him to be his servant until he
comes of age."[48] Cases were brought against masters for mistreating their
apprentices, however. Phineas Cook was charged for the ill treatment of
"one Robert Cromwell, a poor, helpless, decrepit boy, an apprentice to
said Phineas for a term not yet expired."[49]

Sometimes children who were exceedingly unhappy with their placement ran away. As previously noted, Benjamin Franklin's father had
considerable difficulty settling his son in a trade. Originally, the elder
Franklin thought to give Benjamin "as the tithe of his sons, to the service
of the church,"[50] but he soon realized that he could not afford the necessary education. When working the family's tallow chandlery proved
unsuitable, the elder Franklin feared that his son would "break away and
get to sea, as Benjamin's brother, Jonah, had done, to his great vexation."[51]
Benjamin later wrote, " My father at last fixed upon the cutler's trade, and
my uncle Benjamin's son Samuel ... I was sent to be with him some time
on taking. But his expectations of a fee with me displeasing my father,
I was taken home again." Continuing to worry about Benjamin, his father
decided to capitalize on his son's "bookish inclination" and determined
"to make me a printer, though he had already one son of that profession."
Young Franklin admitted that he "still had a hankering for the sea. So
to prevent the apprehended effect of such an inclination, my father was
impatient to have me bound to my brother, I stood out some time, but at

last was persuaded, and signed the indentures when I was not yet but twelve years of age."[52]

Samuel Sewall also had difficulty in placing his son. At first young Sam was expected to follow in his father's footsteps. At nine, he was sent to Latin school, but in less than two years, it was clear that he was not suited to these studies. Sewall sent Sam to writing school and then set out to place him in a career. The elder Sewall recorded, "I have Sam to Michael Perry [a book seller] to live with him upon trial."[53] Three months later. he wrote, "I go to Mr. Perry and speak to him to send home Sam from the shop, that so his sore and swollen feet might be cured, which standing in the cold shop would prevent. He sends him home."[54] Six months later, the elder Sewall reported, "I discourse Capt. Sam Checkly about his taking Sam to be his [ap]prentice. He seems inclined to it, and in a manner all I mention is to encourage me."[55] This, too, proved unsatisfactory. "Last night Sam could not sleep because of my brother's speaking to him of removing him to some other place, mentioning Mr. Usher's." Young Sam was so greatly stressed that he fainted when he went to get wood. Conversation between the two Sewall brothers included reference to Wadsworth's sermon on idleness:

Sam overheard him, and now alleged these words to be against his being where he was because of his idleness. [He] mentioned also the difficulty of the employment by reason of the numerousness of goods and hard to distinguish them, many not being marked, whereas books, the price of them was set down, and so could sell them readily. I spoke to Capt Checkly again and again, and he gave me no encouragement that his being there would be to Sam's profit; and Mrs. Checkly always discouraging."[56]

The worried father prayed "give rest unto my dear son, and put him unto some calling wherein he will accept."[57] A week later, Sewall wrote that he "was very sorrowful by reason of the unsettledness of my Samuel."[58] Two years later, Sewall "agreed with Mr. Wilkins about Sam's living with him."[59] This last placement seems to have agreed with Sam, and he remained with the bookseller Richard Wilkins. After his marriage to the governor's daughter in 1704, Sam turned to farming.

If the parents could not convince the child of the benefit of the apprenticeship, or if they were concerned about the conditions under which the child served, they might seek to nullify the contract and find a more suitable placement. Nancy Hannah, a free black of Virginia, successfully appealed to the courts on behalf of her three children, Sarah, Thomas, and Joe, who were being abused by their master. They were removed and placed with a new master, who took the boys as carpenter's apprentices and promised that Sarah would be taught to "read and spin."[60]

Virginia recognized poor children as an excellent labor source very early. In 1646, counties were directed to send two poor boys or girls at least 7 or 8 years of age to Jamestown to work in the two operations for linen manufacture so that they might "be instructed in the art of carding, knitting and spinning."[61] The Assembly estimated that five children under the age of 13 could spin and weave enough to keep 30 persons clothed.[62] Even in New England, the commercial value of child labor was recognized early. In 1682, Boston's leaders recommended that the almshouse and workhouse be rebuilt so that children who "shamefully spend their time in the streets" could be put to work "at the charge of the town."[63] In 1720, a committee was assembled to consider the establishment of spinning schools. The committee recommended that 20 spinning wheels be provided "for such children as should be sent from the almshouse."[64] At the same time, a philanthropist established a "Spinning School House" which he bequeath to the town "for the education of the children of the poor."[65] The Reverend George Whitfield established Orphan House in Georgia as a charitable institution for the care and education of orphaned boys and girls. The children's day was broken up into two-hour segments of alternating work and school, with breaks for meals and prayer. A description of the daily schedule was recorded by one resident:

From eight to ten, the children go to their respective employs, as carding, spinning, picking cotton or wool, sewing, knitting. One serves the apothecary who lives in the House, others serve in the store or kitchen; others clean the house, fetch water, or cut wood. Some are placed under the tailor, who lives in the house; and we expect other tradesmen, as a shoemaker, carpenter, etc. to which others are to be bound.... At noon we go to dinner all in the same room, and between then and two o'clock every one is employed in something useful, but no time is allowed for idleness or play, which are Satan's darling hours to tempt children to all manners of wickedness.... [F]rom four to six [the children] work in their respective stations as before mentioned.[66]

As time progressed, the gainful use of children's time became less a matter of virtue and more a practical use of available assets, particularly in the latter half of the 18th century when the importance of domestic manufacture became more critical. In 1751, the Society for Encouraging Industry and Employing the Poor was organized in Boston Its stated dual purpose was to promote the manufacture of woolen and other cloth and the employment of "women and children who are now in a great measure idle."[67] Provincial laws of 1753 imposed a tax on carriages to further the production of linen, which would provide employment for the poor women and children and lessen the burden of caring for them.[68] In 1770, William Molineux petitioned the Boston legislature to help him in his plan for "manufacturing the children's labor into wearing apparel." This proposal met with great approval as "the female children of this town ... are not only useful to the community but the poorer sort are able in some measure to assist their parents in getting a livelihood."[69] Boston was not alone in its position. In 1767, New York governor Henry Moore reported to the Lords of Trade that "every home swarms with children who are set to spin and card."[70] The New York Linen Manufactory advertised, "The Directors are disposed to take young boys as apprentices to the linen and cotton branches" and encouraged parents to apply on behalf of their children. An establishment in Bethlehem, Connecticut, sought boys and girls from 10 to 14, and another wanted "a number of lively boys from eight to eighteen."[71]

The high profitability of employing children was a keystone in the scheme of those planning to establish early manufacturing industries. Children were a welcome alternative to relatively scarce and higher-priced adult men, many of whom distrusted factories and considered such work beneath them. Moreover, a healthy teenage boy could usually do as much unskilled work as a man. Some manufacturers found that children as young as three years old could gather the waste cotton that collected near the machines. Children aged seven and older could operate simple spinning and carding machines.

Samuel Slater, alternately considered the Father of American Industry and the founder of the American Industrial Revolution, was among the first to build a successful water-powered textile mill in America. With his staff of four boys aged 7 to 12, hired to operate three carding machines, two water frames, one carding machine, and one roving machine, he successfully demonstrated the profitability of spinning yarn using child labor. A week later he hired a girl, and within days added three more boys and another girl, recruiting the children on contract. They worked 12 hours a day in winter and 14 to 16 hours in summer, six days a week. Jobs ranged from picking foreign matter such as leaves, pods and dirt from the cotton to operating the carding and spinning machines. The children proved to be good workers who produced high-quality yarn under Slater's supervision. Families welcomed the additional income their children brought to the household and soon became dependent on it. A new and improved mill brought additional dependence on child labor. When Slater tried to hire women and children who lived a distance away from the mill, as was the practice in England, he found the New Englanders resistant to breaking up the family and introduced pauper apprentices to his workforce instead. However, he found the latter system restrictive and more expensive than he had hoped because he was forced to conform to indenture specifications.

Child contract workers and apprentices worked together under similar conditions. Both attended Sunday school where they learned basic reading and writing from students at Brown University. Ultimately, the mill had more than 30 workers, mainly children, but Slater did hire men as watchmen and construction workers. As the mill continued to expand, so did the need for children to work in it. A mutual dependence developed as the mill relied on the children and the families relied on the money the children earned. Some families had more than one child working at the mill. By 1796, two houses had been built for factory children's families and multiple-family dwellings soon followed. These houses were better than these families could otherwise afford. Household needs were available at the company store. Slater deducted the rent and the purchases from the children's pay.

Many applauded the employment of children in the manufacturing industry. Supporters touted the additional value received from girls between 10 and 16, "most of whom [were] too young or too delicate for agriculture." This work was thought to save the youngsters from the "vice and immorality to which children [would be] exposed by a career of idleness."[72]

Criticism of child labor in manufacturing was most likely to come from abroad. Brissot de Warville, a French traveler in America at the end of the 18th century, wrote, "Manufactures are much boasted of because children are employed therein from a most tender age. [M]en congratulate themselves upon making martyrs of these innocent creatures for is it not a torment to these poor little beings ... to be a whole day and almost every day of their lives employed at the same work in an obscure and infected prison?"[73]

The trend toward employing children in factories rather than in a cottage industry continued well into the 19th century when attitudes toward child laborers and the benefits of unfettered industrialization finally began to change, in large part through the work of such amateur social reformers as the novelist Charles Dickens. Despite many good intentions and grand schemes, the poor remained in their crime-ridden environment, children worked without seeing daylight, and servants and slaves remained on the bottom rungs of social and economic life. Yet, despite the incongruity between the utopian ideals of the reformers and the actual conditions, mindless social tinkering and disgraceful forms of public altruism persisted and proliferated until well after the Civil War. Child labor in the 18th century was not created by unfeeling parents, callous governments, or avaricious mill owners although the financial and social advantages to each group were obvious. The mills merely altered the venue and type of work in which colonial children were engaged at a time when children were always expected to be productive members of the household.

NOTES

1. Quoted in Edmund S. Morgan, *The Puritan Family Religion and Domestic Relations in Seventeenth-Century New England* (New York: Harper and Row, 1944), 67.

2. William Bradford, *Bradford's History of Plymouth Plantation* (Westminster, MD: Heritage, 1999), 23.

3. Quoted in Edith Abbott, "A Study of the Early History of Child Labor in America," *American Journal of Sociology* 14 (July 1908), 16.

4. "Spinning upon the rock" meant using a handheld distaff to spin. While it required a certain skill, it was a simple way to spin twisted thread. Some spinners were so adept at this that they could spin while they walked.

5. Small tape looms such as belt looms were light enough to be taken out to a field or pasture. Simply a heddle frame, these primitively shaped boards were cut so that the center of the board had a row of narrow slats pierced by a small hole through which the warp threads passed. The board could be held at the bottom by the weaver's knees and steadied at the top by being tied to the back of a chair, fence or tree.

6. Quoted in Abbott, "A Study of the Early History of Child Labor in America," 16, 17.

7. Quoted in ibid., 16.

8. Alice Morse Earle, ed, *Diary of Anna Green Winslow, a Boston Schoolgirl of 1771* (Bedford, MA: Applewood Books, 1996), 40.

9. Usually the knots, or lays, consisted of 40 threads, and 20 lays made a skein. The number of threads varied regionally. Spinning two skeins of linen thread was a good day's work.

10. Abigail Foote, quoted in Carl Holliday, *Women's Life in Colonial Days*, (Minneola, NY: Dover Publications, 1999), 116.

11. Sally Wister, *Sally Wister's Journal: A True Narrative* (Bedford, MA: Applewood Books, 1995), 61.

12. Quoted in Edmund S. Morgan, *The Puritan Family: Religion and Domestic Relations in Seventeenth-Century New England* (New York: Harper and Row, 1944), 67.

13. Alice Morse Earle, *Child Life in Colonial Days* (New York: Macmillan, 1940), 168.

14. Ibid., 168–69.

15. Spinning bees became extremely popular as the spirit of revolution brewed. Women of means gathered with their spinning wheels, producing linen fiber as a sign that they were not dependent on cloth imported from Britain. Spinning became a manifestation of a woman's patriotism. Of course, for less well-to-do women, spinning remained an essential means of supplying clothing and linens to their families.

16. Earle, *Diary of Anna Green Winslow*, 20.

17. Ibid.

18. Ibid., 22.

19. Margo Culley, ed., *A Day at a Time* (New York: Feminist Press, 1985), 69–73.

20. Ibid., 70.

21. Ibid., 76.

22. The niddy-noddy was a hand held device used to wind yarn into skeins. The person using the implement would count the number of wraps so that skeins would be of equal amounts. The clock reel, also known as a click reel or weasel, was a free standing device that also wound the wool. It featured a wooden gear that would count the number of wraps of a skein. When the skein was complete, the gear would make a pop to alert the operator.

23. The rhyme has a four-count beat that coincides with the four movements involved in using the device: "Niddy-noddy, niddy-noddy, Two heads, one body."

24. A speedy and accomplished spinner could spin six skeins of yarn in a day.

25. Earle, *Diary of Anna Green Winslow*, 25.

26. Ibid., 27.

27. Goose picking was a particularly unpleasant task. Several times a year, the down was harvested from live geese. The pickers had to cover the heads of the geese with specially made baskets or with a heavy stocking to avoid being pecked. Down flew everywhere while the unhappy bird displayed its displeasure. The feathers were used to stuff mattresses that were particularly popular among the Dutch.

28. Elizabeth George Speare, *Life in Colonial America* (New York: Random House, 1963), 83.

29. Anna Neuzil, appendix to *Women in Plymouth Colony, 1633–1668* (Raleigh: University of Virginia, 1998), x.

30. M. Halsey Thomas, ed., *The Diary of Samuel Sewall, 1674–1729*, vol. 1 (New York: Farrar, Straus and Giroux, 1973), 314.

31. Kathleen M. Brown, *Good Wives Nasty Wenches and Anxious Patriarchs: Gender, Race, and Power in Colonial America* (Chapel Hill: University of North Carolina Press, 1996), 230.

32. Nathaniel Shurtleff and David Pulsifer, *Records of the Colony of New Plymouth in New England*, vol. 2 (New York: AMS Press, 1968), 112.

33. Anna Neuzil, x.

34. Alden T. Vaughan, *America before the Revolution, 1725–1775* (Englewood Cliffs, NJ: Prentice-Hall, 1967), 43–44.

35. Alvin E. Conner, *Sectarian Childrearing: The Dunkers, 1708–1900* (Gettysburg: Brethren Heritage Press, 2000), 61.

36. Brown, *Good Wives*, 295.

37. Julia Cherry Spruill, *Women's Life and Work in the Southern Colonies* (New York: W. W. Norton, 1973), 284.

38. Connecticut Historical Society, *Children at Work* (Hartford: Connecticut Historical Society, 1993), 6–7.

39. Ibid., 11.

40. Neuzil, x.

41. Connecticut Historical Society, *Children at Work*, 14–15.

42. Ibid., 12–13.

43. Abbott, "A Study of the Early History of Child Labor in America," 16.

44. Ibid., 16.

45. Ibid., 18.

46. Ibid.

47. Ibid., 19.

48. Ibid.

49. Ibid.

50. Vaughan, *America before the Revolution*, 79.

51. Ibid., 80.

52. Ibid., 60–61.

53. Thomas, *Diary of Samuel Sewall*, vol. 1, 321–22.

54. Ibid., 327.

55. Ibid, 336.

56. Ibids, 347.

57. Ibid., 348.

58. Ibid.

59. Ibid., 371.

60. Brown, *Good Wives*, 231.

61. Abbott, "A Study of the Early History of Child Labor in America," 20.

62. Alice Morse Earle, *Home Life in Colonial Days* (Stockbridge, MA: Berkshire House Publications, 1993), 189.

63. Abbott, "A Study of the Early History of Child Labor in America," 16.

64. Ibid., 21.

65. Ibid.

66. Spruill, *Woman's Life and Work in the Southern Colonies*, 192–93.

67. Abbott, "A Study of the Early History of Child Labor in America," 21.

68. Ibid., 22.

69. Ibid.

70. Ibid.

71. Ibid., 23.

72. Ibid., 25.

73. Ibid., 26.

Part V

The Role of Servants and Slaves

15

Servants

We should never think of bereaving our fellow creatures of that valuable
blessing, liberty, nor endure to grow rich by their bondage. To live in ease
and plenty, by the toil of those, whom violence and cruelty have put in
our power, is neither consistent with Christianity nor common justice.
—Anthony Benezet, a Quaker (1754)

SERVITUDE

Three quarters of all immigrants to British North America during the
colonial period were enslaved or experienced forced servitude during
some part of their lives, and half of the remainder came as paid servants
or wage laborers. Even in the earliest colonial settlements servants were
often included as part of the household structure, and they were a large
part of the overall colonial community.

Between the 1640s and 1670s, many free white settlers immigrated to the
American colonies as servants. Most were drawn from among British agricultural workers. Agents scoured the countryside of England and Wales
making grand promises about the opportunities that awaited workers if
they accompanied a family of supposedly wealthy patrons to the colonies.
A ballad relating the miseries of one poor maiden who was deceived
by such unscrupulous assurances became popular in 17th-century
England. It opened with:

> This girl was cunningly trappan'd,
> sent to Virginny from England

Where she doth hardship undergo,
there is no cure it must be so
But if she lives to cross the main,
she vows she'll ne'er go there again.[1]

These servants entered into a contract for a set number of years, which paid for their transportation to the colonies and usually limited their responsibilities somewhat. The number of years varied greatly but averaged a little more than four. At the end of that time, the indentured servants were free to return to Europe, renew their agreement with the employer, or find other work in the colonies. Contracts could be made directly with the future employer or with other merchants, who would sell the contract on arrival in the colonies.

A small percentage of servants were drawn from the English prisons. Convicts were released from incarceration on the condition that they would immigrate to America as servants. Usually, their contracts were for double the term of service of those who accepted servitude voluntarily. While some colonial families saw them as good value for their money, others avoided employing former convicts because they were uncomfortable with the thought that there might be behavioral difficulties with such persons.

Servants were forbidden to engage in any activity that had the potential to interfere with their work. Since they usually lived under the same roof as their employers, this factor often served as a cause of friction between them and their employers. They could be forced to attend church services with their masters' family even if they were not of their employers' denomination. Employers could physically discipline their servants, and cuffs upon the head or back and whippings were not uncommon. Servants were not permitted to drink excessively and certainly not to marry during the term of their employment. A female servant who became pregnant was liable to her employer for the additional costs incurred for a midwife, a nurse, and any subsequent child rearing. Since few servants were in a position to pay for the expenses of having a child, their time of servitude was commonly extended by 18 to 24 months.

The low ratio of women to men in the colonies made it easy for female servants to find men interested in becoming their husbands, but it was illegal even for a free man to marry an indentured servant without compensating the employer. British law at the time allowed employers to demand the specific performance of a personal service contract.[2] Pennsylvania servants, James Hall and Margaret Ryan, ran away and married without permission. After 13 days, they were caught by bounty hunters and returned at a cost to their employers of nine pounds. As punishment, the town court ordered both of them to serve an additional 30 days for running away, five additional months for the £9 expense, and a one-year penalty for marrying.

This photograph shows a group of servants from Plymouth Plantation in practical woolen clothing typical of their status. The picture was taken in October. Although many summer clothing items would have been made of coarse linen, woolens were used year round.

Domestic servants "with hardly an exception" were white women.[3] They spent their days engaged in the same types of activities as their mistresses. They cooked, cleaned, sewed, washed, tended the fire, worked in the garden, and looked after the family children. If the mistress saw fit, servants could be hired out to work for another family who might need temporary help, to assist with a labor intensive activity such as the autumn slaughter of livestock, or to provide nursing to an ill or infirmed person. If the mistress was truly generous, the servants might be permitted to keep all or part of any fees earned while on assignment, but the fruits of such employment were legally those of the employer unless otherwise stated in the original contract.

It was common for domestic servants to sleep in a garret or in the kitchen. For many their bed was nothing more than a linen ticking filled with straw rolled out into a convenient place on the floor. This could be quite comfortable, but it lacked the refinement and the sense of ownership supplied by a bedstead or a separate sleeping chamber. The entire household probably shared the same lavatory facilities on the margins of the property.

In addition to permanent servants, the mistresses of northern households often relied on short-term help from the young women of the neighborhood. These were often the supernumery daughters of local families from the middle range of the local social hierarchy. The labor of their brothers was usually reserved for the benefit of the family. The vast majority of these part-time servants seem to have been single women between 15 and 25 years of age who fully expected to become mistresses of their own homes in time. They often alternated work in their family home with that in the homes of their neighbors. "Such shuffling and reshuffling of workers was part of a larger system of neighborly exchange that sustained male as well as female economics in the period."[4]

Strong, well-formed sons were the principle engines of the family farm economy, but many families required more male help than nature provided. The supervision of hired men, male servants, and any apprentices, fell to the husband. Like their female counterparts, male servants often worked side by side with their masters plowing, harvesting, and tending animals. Male servants were often required to do the heavy physically demanding work: digging drainage ditches, postholes, or holes for outhouses, and demeaning work shunned by family members such as clearing trees and brush, and splitting firewood to feed the unending needs of the kitchen and bedroom fireplaces. Male servants might also provide specific skills in agriculture, animal husbandry, building, milling, woodworking, record keeping, or surveying that were not in the householder's repertoire of personal skills. As with female servants, the householder could hire out their male servants to work for others and keep all the profits or that portion agreed to in the initial employment contract.

Trusted male servants often served as managers for gristmills, sawmills, lumberyards, shipping concerns, or on farms and plantations with a large number of workers. These men were almost always well educated, and they were often difficult to distinguish from the actual owners of the business or property by their clothing or accommodations. Such persons, not to be confused with the plantation overseers who dealt primarily with slaves, were sometimes called factors or agents.

Free white laborers were scarce in colonial America at all times, and they were considered expensive and generally unreliable workers. The opportunity for any capable and healthy free white man to establish his own farmstead made voluntary service to others less attractive to white laborers in America than it was to those in Europe. The opportunity to work for oneself created a decline in the availability of free laborers that can be traced from the time of the earliest settlements to the extinction of the colonial period at the end of the 18th century. "All the correlations are consistent: the rising numbers of indentured servants through the 1650s, then the falling away in the sixties, as English population growth slackened, as fire [the Great London Fire of 1666] and plague both reduced the available labor supply in London and created a greater demand there, and hence as real wages rose."[5]

Male workers often did the heavy work like splitting out shingles, clearing land, and digging trenches and foundations.

FORCED SERVICE

Lacking the ability to hire free wage laborers, employers turned to indentured servants. Most persons working under an indenture in the colonial period came from a lower social class than their employers. Colonial proprietors and plantation owners soon found, however, that indentured servants and wage earners resisted discipline, ran away, more often attacked their employers and generally demanded better treatment than black slaves freshly imported from Africa. Consequently, as the number of white indentures diminished with time, the number of African slaves increased. With the decline of the indenture system in the 18th century, plantation owners in particular seem to have become addicted to the use of slave laborers.

In 1619, a Dutch ship arrived in Virginia with a cargo of no more than two dozen black laborers. Until recently these were all thought to be slaves, yet there is convincing research that suggests that at least some of these blacks were indentured servants or free craftsmen. In 1625 there were only twenty-two blacks in all of Virginia, but there were twenty times their number of white servants and laborers. By 1671, among a population in Virginia estimated at 40,000 during a census, there were 6,000 persons deemed white servants and 2000 recorded black slaves. This meant that twenty percent of the population of early Virginia was in servitude; yet only one resident in twenty in the colony five percent were actually enslaved. The English were only minimally involved in the slave trade before the Restoration in the 1660s, and black slaves did not outnumber white indentured servants in the colonies until the turn of the 18th century. These data have forced historians to revise the common vision of the colonial Chesapeake somewhat. Until 1700, it was generally not slaves but "servants who guided the plough or wielded the spade, the hoe, or the axe."[6]

The term *indentured servant* has been misinterpreted by many students of the period. In its colonial interpretation, servants as a class of people "included all who had bound themselves under the provisions of an agreement, embodied in a formal legal document ... which had the force and sanctity of law, to continue for a prescribed time in another's employment." A servant might be a farm worker or laborer working for a wage, an artisan or craftsperson under contract to produce a piece of work or complete a project, and all those who served an apprenticeship. Indentured servants were not slaves, but they were legally bound to serve for a specified period. Moreover, the term *indenture* was much more encompassing than many people believe and probably should be read as "under contract." As such, it sometimes implied no more menial status than that of a modern sports superstar under a multimillion-dollar contract to a professional athletic team.

Contracts in the colonial period were usually written in duplicate on both sides of the center of a piece of paper. Both contracting parties then signed each side, and the document was ripped down the middle. Each of the principals to the contract would be given a half, which contained all the points of agreement. If questions occurred concerning the terms of the contract or its authenticity the two halves could be brought together and the irregularities of the tear, or indentures, matched to indicate that each was part of the original document. Similar systems were used to verify banks drafts, bonds, and promissory notes into the 20th century.

Indentures could be sold to third parties, but only if this procedure was not forbidden by the initial contract. Many servants tied themselves to a particular family by careful wording of their indenture for personal service. This provided continuity, stability, and a modicum of security for the servant. Ironically, the indentured status also insured a social position and economic status that many unskilled workers sought out because they feared the chronic under-employment that characterized most European economies. Many indentured servants found that willing workers were a scarce commodity in America, and they became relatively sophisticated concerning the process, negotiating better terms in their indentures in the colonies than were offered in Europe.

The largest difference between an indentured servant and a modern contract worker was that those persons under indenture could be forced to remain on the job and complete the manual labor or serve the whole time for which they had contracted. In other words they could not quit. In this regard indentured workers were "bound" to their employers in a way unlike any that we know today. Consequently, the term *bondsman* is sometimes used interchangeably for either a *slave* or an *indentured servant*. A few persons were able to purchase a release from their indentures, but only at an extraordinarily inflated price. Absolute freedom was usually not otherwise extended to any indentured person until the full terms of the contract were fulfilled.[7]

Through the institution of indenture, tens of thousands of persons came to America as servants with the hope of receiving land or carving out a farmstead of their own at the end of their terms of service. These were given a social status, which was little more than that of slaves, and many of them failed to survive the rigors of their contracts. Moreover, since indentured servants could lose themselves among the immigrants on the frontiers, the number of runaways among colonial indentures was significantly higher than among the same class of persons in Britain. Others voluntarily renewed their indentures at the end of their initial term and never achieved the status of freemen.

English authorities placed no obstacles in the way of emigration to the colonies other than to enforce any existing contracts, maintain the continuity of apprenticeships, and require that emigrants extinguish any outstanding debts before leaving England. It was hoped in fact that the colonies might provide homes and work for the chronically unemployed and thus relieve the local English parishes of men and women who made demands on the public dole. It was also anticipated that the emigration to the colonies "would diminish crime in the kingdom by drawing away a large number of the inhabitants who otherwise might be tempted, by the small opportunities within their reach of earning a livelihood, to drift into vagabondage, beggery, and lawlessness."[8]

There was an earnest attempt to find young women of good character and marriageable age in Britain to serve as wives for the colonists. Each of these women was provided with a dowry for personal moving expenses, for clothing, and for passage. Sometimes a hope chest was also included filled with necessary household items. Colonial men would buy a wife by taking up the indenture entered into by the woman or her parents with an agent. The marriage generally resolved the debt and fulfilled the contract. Although they were supposed to be at least sixteen, some of these women were actually girls as young as twelve and a very few others were women as old as forty-five. The men's preference was for mature peasant girls who were healthy, robust, and industrious rather than nubile adolescents. The young women who exhibited these qualities had some choice among prospective husbands while the old and the very young had little in the way of selection. A plump but healthy figure was considered an asset as it was considered a sign of fertility.[9]

The women were expected to make their choice of a husband on arrival, and very little ceremony took place with regard to extensive questioning or courtship between couples. Under the circumstances the men could be expected to be on their best behavior, but at least some of the girls had been sent out by their families against their own wishes. Nonetheless, if they behaved badly or were overly uncooperative, they were made to understand that they would forced to serve out their indentures as servants. Prostitutes from the streets and allies of English cities were sometimes knowingly included in a likely batch of brides by unscrupulous agents, and many girls arrived in the colonies pregnant having been sent off in disgrace by their parents.

Unmarried women indentures had unusual opportunities of advancing their social position in life. Given the shortage of potential brides, few of the women failed to find a suitable husband at the end of their term "if they enjoyed an honorable reputation." A colonial observer noted that no maiden brought over from England "failed to find a husband in the course of the first three months after she had entered into his service." Nonetheless, a large number of these imported women did not come with the requisite status of a maiden, and these "were considered to be worthless."[10] In the Chesapeake region an average of only two women per year voluntarily emigrated as indentured servants from 1718 onward. This was due in part to an improving economy in England, which left fewer individuals willing to leave their home in order to sell themselves into bondage in the wilderness.[11]

Placing unsupported or orphaned children as indentured servants with families in need of additional labor was common. The practice relieved the community of the need to maintain the unfortunate youths and provided them with skills to enter society as productive adults. Many of these children were apprenticed to learn simple tasks such as farming, husbandry, or the skills of a stockman. As early as 1620, one hundred destitute children above the age of fifteen years were swept from the streets of London by the Virginia Company to be sent to America with £5 allowed for the clothing and transportation of each. Based on a review of the available muster lists from some of the Company's transport ships, it is clear that in many cases these cargoes of children were composed of both boys and girls. Many of these youths were bound out by their own guardians or parents in the hope of providing them with a better future than they might have had on the streets of London. The company bound itself to give each boy training in a trade or a profession, and each girl was to be trained in proper housewifery. Some female indentures were also promised reading lessons during their tenure. In 1627 alone almost 1500 children were sent to Virginia, and in 1657 a single transport ship was documented to have almost two dozen servants aboard none of whom was over 19 years of age.[12]

According to one 19th-century historian, "The preference displayed in the introduction of so many young persons [to the colonies] had its origins in considerations, the influence of which lasted throughout the [17th] century. Boys were not only more easily controlled [then men], but their terms continued for a greater length of time than those persons who had reached maturity, and in consequence, their masters were not called upon to supply their places so often or so soon." A healthy youth, male or female, could perform most of the tasks of an adult, and as time passed, they became adults themselves. Forcing children to work under harsh conditions away from their families seems cruel from the present-day perspective, but in an era when education was a privilege reserved for the well-to-do, the practice of indenturing unfortunate youngsters may

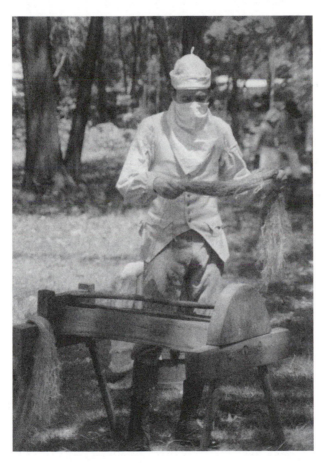

Textile production is thought of as women's work, but this man is performing one of the initial stages of linen production. He is using a cane break to remove the bark-like casing of the flax surrounding the interior threads that make line. The work is dusty and slow.

actually have benefited them in their adult lives. During their terms, they formed habits of obedience and industry, and they acquired the advantage of training through long service.[13]

Nonetheless, under these conditions, a large and valuable portion of Britain's future labor force was sent from the home islands to American shores. The overwhelming popularity of Chesapeake-grown tobacco alone created a demand for labor in America that white laborers from Britain simply could not continue to supply. The natural tendency of tobacco to exhaust the available land required the constant clearing of virgin ground for new fields. This was brutal and unrewarding work even for those working their own land. Without indentured labor or slaves bound to their masters, the southern colonies would have become regions of petty peasant proprietors, each forced to clear and tend his own tiny plot of ground just to survive. Similar conditions existed on many frontier farms established by free laborers who came to be known as poor whites or white trash in the years before the American Civil War.

The London plague and fire of 1666 decimated Britain's population of available workers, and the number of indentured servants choosing to emigrate to the colonies fell steadily throughout the remainder of the colonial period. Historians and social scientists have also noted the shift from a traditional social order characterized by minimal conflict between masters and servants to one that featured harsher dealings with bondsmen, including the vigorous enforcement of written contracts, the failure to honor oral agreements, and the insistence on increasingly longer terms of service. So fractious did the situation between masters and servants become in England that Parliament took steps in 1717 to insure that persons other than slaves could not be carried off to the colonies without their freely given consent. Without resorting to these facts historians have been hard pressed to otherwise explain the sudden shift from white indentured labor to black slavery.

Neither poverty nor race was an obstacle to becoming an indentured servant. There was always some person willing to bear the expense of transportation in return for the right of disposing of the indentured servant's labor after arrival in the colonies. The salable value of both white and black indentured men was generally tied to the number of years remaining in their contracts. "A man still having one year unexpired, ranged in value from £2 sterling to £4; having two years, from £6 sterling to £8; having three years from £8 to £14 sterling; having four years from £11 to £15 sterling." The value of female indentured servants was usually fixed at lower rates, starting from about £1 and rarely exceeding £15 even for six or more years of service.[14]

As the period progressed, shrewd persons generally avoided fixed indentures, preferring flexible contracts that could be cancelled on payment of the cost of passage on disembarking. Such persons, tied to the price of their voyage rather than to duration of service, were known

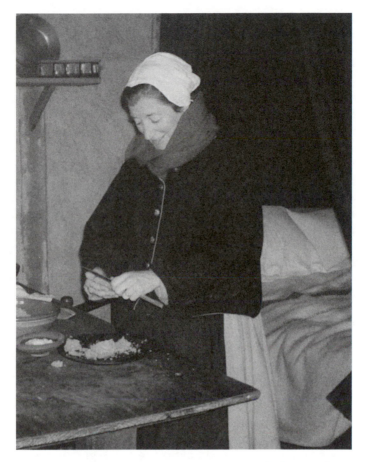

Women did the usual household chores, including cooking, cleaning, sewing, and tending the garden. In many households, only the quality of the clothing distinguished the servants from the mistress.

as redemptioners. In 1700, the cost of transportation was about £10 per person, and redemptioners who found the money to pay off the debt when they arrived could proceed on their way as free laborers. The payment was often made with the help of friends and family already in the colonies. The method of contracting oneself as a redemptioner was complicated, and many of the protocols are hard to define precisely. Most redemptioners emigrated in the 18th century from Germany, and they left few written accounts of how they accomplished the process. A few businessmen are known to have purchased the redemptions from the owners of transport vessel, moving the poorest of these indentured people around the colonies in order to sell their labor contracts at a profit.

The business was filled with risk for the dealer, however, because so many redemptioners escaped during this process.

An amateur 19th-century historian recorded the following amusing confrontation between a redemption dealer and one of his charges. The redemptioner had contrived to be the last of a group of servants to remain unsold, and for several days he traveled about with his master, a dealer named McCullough, without companions. One night they lodged at an out-of-the-way tavern very late at night. In the morning the young indentured fellow rose early and, noting that the innkeeper had mistaken him for the dealer, sold his master to the landlord after some hard bargaining, pocketed the money, and marched off. By the time the dealer had convinced the innkeeper that he had been deceived, the redemptioner had gained such a start that his pursuit was rendered hopeless.[15]

Until late in the 18th century, English justice eschewed imprisonment as a sentence for crime, choosing rather to inflict corporal punishments such as floggings and branding on criminals. A common alternative to physical punishment was transportation to the colonies as an indentured servant or laborer. Many criminals were made to serve as indentured servants for seven, fourteen, or more years. Indenture for life was not unheard of as an alternative to death for capital crimes. A sentence of indenture for life was equivalent to enslavement, but it did not pass on the state of bondage to the person's offspring, if there were any. Initially there was no plan to use the colonies as a place of retention for social miscreants. Nonetheless, proposals to transport criminals were made by the Virginia Company as early as 1611, but the number transported remained insignificant in the overall colonial labor picture. In 1661 a special committee of the Privy Council was appointed to consider how "felons condemned to death for small offenses" might be disposed of for use as laborers in the colonies.[16] Following the Restoration, a somewhat larger number of convicts were sent to America than might otherwise have come. Among these may have been some holdovers from the supporters of the Puritan Republic. It was not until the imposition of the Transportation Act of 1718, however, that a significant number of convicts arrived in America as indentured servants.

The influx of indentured convicts after 1718 had a negative effect on the perceived status of persons who voluntarily entered into indentured service for financial or other legitimate reasons, and it caused many honest persons to avoid entering into service contracts at all. The Transportation Act served the needs of Parliament to banish felons and other persons thought to "chargeable, dangerous, or troublesome."[17] Yet this policy addressed the needs of Britain more than it did those of America. Benjamin Franklin, speaking for the colonies, suggested that the colonial governments respond to the influx of convicts from Britain in kind by depositing a thousand rattlesnakes on the shores of England.[18] A number of colonies attempted to pass their own laws prohibiting the landing of indentured felons. Nevertheless, the government in London continued to think of the colonies as a dumping ground for the undesirable, the unemployed, and the untrained, hoping all the time that such forced immigration would somehow benefit the Empire.

FREE BLACK WORKERS

In Virginia, the status of black freemen was carefully defined by the colonial government and the courts, which reflected many of the same prejudices toward free Negroes that they held toward black slaves. Such views were common in many other colonies, including those in the North. "Consequently the free Negroes in the eighteenth century were a small and despised group." Free blacks were denied the right to bear witness against whites in court and could not bear arms, vote, or hold office. Even persons of mixed race were forbidden to marry whites. In the 17th century, almost all manumissions (legally freeing a slave) seem to have been accomplished by white fathers for their mixed-race children. Statistics for the 18th century, when records are more abundant, suggest that the number of freemen grew at about the same rate as the population and hovered at about four percent (4%) in the decades before the Revolution. In the North free blacks generally lived in separate areas of the town, unless they were given quarters in the homes of their employers. Thomas Jefferson noted, "Among the Romans emancipation required but one effort. The slave when made free, might mix with [other Romans], without staining the blood of his master. But with us a second [effort] is necessary, unknown to history. When freed he is to be removed beyond reach of mixture."[19]

There are many indications that in all the colonies, but primarily in the south, there were many mixed-race persons serving as free or indentured laborers "who had either been set free by their white fathers or were sprung from emancipated African mothers." Many of these persons served under contracts indistinguishable from those of white laborers. Some of these contracts were for comparatively short terms, and others ended when the servant attained his majority, generally considered to be 25 for blacks. In the South, the mixed-race child of a black man by a white woman was considered a bastard and the property of the courts, which might extend servitude until the person's 30th year.[20]

Free blacks seem to have preferred to live in the urban setting of the North and were twice as likely to live in coastal towns as slaves, who were primarily agricultural workers. Former slaves or freeborn blacks could more easily earn a living along the coast, especially as artisans, shipwrights, sailmakers, and stevedores. In towns, black craftsmen and other free blacks found opportunities for employment, exposure to black culture and religion, and the company of other freemen. However, the majority of free blacks lived on the margins of poverty and were subject to detention and questioning by the authorities without cause.

Free blacks were continually encouraged to sell themselves back into servitude. There were advantages in doing this. A freeman could sell himself as an indenture for life, contract his conditions of employment, choose his master, provide for his retirement, and retain the cash under the laws of Virginia and many other colonies. Incredibly, many free black tradesmen and artisans entered their own children into these contracts, often in lieu of an apprenticeship agreement, because they gave their offspring as indentures the protection and cover of the law that they would have been denied as free persons.[21]

AND JUSTICE FOR ALL

Many laws governed the manner in which indentured persons could be treated. They were entitled to care during illness, and the time of service lost to illness could not be held against them. They could not be sold out of the colony in which they arrived nor could they be cheated out of their freedom dues—those items due them at the conclusion of the indenture. Overall, indentured servants were given a legal status similar to that of children. The Pennsylvania colonial assembly passed legislation that gave indentured servants two suits of clothing, a new ax, a grubbing hoe, and a weeding hoe as freedom dues.[22]

Disputes between indentured servants and masters occasionally made their way into the courts. The most common complaints by servants were that the master or mistress was not attending to their physical welfare. There were also specific claims that the master had failed to provide proper clothing or food. The majority of charges against servants were for running away, or for stealing. Other common complaints included unruly behavior, fornication, profanity, and sexual misbehavior. Mary Dudley of Massachusetts wrote to her mother complaining of her indentured servant, "If I bid her do a thing she will bid me do it myself .... If I should write you all the reviling speeches and filthy language she hath used towards me I should but grieve you."[23] Penalties for offenses varied from one colony to another and evolved as time progressed. In cases of a servant's unlawful absence from duty, Maryland extended the contract by twice the number of days absent. In 1666, the penalty was increased to 10 days for every day absent. In 1683, Pennsylvania added lashing to the imposition of 5 additional days for each day of unlawful absence. Anyone found to be assisting a runaway was required to pay the master £20 and an additional £5 to the court.[24]

Respect for authority extended beyond the bounds of the indenture to the trial and punishment for all persons accused of a crime before the colonial justices and courts, and defendants seem to have respected the system even though it was filled with apparent cruelty and diabolical inventiveness.[25] As an example, after a free white defendant pleaded guilty to a stabbing in 1730, a Virginia court "ordered that for the offense

This detail from an antique linen postcard shows the stocks used to punish minor crimes in colonial Virginia.

the sheriff take him and set him in the pillory and nail both his ears [to the board], therefore to stand for one hour, and at the expiration of the same, to cut them [his ears] both off."[26] English justice, even for whites, rarely resorted to imprisonment as a sentence for crime. Whipping, flogging, branding, ear cropping, and other immediate physical punishments were thought to be much more effective in deterring unwanted behaviors than simple confinement. While colonial jails were "dirty, cramped, and foul smelling," they were used only as temporary holding facilities, not for long-term confinement. Town courts in some colonies were limited in their sentencing strategies to whippings and banishments, but the right of most county courts "to take life and limb" was absolute.[27]

From 1711 to 1754, only six white men brought to indictment before the courts in Virginia chose a jury trial. A jury trial rarely mitigated a just punishment and was only effective if the defendants had something material to say in their defense. In general, it did not improve the defendants' chances very much to put themselves before a jury. Those that pled their quilt were punished, but they usually saved the additional costs of a trial and the series of fines that would inevitability be assessed against them. Even if found innocent, defendants might be forced to post cash and sureties to bond themselves to future good behavior.[28] Newcomers, men and women on the fringes of the community, former convicts, and servants or slaves were usually presumed guilty before trial.[29]

Most colonial courts gave high regard to the body of English common law accumulated before 1609 and to colonial precedents thereafter. Local exigency seems to have determined how cases were tried in many colonial jurisdictions. In Massachusetts, all felony and homicide cases were heard by at least one justice; in Connecticut, a system of justices sitting together heard such cases. Consistent with English practices witnesses testified under oath, but defendants often did not testify so that they would not be forced to perjure themselves in making a defense. Common in England since the thirteenth century for the trial of serious crimes, Oyer and Terminer courts were also fixtures of Anglo-American justice. In Virginia they were given specific charge to hear capital cases against bondsmen and slaves. In Pennsylvania, Delaware, Georgia, and the Carolinas in the 18th century freeholders courts composed of two or more local justices and three to five local landowners were establish to provide the same function. In New York, Massachusetts, Connecticut, and New Hampshire felony cases involving bondsmen and slaves were brought before a grand jury before being heard by a trial jury at a regular session of the superior courts. New Jersey established freeholders courts but limited their jurisdiction to murder, rape, arson, and dismemberment allegedly committed by bondsmen; and Rhode Island stopped just short of creating a similar system by creating town courts presided over by county justices and town wardens. The characteristic slowness of the English court system seems to have been taken to heart by the colonists, who everywhere in varying degrees valued expediency over protocol when dispensing justice to those in servitude.[30]

In almost all cases involving bondsmen, there was no jury trial, and the bench determined the facts and set the sentence. The county immediately meted out punishment to defendants found guilty of serious crimes. In the absence of a local justice of the peace, the hearing officers came from the community of white freeholders and masters. White bondsmen had all the rights generally held by free persons and could mount a similar form of legal defense if they chose.[31] A wide range of crimes regarded as misdemeanors today were considered felonies in the colonial period, and almost all felonies warranted capital punishment. Ironically, a similar expansion of the definition of capital crime was going on in England. One of the oddities of American economic history made it more likely that a free white in England would be executed for his crime than a slave or indentured servant in the same legal circumstance in the colonies.

In the South, crimes against slaves by whites were treated with extreme leniency. In Virginia, Governor William Gooch noted that an overseer charged with the murder of a slave and found guilty might "have his life spared not only because it did not appear that he had the intention to kill the Negro, but in regard as the executing of him for this offense may make the slaves very insolent and give them occasion to condemn their masters and overseers, which may be of dangerous consequence in a country where Negroes are so numerous."[32] In *The American Slave Code in Theory and Practice* (1853), William Goodell noted, "[F]rom the very nature of slavery, and the necessary degraded social position of a slave, many acts would extenuate the homicide of a slave, and reduce the offense to a lower grade."[33]

Throughout the 18th century, colonial law and procedures progressively abandoned the common-law precedents of English jurisprudence in order to control the bound population of the colonies and appease the employers or slave owners. Yet the trials of slaves and servants, even if they were found not guilty, sent a message to other bondsmen that any offense would result, at the least, in their arrest and incarceration. A few well-chosen public punishments and executions were thought to be excellent deterrents, making bondsmen more likely to consider the punishments meted out by their masters lenient by comparison.[34] A report on the history of American legal practices notes, "[Bondsmen and] slaves were valuable property, not to be regarded lightly by their masters or other slave owners. The legislature might compensate masters for a slave hanged for a crime, but it did not compensate them for the lost time and labor of trial and punishment. Some masters … may have intervened for them [their bondsmen] even when their guilt was established." Robert Carter's journal recorded his own combination of "paternal kindness, exasperation, and offhanded cruelty" used to chastise those servants that were "valuable." He noted that these efforts "had some good effect."[35]

APPRENTICESHIPS

The contracts that legalized the apprenticeship were considered indentures. They specified what duties and behaviors were expected of the servant and what the master or mistress was required to provide in return. It was not unusual for certain social prohibitions to be specified in the indenture.[36] The term of service could last for a specific time or until the child reached a certain age. At the satisfactory conclusion of the term the apprentice would be given certain essentials that would allow them to go out on their own. Generally this involved a provision of clothing and a set of essential tools for the former apprentice to ply their newly learned trade.

Servants and apprentices formed communities of their own within the wider community where they were usually a majority of the population. Yet the minority composed of the householders for whom they worked, ruled them absolutely. The difficulties encountered by most servants and apprentices in dealing with freeholders and masters were mitigated somewhat because there were so many of their fellow citizens in servitude.

NOTES

1. Selma R. Williams, *Demeter's Daughters: The Women Who Founded America, 1587–1789* (New York: Athenaeum, 1976), 55.

2. A contract specifying performance of a personal service is forbidden by the U.S. Constitution. An employee can be sued for monetary damages but not forced to serve.

3. See William S. Sachs and Ari Hoogenboom, *The Enterprising Colonials: Society on the Eve of the Revolution* (Chicago: Argonaut, 1965), 19; quotation from Philip A. Bruce, *Economic History of Virginia in the Seventeenth Century: An Inquiry into the Material Condition of the People, Based on Original and Contemporaneous Records* (New York: Macmillan, 1896), 575.

4. Laurel Thatcher Ulrich, *A Midwife's Tale: The Life of Martha Ballam, Based on Her Diary, 1785–1812* (New York: Vintage, 1990), 82.

5. Bernard Bailyn, *The Peopling of British North America: An Introduction* (New York: Alfred A. Knopf, 1986), 28.

6. See Sachs and Hoogenboom, *The Enterprising Colonials*, 19; quotation from Bruce, *Economic History of Virginia in the Seventeenth Century*, 575.

7. Bruce, 574.

8. Ibid., 583.

9. My own great-grandmother came to America in the 1880s as a mail-order bride. Finding that her intended husband (buyer) had married another woman in the interim, she married one of his friends, who paid her passage and costs. The couple produced nine healthy children, three of whom lived to be more than 100. The other six died in their 90s.

10. Quoted in Bruce, *Economic History of Virginia*, 51.

11. Carol Berkin, *First Generations: Women in Colonial America* (New York: Hill and Wang, 1996), 108, 152.

12. Bruce, *Economic History of Virginia*, 601.

13. Ibid., 596.

14. Ibid., 52–53.

15. Joseph J. Lewis, "Sketches of the History of Chester County," *Village Record* (1824), http://www.delcohistory.org/ashmead/ashmead_pg202.htm (accessed March 2005).

16. Bruce, *Economic History of Virginia*, 604.

17. See Kenneth Morgan, *Slavery and Servitude in Colonial America* (New York: New York University Press, 2000), 4; and Bruce, 593.

18. Cedric B. Cowing, *The Great Awakening and the American Revolution: Colonial Thought in the 18th Century* (Chicago: Rand McNally, 1971), 144.

19. Quoted in ibid., 112.

20. Bruce, *Economic History of Virginia*, 52.

21. Dorothy Denneen Volo and James M. Volo, *Daily Life in Civil War America* (Westport, CT: Greenwood Press, 1998), 65–66.

22. Elaine Forman Crane, ed., *The Diary of Elizabeth Drinker* (Boston: Northeastern University Press, 1994), 63.

23. Selma R. Williams, *Demeter's Daughters*, 60.

24. Cheesman A. Herrick, *White Servitude in Pennsylvania: Indentured and Redemption Labor in Colony and Commonwealth* (Philadelphia: John Joseph McVey, 1926), 166.

25. Peter Charles Hoffer and William B. Scott, xxxii.

26. Ibid., 123.

27. Ibid., xlviii.

28. Ibid., xxx.

29. Ibid., xxxv.

30. Ibid., xlvi–xlvii.

31. Volo and Volo, *Civil War America*, 70–71.

32. Hoffer and Scott, li.

33. William Goodell, *The American Slave Code in Theory and Practice* (New York: American and Foreign Anti-Slavery Society, 1853), 92.

34. Hoffer and Scott, lii.

35. Ibid., xlix.

36. The Connecticut Historical Society, 11.

16

Race-Based Slavery

The slave, to remain a slave, must be made sensible that there is no appeal from the will of his master.

—The Black Codes[1]

THE SLAVE TRADE

For determining the extent of English involvement in the slave trade to British North America, the records of the Royal African Company are an important resource. This company held a monopoly from the British Crown on legal slave trading on this route. From 1673 to 1689 an annual rate of just over 4,000 slaves per year can be calculated. However, other sources suggest that the colonies seem to have taken in almost 7,000 African slaves, but it is possible that these estimates are 10 to 15 percent too high. The Company's own accounting suggests that English and Dutch interlopers actually had a large share of an illegal trade in slaves that flourished until the late 18th century. The practice of re-exporting slaves among the colonies, more widely practiced than historians formerly thought, also confounds precise estimates.

For example, New York and New Jersey imported almost 5,000 black slaves from 1715 to 1767 but only about 900 seem to have been African born. In the same period, 86 percent of the slave ships entering Virginia came from the West Indies or nearby colonies, not from Africa. Yet, historians insist that "the proportion [of slaves] from Africa increased with the passage of time. In the earliest period, 1710–1718, only 56 percent of the slaves were direct exports from Africa, the remainder being re-exports from other colonies."[2]

The method employed by many researchers of taking a one-year esti-mate of the total number of slaves carried in British ships and treating it as an annual average has often yielded unacceptably high estimates both on the score of double-counting slaves and of neglecting re-exports. A recent search of the historical literature produced a number of separate one-year estimates scattered throughout the 18th century. One report for 1720 mentions a total of 146 ships in the British slave trade, capable of carrying 36,050 slaves. A second gives 87 ships from London in 1725, with a total capacity of 26,400 slaves, plus 63 ships from Bristol, with a total capacity of 16,950. In 1749, Bristol and Liverpool together sent out 117 ships, with a total capacity of 39,840, while London sent out 80 additional ships capable of holding 27,200 slaves. Other reports, more often repeated in the litera-ture, give an export capacity for the British slave trade of 53,100 slaves in 1768 and 47,100 slaves in 1771. A semiofficial study of the slave trade by the Board of Trade estimated a slave ship capacity of 41,000 on the eve of the American Revolution. Researchers arrived at these data by using a common rate of two slaves per ton to convert the ship burden in tons to a number of slaves loaded, yet many ships were known to sail with far fewer slaves than full capacity. Similar devices were used for guessing the extent of the slave trade in the 16th and 17th centuries, casting "consider-able doubt as to the reliability of the process."[3]

Before the arrival of oceanic steam navigation in the 19th century, ships were at the mercy of the prevailing winds and ocean currents. A voyage from Europe to America and back was best accomplished by sailing a large clockwise loop from Gibraltar down the West African coast to the latitude of the Cape Verde Islands and then across the Atlantic to the West Indian islands of Barbados or Guadeloupe. Vessels could then beat northward out of the Caribbean with the help of the Gulf Stream and catch the prevailing westerlies on the way home to Europe. This route, which brought ships within a few score miles of the African coast, helps to explain why so many of the earliest Africans brought to America as slaves came from the regions around the Senegal and Gambia Rivers. "[I]t all fit devilishly well into the export of West Africans to the Caribbean and North America and concentrated the higher risks of unfavorable winds in the legs of the voyage in cargo—European manufactures outbound, coffee, rum, and sugar homeward bound—that was least perishable." Barring adverse winds or dirty weather, the slave-carrying leg, known as the Middle Passage, commonly took seven or eight weeks, "a long time under slave-ship conditions, and losses were often sickeningly high." An alternative route that drove eastward under the chin of Africa toward Benin became popular later in the period.[4]

The losses from disease, violence, and other causes (accident or lack of water and food) during the ocean crossing seem to have been about

5 percent, but estimates as high as 25 percent are commonly found in modern textbooks. Slavers who tolerated such high losses as a common practice were bitterly assailed even by the slave-owning portions of society. Nonetheless, it was this particularly hideous characteristic of the slave trade that seems to have most inflamed the few abolitionists to be found in colonial society.[5]

A study of the Nantes (French) slave trade indicates that the number of slaves purchased in Africa was 22.2 percent higher than the number landed during the long world peace of 1715 to 1741. Although this figure for mortality among the slaves from Africa in transit is often accepted as a general coefficient of loss for the whole colonial period, other evidence concerning the slave trade "hardly justifies such a fine calculation." The period from the dawn of the 16th century to the first decades of the 19th century was one of almost continuous warfare at sea, with the years 1715 to 1741 providing an uncharacteristic respite in attacks upon ocean commerce. These peacetime years represented a period when slave ships were "probably loaded more nearly to capacity" than was possible during periods of war when lighter cargoes of slaves and fleeter vessels were needed to escape capture.[6]

SLAVE LABOR

Slave markets provided an abundant source of labor in the colonies that employers found to be less restrictive than indentured servitude, and the increasing number of slaves being brought from Africa easily filled any shortfall in the number of available indentured workers. Once purchased, slaves were the master's property until death or sale. Indentures were limited by time. At the end of the contract, the bondservant, but not the slave, was free to leave. Additionally, indentured servants were more likely than slaves to bring grievances against their masters to the attention of authorities or to seek legal action in the courts.

The Dutch colony of New Amsterdam was founded in 1626. Among the first residents were eleven male African slaves. Female slaves were brought to the colony later. The Dutch placed a great reliance on slave labor, employing small numbers of slaves both in their households and on their farms. The social climate on Dutch farms was often different from that on southern plantations. Dutch owners commonly absented themselves from their properties for long periods to luxuriate in the more amenable surroundings of the town, especially during the winter months. The slaves were left virtually on their own to manage the property during the owner's absence. Moreover, Dutch slave owners initially seem to have placed slaves on the same level with indentured servants who might be freed after a specified period. In 1661, a black couple, formerly slaves, successfully petitioned Governor Peter Stuyvesant for the release of their son from bondage. However, after the Dutch colony was lost to the English, race-based slavery became a perpetual condition, with fourth- and fifth-generation slaves serving fourth- and fifth-generation colonials of both Dutch and English descent.[7]

In the first quarter of the 18th century, northern farmers were increasingly likely to replace indentured servants and wage laborers with black slaves, especially in New York, New Jersey, and Pennsylvania, but these slaves were owned in ones and twos, with total numbers that were insignificant when compared to those on southern plantations. Nonetheless, as a source of black slaves Rhode Island was second only to South Carolina, and the little colony had many farmsteads and shipping companies, each employing many dozens of slaves. In contrast, the Chesapeake colonies held many thousands of black slaves. By 1700, the number of enslaved persons in the South equaled that of the entire free and indentured white population.

DOCUMENTING SLAVERY

There seems to be an academic coerciveness about the study of slavery that brings historians back to it again and again. Possibly it is the nature of the institution, being so far removed from the living memory of Americans—black or white. One historian noted, "The same tests for

The Dutch that came to New York were among the most cosmopolitan and sophisticated people in Europe, yet they were comfortable with the concept of slave ownership.

the righteousness or wrongness of slavery remain in use year in and year out." Yet, there can be no doubt about the inevitable findings of such a debate regardless of how often the traditional sources "have been mined and re-mined." However, when researching the nature of slavery, rather than the proslavery or antislavery arguments and debates of the past, historians can play the light of research on different questions. For example, historians reference the daily business accounts written by slave owners sparingly and with great caution even though they are plentiful and filled with detailed information. These sources of information about slave society reside largely in the daily reports of plantation activities and the internal records of slave trading establishments. Nonetheless, they provide first hand accounts, rather than hearsay evidence, concerning slavery. They were written contemporary with events and are considered by most open-minded historians to have "the substantial integrity needed for accuracy in business accounts." Moreover, historical archaeologists have produced a mass of work concerning the housing, feeding, and clothing of slaves just in the last few decades that has overturned many of the traditional views of slavery that were based on anecdotal evidence accumulated in the 19th century. Together with contemporary published tracts on the "Management of Negroes," private letters and papers of slaveholders, and advertisements for fugitives, these sources provide an accurate picture of what slaves looked like and how they occupied themselves, even if they cannot supply a reliable indicator of how they felt or what they thought.[8]

SLAVE LAW

Traditional historians, misled by anecdotal evidence, believed that the American form of slavery was "the most awful the world has ever known" and characterized by "frightful Barbarities." Slave owners were thought to have opposed every scheme to make the lot of the slave more tolerable with every legal obstacle that they could devise. This view requires some revision to better align it with the facts. Certainly slavery was a cruel and abhorrent institution. Yet, it was centuries old in Europe, and the customs, attitudes, and regulations surrounding it had been fixed in the law since Roman times. The emperor Justinian's code was often referenced in this respect. Moreover, the early Roman Catholic Church in its writings had preserved and perpetuated the traditions associated with slavery in the Law of Moses. These ancient works not only recognized the keeping of slaves but also made endless rules for their treatment and governance. Under these traditions, slavery was not reserved for blacks. Most of the peoples of Europe had been enslaved at some point in their ethnic history. Moors, Jews, and Spaniards had been held in slavery as recently as the 15th and 16th centuries, and the first people to practice slavery and to be enslaved in America were the natives of the New World themselves.

Indians were rounded up by the hundreds by competing tribes and shipped as slaves by the Europeans to the islands of the Caribbean.

The logic of the legal precedents involving slavery, both biblical and classical, is incomprehensible to us today and probably also escaped the understanding of 19th century partisans "both North and South, even though each drew upon [them] for their arguments." Nonetheless, European law clearly recognized and implicitly sanctioned the institution and legality of slavery. "[N]owhere was it denied." At the same time, there was the universal presumption among philosophers and intellectuals that involuntary servitude of any kind, violating the divine and natural rights of man, was against both reason and nature. These ideas posed difficult dilemmas for the colonials—dilemmas that were incapable of solution even during the founding of a great nation.[9]

Notwithstanding the need to indict the entire concept of human bondage as morally contemptible, it was always implicit in the body of law that governed slavery that the slave had some rights, although of a very limited nature. "It is important ... to keep in mind that for all the system's cruelties there were still clear standards of patriarchal benevolence inherent in its human side, and that such standards were recognized as those of the best Southern families."[10] Among these standards was the slave's right to buy his own freedom and to have time in which he might work for himself and accumulate the purchase price. Even in rural areas, slaves might sell the produce of their own garden plots or the products of their craftsmanship and retain the profits. Moreover, they had the right to practice religion under rigidly specified conditions, and a body of law (if not justice) had accumulated that applied to most foreseeable circumstances. Slavery in the English colonies may have been milder in terms of the physical comforts afforded the slave than it was elsewhere in the Americas (the Spanish, for instance, were particularly inhumane). However, "it would be missing the point to make the comparison in terms of physical comfort. In one case [Spain] we would be dealing with the cruelty of man to man, and, in the other [England], with the care, maintenance, and indulgence of men toward creatures who were legally and morally not [considered] men."[11]

England recognized a large body of law dealing with indentures, apprentices, and other contract workers, but in British North America there was no true body of slave laws or legal precedents from the beginning of colonization. Because slavery was uncommon in Britain, the issues proceeding from the institution devolved on to each of the colonial legislatures separately, and legislation was crafted in decidedly differing forms from colony to colony. Under English common law, the bondsman retained a legal personality and his children retained their status as freemen. The state of villeinage, which had once flourished in England, came closest to the condition of slavery. However, the legal condition of villeinage had become extinct by the 17th century. It was almost out of memory.

The legal suppression of the individual personality—the idea that the black slave was chattel rather than human—unified the conceptual threads of colonial slavery everywhere that it could be found. "Perhaps it is due to this circumstance that the slave legislation of the English colonies was more severe [in its consequences] ... that the master's power ... was more absolute and uncontrollable."[12]

Regardless of the benevolence or lack of it imputed to the colonial regime, the key to the nature of slavery as a social system was the patriarchal ideal.[13] Social historians have identified four major spheres of interest that help to define the status and condition of slaves in colonial America: their term of service, their status in marriage or as a family member, the limits of their master's power over them, and their civil and property rights. Those who state categorically that they already know the facts regarding these areas of concern should note that a great deal of misinformation and misdirected rhetoric surrounds the history of slavery.

Unlike white employees, slaves were not free to change their condition when it became too burdensome. Although slavery was assumed to be for the life of the slave, no part of English law allowed for slavery to be based solely on race. Almost every colony felt the need for some kind of statutory recognition of the status of slaves to underpin this characteristic of the institution. Legislation recognizing slavery occurred as follows: Massachusetts (1641), Connecticut (1650), Virginia (1661), Maryland (1663), New York and New Jersey (1664), South Carolina (1684), Rhode Island (1700), North Carolina (formed in 1710), and Georgia (founded in 1732). No effort was made in any of these enactments to automatically place all Negroes into the condition of slavery, and many of the provisions dealt with Indians, convicts, and apprentices. While slavery was accepted in the northern colonies, it was not as widespread as in the South where the plantation economy demanded an abundant source of low-cost labor. Nonetheless, it was not until 1698 that Massachusetts undertook to consider the important question of the status of children born to slaves, and as late as 1784, children born to slaves in Connecticut were born into slavery that ended at 25 years of age. The last slave in Connecticut was freed by an enactment of the legislature in 1848, only 12 years before tens of thousands of men from that state fought to end slavery in the Civil War.[14]

SLAVE LIFE

The early Dutch settlers of New Netherlands made extensive use of slave labor. Having won their political liberty from Spain in the early 1600s, the Dutch immediately formed a zealous affinity for depriving Negroes of their personal freedom by devising a trading-factory system for slaving on the Gold Coast of Africa. Dutch manors along the Hudson River, like their southern counterparts, required more laborers than their

Slaves were sold at auction, along with livestock and other forms of merchandise. The poster speaks for itself.

sparse settlements could provide. Some large farms in the Narragansett Bay region of Rhode Island and in eastern Connecticut also used slaves in large numbers. However, the small farmers of New England did not need workers in such abundance. Large families and dependent relatives usually supplied the needed labor. Many farmers accumulated a small stock of capital for the specific purpose of buying a slave when more hands were required than the family could supply.

The situation of these slaves must have been vastly different from the lot of the plantation slave. Slaves in the north experienced more intimate contact with white society than elsewhere. Early diaries of northern colonists and many Indian captivity records mention slaves by name as if they were members of the household. It is likely that both male and female slaves in the north acculturated rapidly as they did not receive from newly imported slaves the same level of cultural reinforcement of their African heritage that their southern counterparts did. Slaves in New England also learned more skills than the average southern plantation worker. Besides knowing how to work in the cornfield and cabbage patch, tend the stock and the dairy, and repair a fence or a cradle, many were purchased for their metalworking or crafting skills. Contemporary newspapers offered an abundance of advertisements describing slaves who were "brought up in husbandry," were "fit for town or country," or understood the farming business "exceedingly well."[15]

Nonetheless, slaves in New England were exposed to many of the same restrictions on their freedom as their southern counterparts. An act passed late in the 18th century in Connecticut stated:

Whatsoever Negro, Mulatto, or Indian servant or servants shall be found wandering out of the bounds of the Town or Place to which they belong without a Ticket or Pass in writing under the hand of some assistant, or Justice of the Peace, or under the hand of the Master or owner of such ... shall be deemed and accounted to be runaways and may be treated as such .... Every free person which shall presume, either openly or privately, to buy or receive of or from an Indian, Mulatto, or Negro slave or servant any money, goods, merchandise, wares, or provisions, without order from the master or mistress of such ... shall forfeit to [any injured] party ... the articles (if not altered) and also double the value thereof .... If it appear they were stolen [every Indian, Negro, or Mulatto servant or slave] shall be punished by whipping, not exceeding thirty stripes.[16]

Slaves on the New England frontier were treated in much the same way as whites bound to service. They lived side by side with the owner's family, sharing the same labors, food, and residence. On her journey through the primitive settlements between Boston and New York, Sarah Kemble Knight complained that settlers were "too Indulgent (especially the farmers) to their slaves: suffering too great familiarity from them, permitting them to sit at table and eat with them."[17] Knight also noted a dispute between a master and his slave "concerning something the master had promised him and did not punctually perform; which caused some harsh words between them; But at length they brought themselves to Arbitration." The master was ordered by a justice of the peace to pay the slave 40 shillings "and acknowledge his fault."[18]

The vast majority of small farmers worked the land themselves, and few owned any slaves. However, many white farmers may have harbored the desire to accumulate enough money to buy one or two slaves, as this raised them to a new social status in the eyes of their neighbors. Nonetheless, most frontier farmers who owned slaves before large-scale plantation slavery flourished worked in the fields beside them, ate the same foods, lived in the same house, and wore essentially the same functional clothing.

Many farmers in New England owned a single slave or two that helped them work the fields, and some farmers looked on them in the same way that they viewed any other tool of their trade.

By 1690, the need for additional slaves had become so great that the Royal African Company, which held a monopoly on importation, could not fill the demand. In 1698, Parliament revoked the company's charter and threw open the African coast to independent slavers and traders. The stream of slaves became enormous, with two effects. The annual flow of white indentured servants to the Chesapeake colonies dropped sharply, and initial moves toward purposely breeding domestic slaves so that their children could be sold were put on hold. As long as importation from Africa was possible, breeding slaves to sell on the market was not acceptable anywhere in the colonies. Not until the Atlantic slave trade was outlawed in the 19th century (1808) did raising a domestic stock of slaves become common. The major advantage of second-generation slaves was that they were born to the work and spoke English; the disadvantage was the need to feed, house, and care for them as infants and small children when their labor was at best only marginally productive.[19]

Slave marriage and the sanctity of the slave family had long since been destroyed by the procedures common to keeping slaves, and the law showed no inclination to rehabilitate them. Legal enactments could easily have guaranteed the inviolability of the family unit or given legality to slave marriages, but such laws, viewed as restrictions on the slave owner, would have set human interests and property rights at odds. "It was thus that the father of a slave was 'unknown,' a husband without the rights of his bed, the state of marriage defined as … 'concubinage' … and mother-hood clothed in the scant dignity of the breeding function." Slaves were almost never admonished for fornication or adultery, nor could they take any action against the violator of a wife or daughter. For all practical pur-poses, under such circumstances, the slave family became entirely matri-archal because only through the mother could kinship be determined. Family lines flowed from great-grandmother to grandmother to mother, with generations renewing themselves almost as quickly as the onset of the childbearing years permitted.[20]

That slave owners viewed a natural increase in the slave population as advantageous cannot be denied, but many planters professed an aversion to purposely breaking up slave families by selling black children because the practice increased unrest among the slaves. Nonetheless, the extrava-gant lifestyle of the planters, coupled with the regularity of foreclosures on mortgages and demands for the repayment of loans, caused most slaves to see the auction block at least once in their lives. Slaves could be bought or sold, rented out, gambled away, or left in a will as an inheri-tance to almost anyone; and the law did not provide for the continued unity of the slave family when determining the division of an inheritance or the settling of a debt. Behind the harsh realities of slavery lurked a great fear of the uprising of slaves and bondsmen in general. By 1740, the number of black slaves had increased to such a critical point that fear became epidemic, especially in the South, leading to harsher laws and more public punishments.

LEGAL RIGHTS OF SLAVES

Slaves could be physically punished by their masters for many forms of disobedience or insolence and for petty crimes. Masters held similar rights over their indentured servants and their apprentices, but these rights were greatly limited by law or contract. Incredibly, masters did not have unlimited legal power over their slaves. A slave accused of a felony could not be purposely mutilated, maimed, or killed as punishment without the intervention of a court, and during the 1700s, such extreme punishments seem to have become less common. The jurisdiction of these courts varied from place to place; but, generally, their procedures were set down in a group of laws known to historians as the Black Codes.[21]

A 1669 Virginia law, for instance, declared it no felony for a master or overseer to kill a slave who resisted punishment. A South Carolina law passed in 1712 set the punishment for a violent act by a slave on any Christian person as "a severe whipping for the first offense, branding for the second, and death for the third." The same act also provided the first two punishments for the corresponding attempts to run away and "his ears to cut off for the third, and castrated for the fourth." Nonetheless, it is doubtful that the most repellent of these punishments were often used, but they did come to symbolize the absolute power of the master over the slave.[22]

The Negro Act of 1714 noted, "Whereas it has been found by experience that the executing of several Negroes for felonies of a small nature ... have been a great charge and expense to the public ... all Negroes or other slaves who shall be convicted and found guilty of any capital crime (murder excepted) for which they used to receive sentence of death, as the law directs, shall be transported from this province."[23] A South Carolina law of 1740 noted, "In case any person shall willfully cut out the tongue, put out the eye, castrate, or cruelly scald, burn, or deprive any slave of any limb or member, or shall inflict other cruel punishment, (other than whipping, or beating with a horsewhip, cowskin, switch, or small stick, or by putting irons on, or confining or imprisoning such slave), every such person shall, for every such offense, forfeit the sum of one hundred pounds current money." The need for such protections for human beings boggles the modern mind and disturbs the civilized psyche.[24] Nonetheless, as late as 1791, two Negro slaves were sentenced in a Charleston, South Carolina, court to be burned alive on the site where they were accused of having murdered a white overseer.[25]

Of course, a slave defendant was not entitled to a jury trial, but he did get a hearing. These hearings were generally held in a county court set up for the purpose. A neutral hearing officer was required to determine the merits of the case and to act as a finder of fact. As the hearing officers usually came from the community of free white slaveholders, questions of guilt or innocence were often moot, and only the nature of the punishment hung in the balance. Nonetheless, the slave was allowed to make a defense, generally relying on his own testimony or the testimony of other slaves. Slaves could not subpoena whites to testify, although whites might volunteer their testimony. The county could then sentence and mete out punishment to any slaves found guilty of serious crimes. Both the Black Codes and custom gave great leeway to the officers of the court in determining the nature of any punishment. Slaves were never given the impression during the process that their masters did not have the right to discipline them. "The slave, to remain a slave, must be made sensible that there is no appeal from [the will of] his master."[26]

PUNISHMENT

As slaves were valuable in their persons, masters looked down on any form of physical punishment that permanently devalued his property. Some masters intervened with the court in behalf of their slaves even when their guilt had been firmly established. Hamstringing, various forms of dismemberment, and death were uncommon punishments for mere disobedience or petty crime. If only for economic reasons, the master wanted to maintain a chastised but physically capable slave in his employ, not a worthless handicapped cripple that he could not sell. Punishments most often took the form of an informal "laying on" of the ever-present lash or rod, while a "hitching up" to the whipping post for a formal flogging was reserved for major offenses. Masters also had the option of selling an unrepentant slave to the far South, to the interior, or to the disease-infested sugar plantations in lieu of punishment. The life expectancy of slaves in the West Indian Islands was less than five years.

In colonial times, it was thought impossible for white laborers to survive for long in the tropical climate of the West Indies. Yet, the overseers seemed to function well enough. The concept that the black races were better equipped to labor in the heat- and mosquito-infested islands proved equally incorrect.

Slave owners rarely punished their bondsmen personally. This was left to the overseer. Much of the physical abuse distributed to slaves came from these often coarse and uncultivated men. Overseers came and went on individual plantations, and some were too severe and brutal to retain their positions. These white men were aided by slave drivers, who, although black slaves themselves, could apply the lash with pitiless regularity and were used to chase down fugitives. "They scrupled not to aid and abet the enslavements of other Negroes—in fact, had few scruples about anything."[27] Philip Fithian, a Yale graduate serving as a tutor to the children of Robert Carter on a plantation in Virginia, wrote in 1773, "Mr. Carter is allowed by all, and from what I have already seen of others, I make no doubt at all but is the most humane to his slaves in all these parts!" Fithian also related some of the warped practices used to discipline and punish slaves attested to by a fiendish overseer of Mr. George Leeds named Morgan.

He [Morgan] said that whipping of any kind does them no good, for they will laugh at your greatest severity; but he told us he had invented two things, and by experiments had proved their success. For Sullenness, Obstinacy, or Idleness, says he, take a Negro, strip him, tie him to a post; then take a sharp curry-comb [a metal instrument used to shed hair from horses] and curry him severely till he is well scraped; and call a boy with some dry hay, and make the boy rub him down for several minutes, then salt him, and unloose him. He will attend to his business (said the inhuman Infidel) afterwards! But savage cruelty does not exceed his next diabolical invention.... Lay upon your floor a large thick plank, having a peg about eighteen inches long ... and very sharp, on the upper end set fast in the plank—then strip the Negro, tie the cord to a staple in the ceiling, so that his foot may just rest on the sharpened peg, then turn him quickly around, and you would laugh at the dexterity of the Negro, while he is relieving his feet on the sharpened peg! Good God! Are these Christians?[28]

To place the diabolical inventiveness of the overseer into historical perspective, it should be noted that the last infernal invention described by Fithian was a common punishment inflicted on soldiers in the militia by courts martial not only during colonial period but also during the Revolution and the American Civil War. Violence was the common coin of colonial discipline in society, business, church, and even school. Were it otherwise, many colonial slave owners would seem to be crazed minions of the devil himself. In the late 17th century, there were no abolitionists or racial justice societies promoted by well-meaning whites.[29] The only agitation against slavery came from Quakers and Moravians, and even this rebuke was mild. In a society where indentured servitude was common and free laborers were rare, few people thought in terms of immediate and forthright emancipation of slaves.

In 1671, George Fox counseled his fellow Quakers to take stock of their slaves and eventually to consider setting them free. "Let me tell you it will doubtless be very acceptable to the Lord, if … masters of families here, would deal so with their servants, the Negroes and blacks whom they have bought with their money, as to let them go free after they have served faithfully a considerable term of years, be it thirty years after, more or less, and when they go and are made free, let them not go away empty handed." Nonetheless, Quakers continued to own slaves. Anthony Benezet, speaking for the Society of Friends in Philadelphia in 1754, noted the "uneasiness and disunity" occasioned by the continued "importation and purchasing of Negroes and other slaves" (Native Americans) by his fellow Quakers. "[W]e have with sorrow to observe, that their number is of late increased among us. [W]e have thought proper to make our advice and judgment more public; that none may plead ignorance of our principles therein; and also again earnestly exhort all, to avoid in any manner encouraging that practice, of making slaves of our fellow creatures."[30]

NOTES

1. Quoted in Stanley M. Elkins, *Slavery: A Problem in American Institutional and Intellectual Life* (New York: Grosset and Dunlap, 1963), 57n.
2. Philip D. Curtin, *The Atlantic Slave Trade: A Census* (Madison: University of Wisconsin Press, 1975), 143.
3. Ibid., 147.
4. J. C. Furnas, *The Road to Harpers Ferry* (New York: William Sloane, 1959), 109–10.
5. Ibid., 108.
6. Curtin, *The Atlantic Slave Trade*, 134n. In 1795, the legal capacity for a slave ship was set by the British at 1.6 slaves per ton, and the trade was outlawed in 1808. The last legal date of departure for a slave ship from a U.S. or British port was April 30, 1807. The slave trade remained legal in Cuba until 1903.
7. See James M. Volo and Dorothy Denneen Volo, *Daily Life on the Old Colonial Frontier* (Westport, CT: Greenwood Press, 2002), 95–118.
8. Kenneth M. Stampp, *The Imperiled Union* (New York: Oxford University Press, 1980), 43–45.
9. Elkins, *Slavery*, 64.
10. Ibid., 104.
11. Ibid., 78n.
12. Ibid., 64.
13. Ibid., 104.
14. Ibid., 41n.
15. Lorenzo Johnston Greene, *The Negro in Colonial New England, 1620–1776* (New York: Columbia University Press, 1942), 103.
16. Connecticut Historical Society, *Connecting with Connecticut History* (Hartford: Connecticut Historical Society, 1995), 58.
17. Sarah Kemble Knight, *The Journal of Madame Knight* (Boston: Small, Maynard, 1920), 38.
18. Ibid.
19. Elkins, *Slavery*, 49.

20. Ibid., 55.

21. For further details concerning black rights or legal protocols during court proceedings, see Peter Charles Hoffer and William B. Scott, eds., *Criminal Proceedings in Colonial Virginia: Records of Fines, Examination of Criminals, Trials of Slaves, etc., from March 1710 to 1754* (Athens, GA: University of Georgia Press, 1984).

22. Elkins, *Slavery*, 49n.

23. Peter H. Wood, *Black Majority: Negroes in Colonial South Carolina from 1670 through the Stono Rebellion* (New York: W. W. Norton, 1996), 280.

24. Elkins, *Slavery*, 56n.

25. Wood, *Black Majority*, 278.

26. Elkins, *Slavery*, 57n.

27. Furnas, *The Road to Harpers Ferry*, 119.

28. Alden T. Vaughn, ed., *America before the Revolution, 1725–1775* (Englewood Cliffs, NJ: Prentice-Hall, 1967), 19–20.

29. As noted in the previous chapter, a freeman could sell himself as an indentured servant for life, contract his conditions of employment, choose his master, and retain the cash under the laws of Virginia and other colonies.

30. Clarence L. Ver Steeg and Richard Hofstadter, *Great Issues in American History, from Settlement to Revolution: 1584–1776* (New York: Random House, 1969), 232.

Selected Bibliography

Bailyn, Bernard. *The Peopling of British North America: An Introduction*. New York: Alfred A. Knopf, 1986.

Bennett, Ralph, ed. *Settlements in the Americas: Cross-Cultural Perspectives*. Newark, DE: University of Delaware Press, 1993.

Blassingame, John W., *Black New Orleans*. Chicago: Chicago University Press, 1973.

Breen, T. H. *The Marketplace of Revolution: How Consumer Politics Shaped American Independence*. New York: Oxford University Press, 2004.

Brown, Kathleen M. *Good Wives, Nasty Wenches, and Anxious Patriarchs: Gender, Race, and Power in Colonial America*. Chapel Hill: University of North Carolina Press, 1996.

Conner, Alvin E. *Sectarian Childrearing: The Dunkers, 1708–1900*. Gettysburg: Brethren Heritage Press, 2000.

Cowing,Cedric B. *The Great Awakening and the American Revolution: Colonial Thought in the 18th Century* . Chicago: Rand McNally, 1971.

Cremin, Lawrence A. *American Education: The Colonial Experience, 1607–1783*. New York: Harper and Row, 1970.

Curtin, Philip D. *The Atlantic Slave Trade: A Census*. Madison: University of Wisconsin Press, 1975.

Davis, David Brion. *Slavery in the Colonial Chesapeake*. Williamsburg: Colonial Williamsburg Foundation, 1994.

De Crevecoeur, J. Hector St. John. *Letters from an American Farmer and Sketches of Eighteenth-Century America*. Reprint, New York: Penguin Books, 1981.

Demos, John. *A Little Commonwealth: Family Life in Plymouth Colony*. New York: Oxford University Press, 2000.

Earle, Alice Morse. *Child Life in Colonial Days*. New York: Macmillan, 1940.

————. *Diary of Anna Green Winslow, a Boston Schoolgirl of 1771*. Bedford, MA: Applewood Books, 1996.

————. *Home Life in Colonial Days*. Stockbridge, MA: Berkshire House, 1993.

Elkins, Stanley M. *Slavery: A Problem in American Institutional and Intellectual Life*. New York: Grosset and Dunlap, 1963.

Fabend, Firth Haring. *A Dutch Family in the Middle Colonies, 1660–1800*. New Brunswick, NJ: Rutgers University Press, 1991.

Fischer, David Hackett. *Albion's Seed: Four British Folkways in America*. New York: Oxford University Press, 1989.

Fogleman, Aaron Spencer. *Hopeful Journeys: German Immigration, Settlement, and Political Culture in Colonial America, 1717–1775*. Philadelphia: University of Pennsylvania Press, 1996.

Greene, Jack P. *Pursuits of Happiness: The Social Development of Early Modern British Colonies and the Formation of American Culture*. Chapel Hill: University of North Carolina Press, 1988.

Leckie, Robert. *A Few Acres of Snow: The Saga of the French and Indian Wars*. New York: John Wiley and Sons, 1999.

Loeper, John L. *Going to School in 1776*. New York: Athenaeum, 1973.

Morgan, Edmund S. *The Puritan Family: Religion and Domestic Relations in Seventeenth-Century New England*. New York: Harper and Row, 1944.

Morgan, Kenneth. *Slavery and Servitude in Colonial North America*. New York: New York University Press, 2000.

Rule, John. *The Experience of Labour in Eighteenth-Century English Industry*. New York: St. Martin's Press, 1981.

Russell, Howard S. *A Long Deep Furrow, Three Centuries of Farming in New England*. Lebanon, New Hampshire: University Press of New England, 1976.

Schama, Simon. *The Embarrassment of Riches: An Interpretation of Dutch Culture in the Golden Age*. New York: Vintage Books, 1997.

Smith, Chard Powers. *Yankees and God*. New York: Hermitage House, 1954.

Spruill, Julia Cherry. *Women's Life and Work in the Southern Colonies*. New York: W. W. Norton, 1973.

Swan, Susan Burrows. *Plain and Fancy: American Women and Their Needlework, 1650–1850*. Austin: Curious Works Press, 1995.

Thomas, M. Halsey, ed. *The Diary of Samuel Sewall, 1674–1729*, 2 vols. New York: Farrar, Straus, and Giroux, 1973.

Volo, James M. and Dorothy Denneen Volo. *Daily Life on the Old Colonial Frontier*. Westport, CT: Greenwood Press, 2002.

————. *Encyclopedia of the Antebellum South*. Westport: Greenwood Press, 1999.

Wacker, Peter O. *The Musconetcong Valley of New Jersey: A Historical Geography*. New Brunswick, NJ: Rutgers University Press, 1968.

Williams, Selma R. *Demeter's Daughters: The Women Who Founded America, 1587–1787*. New York: Athenaeum, 1976.

Wilson, Lisa. *Ye Heart of a Man: The Domestic Life of Men in Colonial New England*. New Haven: Yale University Press, 1999.

Wood, Peter H. *Black Majority: Negroes in Colonial South Carolina from 1670 through the Stono Rebellion*. New York: W. W. Norton, 1996.

Wright, Louis B. *The Atlantic Frontier: Colonial American Civilization, 1607–1763*. New York: Alfred A. Knopf, 1951.

————. *The Cultural Life of the American Colonies*. Minneola, NY: Dover Publications, 2002.

Index

About the Authors

JAMES M. VOLO is a science teacher at Norwalk Public Schools in Norwalk, CT. He is co-author of *Daily Life in Civil War America* (Greenwood, 1998), *Daily Life during the American Revolution* (Greenwood, 2003), and *Daily Life during the Old Colonial Frontier* (Greenwood, 2002).

DOROTHY DENNEEN VOLO is a math teacher at Norwalk Public Schools in Norwalk, CT. She is co-author of *Daily Life in Civil War America* (Greenwood, 1998), *Daily Life during the American Revolution* (Greenwood, 2003), and *Daily Life during the Old Colonial Frontier* (Greenwood, 2002).